THE PERSON YOU HAVE CALLED CANNOT BE REACHED AT THE MOMENT:
REPRESENTATIONS OF LIFESTYLES IN TURKEY, 1980–2005

The Person You Have Called Cannot Be Reached at the Moment:
Representations of Life Styles in Turkey, 1980-2005

Meltem Ahıska
Zafer Yenal

1st edition April 2006, Istanbul

Design concept
Bülent Erkmen

Research
Elem Tuğçe Oktay
Maral Jefroudi
Nadir Öperli

Book design and
pre-press production
Burcu Kayalar

Cover design
Emre Çıkınoğlu, *BEK*

Photographs
Serdar Tanyeli

Object research
Doğa Kılcıoğlu

Translation
Ceyda Eldem
Leyla Tonguç Basmacı

Index
Evren Dinçer

Production, editorial
and design consultancy
BEK

Printing
Ofset Yapımevi
Yahya Kemal Mahallesi
Şair Sokak No: 4
Kağıthane, İstanbul

© 2006, Osmanlı Bank Archives and Research Centre

All rights reserved. No part of this publication may be reproduced or transmitted in any form or by any means, electronic or mechanical, including photocopy, recording or any other information storage and retrieval system, without prior permission in writinf from the publisher

ISBN 975-98125-9-2

This work has been realized on the occasion of the exhibition
The Person You Have Called Cannot Be Reached at the Moment: Representations of Life Styles in Turkey, 1980-2005
sponsored by Garanti Bank and organized by the Ottoman Bank Archives and Research Centre, between May 10- September 17, 2006

Exhibition proposal
Sibel Asna

Exhibition curators
Meltem Ahıska
Zafer Yenal

Exhibition design
Bülent Erkmen

Exhibition text
Meltem Ahıska
Zafer Yenal

Research
Elem Tuğçe Oktay
Maral Jefroudi
Nadir Öperli

Graphic design of the exhibition
and exhibition poster
Emre Çıkınoğlu, *BEK*

Display unit design and
exhibition design consultancy
Yeşim Bakırküre, *Ypsilon Tasarım*

Exhibition design preparations
Binnur Özgen, *Ypsilon Tasarım*

Execution of exhibition design
Esin Seven, *BEK*

Digital printing and application
Ora Reklam Hizmetleri A.Ş.

Production, editorial
and design consultancy
BEK

Project coordinator
Sima Benaroya,
Ottoman Bank Archives
and Research Centre

The person you have called cannot be reached at the moment

REPRESENTATIONS OF LIFESTYLES IN TURKEY
1980-2005

Table of contents

i need a new me *8*
    Fitness: a social responsibility *10*
    Men also want to look good *26*
    Do I have a psychological disorder? *40*
    A new age a new person *56*

what, oh what can we get for free? *70*
    To exist through shopping *72*
    Where should we go on vacation? *88*
    Buy now and pay later *102*
    What if we get lucky? *114*

seize the times! *126*
    Fast food comes to Turkey *128*
    Instrument of modernity: the automobile *144*
    Homes leap into the new age *126*
    Got any spare time? *174*

i was like, whoa, you know? *184*
    Where is the Turkish language headed? *186*
    Sex is everywhere *200*
    What a wedding! *216*
    A nation is partying! *230*

connecting people *248*
    Television watches the world for you *250*
    Reaching out to others *266*
    International coffeehouses *282*
    Moving toward a global city *294*

no trespassers! *308*
    Sheltered lives *310*
    Living, unregistered *326*
    Education's hurdle race *336*
    Violence rules *354*

everything old is new again... *368*
    In fashion again *368*
    In search of faraway flavours *382*
    The good old *bayrams!* *398*
    NeoTurkism *412*

Acknowledgements

The realization of the exhibition, *The Person You Have Called Cannot Be Reached at the Moment*, and of its accompanying catalogue was made possible through the efforts and collaboration of a number of people and institutions. We wish to express our deepest gratitude to all those who have contributed and lent their assistance and support to this project – which from the moment of its first conception to its conclusion has taken us a good eighteen months.

Our most sincere thanks go to Sima Benaroya, Manager of the Ottoman Bank Archives and Research Center, and to Bülent Erkmen from BEK Tasarım for their precious contributions, moral support and help at every stage of the process, in the realization and design of both the exhibition and the book. We also wish to express our warmest gratitude to Sibel Asna from A&B İletişim, who played a major part in the initial conception and preparation of this project and backed it from beginning to end.

We cannot thank enough our dear assistants, Elem Tuğçe Oktay, Maral Jefroudi and Nadir Öperli, whose dedicated work and creative input also helped make the project possible.

We acknowledge our debt to Alan Duben, Ayşe Öncü, Fatih Özgüven, Naim Dilmener, Rıfat Bali, Sırma Köksal and Uğur Tanyeli for their helpful suggestions and the inspiration their previous works and research have given our project.

Our deepest appreciation goes to Ceyda Eldem and Leyla Tonguç Basmacı who with their exceptional translations have practically rewritten the book and the exhibition texts.

The technical realization of both the exhibition and the book owe much to the cheerfulness, dedication and efficiency of many people; special thanks to Binnur Özgen, Burcu Kayalar, Emre Çıkınoğlu, Doğa Kılcıoğlu, Esin Seven, Evren Dinçer, Haldun Topal, Kağan Gözen and Yeşim Bakırküre.

Our deepest thanks to the entire staff of the Ottoman Bank Archives and Research Center, starting with Ercan Ünal, Hülya Kök, Lorans Tanatar Baruh and Ümit Servi who have assisted us with great understanding and courtesy every step of the way.

To Serdar Tanyeli, Hüseyin Özçelik and Mehmet Özen for their photographic work;

For kindly sharing their archives with us, to Açık Radyo, Ahmet Z. Sekendiz, Best FM, the Boğaziçi University Library, CNN Türk, Gülten Kaya and Gam Production, Güzin Yalın, the Istanbul Municipality Caricature and Humor Museum, the Istanbul Bilgi University Library, the Istanbul Metropolitan Municipality Atatürk Library, Department of Periodicals, Istanbul Modern Museum, the Istanbul University Library, the Library and Research Center of the Foundation for Women's Studies, Kanal D, Ahmet Ekendiz, Naim Dilmener, NTV, the Ottoman Bank Museum Archives and Research Center Library, the Advertising Foundation and Association of Advertisers, the Archives Department at Kanal 7, TGRT FM, and TRT, and the Turkish Journalists Association Press Museum;

And for their assistance and kind contributions throughout this project to: Altyazı Aylık Cinema Magazine, Arnavutköy Neighborhood Initiative, Boğaziçi University Mithat Alam Film Center, Capitol Public Relations, Durak Copy, Eti Food Production and Trade, Inc., Hedef Stationary, Istanbul Modern Museum, Kanal D, Kuraldışı Education and Consulting, Net Kırtasiye, Post Office, Rec Time Production, the Advertising Foundation and Association of Advertisers, Sinema.com, the Türker İnanoğlu Foundation, the Uçan Süpürge Association, Yunus Kırtasiye, Ani Demirci, Asena Günal, Alper Ayhan, Ataullah Arvas, Aydan Pamir, Ayfer Bartu Candan, Aynur Erdemci, Ayşegül Molu, Başkan Kalezade, Biray Kırlı Kolluoğlu, Can Candan, Cansu Sertlek, Cihan Yavuz, Cüneyt Özdemir, Çiğdem Köstepen, Çiçek Kahraman, Deniz Kologlu, Deniz Yükseker, Ekmel Kangal, Enis Köstepen, Ece Üçoluk, Engin Özendes, Faruk Eren, Fatma Ermiş, Ferhat Boratav, Filiz Akalp, Gökçe Oktay, Gökhan Akçura, Gözde Onaran, Işık Güler, Lütfiye Çakmak, Mehmet Alkan, Melida Tüzünoğlu, Murat Es, Mustafa Arslan, Mustafa Aşcıoğlu, Müge Tanıl, Nazan Sakızlı, Nazan Üstündağ, Nilüfer Ergürler, Orçun Öperli, Orhan Akkaplan, Ömer Ovacık, Özlem Ece, Öznur Şahin, Rıza Teksan, Ruzedar Güler, Şenay Aydın, Şule Yenal, Tamar Demirci, Şükran Yücel, Timuçin Gürer, Turgut Çeviker, Umay Aykut, Volkan Üst, Yalçın Güngören, Yamaç Okur and Zeynep Dadak, our most sincere thanks.

Introduction

We conceived this book as the accompanying catalogue to the exhibition of the same name that opened at the Ottoman Bank Museum in May 2006. Our aim was to document the various *representations* of different trends and lifestyles in Turkey from 1980 to 2005, and provide a platform for their subsequent discussion. First of all, we should explain why instead of simply saying "lifestyles", we use the term "representation." The concept "lifestyle" entered general usage in Turkey with the growing professionalism of media practices after the 1980s. It refers to the creation, through *consumption* habits, of a *differentiated style* in various areas of life. In this period, the term "lifestyle" played a key role in the self-identification of an emerging new elite, which considered itself "modern," "Western," and "global." The ways of living that remained outside these criteria, since they did not conform to the desired style, were labeled "backward," "Eastern," and "rural," and devoid of a lifestyle *status*. "Lifestyle," then, becomes concrete only when reflected through the prism of a particular dominant class.

Despite the close relationship that exists between "lifestyle," class, and status, the concept has deviated rather significantly from former static meanings it possessed when it first gained popularity in the 1980s. Since class rule has become much more anonymous and now takes place within general culture, "lifestyle" has started to carry increasingly fleeting and vaguely defined implications. Another reason is that "lifestyle" models enter *circulation* just like any other merchandise. In particular, magazines, newspapers, television and other "mass media" convey lifestyles created throughout the world to different localities; in Turkey, for instance, it is possible for an American or English lifestyle to become popular. In sum, today, "lifestyles" can be purchased. This is most clearly observed in the union of culture with the market and consumption. If culture defines consumption and consumption defines culture, cultural indicators also constitute a sphere in which social stratification is produced and acquires meaning. The French thinker and cultural sociologist Pierre Bourdieu argued that class differences were correlated to inequities in the field of production and expressed through consumption – the indispensable component of culture. Thus, everyday activities achieved through consumption such as the ways people dress, eat, communicate and enjoy themselves become basic practices that "differentiate" them. Consequently, the field of culture and consumption is a field of *struggle* defined by continually changing indicators. Viewed in this context, a "lifestyle" is simultaneously an indicator of *real* conflicts and differences in society and the *shallow* manifestation of perpetually shifting and transitory styles of living. This is why, when discussing lifestyles, it is not enough simply to examine the way individuals or groups live, one should consider as well how lifestyles are propagated through culture.

In this sense, the representations of lifestyles disseminated by popular culture, which incite *desire* in everyone, are at once *full* and *empty*. They are shallow because various socio-economic processes shape them, and their purpose is to exert power; they create *norms*, produce a sense of need, dictate behavior and provoke fear. Yet, as Barthes discussed in his seminal work on the myths of everyday life (1996), these representations are also laden with significance; by *stealing* the various meanings that constitute the essential parts of individual or collective quests for identity and by remodeling them, they reach a very wide public, provoke desire and define identities. The chronology and interrelationship of lifestyle representations, thus hold up a mirror to both familiar and very different ways in which we see ourselves.

When looking a these representations in Turkey over the two and a half decades from 1980 to 2005, and retracing the major transformations that have occurred in that time, it may come as a surprise to see that certain now-familiar trends and products are actually quite new. Conversely, other themes have prevailed to our day almost unchanged. Throughout this book, we have attempted to address these breaks and continuities, illustrating them with a series of examples and discussions. We have concentrated on this particular twenty-five year period because we believe that the 1980s represent a major breaking point. In his study *Tarz-ı Hayattan Life Style'a*, Rıfat Bali takes as his starting point the Özal period and investigates in detail the efforts of the new elites to open up to the world: their direct links to the financial and services sectors; their predilection for imported goods and brand names; and their ideology based on individualization and competition (2002). Other writers have discussed the cultural implications of the changes generated by the same period, using terms like the "life on display" and the "age of glossy images"(Gürbilek 1992; Kozanoğlu 1992). Our objective in this work is to offer a reading contrasting the *concrete*, *external* images shaped by popular culture in this period, with the *abstract* and *deep-rooted* tendencies of the extensive socio-economic processes that laid the groundwork for them. In so doing, we have tried to avoid moral judgments; it is not our aim to expose the images popularized in these representations as indicators of *artificiality* and degeneration and offer *authentic* and wholesome lifestyles to replace them. Of course, this is not to say that our goal is to embrace and celebrate popular culture. On the contrary, we have approached these popular images as the traces of a specific historicity. By historicizing the present, we aim to facilitate its critical analysis.

In the choice of headings for both the exhibition and its catalogue, we resorted to popular songs, ad slogans or expressions from the decades between 1980 and 2005. Of the seven headings that emerged, none by itself carries any major significance; they are as light and whimsical as the songs, taglines or expressions to which they refer. By separating these popular expressions from their actual constitutions, we turned them into secondary "signifiers." We regrouped under these signifiers the various themes that make up the focal points of lifestyle representations propagated over the past 25 years. As a result, in addition to external and changeable representations, these signifiers now also express the wide-ranging, often indiscernible historical processes of social relations. At this point, a word should be said about the various levels and forms of representation used. Newspaper and magazine clippings from various newspapers and magazines published between 1980 and 2005, selected and scanned for relevant themes, constitute the most accessible and direct level of representation. The printed media's pervasive role in shaping lifestyles, rousing desires and diffusing fears is well established. Still, daily newspapers are easily cast aside and forgotten once rapidly skimmed through and the messages they offer thus not especially durable. On a second level, we use audio representations essentially aimed at controlling and directing lifestyles. Most are excerpts from radio broadcasts and demonstrate the deeper, "authoritarian" impact that voice can exert on people's lives. We also use clips from taped television transmissions involving "ordinary" people in these lifestyle representations; these express people's attempts or struggles to conform to existing scripts. The rift between representation and real life stands out most clearly at this level. It is also this level that best evokes the burden and *violence* these representations impose on individuals. Finally, in both the exhibition and this catalogue we include various objects that have been on the market since the 1980s. Some are still popular today, others have fallen from favor; all are or were objects waiting to be claimed or used within specific lifestyles. However, shown here, abstracted from actual life, they occupy the extreme point on the axis of representation and evoke the actual instant of consumption by exteriorizing the desire they may have produced when they were first glimpsed in a shop window or held in the hand.

This catalogue is not meant as a summary of events experienced over the past 25 years. The interpretations and theoretical references we offer here should be viewed more as an attempt to provide a platform for discussion on the possible meanings of transient representations. The passages quoted from various literary texts serve to enhance the exchange between the different levels of signification. Naturally, entirely different readings, interpretations or representations might be contributed. Finally, we shouldn't forget that both catalogue and exhibition are themselves products of the era we study. Without banks to sponsor cultural initiatives or digital cameras, the internet and other technologies to facilitate access; without expert knowledge in various cultural spheres from the movies to music; and without sociologists who show an interest in culture, this book would probably never have been written.

Enjoy your reading!

The 1980 military coup, followed immediately by the rapid emergence of the free market policies on the agenda, thrust Turkey into an accelerated process of social transformation. A period was cast aside and a "new age" began. Alongside the striking changes taking place in shop windows, we can also observe, in those years, the shaping of a new type of person. This new individual, in whom modern market-based power strategies invest, displays characteristics identified through the market and the changing institutions. The new person ideal is not only a social goal; by motivating the fears dormant in people, it becomes an individualized norm as well. The new age is an age of individualization and individual quests. It is a time to seize opportunities and discover the latest and fastest methods and techniques to reclaiming a healthy and attractive body; attaining and safeguarding psychological wellbeing; or revamping an obsolete male image that resists change. The desire to create a new self is both personal and a duty defined by technologies of social power.

i need a new me

Fitness: a social responsibility

My mother was stroking my hair and murmuring "My beautiful daughter", but I couldn't stand it anymore.

"I don't want you to call me beautiful daughter," I screamed. My mother was surprised, she stood aghast, watching me.

"If I was beautiful, everybody would revolve around me the way they do with Ayşegül. If I was beautiful, at least one person, just one person would invite me to dance. I'm not beautiful, I'm not beautiful like Ayşegül or like you. I'm a fat, pimpled, ugly girl. That's all, so I don't want to hear anymore the words "my beautiful daughter".
[İpek Ongun, *Bir Genç Kızın Gizli Defteri*, 1993, Altın Kitaplar Publications, p. 22]

I don't want to run to improve my health. It's fine if I can just breathe. [Tezer Özlü, *Kalanlar*, 1990, Ada Publications, p. 37]

Jane Fonda's step, aerobics and fitness tapes, very popular in the 1980s

"Is Turkey the Fattest Country in Europe?" and, if so, are we "packing on those extra pounds" because we're happy or because we're sad? Is it true women today are "boosting calorie burn" and "getting in shape for the summer" by training in martial arts? Headlines everywhere keep advising us on how to become slimmer and more attractive and on the ways to pamper our bodies… Women's magazines all chant the same mantra: get in shape and stay fit, exercise regularly, go jogging around the park, work out in fitness centers, eat low fat-products, avoid carbohydrates. Though methods may have changed over the years, the goal pursued never varies: "Beauty, health and fitness." Those who jammed aerobic salons and health clubs in the 1980s hoping to burn fat on treadmills, stationary bikes or aerobic steps today embrace "techno-fitness" or, if they lack the means, walk their way to health wearing everyday clothing (including scarves and long skirts). The common denominator here is they are all female. For a long time now, the road to beauty and health for women has apparently implied getting thinner.

Being beautiful and healthy has always been a major concern. Maybe what has changed today is that greater focus is given to these topics and they are more openly discussed. First of all, it should be noted that publications for women in Turkey have increased over the past two decades. In addition to the growing number of television programs and newspaper articles targeting women, the first magazines specifically dedicated to women, such as *Kadınca* and *Elele*, emerged in the 1980s. On the one hand, these magazines supported the developing feminist movement by articulating topics on women's liberation, on the other, they established the norms of ideal feminine beauty by offering a wide variety of articles on the ways to attain this ideal through various beauty products. Today, the Turkish editions of several women's magazines, including *Marie Claire*, *Cosmopolitan*, and *Elle*, share newspaper stands with magazines dedicated to younger women and teens. The main focus of these publications is the relationship

Zaman Turkuaz
11 April 2004

Running for health in print skirts

'Step'siz yapamaz olduk

Akşam
20 September 1994

Milliyet Aktüalite
26 April 1981

Günümüz modası: Egzersiz

above: **We can't do without step**: *Step, which ever since it first started to be practiced, has been spreading like wildfire thanks to its popularity, has become a passion for Turkish people.*

left: **Today's fashion: exercise**: *The only thing that makes women unhappy is "bulging fat"... Men with a paunch and round shoulders are not regarded with distaste. But, in order to "lose weight", or to have a "shapely" body, to protect your motor system and as therapy everybody nowadays should "exercise"...*

of women with their bodies. Glamorous photographs displaying women's daily fashions and lingerie are displayed alongside articles advocating thin and *fit* bodies as the essential requisite of seduction. Both these ideals and the imperfections they evoke spur women to action. To be attractive and desirable a woman must meet a number of requirements: get rid of extra fat, tone and tend her body and, of course, discover the *correct* ways to do this.

As in almost every other field, there are experts today who specialize in these topics: the doctors, dieticians and beauticians whose "scientific" methods you have to rely on to attain that trim, attractive figure. Weight loss has gradually become a more *technical* issue. Medical research conducted over recent years has established that being overweight can directly result in a number of health problems. Losing weight is thus not uniquely a beauty issue but also a health priority. Simple body weight is no longer sufficient to determine excess body fat and which diet should be followed. Nowadays, you need to calculate your BMS (body mass index) and body fat percentage. And, just as there are a number of diets to chose from – low carbohydrate diets, the Atkins diet, high protein diets, the Montignac diet – there exist various measures for excess body weight, ranging from slightly overweight, to frankly fat or obese, with grossly obese and morbidly obese at the far and fearful end of the scale. In sum, beauty and health now form an inseparable whole. Today, a whole market is entirely devoted to weight loss and its accompanying cosmetic products, fitness and health centers, and weight loss experts. The momentum generated by this self-expanding market has created new areas and spurred the transformation of existing areas in response to market logic and rules. One major new concept to emerge from this process is that of *healthy eating*.

For a long time now, eating has been approached as a *nutrition* issue, and one of the crucial determinants of a person's dietary choices is concern for better health. Already in the 1950s, when margarine was still a new product in Turkish kitchens, a number of doctors were recommending its use as a healthier alternative to saturated animal fats like butter. Also around this time, the topic of *healthy eating* had begun to show up in the curriculum of schools, especially those aiming to produce a new generation of

There wasn't much to do at this time of the morning. Taking a sudden decision, I wore my track suit, I put on an eye-catching headband, I wore with affectation, swagger and faith the running shoes which had been dozing in a corner of the cupboard for a long time and I went for a morning run. As you can see, I was determined on starting the day in a good way and I hadn't been doing this, that is these morning runs, for a long time...
[Murathan Mungan, *Yüksek Topuklar*, 2002, Metis Publications, p. 81]

Pedometre: electronic device used to count steps while walking or running

Anti-cellulite cream

I NEED A NEW ME FITNESS: A SOCIAL RESPONSIBILITY

Sugar-free sugar

The one by her side asked her: What size do you wear?

Can't these girls tell, when they look at you? As soon as you put on weight, the breasts and hips get wider and wider, and the legs thinner. Thirty eight has been left behind, and so has forty, and slowly forty two too. I could manage a forty two, but the waist would ride up.

I need a forty four my girl.

The girl wrinkled her nose: We only do up to forty two.

Somehow she couldn't believe it: Oh? Really? Tonight there is a ceremony in my honour, and I was thinking, that for a day like this, a classy, cheerful blouse…

This time it was the girl standing further away who cut her short: You'd better go to YGB. They do both older people and bigger sizes.
[Adalet Ağaoğlu, *Hayır…*, 1987/2005, Yapı Kredi Publications, p. 55]

Sugar-free chocolate

sensible, modern housewives. But the emphasis on the health aspect of food products, cooking and eating has become increasingly apparent in recent years. *Light*, low-fat, healthy and well-balanced eating is a theme which pops up everywhere we look. Whether in cookbooks, food and cooking articles in magazines and newspapers, or in food programs on television, the same principle is always touted: a healthy diet. This should come as no surprise in a health-conscious society, where most consumers are aware of the existence of good and bad cholesterol and know the difference between saturated and unsaturated fats.

From the 1980s onward, processed foods also "lightened," as a number of low-calorie and diet products began to grace supermarket shelves. Today, there is a "light," "low-cal" or "lean" version available for almost every popular food, from traditional Turkish fare like *helva*, *lahmacun*, or yogurt, to more universal products like milk, sausages, ice cream or soft drinks. Obviously, the growing investments of such multinational companies as Nestle, Unilever and Philip Morris in Turkey and the rapid industrialization of local food production contributed significantly to the emergence of this wide range of products. As a brand new weight loss market developed, the road to a thinner more vital self yet again entailed consuming more, and losing weight became a broad social concern.

Although weight loss seems a generalized concern, products and service lines vary according to segments of society. While upscale consumers benefit from the high-tech equipment of fitness salons and shed those extra pounds following customized regimens under the supervision of their dieticians, the less fortunate walk or jog their way to health around city streets and parks and try the latest fad diet acclaimed by the media. Social stratification also appears in the awareness people have of new ideal body weights and measurements and in their concern to match these. For the middle classes in particular, *fitness* is equivalent to social status. Someone *fit* is giving others more or less the following message: I take care of my body and thus fulfill my responsibilities to those around me, starting with my family. On the other hand, obesity seems to imply laziness, a "couldn't care less" attitude, and, because of the possible health risk implied, irresponsibility both towards the self

right: **Are you overweight because you are unhappy or because you are happy?** *Your overeating is not the only reason why you gain weight. Separation from a loved one, pregnancy, hormonal imbalance, stress and loneliness can also add to your weight.*

below: **A national effort for losing weight:** *Diets, aerobics, surgical methods, hypnosis, electricity, water, heat... For a society which is caught in the madness of losing weight, the alternatives are practically endless.*

Marie Claire
September 2000

Nokta
4 June 1989

Yeni Günaydın
12 August 1992

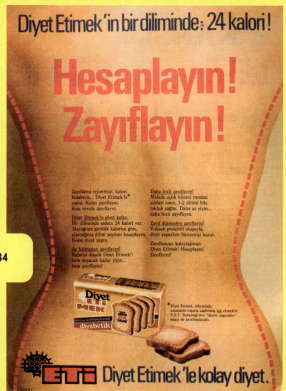

January 1984

above: **A race to lose weight:** *Centres that help weight loss through scientific methods have become very appealing for Turkish people.*

right: **Count calories! Lose weight!** *Go on a weight-loss diet, counting calories... With Diet Etimek... Easy to lose weight...*

Teknoloji ve spor bir araya geldi

Tekno fitness devri!

Eskiden, yaptığınız egzersizin işe yarayıp yaramadığını anlamak için ya tartıya çıkar ya da elde bir mezura "kaç santim incelmişim acaba" diye ölçerdiniz. Şimdi o devirler tarih oldu. Çünkü artık önde gelen spor merkezlerinin kişiye özel bilgisayar programlı sistemleri sayesinde nasıl ve ne kadar form tuttuğunuzu evdeki bilgisayarınızdan bile takip etmeniz mümkün. Nasıl mı? İşte cevabı...

Form Sante
November 2004

July 2000

Hayatı "Light" yaşamak

Üstünde "light" yazılı ürünler, sağlığına ve dış görünümüne özen gösterenlerin, marketlerde daha huzurlu alışveriş etmesini sağlıyor. "Light" sütü Türkiye piyasasına ilk lanse eden firma olan Mis, yoğurt ve peynirleriyle de kilosuna dikkat edenlerin tercihi...

above: **The age of techno-fitness:** *Technology and sport, combined.*

right: **Living a "light" life:** *Products with a "light" label make it possible for people who care about their health and their appearance to feel more assured during their supermarket shopping. The first company to launch "light" milk in the Turkish market, Mis is also preferred by people who watch their weight for its different yoghurts and cheeses...*

Scene from the final episode of the programme "I Want to Lose Weight Now", broadcasted since 2005
[ATV, 7 January 2006]

and others. The television program, *Şimdi Zayıflamak İstiyorum* [I Want to Lose Weight Now] is a case in point: remorseful, fat people are presented to the public as examples of what to avoid. In this context, bodies have become social capital which can easily be turned into economic capital.

However much getting thin may seem an essentially female concern, a substantial number of younger men today have also joined the caravan of weight loss and fitness buffs, and flock to indoor pools and gyms. Our bodies have progressively become a mirror for personal achievement, cultural standing, and self-esteem. In them we see our reflection and the self that others see. In an era where the craze for individualism and self-realization continually increases, the body has become a project to plan ahead for, just like children or a career. It can be reshaped, reduced and improved. But this is no easy process, especially where women are concerned. There are no limits to weight loss; "you can never be too thin." And even thin by itself is not enough. To be "fit", a woman must get rid of the flab on her midriff, the cellulite on her thighs and other localized adiposities. The object is not merely a thin body, but a flawlessly toned and firm one, making ideal beauty a harder and harder goal to reach.

I am sitting in my beautiful house, looking at myself in the mirror... Touching my face with my fingers, stopping for a while at every line, at every crease... I smile... To myself... I caress each thin line, one by one.

My dear lines, my dear wrinkles, how I love you... How much you have taught me... How much you love me... You are my happiness, my struggle, my unhappiness, my pains, my independence... My dear thin, small, graceful lines... My friends. What would I do without you? You are my determination, you are my strength. The things I have been through to create you... the way I suffered... how I fought... in order to be able to look at you with such understanding and happiness... how I struggled.

[Duygu Asena, *Kadının Adı Yok*, 1987/2004, Doğan Publications, p. 180]

As these almost impossibly high beauty and health standards increase our anxiety, so do the demands and responses of those around us. While some tell us to "stick to a diet and lose weight," others falsely commiserate, urging us to eat and stop "starving" ourselves. To add to the confusion, some sources suggest it is possible to ease this arduous slimming task and "shed pounds as you sleep." Actually, the most stressful aspect of the issue comes from the juxtaposition of weight loss and consumerism. In this age of consumerism, newspapers advertise the latest breakthrough diet with guaranteed results alongside gourmet recipes and reviews of the newest "in" restaurants and cafes. It has become more and more common to see "gastropornographic" images of hard to replicate recipes – more design objects than actual meals – sharing the pages of glossy magazines with impossibly thin models. The messages are conflicting; we are instructed to lose weight yet enticed to try new restaurants and foods. In a century where sensuality and self-gratification are continually provoked and every

Hürriyet
8 August 2000

left: **The Turkish woman of the year 2000:** *Beautiful, healthy and sleek*

below: **The fat melts away:** *Winter is over, the Bayram has passed. Summer is approaching. We are going to show our bodies around wearing only swimming suits, t-shirts and shorts. But how? With a big paunch or with a fit body? The furore of losing weight, of becoming thinner and more beautiful has spread to Turkey too. People are working hard in different ways to lose weight. You choose!*

Tempo
13 May 1990

right: **Turkish women are the fattest of Europe:** *Obesity is the problem with the highest budget in the world. Illnesses and syndromes linked to excessive overweight are also on the increase. According to recent researches, Turkish women are the most overweight women of Europe.*

below: **Thin, thinner, very thin:** *You wish to lose weight but you don't know which method is the healthiest and the longest lasting. Rather than choosing a diet at random, have a look at our recommendations on sensible weight loss…*

Sabah
23 July 2005

Options
March 1997

10 soruda selülit

Hürriyet
10 May 2003

Kadın kalça ve bacaklarının en büyük düşmanı...
SELÜLİT

Her kadının korkulu rüyası olan bir hastalıktır Selülit. Özellikle de, kadınların en dikkat ettikleri organ olan bacaklarda ortaya çıkması, olaya ayrı bir önem kazandırır...

Sevim Çağlayan'da da selülit var...
Bir zamanların ünlü şarkıcısı olan Sevim Çağlayan da, selülit hastalığından şikâyetçi.

Haftanın Sesi
24 September 1982

above: **10 questions about cellulite**

left: **Cellulite:** *Cellulite is every woman's nightmare. The fact that it appears especially on the legs, which are such an important feature for women, makes the issue even more serious...*

I run. My left foot, together with my right foot, run away from me. My waist is about to split from my body and my sweat trickles into my eyes, it displaces my tears and throws them out. This still doesn't stop me. I don't stop, because my ugly fat face is reflected in the mirrors. I'm running on the treadmill and I'm disgusted with my flabby stomach. I'm trying to get rid of myself. I'm trying to burn my fat, but I'm burning myself too. My breath is slowing down. Every time I breathe out, a piece of my soul jumps out. I'm tired. [Aydilge Sarp, *Bulumia Sokağı*, Ekim 2002, Remzi Publications, p. 5]

Dolls doing aerobics or using fitness equipment

form of consumerism encouraged, so that consuming becomes an accepted form of existence, how realistic can it be to ask people to turn their backs on eating, drinking and all the other pleasures the world has to offer? It is probably just at this point that the paradoxes of a consumerist culture most clearly reveal themselves.

The body has always been subjected to control mechanisms enforced by different social institutions and customs. Today, this control over the body is exercised circuitously through the markets and emerges to confront us like a personal issue. But maintaining the incessantly motivated desires of people within acceptable limits remains a social issue. The desires of women, in particular, must be curbed because women exist not only for themselves but for their families, husbands and children. The relationship of women with their bodies is expected to reflect the care they lavish on their children, the fidelity and esteem they give their spouse and even modernity criteria. In the articulation of the body-health-beauty trilogy, societal control has acquired an increasingly far-reaching ascendancy. For countless young women who count calories, diet endlessly or resort to an assortment of methods in their endeavor to become fit, the boundaries between personal control and social control have clearly merged. "Total Anti-Cellulite" programs, clinically tested and approved by dermatologists as safe and efficient, may be out on the market, but apparently most women still find it hard to justify such "self-centered" indulgence.

Değer mi hiç?

■ Yiyen, içen, sevişen bir insanla, tıbbın öngördüğü biçimde yaşayan bir insanın sağlık durumu arasında sadece binde 1'lik bir fark olduğu ortaya çıkarıldı

Stuttgart'ta bulunan "İnsan Davranışlarını Araştırma Merkezi"nin 7 yıl önce başlattığı proje ilgi çekici sonuçlar doğurdu. Merkez 7 yıl önce 300 gönüllü seçip, bunları iki gruba ayırdı. Birinci gruptaki 150 denek, alıştığı yaşam biçimini hiç bozmadan bildiği gibi yiyip içip keyfine baktı.

Kafana göre takıl

■ İkinci gruptaki 150 kişi ise, tıbbın son gelişmelerinin öngördüğü sağlık koşullarında yaşatıldı. Bunlara süper vitaminler, mineraller, oligo elementler verildi. Sonuçta robot gibi yaşayan bu biyonik insanların sağlık durumunun, kafasına göre takılanlardan sadece binde 1 daha iyi olduğu anlaşıldı.

Robot gibi değil, dilediğince yaşamak en iyisi!
Araştırma merkezinin seçtiği ilk 150 kişilik grup, tıbbın en son yöntemlerinin öngördüğü biçimde yaşadı. Bunlar hiç içki, sigara içmedi. Erken kalktılar, erken yattılar. Vitamin, mineral hatta serumla bile beslendiler. İkinci gruptaki 150 kişi ise normal yaşantılarını hiç değiştirmeden sürdürdü. Sabahlara kadar diskolarda dolaştı, yedi, içti. Kafasına göre takıldı. Neticede iki gruptakilerin sağlıkları da hemen hemen eşit çıktı.

Bugün
1 May 1993

---

above: **Is it worth it?** *It has been revealed that there is only a difference of one per thousand between the health of a person who eats, drinks and makes love and that of a person who lives in accordance with medical recommendations.*

right: **Lose weight while sleeping:** *Sleep comfortably, in peace... And wake up thinner than the day before, thanks to your pyjama sauna.*

zayıflatıcı pijama-sauna ile

UYURKEN KİLO VERİN

İlaç almadan, perhiz yapmadan, egzersiz yapmadan.

Rahat, huzurlu bir şekilde uyuyun... Ve PİJAMA SAUNA'nız sayesinde bir önceki güne göre daha incelmiş olarak uyanın.

SADECE 129.000 TL

January 1993

Yaza incelmiş girmek isteyen kadınlar tek antrenmanda yüksek kalori kaybettiren dövüş sporlarını tercih ediyor

Döverek zayıflayın

Akşam
5 June 2004

Bujin Fight Club'ta borsacılar, bankacılar ve reklamcılar günlük hayatın stresini kum torbası yumruklayarak atıyor. Zayıflamak için Uzakdoğu savaş sanatlarını tercih eden üyeler, dövüş felsefelerinin de eğitimini alıyor. Hem ruh hem beden terbiyesi sunan merkezde kozlar, bir boks müsabakasıyla dövüş kulübünün ringinde paylaşılıyor.

above: **Fight to loose weight:** *Women who wish to be slimmer for the summer prefer the martial arts, where one can burn a high number of calories in a single session.*

below: **Family discord lies behind overweight:** *Each region, each city has its own characteristic problems. But among these problems, and among the reasons why one eats excessively, unhappy marriages come first.*

Milliyet
5 June 1988

TATİL SOHBETİ
● Muzaffer Kuşhan'a göre, Türk kadını kendine bakmıyor

Aile geçimsizliği şişmanlık nedeni

"Her bölgenin, her şehrin kendine göre sorunları var. Ama genelde bu sorunların başında, kişiyi en çok yediren sebeplerin başında mutlu olmayan evlilikler geliyor. Bazen maddi sıkıntılar. Daha çok erkeğin ilgisizliği"

Milliyet
22 April 1992

Milliyet Metro City
5 March 2005

above: **You must eat:** *You must eat. Yes, you are doing aerobics, fine. You walk everywhere. You are very active, very into sports, but does what and how you eat matter for you as much as it should?*

left: **Be selfish!** *Cellulite, one of the major problems of the summer, ceases being a nightmare for the working woman. A new individualised anti-cellulite programme which offers solutions for cellulite is being implemented in Turkey, for the first time in the world.*

Men also want to look good

Machine for the removal of nasal hair

Attila - that man - had run after girls here and there, he had messed around quite a bit, and he was a so-called good family boy; they got him a Buick with fins, so that he would behave and get himself a job - it was the first taxi in the town, such swagger, such grandeur. One would think that he would have reached a certain maturity, that he must have satisfied every youthful desire he had, that he must know the value of a woman. One would think, I haven't been loved by anyone, he will love me. And he was handsome too, the rascal - for those times - a thin Clark Gable moustache, sideways glances, rolled up shirt sleeves, a lopsided gait on oval high heels, sitting back at the steering wheel and dashing off like an arrow... [İnci Aral, Mor, Epsilon Publications, p. 187]

In recent years, men, just like women, have started to take an interest in their appearance, in the way they dress, and the various fashions and beauty products available to improve their looks. Men today make liberal use of perfume, facials, manicures and pedicures and even resort to cosmetic surgery. This fashion-conscious, well-groomed "new male," gracing the pages of newspapers and magazines, goes by the appellation of "metrosexual." From actors to football players, examples of *metrosexual* men abound, but the definition of *metrosexual* remains somewhat vague.

At first glance, the immediate associations for metrosexuality are obviously sexual; casting men as sexual objects raises a number of interesting issues. From the beginning of modern times, women have always symbolized sexuality. While the female body is an object of desire, it also represents a threat calling for constraints. Woman is both the "seducer" and the "seduced," while male sexuality is generally presented as the norm. This is somewhat reminiscent of the way racial issues are handled in American society: many topics concerning blacks are open for discussion, while being "white" remains an unassailable fact. In the same way, while many societies conduct research on women, and women are considered a legitimate topic of analysis, masculine ideology remains an unquestioned reality. The "boys will be boys" attitude endorses all kinds of male aggressive behaviors, as witnessed by the prevalence of rape. Male sexuality is questioned only when it deviates from this "norm." Homosexuality, for example, much like female sexuality, constitutes a threat and is presented as a *sickness*. Borderline transgressions from masculinity, such as transvestitism and transsexuality, are viewed as pathological cases. In his investigation of a new male masculinity, Jonathan Rutherford (1988) demonstrated, with a striking example from his own experience, the extent to which male sexuality had become a secret norm, internalized and never discussed. The author recalls that, in his early adolescence,

Metroseksüel erkekler kulübüne hoş geldiniz

Artık estetik ve kozmetik dünyasında erkekler de yerini aldı. Estetik cerrahlara gidenlerin yarıya yakınını erkekler oluşturuyor. Göbeklerini aldırıyorlar, kaşlarını ve kırışıklıklarını yok ettiriyorlar. Yani artık devir metroseksüellik devri ● Özlem UÇAR

Özcan Deniz

Müzik piyasasına ilk adım attığı yılların aksine zaman içerisinde büyük değişim gösterdi. Manikürsüz sokağa çıkmayan Özcan, geçtiğimiz yıllarda kemerli olan burnunu yaptırıp kalın kaşlarını aldırttı.

Akşam
28 March 2005

İzzet Yıldızhan

● O da metroseksüel erkekler sınıfında kendine yer arayanlardan. Önce kemerli burnunu küçülttürdü, ardından da vücudunun çeşitli bölgelerine epilasyon yaptırarak fazla tüylerinden kurtuldu.

Hürriyet
1 March 2000

above: **Welcome to the metrosexual men's club:** *Now men are also part of the world of aesthetics and cosmetics. Men constitute almost half of the patients of aesthetic surgeons. They have their bellies reduced, their eyebrows and wrinkles removed. We are in the era of metrosexuality.*

right: **Men take care of themselves too:** *While women are living a revolution from an aesthetical point of view, men too are trying to keep up with this trend. There are formulas that can easily be implemented by men, who wish to take care of themselves almost as much as women.*

right: **Man make themselves beautiful too:** *Taking into consideration the fact that men want a healthier body and skin, hotels present alternative service. Luxury hotels, which compete with each other at offering various activities, meet different needs with their sauna, jacuzzi, pool and gyms.*

below: **I don't know if I am metrosexual:** *Haluk Dinçer says that he is not an expert in anything, but that he knows well how to be a CEO. He takes care of himself, he exercises every evening, he has his manicure done and he goes shopping for his clothes.*

Gazete Metro
12 January 2004

Tempo
26 June 2004

confronted in school by menacing older boys asking whether he was heterosexual, he had panicked and answered "no." Not knowing the meaning of the word, and assuming it carried dangerous sexual implications, he had instantly rejected the labeling. Similarly, metrosexuality, a popular topic in Turkey today, carries obvious sexual connotations. Does the fact that the term has gained acceptance in certain segments of society, particularly the upper echelons, mean that male sexuality is no longer an implicit point of reference but a topic for discussion? In a way, yes. Nowadays, even men are urged to rethink their sexual identity and purposively create a "new self" in greater harmony with a modern lifestyle. The metrosexual as a proposed masculine alternative has polished off some of the rough edges of his macho persona. Yet, as a revised male identity, it remains limited to appearances. The expression, *light erkek* [male], first coined by the popular Turkish sitcom *Çocuklar Duymasın* [Don't Let the Kids Hear], was a reference to the modern man who helped with housework, showed empathy to his woman, and concern to his children. Associating the epithet *light* – more commonly used in association with diet or low calorie products – with male [*erkek*], implied that male identity had been somewhat lightened or reduced. The "light" male is *less male*. Less dangerous, but also less potent. Thus, right from the start, the new role the appellation suggested appeared suspicious and was rejected. The fear men had of losing their male power in a changing society was thus expressed in the *light* male designation. Launched to counter this light male classification, the model of the *taş fırın erkek* [the Turkish equivalent of the "Marlboro Man"] simultaneously succeeded in providing grounds for polemic and legitimizing the fear reaction.

In the end, what had started out simply as a kind of new image and fashion-consciousness in straight men, progressed all the way to a reassessment of traditional masculine gender roles. This may have meant a step forward in reconsidering previously established norms of masculinity, but it was also important to clarify the social processes that put this polemic on the agenda and regulated it. Ayşe Öncü notes that in "contemporary consumer societies," state institutions are not the only means to govern sexual behavior; "this control is exerted through a complex network of influences sourced in the market." (2003: 185) Within a consumer economy

Face mask to clean blackheads on men's faces

(I tug at my body hairs) I am going to tear them all out, each and every one of them! bloody liars! you are not mine! bloody leeches! let go of my body! stop sucking my blood! bloody hairs, barbed wire of my body! all my life you have kept men away from me! Go away, get away from me! What part of me are you protecting? What part of me are you surrounding with your barbed wire?

— Mr Suat! Mr Suat! Are you sick? Is something wrong?

(- What do you think you are, a girl, are you shaving your legs, you scoundrel? That's not how you shave, this is how you shave! Come here, come here!

- Dad don't! My legs are bleeding!

- Of course they are going to bleed, of course they are! You will never forget this!)

— My hairs, my hairs are bleeding, my girl, they are bleeding.

[Murathan Mungan, "ÇÇ", *Son İstanbul*, 1988, Remzi Publications, p. 126]

Zaman
11 April 2004

"Taş fırın erkeği" NASIL PİŞİRİLİR?

HAYAT MEMAT

SENAİ DEMİRCİ

Bu yakınlarda hiç taş fırın erkeği gördünüz mü? Hiç konuşabildiniz mi kendileriyle? Nasıllar acaba? Memnunlar mı hayatlarından? Yoo; öyle kolayca randevu alamazsınız ondan. Sorularınızı da açıkça sorma cesareti bulamazsınız. Sorsanız bile size içinden geçenleri söylemez; söyleyemez. Mutlak bir iktidar sahibidir o. İçini dökerse tahtından aşağı düşer. Dokunulmazdır; sizinle temasa geçerse incinir, yaralanır. Anlaşılmazdır; konuşur ve sessizliğini bozarsa deşifre olur ve esrarını kaybeder. Ketumdur; içinde hiç fırtınalar kopmaz, hayal kırıklığı uğramaz kalbine, çocuklar gibi sevinmez, duyguları her daim durgun bir göl gibidir. Amansız fırtınaların göbeğinde kocaman bir kaya gibi kıpırtısız durur, deniz

How does one cook a Marlboro man?

continually gaining momentum, consumer desires hone in on diverse products and styles, and identities are constantly reshaped and redefined. While stories about the upper middle classes, in other words, the consumerist "rich kids," display their lifestyles, they also demonstrate how this segment of society sets itself apart from "the rest." Öncü examines the *maganda* [coarse, unrefined male] stereotype, popularized by a number of humor magazines in the beginning of the 1990s, as a new form of masculinity. In her words, "The *maganda* variety male, totally unaware of his uncouth masculine aggressiveness – and thus able to contaminate the period's moral discourse by jolting adult etiquette and revealing its inherent shallowness – emerged as a naïve type to be ridiculed." (2003:186) The term *maganda* also reflects the reactions of consumerist contemporary young males involved in a process of identity search to the dominant male codes of the times. "It [*maganda*] can be interpreted as an attempt to challenge the established norms of 'adult' masculinity." (Öncü, 2003:193) But it also expresses the "experience of alienation and otherness" within the new abundance of sexual fantasies and objectified icons and images in Istanbul during those same years. One of Öncü's chief conclusions is that *maganda* humor should be interpreted as "the product of a generation of young men who discovered that masculinity was something to pursue and persistently cultivate but never fully realize." (194) In the same way, the "metrosexual" and tongue in cheek "light" male characterizations – though who or what they defy is never made quite clear – reveal a similar quest for identity within a consumer economy, where objectified icons of masculinity mark the way, pointing to the uncertainty and variability of such market-dependent pursuits. Rather than the linear transformation of social relationships, we obtain a scattering into different male groups; the merging of masculinity and class through consumerism has created its own "others." The modern male image promoted by advertisements and the unchanging *maganda* or macho figures of humor magazines and the illustrated press are in continual interaction.

Now, men just like women feel the pressure to constantly make over their images, but it is the market that determines the techniques and directions. The contemporary male image is conceived in a consumer economy. The most tangible proof of

Since his childhood, Attila always took the Hollywood stars as example and he imitated their clothes, hair and movements to the point of boredom, both his and of others. At one point he had a hair cut with the crest lifted up like a cockscomb, like that of John Travolta in Saturday Night Fever which he saw a video of, and he had started to walk shaking his ass just like Travolta. He used to wander around like a character out of a film, with his ridiculous hair, the shirts and waistcoats that no one wore anymore and his gait, and he was an object of much ridicule because of this much delayed fashion, until Richard Gere in the film American Gigolo came to his aid. He would wear his uncle's expensive chequered jacket, his shirt and shot silk neck tie, he would comb his hair upwards with his fingers, just like Richard Gere, he would move with a bouncing gait and he believed he gave girls a thrill with his looks. [Mehmet Bilal, *Adresinde Bulunamadı*, 2005, Everest Publications, p. 50]

Natürel
1 October 1996

above: **Extreme hair ends are trendy:** *Men's hair styles have become as grandiose as women's. Their hair styles are changing with the changing fashions.*

below: **Zontintellectual Abdullah:** *Abdullah is officially becoming a zonta intellectual!*

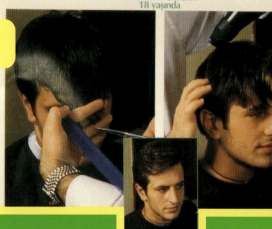

Hürriyet
5 February 1992

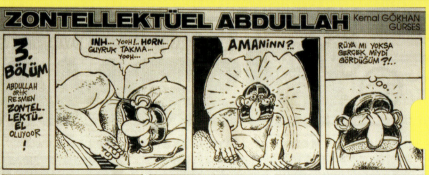

this is that new males are now part of the beauty and cosmetic industry's *clientele*. By purchasing all sorts of merchandise, from diverse personal care products to the services offered in hair and beauty salons, and by keeping up with continually evolving fashions, men are undergoing a transformation. The aim is to become *modern* and acquire visibility as the forerunners of change in the Westernization process which has been going on in Turkey for many years now. The new male ideals circulating in the media today are positioned in relation to Western concepts of modernity. From the 1990s on, men with a moustache are "out" and clean-shaven men are "in." Because it is considered a throwback to tradition and backwardness, the moustache controversy concerns all segments of society today, starting with politicians. Similarly, for certain sections of society, long hair, hair in a ponytail, or an earring have become indicators of the modern male. Celebrities like the pop star Tarkan and the footballer İlhan Mansız are the trendsetters in men's hair fashions. But here again a contradiction is involved. The clean-shaven young male sporting an earring and wearing his hair either casually long or moussed and short is presented both as modern and attractively "bohemian" and caricatured, derogatorily, as an *entel* ["intellectual"]. The term *entel* entered popular jargon in the late 1980s, showing up in cartoons to designate a kind of effeminate and pointless "intellectualism" that embodied just about all of the negative influences of excessive Western aspirations. One of its modified versions is the *Zontellektüel* – derived from the Turkish slang term "zonta", meaning a coarse and vulgar Anatolian male – in reference to the unrefined male [*zonta*] who nonetheless has intellectual ambitions and aims for upward mobility. The makeover he undergoes to become an *entel* involves growing out his hair, styling it into a ponytail, opting for an earring, and donning stylish eyewear. To top it all, this transformation remodels him into a submissive male entirely turned over to a woman's authority. The emphasis here is on the comical aspect of his endeavor, which has led to a purely superficial alteration of his outer appearance only. Through this attack on a particular male trend, a criticism is also aimed at society in general for its dependence on a so-called "liberalized" market. At the opposite end of the spectrum, is the "real" man, who bravely confronts life, ready to forcefully defend disappearing moral values and, tapping

Brut: One of the first shaving lotions to enter the market in the 1980s

One day he asked Şehmuz. Şehmuz couldn't remember Ismayil. He thought for a while.

"Ismayil. Ismayil? What does he look like?"

"He is a porter at the wharf too." Said Salpa.

"At the wharf, is he!"

"He is tall, with a moustache, a thick moustache."

"A moustache," said Şehmuz, "Thank God we all have it." He laughed. [Yılmaz Güney, *Salpa*, 1975/1989, Can Publications, p. 97]

CY: Aslıhan, you were going to tell us a positive aspect of being a woman...

A: I'll tell you a positive aspect, everybody treats you nice. (laughs)

CY: (laughs) So you say even oafs become more refined...

A: Yes, everywhere we go...

CY: Yes, being a woman, that is, being around women really makes one more refined. I saw an example of this, I must confess my dear Aslıhan, during my military service. As it's all men in the military service, you'll get those who don't brush their teeth, those who don't wash their feet, those who don't use any perfume! Since there are no women, who are you going to smell nice for, it doesn't matter if you smell nice for Şehmuz in the bed next to yours! Actually, it's worse if you smell nice (sound effects for laughter).

A. Well, that's why I wouldn't want to be a man.

CY: It's a good thing you aren't… Now, we ask our callers to tell us a negative aspect of being a woman too..

A: Well yes, both working and cleaning house is difficult of course.

CY: Aslıhan, are you married?

A: Yes, I've been married for a year and a half.

CY: Then you didn't know what you were getting yourself into with that signature. This is what that signature means… (sound of laughter)

A: I'm happy, I am… (sound of laughter) [A section from the phone conversation with a listener called Aslıhan, made during the programme "Ceyhun Yılmaz Show" which is broadcast everyday from 6 pm to 8 pm, Best FM, 8 March 2005]

into the rising wave of nationalism, also gains the support of staunch patriots. The male in the popular television series of the 2000s, *Kurtlar Vadisi* ["Valley of the Wolves"], who carries his gun everywhere he goes, may have sacrificed his moustache to fashion but he isn't about to give up other "traditional" codes of manhood. This "new" man takes a stance both against the state and the Western values that have come to symbolize it. Thus, masculinity, hotly debated amidst desires and threats, has not only generated different options in the consumer arena, but taken on a crucial place in politics as well.

At this point we should perhaps ask ourselves how new this "new" male stereotype really is. Studies in the cultural modernization of the Ottoman Empire, from the *Tanzimat* period to the first years of the Republic, suggest that evolving male stereotypes may not have been such a novel topic of discussion after all. It is possible to draw a parallel between the *alafranga* ["Western style"] male, popularized through novels and the press in the beginning of the 20th century, and today's metrosexual and other "new" male categorizations. As in contemporary classifications, what distinguished the *alafranga* male from his contemporaries was essentially his appearance. "Wearing a frock coat, trousers and a European-styled shirt, shaving off your moustache, going to the theater, living in the Beyoğlu side of town, owning a stone or brick house, embellishing spoken or written speech with foreign terms, eating with a fork, engaging in morning gymnastic exercises, marrying a foreign woman, strolling down the street arm in arm with your spouse…" (quoted from Cevdet Kudret by Deren, 2002: 386) were considered *alafranga* behaviors and the term was used to convey popular scorn. Long hair and a clean-shaven face were not only viewed as the main manifestations of the *alafranga* man but could indicate sexual deviance as well. When the protagonist in Ömer Seyfettin's short story, *Kesik Bıyık* ["Cut Moustache"], shaves off his luxuriant moustache to emulate American fashions, his father throws him out on the street and further humiliates him by declaring, "Even if your moustache grows back, your honor is lost for good!" (Deren, 2002: 402) To the extent that *alafranga* defined a lifestyle, it played a key role in identifying the moral criteria that singled out which aspects of Westernization were acceptable and which were not. The new

Bugün
17 May 1990

Şimdi, bıyıksız erkekler moda

■ Artık karşılarında "Güçlü erkek" görmek istemeyen hanımlar "Güçlü erkeğin simgesi" olarak gördükleri bıyığa da karşı çıkıyorlar.. Bazı hanımlar ise, daha ileri giderek bıyığı "İlkel" ve "Banal" buluyor

■ Bıyığı "Modası geçmiş bir alışkanlık" olarak tanımlayan hanımlar eşlerine, ve arkadaşlarına da bıyıklarını kesmeleri için baskı yapıyor.. Hanımlar özellikle Deniz Baykal'ı örnek göstererek "Bak! Bıyıksız da güzel" diyor. Hanımlar en çok Özal'ın bıyıklarını kesmesini istiyor.

DENİZ BAYKAL- "Bıyıksız erkek" isteyen hanımlara "model" oldu...

March 1980

ERKEK SÜNNET OLUR, ASKERLİK YAPAR, RAKI İÇER, PERMA-SHARP KULLANIR!

(Bundan daha doğal ne olabilir ki?)

PERMA-SHARP
"adı yeter"

Erkek yüreklidir, ciddidir, dürüsttür, sözünden dönmez, tıraş olur, Perma-Sharp kullanır!

above: **Men without moustaches are trendy now:** *Women who don't wish to have "strong men" around them, are also against moustaches, which they see as "a symbol of the strong man". Some ladies actually take it further and consider moustaches "primitive" and "banal".*

left: **Men get circumcised, they do their military service, they drink rakı, they use Perma-Sharp:** *Men are brave, serious, honest, they keep their promises, they shave, they use Perma-Sharp.*

dress codes proposed for men during the Republican period, such as the hat and tie, "going beyond simple elements of fashion, take on a transcendental quality, fusing religious, ethnic and social (urban- rural) distinctions, to become a secular uniform demonstrating the wearer's loyalty to the state. Anti-establishment attitudes, on the other hand, are expressed with moustache and beard or differing headgear." (Deren, 2002: 388) A similar symbolization can be observed ten years on, in the wake of the 1980 military coup, with the resistance developed against regulations prohibiting long hair, beards and moustaches. Before the 1980s, diverse moustache styles had indicated political affiliation and the fact that the state was attempting to suppress – if only outwardly – the expression of these various political positions, had met with the opposition of even the police.

Shaving, manicure and pedicure set for men

The shadow of a doubt passes from his continuously shining eyes. Maybe in order to cover this, he smiles slightly under his fair Gorki moustache. I have to say something:

"The men of our mothers' time had Hitler moustaches. Our men have no moustaches, like well shaved Texas cowboys. But there were some with Don Ameche or Clark Gable moustaches..."

His face tenses. He waits. I skip his Gorki moustanche. And I skip the Lenin moustaches on the streets, ever increasing in number. I get up. "Come on, let's go to the Hergele Square. I haven't been there for years." [Adalet Ağaoğlu, *Ölmeye Yatmak*, 1973/2004, Yapı Kredi Publications, p. 252]

Consequently, for a long time now, hair length and facial hair have symbolized political struggle and change. In this sense, both the well-groomed males who emerged in the period spanning the 1980s to the present and today's new masculine stereotypes can be viewed within a broader politico-historical framework. More specific to the last 25 years is the fact that state and market control have become more intensely merged and that market codes have gradually acquired more weight. Today, the male image is rapidly catching up with the female image – which, ever since the Republican period, has held a key position in the showcase of modernity and been under scrutiny from skirt lengths to head scarves – leaving the polemic on men in the shadows. New power strategies indirectly filtered through the market and acquiring momentum with fashion have made men more visible targets. Now, they too are left face to face with the obligation to recreate themselves and revamp their masculinity. Yet, all these changes have not put an end to male violence in society. On the contrary, new masculine ideals keep spurring on the violence. Apparently, the macho male trend never dies.

Erkekler saçlarına taktılar

Erkekler artık saçlarını boyatarak, ilginç modellerde kestirerek ve kazıtarak görünümlerinde değişiklik yapıyorlar. Şimdi kuaför sırasında onlar bekliyor

Milliyet
1 September 2002

Metroseksüel milletvekilleri! TAM LİSTE!

KİMİ SAÇINI BOYATIYOR, KİMİ ÇAPKINLIK PEŞİNDE. METROSEKSÜEL OLANI DA VAR. BAŞBAKAN ERDOĞAN GİBİ GÖZ MASKESİ KULLANANI DA... İŞTE VEKİLLERİN "ACAİP" HALLERİ...

Haftalık
17 July 2004

top **Men are obsessed with their hair:** *Men too have started changing their appearances by having their hair dyed, getting interesting hair cuts or having their head shaved. Nowadays they are the ones waiting at the hairdresser's for their turn to come.*

above: **Metrosexual members of parliament**

right: **They said you are a communist and they cut off half of my moustache:** *Ziya Doğanoğlu, who was attacked by about 20 people in Yozgat and had half of his moustache cut off, said "I have nothing to do with either left-wing or right-wing people. My only crime is to grow a moustache."*

below: **The Istanbul police is not willing to cut off its moustaches!** *In a letter sent by the Istanbul Chief of Police to the Police Departments, policemen have been asked to cut off their moustache completely and to cut their hair short within 48 hours.*

Günaydın
13 January 1980

"Sağla solla ilişkim yok"
Yozgat'ta 20 kadar kişinin saldırısına uğrayan ve bıyığının bir tarafı olduğu gibi kesilen Ziya Doğanoğlu "Benim ne sağ ile ne de sol ile ilişkim var. Tek suçum bıyık bırakmak" dedi...

"Sen komünistsin diyerek bıyığımın yarısını kestiler"

48 saat mühlet tanındı

İstanbul polisi bıyıklarının kesilmesine razı olmuyor!

Günaydın
28 January 1980

SADETTİN TANTAN — UĞUR GÜR

Bıyıkları ile ünlü iki polis şefi

İstanbul Emniyet Müdürlüğü'ne bağlı polislerin yarısından fazlasının bıyığı vardır. Halen Turizm Polisi Müdürü olan Sadettin Tantan ile Yıldırım Ekipler Amiri Uğur Gür de bıyıklarıyla ünlü iki emniyet görevlisidir. Bazı polisler bıyıklarını kesmektense meslekten ayrılmayı tercih edeceklerini söylüyorlar...

SÜSLÜ ADEMLER

ADEM'İN TORUNLARINDA BİR SÜS, BİR PÜS GÖRMEYİN. KERATALARA YAKIŞIYOR DA... ERKEK OLMAYI BAŞLIBAŞINA BİR NİMET GÖRÜP, KENDİNE BAKMAYAN ECİŞ BÜCÜŞ ERKEKLER GÜRUHU İÇİNDEKİ BU FARKLI ERKEKLER RUHUMUZU AÇIYOR, İÇİMİZİ KIPIRDATIYOR, GÖZÜMÜZÜ ŞENLENDİRİYOR. İŞTE ONLARDAN BAZILARI...

MURAT ERSAN

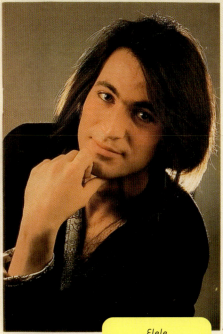

GÜR AKAD

DEHA AKGÜN — İLHAN İREM

SİNAN ÇETİN

Elele
July 1989

Milliyet
18 September 2002

Şimdilerde maço erkek moda!

İmajınızı yenileyin
Şükran Pakkan

Dizimizin bu bölümünde iyi bir izlenim için gardırobunuzda bulunması gereken giysi ve renkleri öğrenecek, önemli ipuçlarını yakalayacaksınız... 'İmaj yapıcısı' İnci Beydeşman da, ünlülerin imajlarına, günümüz modasına açıklık getiriyor...

above: **Glamorous Adams:** *How glamorous the descendants of Adam are! But it must be said that it suits the scoundrels too... Within the group of misshapen men, who believe that being a man is a blessing in itself and that they don't need to take care of themselves, these exceptional men stir our soul, they are good for the heart and pleasing to the eye.*

left: **Macho men are trendy now!** *In this part of the series, you will discover which clothes and colours you should have in your cupboard in order to make a good impression and you will pick up important clues... Image maker İnci Beydeşman tells us of the image of famous people and of contemporary fashion.*

Do I have a psychological disorder?

"Aysel? Aysel, are you there?" No answer. Or rather, the answer is, in quick succession: "I was afraid… I was afraid… I was afraid…" It is said and written casually here and there that somebody was afraid of the military service, somebody of the martial law, somebody of the government, somebody of the future, and so on. Before you come to these, people have many fears that are more daily, more ordinary, more close to one's heart, more to do with themselves. There is the fear of getting wet like a cat in the rain and being caught like that by one's student. There is the fear of being pitied. … Then there is the fear of finding oneself out of the blue without the protection of a man, of someone close… Small and very personal fears…
[Adalet Ağaoğlu, *Hayır…*, 1987/2005, Yapı Kredi Publications, p. 238-239]

While the police was taking away the body riddled with holes, a few workmen returning from the nighshift showed their identity cards and passed the police barricade. … They were hurrying to get home. One of them, a short, dark skinned, dried up looking man asked the police "What happened chief?" "There was a shoot out, a terrorist died" said the police coldly. "God, isn't that over yet!" said the man. When there was no answer from the policeman, the man pulled the collar of his jacket further up around his head to protect himself from the snow and he walked fast towards the houses… [Ayşegül Devecioğlu, *Kuş Diline Öykünen*, 2004, Metis Publications, p. 204]

The beginning of the 1980s was a time of considerable anxiety in Turkey. Yet, neither the dailies nor the newly emerging weekly magazine press alluded to one of its most obvious causes: the 1980 military *coup* and its consequences for everyday living. Following the *coup*, soldiers and military vehicles patrolled the streets, houses were raided, and people were violently apprehended inside or outside their homes and taken into custody. Radio stations ceaselessly broadcast information about the various prohibitions enforced. A number of documentary films, novels and short stories, which today grab the public's attention, reveal that during this period many people were put in jail, tortured, died under torture, or "disappeared" while under custody. The intrusion of the inhumane practices of jails into "normal" everyday life inevitably results in *fear*. In a country where the uncertainties that go with a period of transition already prevail, political violence and oppression associated with an economic crisis can create a form of generalized mass anxiety. In such a context, health experts ponder whether these fears are justified and suggest we may be "too anxious" for our own good. Newspaper and magazine articles focusing on these issues are not necessarily aimed at suppressing or evading unpleasant realities, they may also be considered part of a discourse seeking to reshape individuals.

First, anxiety is said to have pervaded all levels of society, working men and women, housewives, the young and old alike. Society as a whole is declared *anxious* and there is talk of the need for a national mental health policy. In this manner, people are gradually familiarized with *psychological* discourse, which naturally articulates issues on a separate level from the period's dominant political discourse. Whereas political discourse identifies an ideology, a group or a segment of society as a threat, psychological discourse internalizes this threat and addresses people as *individuals*. While in society as a whole the focus is usually on "togetherness," individuals seem urged to separate from others and discover within *themselves* the *sickness* at the root of their

güzin abla
Dertleriniz için buradayım

Korkuyorum

ORDU'DAN — Güzin Abla 17 yaşındayım. Bazı alışkanlıklarım yüzünden çok zayıfım. Ayrıca beni çok üzen başka bir endişem de var. Bunun ilerde evlendiğim zaman gerdek gecesi başarısızlık yapabileceğimden korkuyorum. Şayet cinsel gücüm zayıf olursa ne yapmalıyım? Şu andan itibaren vereceğiniz bilgi için teşekkür ederim.

Evlatcığım, bir kere böyle korkuları kafandan atmaya bak, ruhsal yönden bu gibi çekingenlikler cinsel yaşamını etkileyebilir. Sonra daha çok erken olmakla beraber bir şeyi kesinlikle kabul et ki, gerdek gecesi ille de başarılı olmak ya da muhakkak o gece cinsel ilişki başlamalı diye bir kural olmamalı. İki taraf da arzu ettiği zaman başlamalı. Çünkü kendin kadar evleneceğin genç kızı da düşünmelisin. Bu kimsenin de ilk defa yepyeni bir dünyaya girdiğini ve istediği kadar rahat da görünse onun da bir takım korkuları olacağını unutmamalı. Ayrıca iki taraf da bu konuda açık açık konuşmaktan kaçınmamalı. Önce aralarında konuşarak bir anlaşma sağlıyabilmeli. Genç karı-koca ancak karşılıklı güven üzerine kurulmuş bir ilişkiye ulaşabilmişlerse her iki tarafın da mutsuz olması için sebep kalmaz.

Saklambaç
17 August 1980

I'm afraid: *Dear Güzin, I'm 17 years old. I'm very thin, because of certain habits of mine. I also have another worry which is a great source of concern for me. I'm afraid that when I get married I might be unsuccessful on my wedding night. What should I do if my sexual drive is not strong enough? Thank you very much for any information you might provide from this moment on...*

left: **We are all afraid:** *Why, how, when are we afraid... Here are all your questions answered by an expert...*

below: **Are your fears real, or are you sick?** *In some of us fears are pushed into the subconscious, in some of us they are more obvious, they really stick out. There are those who can't stay at home alone, those who can't sleep in darkness, those who are afraid of death, afraid or animals, and so on...*

Haftasonu
17 September 1982

Kadınca
July 1982

fears and anxieties. The "sickness" metaphor is actually the one most often resorted to in post-1980 Turkey. In a 1981 speech, Kenan Evren compared the September 12 *coup* to a medical intervention: "... if a sickness is not diagnosed, proper medication cannot be prescribed. Because proper medication had not been administered, sickness spread through the entire body. At this point, the Turkish Armed Forces, with the power delegated by the people, had to intervene once again to initiate medical treatment." (Gürbilek, 1992: 73) The sickness metaphor simultaneously legitimizes tracking down the "unhealthy" aspects of society (i.e. the elements that threaten social order) and the actions required to eradicate them. It also puts Evren in the doctor/surgeon position, making it easier for him to embellish his "interventions" with technical analogies while ridding them of political meaning. In the name of healing society, the health theme was merged with concepts of order and control, revealing the basics of the modern power techniques applied. Still, in the discourse of the 1980 *coup*, modern approaches were entangled with overt oppression and violence. In contrast, psychological discourse, which functioned on an individual level, was able to expand on and apply modern power techniques by joining forces with another contemporary discourse: *individualization*.

The Özal period, which started a few years after the 1980 military intervention, took the first step toward "liberalization," as if totally rejecting any connection to the *coup*'s repression and violence. With the emphasis on free markets, a new period of *opportunities* began. During this period, remembered today as one where the "make it big" ideology spread, individualization and individualism were proffered as new ideals under the emblem, "be the master of your own destiny." A central feature of individualization is the return to the self and accepting the *responsibility* to optimize one's own health and competence. At this level, issues can no longer be resolved by "collective surgical intervention;" individuals have to become aware of the sources of their own problems, seek help from a professional and recover their mental health through adequate treatment and medication. Thus, the basic procedure of psychological discourse is established: 1) *Individual awareness and responsiveness*, 2) *professionals*, 3) *techniques and products*.

"When the doctor said "Mr Alkan, sit next to me", he relaxed and sat next to the doctor.
"How are you?"
"I'm fine."
"Are you getting used to us?"
"I am getting used to you, doctor, but I still feel as if I'm going to die, it's as if the medicines weren't of much use."
"You are in such a rush Mr Alkan, just wait, and anyway, if it were just the medicines which were supposed to make you get better, we wouldn't have admitted you here."
"But then what do I need to do, doctor, I'm following all the rules."
"Do you think it's enough to simply follow the rules?"
"No doctor, I'm not thinking of anything. Anyway, it's thinking that makes me like this, that's why you should give me medicines but not tell me to think. You cannot imagine how bad one feels when one thinks, doctor."
"Alright, Mr Alkan, thank you. You can go now, but for the time that you are here you will have to think, just as long as you know."
[Meltem Arıkan, *Ve... Veya... Belki...*, 2003, Everest Publications, p. 32-33]

Her iş bitti, sıra buna geldi!
Ulusal ruh sağlığı politikası istendi

Akşam
14 October 1981

left: **National mental health policy demanded**

below: **The country of mad Ziyas:** The 15 year old boy who was informed on by his school principal for the crime of "making communist propaganda" was in prison for 87 days. He was held at the Forensic Medicine Department for 33 days by the glorious Professor Ayhan Songar who didn't even let him see his family. And he is still made to suffer in various tribunals.

Gırgır
19 February 1989

TÜRK - İŞ'İN İLGİNÇ ARAŞTIRMASI
GEÇİM DARLIĞI İŞÇİLERİ RUH HASTASI YAPIYOR

■ İŞÇİLERİN GEÇİM DARLIĞINDA «RUH SAĞLIĞI GINA» YAKALANDIKLARINIB ELİRLEYEN ARAŞTIRMA SONUÇLARI YÜKSEK HAKEM KURULU ÜYELERİNE GÖNDERİLECEK. TÜRK — İŞ 8'İNCİ BÖLGE TEMSİLCİSİ TOPUŞ «BİR OTOMOBİL FABRİKASINDA ÇALIŞANLARIN BÜYÜK ÇOĞUNLUGUNDA RUH HASTALIĞI VAR DEMEKTİR» DEDİ...

Akşam
21 December 1981

above: **The struggle for livelihood makes workers mentally ill:** *Research results which show that workers with livelihood problems become mentally ill, will be sent to the members of the Higher Council of Referees.*

below: **Young people are depressed:** *According to a research published by the State Planning Organisation in February 1985, one third of university age youth show "symptoms of depression".*

GENÇLİK
Gençlik depresyonda
Devlet Planlama Teşkilatı tarafından yayınlanan Şubat 1985 tarihli bir araştırmaya göre üniversite gençliğinin üçte birinde "depresif belirtiler" bulundu

Nokta
26 May 1985

Stress bracelet

"Isn't the greatest success of psychiatrists to open up their patients, to find and bring out the fears and pains lying in the depths of their hearts or of their unconscious? Do patients open up more easily in sterile offices, or in spaces where they would feel more comfortable?" [Ayşe Kulin, *Adı: Aylin*, 1997, Remzi Publications, p. 136]

Acar Baltaş and Zuhal Baltaş, Ways to Deal with Stress, *1983, Remzi Publications: one of the first and most popular examples of books dealing with stress, published in the 1980s.*

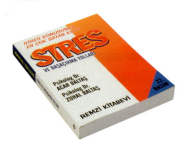

Interestingly, the best way to create awareness and responsiveness in individuals is by tapping into their anxieties and fears. This would explain newspaper and magazine headlines inquiring "are you depressed?" and the frequency of editorial texts related to health, mental or otherwise. We are informed that fatigue, loss of appetite, lethargy and various other symptoms could be the signs of an illness, for instance, of depression. Popular media thus rouses the fear of sickness dormant in most of us. The chief targets of this psychological discourse are women, adolescents and children, the more "vulnerable" components of society. Women, whose personalities and labors have vanished into the "housewife" category, are instructed to view their problems and emotional crises as individual rather than social issues. It is generally accepted that depression occurs more frequently in women, perhaps even more so in housewives, and it is therefore considered crucial for the welfare of both family and society that women deal with their depression. In case this weren't enough, women are also expected to be on the alert for signs of psychological disturbance in their children. Cautionary examples abound in the press: your lack of drive may actually be masked depression; if your child "can't sit still" he could be hyperactive; are you facing up to the "psychological" causes of your marriage problems? – and all lead to the same recommendation: seek professional help. Similarly, it is hinted that undiagnosed personality disorders may lie beneath the emotional turmoil of adolescence. The frequency of mental illnesses within specific segments of society is determined "scientifically," making it easier for individuals to fit themselves into categories and put a name to their condition. *Health professionals* play an essential role both in spreading the fear of illness and offering advice for recovery. After the 1980s, in Turkey, as elsewhere in the world, there was an increasing demand for expertise in every field and for the experts who provided it. At the same time, expertise of all forms in areas like health, sexuality, child care and education were popularized. As the fields of specialization expanded, experts previously bound to specific institutions became more "liberated" and began to communicate their knowledge through other channels, in particular, the media. Articles in print nowadays often include the opinions of authorities

Natürel
November 1996

Haftalık
2 December 2005

above: **Depressive people who are not aware of their depression:** *They are not aware of it, but they are among us.*

right: **Are you manic-depressive?** *Have you been acting irrationally recently? Maybe you have become manic-depressive. Take a look at the clues, but for your trouble to be identified, it is better if you consult with an expert.*

Bilinçaltı intiharın bilimsel adı: STRES
...Ve, yenmenin yolları

Türkiye şartlarında ev sahibine kızmanız, trafik karmaşası karşısında çılgına dönmeniz, orta çapta stresler. Bunların herbirinin beyin hücrelerinin 1 milyonunun ölümüne yol açtığını biliyor muydunuz? Bugün yetişkin insanların yüzde 15'inin sorunu olan depresyon geçiren hastaların ancak yüzde 10'u hekime gidiyor. Amerika'da stresin yol açtığı hastalıkların maliyeti ise 100 milyar doları buluyor. Ancak bu tehlikeli düşmanınızı tanırsanız, onunla baş edecek yöntemlerden birini de tercih edebilirsiniz.

Stresten kendinizi koruyun — Doç. Dr. Nevzat Tarhan, stresle mücadelenin yolunun önce stres belirtilerini tanımaktan geçtiğini belirtiyor. Tarhan, stresi önlemek için kendinize bir uğraşı bulmanızı öneriyor.

Stresle mücadele edin — Toplumsal uyumu bozulan kişilerin ruhsal tepkilerinin değiştiğini söyleyen Prof. Dr. Özcan Köknel, insanların değişikliklere uyum sağladıkları sürece mutlu olacağını belirtiyor.

above: **Stress and methods for overcoming it:** Under the living conditions of Turkey, getting mad at one's landlord, going crazy because of traffic jams are medium sized stresses. Do you know that each one of these causes the death of 1 million brain cells?

below: **Housewives are having mental breakdowns:** Professor Çiğdem Kağıtçıbaşı and Psychologist Suna Tanaltay have stated that housewives have mental breakdowns due to lack of love and to not making good use of their free time.

Günaydın
20 July 1991

Milliyet
1 June 1988

● Hastaneye başvuranların sayısı 9 yılda 5 kat arttı

Ev kadınları bunalımda

● Profesör Çiğdem Kağıtçıbaşı ile Psikolog Suna Tanaltay, sevgisizlik ve boş zamanları değerlendirememek yüzünden ev kadınlarının psikolojik rahatsızlıklara yakalandığını söylediler

Seks terapistinden çiftlere ev ödevi

Cinsellikle ilgili sorun yaşayan çiftler, bu konuda eğitim alan seks terapistlerine başvuruyor. 25 yıldır cinsel terapi yapan Dr. Nesrin Yetkin; "Vajinismus, erken boşalma terapiyle genellikle 2-4 ayda çözümleniyor" diyor

Akşam
27 March 2005

Haydar Dümen

Vajinusmus'u bir seansta çözerim

Nöroloji ve Psikiyatri Uzmanı Dr. Haydar Dümen, kadınlarda cinsel ilişkiye girmeye engel olan vajinusmus (cinsel ilişkiye girememe) geliştirdiği tenikle tek seansta ortadan kaldırdığını ileri sürdü: "Kızlık zarı korkusu, cinsel bilgisizlik ve yanlış inanışlar ülkemizde vajinusmua neden olan faktörler. Bu sorunu tek bir seansla çözüyorum. Hasta sayısı artınca bilimsel kongrede geliştirdiğim yöntemi sunacağım." Dümen, tekniği konusunda daha fazla bilgi vermekten kaçınıyor.

Hürriyet
22 May 1985

Temizlik yapmak, düzenli olmak iyi fakat her şeyin fazlası zarar.

Saplantıların esiri olmayın...

Kimi elinde toz bezi hiç durmadan görünen ve görünmeyen tozları siler durur, kimi evden çıktıktan sonra tekrar tekrar geri dönerek etrafı kontrol eder, kimi durmadan orayı burayı düzeltir.

above: **Homework for couples from a sex therapist:** *Couples that have sexual problems turn to sex therapists who receive training in this field. Dr Nesrin Yetkin, who has been carrying out sexual therapy for 25 years, says: "Vaginismus and premature ejaculation can be treated in 2-4 monts."*

left: **Get rid of your obsessions:** *Cleanliness and orderliness are good but overdoing them is harmful.*

A man went to the doctor. He said I'm a doctor too, don't you go thinking you are a fucking shit.

A man went to the doctor. He said can we have a picture taken together.

A man went to the doctor. He said it doesn't say on the bell, is your name Zhivago.

A man went to the doctor. He said the Indians will attack the mail coach at dusk.

A man went to the doctor. He said what do you say we form a comedy duo together.

A man went to the doctor. He said how many sugar crystals do you think there are in a lump of sugar.

A man went to the doctor. He said I wanted to talk to you about the state of your gadget.

A man went to the doctor. He said if you'd been a lawyer I would have hired you.

The same man that day didn't go to the doctor. The doctor was very worried! [Küçük İskender, *Balık Burcu Hikayeleri*, "profesör doktor stres kıyamet II", 2000, Parantez Publications, p. 51]

Some of the medications used in the treatment of psychological "illnesses"

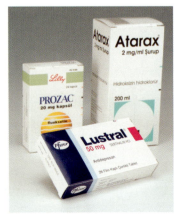

on varied topics and professionals appear on TV shows and even commercials. Professional advice frequently turns up on the packaging of consumer products and specialized product information has become directly accessible to the general public via the market. Along with the greater accessibility of expert knowledge, the scope of psychological discourse has broadened. Health professionals now warn us about correctly diagnosing a complaint. The terms, "mental illness" or "psychological disorder" have become too vague. *Depression*, *anxiety disorder* and *panic attack* all belong in distinct categories. At the turn of the millennium, the fusion of psychiatry and psychology has resulted in more varied and technically sophisticated classifications.

If one way of determining possible psychological disturbances in individuals is to familiarize them with the topic and provoke the necessary concern, the next step is to label the syndrome. Newspapers and magazines offer popular tests and quizzes to determine mental health and identify disorders. Certain publications run serials categorizing disorders and listing their main symptoms. Referring to the 1980s, Nurdan Gürbilek talks about a sudden "explosion of words." "A number of previously unidentified lexical areas dubbed today, 'individual,' 'generation,' 'private life,' or 'sex,' first entered our terminology in this decade," she writes. "This led to an explosion of new words, distinct meanings and definitions." (1992: 37) In the same manner, mental disorders took on separate names and emerged as the "objects" of a new discourse. Once experts had identified the psychological disturbances and crises people were experiencing, it was time to introduce the methods to deal with them. Popular psychological discourse advocates various forms of treatment, with somewhat inconsistent claims. For some, it's a new miracle drug, for others, psychotherapy is the only course to follow. The 1980s are also a time when Turkey was introduced to Prozac, the hugely popular and just as controversial "happiness pill." As doctors began to prescribe the newer antidepressants more and more, psychotherapy was relegated backstage as a more time-consuming and expensive form of treatment, best reserved for an affluent minority. Nonetheless, psychotherapy did gradually develop a large and differentiated range of therapeutic approaches and achieved reasonable popularity with a particular segment of society. Being

Hürriyet
5 January 1997

Biba
January 1998

above: **I am a family matchmaker:** *It is necessary to have psychological check-ups. Whenever we talk about check-ups, we think about check-ups for physical illnesses. But one's soul also needs a check-up. This is also as important as physical illnesses. It is necessary to have a check-up done before a part of the soul dies.*

left: **Discover your soul during psychotherapy**

Hello, I am Nil Gün. We are going to take an internal voyage together. You can make use of this tape in the office, at home, whenever you feel under stress. At the end of this stress meditation you will feel energetic, lively and at ease. A stress meditation held before an important meeting or before taking a decision will be of great advantage to you. Your daily productivity will increase. Meditation done regularly, every day, will be beneficial to your health. You are precious enough to dedicate some time to yourself every day. You can meditate either sitting up or lying down on your back. If you are wearing a belt please loosen it. Don't ever do stress meditation while you are driving. Now put yourself in a comfortable position, close your eyes, follow carefully what is said. [From a hypnomeditation CD prepared by Nil Gün for managing stress related problems, *Hypnomeditation Series 2*, 2004]

Stress balls

The miniature fountain which according to the Feng-shui trend is believed to bring peace, quiet and abundance to houses

in therapy is no longer considered so out of the ordinary. Turkey reached the new millennium with a significant upsurge in the diagnosis of mental illness. According to statistics, 15 million people are affected by psychiatric disorders. Newspaper headlines across the country proclaiming "We're depressed," have become a daily occurrence and pop songs climb the charts with lyrics like "depresyondayım"["depression's got me"] or "psikopatım" ["I'm a psychopath."] Psychobabble has definitely entered everyday language and, in the growing craze for self-help manuals, well-known psychologists publish book after book. Psychological discourse has infiltrated everyday life and the techniques to achieve emotional health now form part of a much more diversified field. TV talk shows, radio programs, hotlines, helplines and free counseling websites have placed psychological discourse even beyond the authority of health professionals. The ubiquitous term *stress*, for instance, seems trend-proof. In the frenzied tempo of modern life everyone has their share of *stress*; a number of personal issues are related to *stress* and we're all seeking ways to cope with *stress*. *Dr. Stress* is here to give his advice on stress management, and you can buy *stress*-lowering herbal teas in the supermarket. As psychology has become more mainstream, it has also fused with the health care consumer market.

In the quest for psychological wellbeing, a number of alternative therapies are out there, countering traditional western medicine, challenging psychiatry's conception of what defines a "normal" individual, and proposing techniques for "alternative healing." Alternative health practitioners offer a wide range of services and programs in yoga, NLP (neuro-linguistic programming), and reiki, to name but a few, to manage stress and promote both physical and mental health. Despite the assortment of unconventional techniques and futuristic approaches now on hand to guide us on the path to "spiritual" wellness, psychological discourse has not yet achieved total liberation from specific norms and value judgments. Being a "normal" member of society is perhaps no longer an absolute requirement, but there are other crucial criteria as well for the modern individual: a striving for inner self-knowledge and for the ways to reconstruct identity. In this quest any stress-reducing method is justified; if it works for you, even belly-dancing in a tavern will do.

Piyale Madra, Ademler ve Havvalar **2005**

left: −My depression must have a name. It's like psychomatic nevrastenic paranoia.
−Couldn't you only be having depression?
−It's not that simple Mister... It's not that simple!

below: **We are going insane:** *The nervous breakdowns resulting from the economic crisis bring about murders too. The number of people who go insane and kill family members or rain bullets on relatives or cut off arms with axes is increasing day by day.*

Yeni Şafak **2 July 2001**

Cinnet getiriyoruz

Krizin doğurduğu bunalımlar beraberinde cinayetleri de getiriyor. Cinnet geçirip ailesini vuranlar, yakınlarına kurşun yağdıranlar ve baltayla kol kesenlerin sayısı giderek artıyor.

AİLESİNİ SİLAHLA VURDU

AVCILAR'da cinnet geçiren baba, biri kız iki çocuğunu ve kendisine engel olmak isteyen eşini silahla vurdu. Nurettin Ateş isimli baba belirlenmeyen bir nedenle cinnet geçirerek evinde bulunan ruhsatlı tabanca ile önce 14 yaşındaki oğlu Musa'yı ardından ise 5 yaşındaki kızı Ezgi'yi silahla yaraldı. Asabi baba polis tarafından gözaltına alındı.

BALTAYLA KOLUNU KESTİLER

ADANA'da 2 aile arasında alacak-verecek meselesi yüzünden çıkan kavgada, 8 kişi yaralandı. Bıçak, satır ve av tüfeğinin kullanıldığı kavgada, Cahit Kılıç, Rukiye Kılıç ve Hüseyin Kılıç, Süleyman Demir, Celal Kalaycıoğlu ve Zühre Besler yaralandı. Tedavi altına alınan yaralılardan Zühre Besler'in baltayla kolunun kesildiği bildirildi.

ENİŞTESİNE MERMİ YAĞDIRDI

ADIYAMAN'da bir vatandaş kızkardeşini 8 ay önce kaçırarak evlendiği için eniştesi Abdulkadir Gürbüz'ü (27) öldürdü. Lisenin arkasına saklanıp eniştesini bekleyen Aziz Delice eniştesini gördüğü an 3 el ateş etti. Kaçmaya çalışan eniştesinin dengesini kaybetmesini fırsat bilen Delice üzerine oturarak göğsüne 6 el ateş ederek ölümüne yol açtı

DEPRESYONDAYIZ!

İstanbul'da yapılan bir araştırma şehrin ruhsal durumunu gözler önüne serdi Çalışma sonuçlarına göre Şişli, Bakırköy ve Kadıköylüler ağır depresyonda...

Sabah
14 October 2005

Eleme, kedere, acıya ve gözyaşlarına son!
Mutluluk hapı Türkiye'de

İşte! Mucize hap!

Bunalıma giren, yaşama küsen ve intiharı düşünen insanları bir anda mutlu eden hap Türkiye'ye geldi

- Şimdilik kaçak olarak Tahtakale'de kutusu 75 bin liradan satılan Prozac ve Fluctin adlı ilaçların, beyin ile sinir hücreleri arasında uyum sağladığı ve bunalımları hemen yok ettiği bildirildi.
- Amerika ve Almanya'da doktor reçetesi ile isteyen herkese satılan hapların uyuşturucu ve bağımlılık yapıcı hiçbir etkisi olmadığı da ifade ediliyor.

Bugün
4 May 1990

EV HANIMLARI ARASINDA NLP İN, ALTIN GÜNLERİ OUT
Hayat yeniden başlıyor

Altın günleri düzenlemek artık ev hanımları arasında demode oldu. Şimdi yeni moda kişisel gelişim kurslarına katılarak evde ve sosyal yaşamda yeni ufuklar açmak.

Yeni Şafak
31 March 2004

top left: **We all have depression!** *A research carried out in Istanbul has shown the psychological situation of the city. According to the results of the research, the inhabitants of Şişli, Bakırköy and Kadıköy have serious depression.*

above: **The pill of happiness is in Turkey:** *The pill which instantly gives happiness to people who are having a mental breakdown, who are depressed and who are considering suicide is now in Turkey.*

left: **Life starts anew:** *Organising gold lottery days among housewives is now out of fashion. The new fashion is to participate in personal development courses and discover new horizons at home*

Marie Claire
October 2004

left: **We fly collectively!** *It is as if the whole world has resigned itself to the unbearable lightness of being. Reiki, yoga, bioenergy, EFT or NLP... If these terms are not unfamiliar to you, and if hearing of concepts such as "power of thought" and "global life energy" give you positive thoughts, then welcome to the club!*

below: **Belly dance to get rid of stress!** *Experts have said that one way to get rid of stress, which is the cause of so many illnesses, is doing lots of belly dancing.*

Meydan
1 August 1993

A new age a new person

One of the most popular expressions going around in the eighties was "making it big." Those who managed to latch onto a fast and relatively painless way to make money and achieve a higher quality of life were considered to have "made it big." Stories about new celebrities who had become rich overnight and moved up the social ladder turned up more and more frequently in the press. Hülya Avşar, for instance, had succeeded in acquiring an apartment in Ataköy and a luxury car with the money she made from her films. Again around that time, serials featuring the life stories of the country's leading bankers and tycoons began to appear in newspapers and magazines. Sakıp Sabancı wrote series for the press and published books in which he gave lengthy advice on the ways to make money and become rich. Sabancı wasn't the only one to consider that personal wealth was the "reward of success." A number of other "prominent" personalities shared his views on the subject. In a consumer's paradise, money was the key to open all doors. This was also the decade when a growing number of young people entered college hoping to study either economics or management. Accordingly, universities offering programs in these disciplines gradually came to occupy the highest ranks on a college candidate's list of preferences. Parallel to these developments, there was an upsurge in the number of people who considered the emerging new generation increasingly devoid of "idealistic" aspirations and "materialistic."

Scene from the contest "Apprentice". The aim of the contest is to choose among the contestants the most successful entrepreneur. [Kanal D, 3 April 2005]

These examples show how material wealth and the appeal of prosperity were related to and represented in different social segments in the post-1980 period. Despite their complexity and diversity, they can be considered the first indicators of alterations in the discourse encompassing the neo-liberal economic and political restructuring process Turkey has been undergoing for the past 25 years. A closer look at this process reveals that economic issues were becoming progressively more central to public concerns. On the one hand, the

3 ayda 3 film çevirdi... Son model bir BMW'si, Ataköy'de bir katı var...

Hülya Avşar'dan "köşeyi dönme" sanatı

Haftanın Sesi
1 January 1984

25 milyonluk daire
Sinemanın çilekeş aktörü Cüneyt Arkın, film üstüne film çevirip ancak bir evle, bir yazlık alabilirken, üç ayda üç film çeken Hülya Avşar, Ataköy'deki bu lüks daireye gözünü kırpmadan 25 milyonu sayıverdi... Ya da saydırıverdi...

Bu da 4 milyonluk BMW
Hülya Avşar, kurşuni renkli 4 milyonluk BMW'sini (solda) alnının teriyle aldığını söylüyor. 1984'e, 83 model BMW ile giren taçsız güzelimizin (üstte) şimdiki hedefi yazlık almakmış. Zor mu yani?... Hele bir milyona bir film daha çevirsin onu da alır.

Lessons on how to make it, from Hülya Avşar:
Would you like to spend only 6 million and own goods and property worth 29 million? Then come and listen to the economy politics of this beauty without a crown.

May 1987

Sakıp Sabancı has written his second book: *Money is the reward of success. "Can there be a recipe for earning money?" Following his first book "From My Life" where he tells of his life, the famous businessman this time has written about the beliefs and principles behind his 40 years of business life and of success.*

right: **Make a bank manager of your son:** Atilla Uras, General Manager of Manifacturer Hannovers Bank, has become the boss of Netbank.

below: **"Materialist" brats: 68 - 88.** It's been 20 years since the legendary student movements. Like its Western contemporaries, Turkish youth has also lost its enthusiasm for politics and has identified a new ideal, a new aim: the new urban professionals, that is the "yuppies".

bottom: **The professionals**

Aktüel
25 July 1991

Nokta
3 January 1988

Para
1 June 1981

Süleyman exasperates me... Although the three of us are partners in this, he gathers his files and without requesting a general meeting he goes and secretly talks to Mr Doğan. During a conversation Mr Doğan said that he liked very much Süleyman's most recent idea. Apparently it's a great idea. Half of that idea, actually more than half of it is mine. He seems to have gone and sold it to Mr Doğan as if it was his own idea. God damn him. He just added a couple of things to the beginning and end. As if it was his own idea. I feel the blood rushing to my head, what should I do, what should I say? Suddenly I turn back and look at Süleyman, he ignores me, but he is actually avoiding looking at me, he cannot come eye to eye with me. If only he would look me in the face. (God damn you Süleyman, you imbecile, so you were educated abroad with your father's money and you think you have become a respectable man? How far can you get with other people's money and other people's ideas? You bloody man.)

What if I said "Mr Doğan, more than half of the project of Süleyman you like so much belongs to me, the three of us talked and I came up with this section, what you like is mine, not his"... what would happen? I must think and I must find a much better project... I must find it... God damn him.
[Duygu Asena, Kadının Adı Yok, 1987/2004, Doğan Publications, p. 137]

world of business and finance, that is, money, the dollar and the mark, inflation rates, and the stock market, were becoming the stuff of everyday conversation, on the other, in an increasingly consumerist world, money and the excess or lack of it, both highlighted social inequalities and regulated dreams for the future.

In the 1980s, while most peripheral countries were experiencing severe debt crises, the Turkish economy was becoming more export-oriented and internationalized. The post-World War II import-substitution strategies underpinning national developmentalist policies ceded the way to new economic policies. Starting with the IMF and the World Bank, all of the international institutions with which Turkey negotiated its debt payments were convinced that property, money and capital markets had to liberalize rapidly for an economy to enter world markets and attract foreign capital. The Turgut Özal governments supported and pursued these views, and state institutions, which from the early years of the Republic on had always played an active role in the economy, gradually receded to the backstage. As the walls of protection in foreign trade were lowered, privatization policies led to radical changes in the economy. In the first place, there was a shift from economic development to growth and the term *market* became progressively more centralized, ending up as the magic solution to every issue. Companies, the main actors of the market, and their field of activity, the business world, secured the seat of honor in social life. When looked at from this perspective, it comes as no surprise that money, wealth and business should have been so high on the agenda in Turkey in the 1980s.

A new term to enter everyday usage in the 1980s was *yuppie*, short for "young, urban, professional" and used to designate the members of a relatively young, upwardly mobile, well-educated, consumerist, upper middle class, holding jobs with high incomes in the upper echelons of the corporate world. The word *yuppie* became popular in Turkey at the same time as it did in a number of other countries. The wave of *neo-liberalism* that affected the entire capitalist world and which accompanied the global economic crisis of the 1970s and the economic restructuring immediately following it was no doubt the main cause of this simultaneity. Therefore we can view *yuppies* as the most

GİRİŞİMCİLİK / AİLE YAPISI
Patron olacak çocuk...
Doç. Dr. Acar Baltaş otoriter aile yapısının çocuğun girişimci olma özelliğini ters etkilediğini vurguluyor.

Nokta
29 November 1987

Zaptedilemeyen kuşak: Gen X

Sabah
5 June 2005

Şirketlerin aradığı yetenekler, gelenekleri reddeden bir kuşaktan çıkıyor. İstekleri farklı bu kesimi elde tutmak rekabetin ön koşulu olacak

above: **The boss of the future:** *Assoc. Prof. Dr Acar Baltaş emphasises that an authoritarian family structure influences negatively a child's potential for entrepreneurship.*

left: **The unstoppable generation: Gen X:** *The talented people that companies are searching for, come from a generation which rejects traditions. Holding on to this segment of society, which has different demands, will be a pre-condition for success in competition.*

... In the compulsory training that I had to attend together with Brits graduated from Oxford, Cambridge, the London School of Economics and the Imperial College, the message given between the lines was "You are going to work hard, you are going to get very tired, but you are going to learn a lot. Before you are 30 you will become a manager, and before you are 40 some of you will become partners to this company. And then, even if you retire when you are in your 50s, you will have become a sterling milionaire. If you leave earlier, you will be readily invited to take up respectable jobs, because of the assets deriving from having worked for Arthur Andersen." And I think that these messages energised everyone but me. In the orientation course where I kept hoping it would be over so that I could read Raymond Carver, my only consolation was that all that I suffered would give me three years later an advantage in being accepted at the business administration master programme at the Columbia University, Paul Auster's school in New York, the capital of the world, unless my uncle objected. [Selçuk Altun, *Yalnızlık Gittiğin Yoldan Gelir*, 2004, Yapı Kredi Publications, p. 63- 64]

Whisky container

"valuable" and privileged children of *neoliberalism*. The state's gradual movement away from control or intervention in the domestic economy, the opening of markets and free trade and the increasing power and monopolist tendencies of multinational corporations over the world economy are the dominant features of neoliberalism from the 1980s to our day. The values on the rise that determine the cultural climate of our times are: competitiveness, initiative, risk taking, individualism, rapid adaptability to changing work conditions, and openness to the world. With the increase in the local investments of multinationals, the engineers, computer programmers, managers, marketing managers, economists and lawyers employed by rapidly internationalizing companies may be considered the members of a new middle class. Considering the growing inequality in income distribution and the decline in real wages that Turkey began to experience in those years, this new middle class can in fact be said to have been relatively privileged. At a time when the bulk of the traditional middle classes – in other words, the self-employed and those employed in the public sector – had become *orta direk* [a popular term widely used in the 1980s to refer to the lower segments of middle classes] and impoverished, certain specific qualities set apart those who met the demand for new skills and succeeded in securing high paying jobs in the private sector. The prominent qualities distinguishing this segment of society were: being a graduate from a prestigious university, such as the Middle East Technical University or Boğaziçi University; holding a master's degree or, better still, an MBA; and being fluent in (a) foreign language(s); this was a social segment which had successfully converted its cultural capital to economic capital. In recent years, universities have started offering career-enhancing courses and leading figures of the international corporate world give conferences and seminars in Turkey. This has contributed to an accumulation of knowledge in the field. The emphasis on cultural capital continues in professional life. A number of companies have adopted short-term professional training programs to develop leadership, initiative and perhaps most importantly, a sense of corporate identity.

Another characteristic common to the new middle classes – outside of their business practices and work conditions – are their

Hürriyet
2 July 2000

Sabah
17 August 1987

above: **We are young and fast and we care for money**

right: **A new manager for a new era:** They are managers... They are the key people in holdings and companies. But what do they do when they are not working? Here is an interesting research which reflects the social life of managers in Turkey.

Capital
December 2005

right: **Companies that raise entrepreneurs fulfill their goals:** *The famous management guru Tom Peters believes that we are in the century of entrepreneurship. But what he draws attention to is not just the people who found businesses. He means also the entrepreneurs within companies. Exemplary practices are seen not only in giant companies such as Apple and IBM, but also in Turkey.*

below: **Determinatıon, belief, success:** *She is both an architect and an interior designer. She founded her own firm by chance, and has set up a partnership with Frederick Fisher & Partners, one of the 100 best architecture firms in the world.*

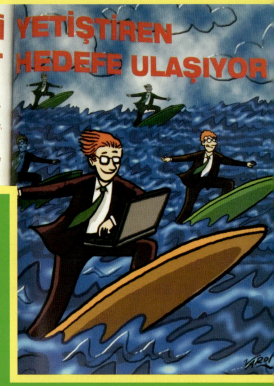

Hürriyet
4 August 2002

common consumption patterns. Specific brands and fashions determine everything from their selection of residence and interior decoration, to their leisure activities, culinary preferences, mode of dress and choice of body care products. In short, the important thing here is to achieve a distinctive style. Both professional life and consumption transcend boundaries and become global. One way of separating yourself from other social classes and flaunting your "individual" style is to have the "select" consumption patterns determined by global criteria. Obviously, this was a class made up of a small minority situated at the peak of Turkey's gradually increasing income polarization. Still, their choices, tastes, adopted values and ideals seemed to have become hegemonic, and it was possible to observe this hegemony in a number of different areas.

Cross fountain pen

Cigar box

It showed up first of all in the greater space allotted to economic and business news in the media. Famous economists, business executives, and professors in economics and management began writing columns and articles. Newspapers offered human resources supplements providing information on evolving work conditions and employment opportunities. One of the most obvious signs of the infiltration of economics into everyday life was the increase in the number of television shows addressing the topic. Finance news and business programs were launched on primetime networks. Magazines printed on glossy paper, such as *Kapital*, *Para*, and the Turkish versions of the world's leading economic publications, like the *Economist* and *Business Week*, emerged to offer reports on economic, business and financial developments, and present interviews with the owners or chief executives of well-known companies. By the time we reach the 1990s, books dealing with the world of business and finance or written by "self-made" tycoons and the famous rich had become some of the best-selling publications at newsstands and supermarkets.

The life stories of the extra-rich had, without a doubt, fascinated the public in previous eras as well. The factory owner character, usually associated with Hulusi Kentmen and popularized by the Yeşilçam movie industry; the photographs gracing the pages of society and celebrity magazines; and the 1950s cartoons of the *hacıağa* (newly rich villager) come from his village to flaunt his

Bastards have backgrounds that are ostentatious enough to keep them alive. Life, which ruthlessly flays people who implement Gandhi's passive resistance to everything but themselves, is more affectionate towards bastards. Because bastards have birthday gifts in their backgrounds and private schools with high fees and families where they learn to talk, where Turkish is spoken correctly. Being crushed by life and being turned into mud happens much later to bastards, when compared with the squashing of ordinary people. But the result is no different. Like all people who have given up on life, bastards too will get trampled under other people's feet at some point or other. [Hakan Günday, *Piç*, 2004, Doğan Publications, p. 175]

wealth in the city are all cases in point. But in the times referred to by these examples, although the rich were a topic of discussion, they themselves did not elaborate on their life stories. In the new era, this changed; the famous rich now held forth unreservedly on their own lifestyles and freely offered their advice on business, finance and a variety of other issues. These were also the decades when businessmen and investor institutions like TÜSİAD, TOBB or MÜSİAD began to show a keen interest in politics and actually intervene in it from time to time. Typical of this trend was Cem Boyner's *Yeni Demokrasi Hareketi* (New Democracy Movement) which entered the political arena in the 1990s. Again around this time, investment in the arts started to acquire prevalence. In recent years, large corporate groups such as Eczacıbaşı, Koç and Sabancı have founded their own museums; banks and companies have opened exhibition galleries and sponsored exhibitions and art events. In other words, the post-1980s have been an age when the bourgeoisie simultaneously acquired greater social visibility in a number of spheres and became more diversified and fragmented. Not only are there frequent displays of groundbreaking and taboo-breaking initiatives, but even the more "conservative" segments are adapting to rising popular trends. The Muslim bourgeoisie of the 2000s emerges at the junction of money and religion. Only by taking these developments into consideration can we explain AKP's arrival to power and its single-party control of government or the tensions that have erupted today between TOBB and TÜSİAD.

For the majority of the population, adjusting to a new era determined by capital, business and markets is no easy task. The new age is one of fierce competition and uncertainty, both of which even the privileged members of the new middle class get their share. As firms grow more flexible, so do their employment policies. To handle a rapidly fluctuating market, companies restructure, creating widespread employee anxiety. It is hardly possible to forget that, first in 1994, then in 2000, Turkey experienced two of the worst economic crises in its history. Nor can their consequences be ignored. Hard times lie ahead for the protagonists of the new era; in the race to succeed, they are expected to set up their own rules, seize opportunity when it knocks, and persevere in the face of adversity.

Nokta
May 1988

Milliyet
5 October 2003

above: **When money meets faith:** *The Muslim segment of society that developed after the 1950s has created its own high society. What is this life style, which was born from the blend of money and faith? How do high society Muslims live, how do they entertain themselves and how do they worship?*

right: **A Muslim bourgeoisie:** *There are visible changes in the life style of a segment of society that emphasises that they are Muslim with their clothes and way of life. Whether you call them "Islamic Bourgeoisie" or "Islamic High Society", their life style is no different from that of the other well-off people of this country.*

Sabah
24 November 2001

Krizin yarattığı yeni hayatlar!

Büyük şirketlerde, bankalarda parlak kariyerlere sahiptiler... Kimi işsiz kaldıktan sonra, kimi ise istifa edip yepyeni bir mesleği seçerek ayakta kalmayı deniyor. **İşte krizin ikinci baharları**

14 yıllık bankacı Dilek Bağdatlıoğlu istifa edip telekomünikasyon alanında kendi şirketini kurdu. Fotoğraf: TOLGA BOZOĞLU

New lives created by the economic crisis:
They had brilliant careers in big companies and banks... Some lost their jobs, some resigned and chose new professions, all in order to survive. These are the second chances resulting from the economic crisis.

right: **Choose your own race:** *In order to be successful in the 21st Century, the question one must ask oneself is not "how" to run, but "which race is it important to run in?"*

below: **Overcome borders:** *International companies are making it possible for young people to develop a career abroad. Young people are given the opportunity to build up their experience over the borders and get prepared for higher positions.*

Kazanmak İçin: Yarışını kendin belirle

21'inci yüzyılda kazanmak için "nasıl" koşmak sorusunun yerine, kendimize "hangi yarışta koşmak daha önemlidir?" sorusunu sormak gerekiyor

Milliyet
3 September 2000

SINIRLARI AŞ

ULUSLARARASI FİRMALAR YURTDIŞINDA KARİYER YAPMAK İSTEYEN GENÇLERİN YOLUNU AÇIYOR. GENÇLERE, SINIRLARIN ÖTESİNDE İŞ TECRÜBELERİNİ ARTIRMA VE DAHA ÜST DÜZEY GÖREVLERE HAZIRLANMA FIRSATLARI SUNULUYOR

Milliyet
3 April 2005

The restructuring of capitalism in the wake of the 1970s global recession began to noticeably affect Turkey in the 1980s. The rapid transformations occurring in the finance and service sectors also had a direct impact on the lives of people. At the individual level this was reflected in the fact that consuming became the key social and leisure activity. Consumerism became the fundamental path to a western lifestyle, identity formation, self-actualization and individualization. Consumerism assimilates various desires and then reproduces them. On the one hand, by giving the illusion of limitless choices, it seems to promote individualization and diversification. Yet, at the same time, by integrating the production, organization and control of *consumer choices, it implies massification. The chief areas where individualization and massification are simultaneously present are shopping malls,* which offer diverse activities and services under one roof; the tourism sector, *which provides numerous alternative leisure or travel "packages;"* credit cards, *which supply a virtual source of income for consumption;* and finally, lotteries and other games of chance, *which represent our hopes and dreams for the future.*

what, oh what can we get for free?

To exist through shopping

Perigot brand container for nylon bags

Yes, I could live here. This could be my home. It wouldn't be bad to live in a supermarket. As expiry dates pass, goods would be changed. Apart from that, there would be no need for change. The shelves, the departments, the cash registers, the cameras could all stay. I wouldn't mind. But it would be necessary to change the writing outside. I should cross out the S and write a P next to it. The house should be called Migrop.
[Hakan Günday, *Piç*, 2004, Doğan Publications, p. 11]

Turkey was once a country where unnecessary spending was considered *wasteful* and thriftiness was celebrated as a virtue. Needlessly "leaving the taps open," "turning on all the lights," "throwing out food," or buying new shoes when the old ones could be "resoled" were all careless behaviors to avoid if one wished to protect the "family budget" and contribute to the "country's economy." With the 1980s, this attitude changed radically and Turkey was rapidly introduced to the new norms and values of the *age of consumerism*. Along with new brands came new values. *Special days*, borrowed from the west, appeared on the calendar, so that on *Valentine's Day* you could prove your love to that special someone with an expensive gift. Adidas sneakers, Toblerone chocolates, Givenchy perfumes and Levi's jeans once ordered from people going *abroad* were now sold at new "hypermarkets" offering "22,000 different products." Through its new stores in Turkey, Toys "R" Us "opened the doors of a colorful world to kids," so that *children*, like their elders, learned to become *customers* of the dazzling and entertaining experiences provided in these places. The path to the *colorful* world of consumerism necessarily entailed shopping.

Today, the new shopping spaces that turn up everywhere you look are the clearest indicators of change. In those years, *supermarkets* were the first to grow, increase in number and diversify. As *super*, *hyper* and *gross* markets gained ascendancy, the "courageous" grocers, corner stores and local neighborhood stores entered a life struggle to defend their businesses and shares of the urban market. One of the chief developments triggering this process was the market entry of major European chains, such as Carrefour, Metro and Spar, and of such leading Turkish corporate groups as Sabancı, Koç, and Tekfen. A certain stratification stands out here. Supermarkets like Macro, with their spacious aisles, *wide variety of products* and *brand names*, and tasteful product display, cater to the upper classes. At the other end, supermarkets like BİM

right: **Consumption madness is a great waste:** *The fact that people with almost no money and who are barely able to buy bread for their homes, should smoke Marlboros instead of local brands, that people should wear imported boots or silk suits instead of local goods just for the sake of it, that people should buy their children expensive imported toys, all these do nothing but encourage the consumption madness, which is a great waste and the most dangerous kind of waste.*

below: **The consumption day for lovers:** *All sectors are getting prepared for 14th February, Valentine's Day.*

Son Havadis
3 October 1988

Hürriyet
9 February 1999

The first shopping mall of Turkey

attempt to draw in customers with their *cheap prices*. Some companies opt for store ranking within their own structure to target different consumer segments; the "Şok" and "Migros" supermarket chains, both part of the Koç Group, are good examples of this. While the former pushes *economical* shopping to the fore, the latter emphasizes *diversity* and *quality*. Large-scale capital is besieging the market on every front with its expertise and research-based flexible marketing policies. In Turkey, as everywhere else in the world, the process of supermarkets "impressing their stamp on the market" is directly related to the growing weight of large-scale capital in the expanding services sector.

Scene from the contest programme "Supermarket", where contestants filling their trolley with the highest number of goods win [Kanal 6, 1992]

Another major aspect of the change taking place in those years was the emergence of large shopping centers. Galleria, which opened in 1988 under the slogan, "Turkey's first shopping mall," stressed in its ad campaign the diverse shopping experience and services it could offer in a single shopping area. In Galleria it was now possible to refresh your wardrobe and have a facial; shop for records while waiting for your credit card authorization; make reservations for your vacation while picking out your husband's suit; and grab a bite at one of the eateries in the *food court* while your kids were ice-skating. Galleria was one of the first examples of a single enclosed shopping area where different services were available for consumption, and as such it became a major attraction. Leaving their cars in the mall's parking lot, people came for a day of shopping or simply "to look." Mainly, people were curious about the "modern" shopping concept of the mall. Among those eager to discover the new shopping center were families from the slum areas surrounding Bakırköy, who walked over to Galleria to roam around the new stores. (Navaro-Yaşın, 2002)

Today, shopping malls have become a way of life in Istanbul and similar – if diverse sized – *concentrated shopping* centers are frequently found in other major Turkish cities. "Proliferating like mushrooms," these are also "European" spaces, a term equated with "modern." Going to Akmerkez, Olivium, Karum or any of the big shopping malls that bring Europe "to our feet" with their western chain stores, like Top Shop, Nine West or Marks and Spencer, their foreign name brands and wide selection of products,

I felt privileged in supermarkets. I could fill my cart till it was jam-packed, and I could still be seen the next day at the same supermarket, doing another bout of exagerated shopping, I could even do this every day, and I would still not be regarded as weird. I had the right to do easily many things which would not be tolerated in others. I could try as much as I wanted of the cheeses and olives set on the counters to be tasted, I could open up bags of biscuits, wafers and crisps; I could drink cold drinks from the fridges. Sometimes I would finish immediately the goods I opened. On the way out the cashier girls would throw these empty bags or bottles in the rubbish bins by their side, while smiling understandingly and they would take the money for these goods almost reluctantly. I wasn't to be reproached for what I did. I could even be considered cute. My fatness was the excuse for my greediness. And in supermarkets my excuse was always valid. [Elif Şafak, *Mahrem*, 2000, Metis Publications, p. 77-78]

has become one of the most crucial indicators of a lifestyle *modeled* on the west. In fact, what these large shopping centers are offering with their movie multiplexes, restaurants, entertainment spaces, fitness and beauty salons and parking garages is *a new lifestyle defined by consumerism.*

Indicators of all that is "modern" and representative of a "western" outlook, malls have also largely transformed living patterns. Through these new public spaces, a large part of our leisure activities and time spent outside the home now identifies with shopping. But this is not to say that these new shopping spaces have created a typical consumer profile. Shopping malls are able to adapt a very similar structure to different identities. The Navaro-Yaşın study conducted on the *Tekbir* [literally "Allahuekber"] shopping center in Fatih, illustrates how popular consumer patterns and objectives can be revised to satisfy the requirements of Islamic modesty (*tesettür*). Aiming to "put its mark on world fashions," and "spread Islamic style throughout the world," the Tekbir shopping center offers its alternative to modern shopping. (Navaro-Yaşın, 2002) "Islamist" or "secular," various identities asserting their "authenticity" are re-created in the market around corresponding consumer axes. Differences in comparable consumer practices are expressed through cultural means. The most extreme examples of culturalization show up in the cultural events organized in shopping centers. For instance, Akmerkez recently hosted an exhibition where statues, installations and oil paintings were displayed in shop windows and aisles, turning the shopping area into a cultural space. But these spaces can also be the centers for more ordinary cultural activities. Some people now prefer the movieplexes of shopping malls when they want to see a movie. Thus, doing a little window-shopping, grabbing a bite to eat and even doing the grocery shopping becomes part of the experience of going to the movies.

Actually, maybe the goal here is reuniting in one place various consumption practices distributed all over the city, and through this vertical layout making them easier to organize and control. There are today consulting companies specializing in the interior and exterior design of big shopping areas. These companies advise and guide their clients on a number of topics, from the choice of

---

They leave the house and go together to Akmerkez.

Handan is a real Akmerkez child. Behiye sees this the minute they go through the entrance. Like an ornamental fish reunited with its bowl, she starts wagging her tail and breathing happily. She knows each and every corner of this place. All of its possibilities. And its impossibilities, in a sense. Because Handan has no money. Handan knows all the goods that Akmerkez cannot offer her, one by one, she knows their quality, their labels, their prices. Such a terrifying memory! Such an unbearable weight to carry around!

They go to the top floor, where the fast food places and the cinemas are. Handan feels like having a "donut" apparently... She eats two doughnuts with pistachios and drinks a coffee. Behiye watches her and she drinks water. Handan is so beautiful. She slowly fills up. She feels better. What hurt before, now feels good. [Perihan Mağden, *İki Genç Kızın Romanı*, 2002, Everest Publications, p. 111]

right: **Children are certainly lucky:** Toys'R'Us, which is about to open its seventh store, has opened the doors of its colourful world not only to children but also to adults.

below: **The Europe in Istanbul:** The German store "Metro", which opened on a 12,000 square metre area close to the Yeşilköy-Mahmutbey highway, is a point of attraction not only for the residents of Istanbul, but for customers from all over the country.

Milliyet
28 November 1999

Hürriyet
15 December 1990

Hürriyet
8 November 1990

Tüketim çağındaki Türkiye

● İthalatın serbest bırakılması, medyanın tüketimi pompalaması, Türk insanının kolay yoldan çağ atlama isteği ile birleşince, kaçınılmaz son: Tüketim kaosu. Devlet İstatistik Enstitüsü'nün, gelir, tüketim harcamaları araştırmasına göre, son 10 yılda, aile bütçesinin aslan payını gıda, konut ve giyim alıp götürüyor.

● İktisat Profesörü Asaf Savaş Akad, 80'lerde, dayanıklı tüketim maddelerinde bir "demokratik devrim" olduğu görüşünde. Beyaz eşya sahibi olmak, artık "doğal bir hak". Üreticiler, ürünlerinin piyasaya yayılma hızının, son 20 yıl içinde yüzde 20 olduğunu söylüyor. Buzdolabı, artık alt orta gelir grubunun evinde.

● Büyük kentlerdeki tüketim kaosunun yeni aktörleri, artık neredeyse hiç tasarruf yapmıyor, enflasyondan korunmak için, dayanıklı tüketim mallarına sarılıyor. Nüfusun yarıdan çoğunun borçlu olduğu büyük yerleşim merkezlerinde, insanlar bir zamanlar hayal bile edemedikleri eşyalara taksitle hemen sahip oluyor.

Beyaz eşyalar gözde
Üst gelir grubunda moda olgusu ve teknik gelişmeler, dar gelirlilerde enflasyondan korunma beyaz eşyaya talebi artırıyor. Tüketici buzdolabını ya da çamaşır makinesini değiştirmek için bozulmasını beklemiyor.

Süper markete süper tüketici
Büyük süper marketlere artık yalnızca alışveriş için değil, aynı zamanda gezme ve vakit geçirme amacıyla da gidiliyor. Tüketici çoğu kez ihtiyacı olmayan mallarla tezgahta gördüğü için sepetini dolduruyor.

Televizyona olan tutku
Tüketici için televizyon iyi bir yatırım. Uzaktan kumandalı, birkaç sistemli "kutuların" hepsi birbirinden farklı. Dar gelirli aileler bile siyah beyaz televizyon almaktansa borca girerek renkli almayı tercih ediyor.

above: **Turkey in the age of consumption**

right: **Shopping centres are mushrooming**

Hürriyet
21 November 2003

Alışveriş merkezleri mantar gibi çoğalıyor

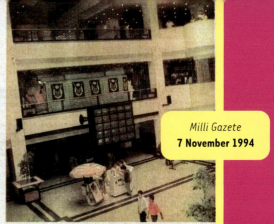

Milli Gazete
7 November 1994

Türkiye'nin iki yüzü...

Türkiye'den geçinenler (zenginler), Türkiye'de geçinenler (fakirler)' şeklinde kısaca formüle ettiğimiz toplumumuzun gerçeğini alış-veriş yaptığı mekanlara yaptığımız kısa bir geziyle daha iyi tahlil etme imkanı bulduk. Dargelirli vatandaşlarımızın durumunu ortaya koyması bakımından Topkapı daimi semt pazarını model aldık. Hatırlı vatandaşlarımın durumunu ortaya koyması bakımından da mega süper, ultra, hiper artık nasıl anlarsanız alış-veriş merkezi Capitol'u baz aldık.

Ünlü markalar 'alışveriş'e geldi

Şişli, Levent, Etiler üçgeninde birbiri ardına açılan alışveriş merkezleri, bazıları Türkiye'ye ilk kez gelen pek çok ünlü yabancı markayı da peşinden getiriyor. Markalar 1074 mağazada yer almak için sıraya girdi

Sabah
21 October 2005

above: **The two sides of Turkey:** *We paid quick visits to shopping centres and had the opportunity to examine more closely the reality of our society, which we can easily divide into those who earn a living from Turkey (the rich) and those who earn a living in Turkey (the poor).*

below: **Famous brands have come shopping:** *The shopping centres which have opened in the Şişli, Levent, Etiler triangle have brought along many famous foreign brands, some of which have come to Turkey for the first time. The brands are waiting for their turns to take up one of the 1074 stores available.*

right: **Stores for the religious conservatives are considered frumpy:** *Most women who cover their heads find the clothes in the stores for the religious conservatives too fancy and frumpy. The brands they prefer are Zara, Derimod, Beymen and Lacoste.*

below: **The shopping temple of Istanbul:** *There possibly isn't anybody who can fall into the Teşvikiye-Nişantaşı-Maçka triangle and leave without any shopping. But being neighbours with the world-famous brands in Nişantaşı, capital of luxury, doesn't come cheap.*

Milliyet
15 February 2005

Sabah Emlak
3 June 2005

site for the proposed shopping center to parking lot capacity, type of stores, and optimal size of the food and beverage areas. In short, there is deliberate and organized top-to-bottom planning involved in the integration of diverse consumption areas in these new shopping areas. This would imply that living patterns are thus also designed according to a well-defined model.

On a different level, this process is reflected in market research. In our day, there exists a science of consumerism. In this "age of consumerism," possessing knowledge on consumption practices and consumer profiles acquires more and more significance for companies. Creating a lucrative enterprise and optimizing sales implies a better knowledge of consumerism, the classification of consumer types, and gaining insights into consumer psychology. As a result, the market research sector has expanded. Whereas before the 1980s there were very few companies involved in this area, today, numerous agencies, both domestic and foreign, carry out market research aimed at providing insights on consumer attitudes and behaviors. When launching new products or services, developing ad campaigns or determining "target markets," businesses now act according to research findings. In other words, it has become easier now for modern retail facilities to *produce consumerism*.

Imitation Lacoste brand t-shirt

Though shopping centers revamp their image to accommodate cultural diversities, they also contribute to homogeneity by drawing same-profile consumers or actually pushing people to sameness. Because they are insulated from the outside world, malls allow people from similar socio-economic and cultural backgrounds to engage in every kind of purchasing without coming into contact with *others*. This applies to the various segments of the middle classes as well. As a result, the social distance and differentiation between different groups has become more pronounced. The gradually rising socio-economic polarization witnessed in recent years is replicated in shopping centers. At the top end of the scale, there are now high-end retail malls targeting the small extra-rich minority. Another recent development parallel to the stratification process taking place

I know the cherries are decaying. And the peaches are dejenerated. The fish have long been dead. Two bunches of parsley cost one lira, eight lemons cost five lira. I'm never fooled by the tomatoes. I am an expert at selecting cucumbers. The apricots are sprawled all over the place, the peppers are of a green that makes me lose my head. I have been carrying home the summer, winter and spring of the market for years now. A single shopping bag is enough nowadays. [İnci Aral, "Haziranlarda", *Ağda Zamanı*, 1999, Can Publications, p. 9]

in metropolitan areas is the growing identification of certain neighborhoods and streets with luxury consumerism; for instance, Istanbul's "shopping mecca, the Teşvikiye-Nişantaşı-Maçka triangle," with its upscale restaurants and cafes and designer brand shops and boutiques is considered the "capital of luxury."

Imitation Gucci wallet, generally sold in small district markets

Meanwhile, at lower echelons of the retail hierarchy, the alternatives range from more modest shopping centers to neighborhood stores for those who cannot afford quality supermarkets or shopping malls.

In the 1980s and subsequent periods, when poverty significantly increased, open-air markets and street vendors continued to be first choice for the majority of lower income groups. But even the goods sold there reflected the craze for *brand-conscious* consumerism. Those unable to buy expensive designer label shirts, shoes or handbags, could purchase cheap knockoffs of the genuine articles from neighborhood street markets or street vendors: fake Lacoste shirts, Versace jeans and Samsonite suitcases...

Nowadays, through celebrity shows and entertainment news on TV, and advertisements and stories in the press, *authentic* designer labels or their *copies* have become accessible to the great majority without class or status distinctions. As the general public acquires greater fashion-consciousness and awareness of the representations of modernity disseminated through the media, its *desires, aspirations* and *dreams* become increasingly *correlated with consumption*. Given the circumstances, it should come as no surprise then that outlet stores are so popular. *Retail factory outlets* or *end of line stores* have become the life-savers of the middle classes, who crave designer labels, envy the beautiful people and look down on the masses. Quality rejects, cut out inside labels, or last year's fashion, no matter; for the brand-conscious, outlets answer their demand for top brands and designer clothing at bargain prices.

Alongside new retail spaces the urban landscape is also changing; *as consumption becomes more conspicuous*, the places of

above: **Street vendors have become part of our lives**

below: **Profilo shopping centre:** *The building in Mecidiyeköy, belonging to Profilo and used for many years as a factory, is being transformed into a huge shopping and entertainment centre like Akmerkez.*

Yeni Gündem
21 June 1987

Sabah
25 August 1997

When we finally left Akmerkez, the shopwindows made my head turn, the gluey coffee in the cardboard cups made me famished, I was tired in the endless labyrinth of having to search every floor again and again for toilets, I had held all the promises which I remembered or didn't remember making to Tuğçe and I was dumbfounded by the crowds who walked elbowing each other. I took a deep breath. Suddenly the street seemed heaven to me. So this is how it could be? Should I go to a shopping mall everyday, in order to endure the streets' normal everyday reality? Tomorrow it's Galleria! The day after Carrefour!

[Murathan Mungan, *Yüksek Topuklar*, 2002, Metis Publications, p. 61]

production move further from the city. Shopping malls have replaced what were once open spaces, factories and garages. In Istanbul 10 to 15 years ago, for example, there were factories on the sites where the Olivium and Profilo shopping centers stand today. The boom in real estate prices and environmental regulations count among the factors leading to this relocation of large-scale production to the outskirts of the city. Concurrently, the increased weight of unregistered manufacturing production activity, usually carried out in the basements of apartment buildings, is no doubt significant. The *removal of production from the public's eye* also means the gradual demise of production-based forms of social identity and opposition. Instead of *workers* and *classes*, the denominations now used are *consumers* and *non-consumers*. Consumer issues are at the fore of newspaper columns and experts offer tips on how to be a savvy shopper. In this context, Türk-İş, the biggest workers' union in Turkey, conducted a survey in 1996 to determine the consumption patterns of families belonging to its union. The name given to the study is particularly interesting: "Research on consumption issues conducted with 5000 consumer families."

Turkey is experiencing a major discourse transformation. The jargon of market researchers and publicity writers is becoming popular. Starting with the word consumer, terms used to classify *socio-economic status* (SES) groups and types of consumers have entered everyday usage. In the wake of the 2001 crisis, many Turkish businesses launched a VAT-reduced shopping campaign to revive sales under the slogan, *bu ülke için seve seve*, [anything for our country]. Headlines in the press read "Back to Life." Clearly, life has become *consumption* and consumption means *existing*.

Çalışanlar hafta sonlarını "ucuzu aramaya" harcıyorlar...
Ortadireğin tatili pazarda geçiyor

● Bakkal-manav fiyatlarının aile bütçesini sarsar hale gelmesi nedeniyle çalışanlar dinlenme günleri olan hafta sonlarını pazar alışverişine ayırmak zorunda kalıyorlar. Halk pazarları ve semt pazarları gibi ucuz yiyecek ve giyeceğin satıldığı alışveriş merkezleri hafta sonlarında satış rekoru kırıyor...

Remzi Akkılınç (Konfeksiyon işçisi)- "Marketten aldığımda 250-300 bin liradan aşağı düşmeyen mutfak alışverişimi, hafta sonları pazardan yapınca 100-150 bin liraya kurtuluyorum. 400 bin lira maaşla geçim zor."

Gülçin Öcel (Şirkette çalışıyor)- "Yarım saat içinde bitirebileceğim alışverişi, kesemize uygun diye yakınımızdaki bakkal marketten değil, hafta sonunu harcayarak çarşı pazar dolaşarak yapıyorum."

Nurettin Çardak (Beşiktaş Belediyesi Halk Pazarı Müdürü) "Haftanın yedi günü açık olduğumuz için, sadece Beşiktaş'takiler değil, çevre semtlerde oturanlar da hafta sonu yararlanıyor."

Tan
4 January 1990

Milliyet
28 November 1999

SEMT PAZARLARI ÖLDÜ... YAŞASIN HİPERMARKETLER!

Yeni tüketici tipi

Tüketici profili her geçen gün değişiyor. Araştırmalara göre 2000'li yıllarda tercih büyük alışveriş merkezlerinden yana

above: **The middle class takes time off in the market.**

left: **A new type of consumer:** *The consumer profile changes every day. According to research conducted, large shopping centres are the favourites of consumers in the 2000s.*

Hürriyet
16 February 2002

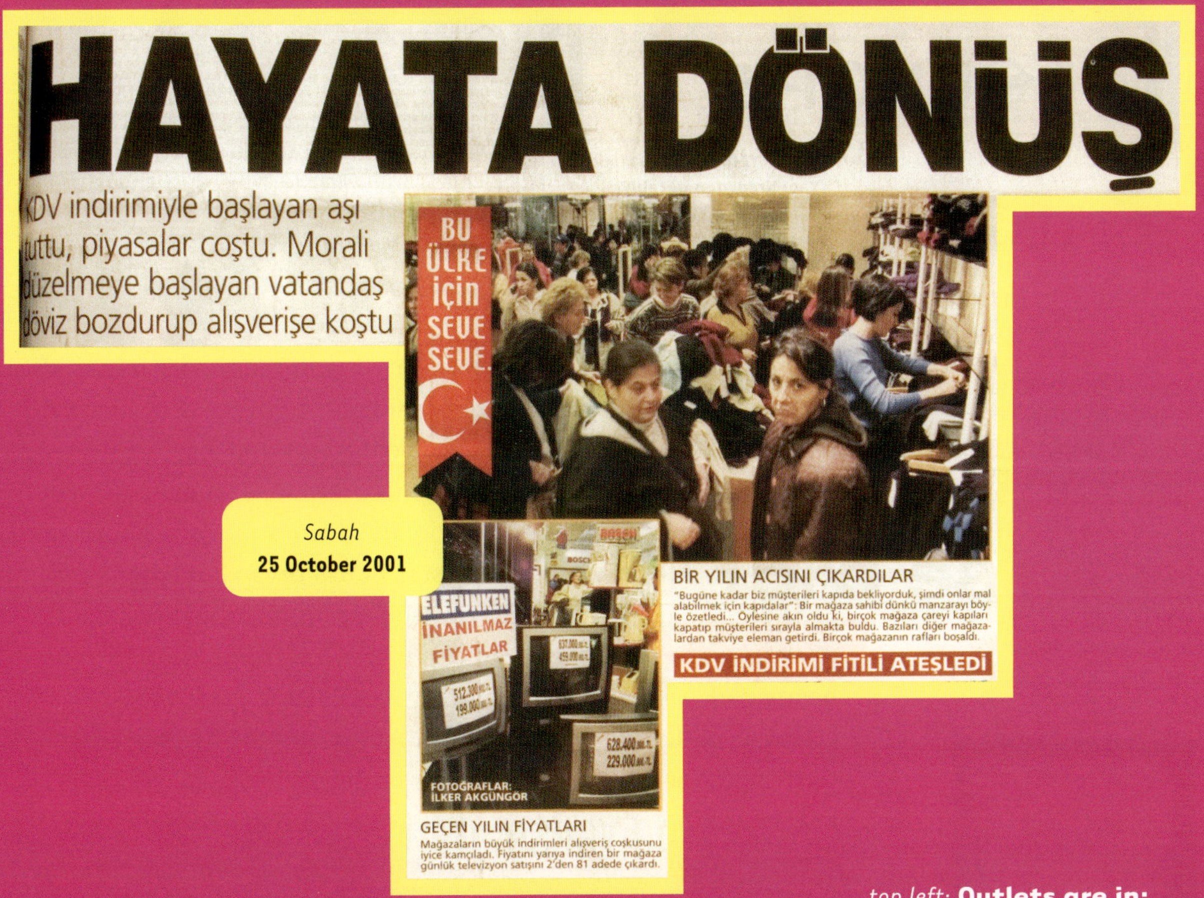

HAYATA DÖNÜŞ

KDV indirimiyle başlayan aşı tuttu, piyasalar coştu. Morali düzelmeye başlayan vatandaş döviz bozdurup alışverişe koştu

BU ÜLKE İÇİN SEVE SEVE

BİR YILIN ACISINI ÇIKARDILAR

"Bugüne kadar biz müşterileri kapıda bekliyorduk, şimdi onlar mal alabilmek için kapıdalar": Bir mağaza sahibi dünkü manzarayı böyle özetledi... Öylesine akın oldu ki, birçok mağaza çareyi kapıları kapatıp müşterileri sırayla almakta buldu. Bazıları diğer mağazalardan takviye eleman getirdi. Birçok mağazanın rafları boşaldı.

KDV İNDİRİMİ FİTİLİ ATEŞLEDİ

TELEFUNKEN İNANILMAZ FİYATLAR

FOTOĞRAFLAR: İLKER AKGÜNGÖR

GEÇEN YILIN FİYATLARI

Mağazaların büyük indirimleri alışveriş coşkusunu iyice kamçıladı. Fiyatını yarıya indiren bir mağaza günlük televizyon satışını 2'den 81 adede çıkardı.

Sabah
25 October 2001

top left: **Outlets are in:** ***Where can one find at lower prices the brands sold in elegant stores and big shopping centres? Here is a guide for our new shopping tradition...***

above: **Back to life:** ***The graft that started with the VAT reduction has caught, the markets are exuberant. Encouraged, people changed their foreign currencies and rushed to do shopping.***

Where should we go on vacation?

Whereas dreaming of holidays was so nice. Warm and sunny places, instead of the cold weather of Istanbul. Places where I can live with just a t-shirt and shorts instead of layer upon layer, where I can eat tropical fruits continuously and go swimming, where I can lie on the beach reading books and look at naked men with swimmers' bodies passing in front of me and sigh. [Mehmet Murat Somer, *Jigolo Cinayetleri*, 2005, Everest Publications, p. 184]

Factor 60 Vichy brand sunscreen lotion for children

As everywhere else in the world, tourism has become a major *industry* in Turkey. It is a *dynamic sector* made up of enterprises that range in size from small family-run pensions to large company-owned international hotel chains. The impact of tourism is not only on the world we inhabit, the environment and social life; it directly influences and transforms people's world view and perception of reality. Looking at the main aspects of this transformation may provide clues to a better understanding of the overall pervasiveness of consumerism in our society today, the trends involved in this process, and the unease and concerns it is producing.

Tourism became a major investment area in the service sector after the 1980s, in large part due to considerable government incentives for tourism investors, such as tax deductions and, especially, access to public forest land. The aim was to promote economic growth and, with the foreign exchange obtained from tourism, eliminate the current account deficit; five-star hotels became the hope of the future. This was also the course that international financial institutions recommended for countries like Turkey with serious balance of payment problems. In the 1980s, a great many countries in Latin America, North Africa and the Middle East were investing in tourism and converting their coastal regions into international tourism centers. Mass tourism, with its travel agencies, tour operators, hotels, and airline companies, was developing into a major industry. During this period, both large domestic companies and foreign capital in Turkey also started to invest in tourism. Alongside the luxury hotels and holiday complexes opening chiefly in the metropolises and on the coast, new subsectors like *congress tourism*, *golf tourism*, and *winter tourism* emerged. As a result, the last thirty years have witnessed radical changes in the environmental and socio-economic structure of coastal regions. Land which had once been crop fields, pastures or forests was rapidly cleared for tourism. Again, during the same years, regions not really up to par in terms of infrastructure and

ANAP artık maceraperest turist istemiyor
Umudumuz beş yıldızlılar
Patlama edebiyatına rağmen turizm gelirleri bir türlü artmıyor. Yeni hedef çok paralı turistlere kaliteli hizmet

Yeni Gündem
20 December 1989

5 yıldızlı tatil şart değil
Turistik beldelerimizde 5 yıldızlı otellere her geçen gün bir yenisi ekleniyor ama pansiyonlarda da gönlünüze göre tatil yapabilirsiniz.

Yeni Günaydın
4 May 1995

above: **Our hope lies in the five stars:** *In spite of the theories on soaring figures, there has been no increase in tourism incomes. The new objective is to offer services to very wealthy tourists.*

below: **No need for a five star holiday:** *New five star hotels are added every day to the existing ones in our touristic regions, but you can also take the holiday of your dreams in a boarding house.*

Şimdi su sporları "in"

Müzik eşliğinde, suyun içerisinde ritmik hareketlerle hoşça vakit geçirmek mi istiyorsunuz? O zaman doğru 5 yıldızlı otellerin sıcacık sularına bırakın kendinizi...

Aktüel
January 1994

right: **Now, water sports are in!** *Do you wish to enjoy yourselves moving under water, to the rhythm of music? Then let yourself go in the warm waters of five star hotels.*

top right: **Diving is trendy now:** *Scuba Diving, known shortly as SDC, is the first and only holiday village on the coast of the Saros Bay for water afficionados.*

bottom right: **It's time for individualised vacations:** *The concept of rich, fun but "remote control" vacations in holiday villages is being replaced by a new concept of vacations planned by the holiday-goers themselves.*

Şimdi *dalmak* moda

Scuba Diving Center ya da kısa adıyla SDC, Saroz Körfezi kıyısında sadece deniz tutkunları için kurulmuş ilk ve tek tatil köyü. Balıkadamlara, sörfçülere hizmet veriyor. Hafta sonunda, sualtıyla tanışmak isteyenlere teknik donanım ve eğitim programı sunuyor. 70 kişinin konaklayacağı imkanlara sahip tesisler Edirne'ye bağlı İbrice Köyü'nde.

Sabah
7 May 1995

Aktüel
July 1991

TATİL KÖYLERİ OUT!

Şimdi bireysel tatil zamanı

TATİL KÖYLERİNDEKİ ZENGİN, BOL EĞLENCELİ AMA "UZAKTAN KUMANDALI" TATİL ANLAYIŞI, YERİNİ DAHA ÖZGÜR, TATİLCİNİN KENDİSİ TARAFINDAN PLANLANMIŞ YENİ TATİL YAKLAŞIMLARINA BIRAKIYOR. GÜNLÜK YAŞAMI YILIN ON BİR AYINDA İŞYERLERİ VE TELEVİZYON TARAFINDAN BELİRLENEN BÜYÜK ŞEHİR İNSANI, HİÇ DEĞİLSE TATİL GÜNLERİNDE NE YAPACAĞINA KENDİSİ KARAR VERMEK İSTİYOR.

left: A boom in boarding houses: *Gümüldür, a touristic paradise renowned in Europe.*

below: This is called time-share: *If you have between 8-10 million, you can spend 3 periods of 15 days each in a magnificent villa in Bodrum, the deed of which is yours for a lifetime... Unless you are middle class.*

Milliyet
17 July 1988

Milliyet
3 April 1988

international transport were opened up to local vacationers as *cheap summer homes*, *timeshares* and *pensions*. The countless identical summer housing developments aligned side by side along the Aegean and Mediterranean coastlines are, unfortunately, an extremely familiar sight today.

How should we interpret this expansion and diversification of tourism activities? With reference to the post-1970s period when non-material products such as image, appearance and symbol became dominant, John Urry talks about the expansion of tourism beyond its specific characteristics to include other social practices. This expansion has also reversed the differentiation between areas like the *arts*, *sport*, *education*, *shopping* and *popular culture* that epitomize the modern age and, by *minimizing their differences*, has united them in the act of consumption. At the same time, it has also made everyday life more aesthetic (Urry 1995: 148-151). During this process consumption has gradually become *less functional* while different consumption areas have started to overlap. A significant reflection of these developments in tourism is *diversification*. This trend, in turn, can be related to the dissatisfaction of the new middle classes with existing standard vacation packages and their search for alternative solutions. In other words, at the back of the diversification in tourism, lie the new class dynamics and changes in consumption patterns that emerged as a result of the post-1970s restructuring of capitalism.

Actually, definitions of tourism have always stressed the break with the humdrum routine of everyday life and the appeal of fresh experiences. Discovering new places, meeting people from different cultures and embarking on out of the ordinary activities are all considered requisites for a tourist. Most of the time, advertising, the press, TV and travel books are at the basis of the idealized, stereotyped and limited narratives shaping these expectations. When people left cold by the prepackaged aspect of mass tourism turned to *alternative* vacation plans, more specialized forms of tourism became popular, such as *adventure tourism* for those who enjoy *rafting*, *trekking*, *scuba diving*, *mountain biking* and various other outdoor activities. *Ecotourism* (also known as nature or culture tourism) offers tourists seeking *authentic experiences* opportunities for a sojourn in a village of the Black Sea region,

Promotional beach ball

Internal tourism is actually a very good thing. First of all, people living in villages and towns get to earn some money. And they get accustomed to civilisation, they meet with civilised people. They learn the meaning of cleanliness. For sure, they do. They turn their homes into boarding houses. Did anything like that ever happen up to now? No, it didn't. And some of them are so clean... Your beds are covered with these snow white, fragrant sheets. They are a hundred times better than hotels. They scrub and bleach the wooden floors. I actually find it hard to enter these houses with my shoes on. The way they dress has also changed a little. That wild look in their eyes has disappeared. They are earning some money. They entertain guests in their homes. Civilisation is coming to their towns. They don't mind it. They have got accustomed to it. The provinces are waking up.
[Oğuz Atay, *Tutunamayanlar*, 1972/1990, İletişim Publications, p. 302]

After having checked in at the hotel, he went straight down to the beach, without even going up to his room. Although he had run straight to the seaside in order to take refuge in the stillness of nature, it was impossible for him to avoid the reality that he would stay for five days in this unfamiliar city and in this completely unfamiliar hotel. Even if he was by the sea, among the rocks, this was the reality of the situation. He was here and he would be here for another five days...
[Meltem Arıkan, *Zaten Yoksunuz*, 2005, Everest Publications, p. 7-8]

But one day at the end of spring, when the postman appeared with the books that Mrs Belkıs sent to herself, at the hotel address, from Paris, or with magazines sent to her from various friends, the hotel management would understand that we would come to stay that summer too. Because there was an agreement between us that was neither written nor verbal, but the conditions of which we would follow precisely. We would come back, we would stay in our old rooms, we would quickly have breakfast at separate tables in the wide paved area we called "dining hall" (some of us would have two or three olives, a slice of bread, five glasses of tea, some of us two beers and cheese, Mr Numan votka and sour cherry juice and shrimps), we would glance at the papers which the earliest riser among us would get from the town centre, we would go and have a coffee under the plane tree and when the day grew really hotter, we would return to the hotel, wear our swimming suits and go for a swim. And we would do our best not to run into each other for the rest of the day. It was as if we had silently

a stay in a yet unspoiled corner of the Mediterranean, or a visit to the mountain pastures (yayla) of Central Anatolia. Another response to this demand for greater meaning in our vacation times is provided by *boutique hotels*, which entered the sector by renovating old buildings to create more personalized spaces, and have flourished in recent years. Nonetheless, even these smaller, more personal forms of alternative tourism fail to entirely avoid some standardization, and in that sense also display a certain *uniformity*. Since their target markets are similar, the services they offer are also more or less the same. Travelers planning a vacation, alternative or otherwise, usually consult tourism brochures, internet sites or apply to travel agencies, the experts in the field. The information acquired from any one of these sources is far from accurately representing the complex and diverse reality of the place advertised. If we also take into account the unfamiliar and transitory element that any vacation contains, it becomes almost inevitable that the travel experiences of tourists are shaped by preconceived notions about their destinations which render them incapable of appreciating the actual reality and culture of that place. In this sense, all of the above is also valid for alternative tourism, since its media-generated narrative and the preconceived notions and self-created categories it produces in us may conceivably nourish and reinforce fantasies about the "other." Furthermore, by opening up previously untouched environments to visitors, these alternative ventures can contribute to their eventual conversion into overcrowded tourism centers. In Turkey, Bodrum, Ayvalık or Assos are all cases in point.

Despite the growing diversity of tourism activity in recent years, package tours are still very popular. Perhaps the main change here has occurred in the increase in top to bottom *supervision* and *regulation*. According to İhsan Bilgin, in the last quarter of the 20th century, the services sector started to organize time spent outside the house and leisure activities into "prearranged and processed recreation choices." (2006: 171) Tourism was one of the areas where this was most evident. While tourism activities expanded and diversified into a number of *subsectors*, like sport, congress, safari, golf or hiking tourism, they were conceived of as a slice of time to be intricately designed and organized down to the most minute detail. Obviously, this process led to major

Küçük olsun benim olsun diyenlere

Butik oteller artık büyük tatil merkezlerini de geçti. İçlerinde şarap mahzenleri, sanat evleri bulunan 10 butik oteli turizmin uzmanları ile birlikte sizler için seçtik

Milliyet
3 May 2003

Tekeli Konakları
Yer: Antalya Kaleiçi. 6 evin birleşmesiyle yapılan 17 yatak kapasiteli bir butik olan Tekeli Konakları 200 yıllık mimari restore edilerek yapılmış. Küçük bir otelden çok bir resortu andıran otelin içinde sanat evi, porselen mağazası da bulunuyor **Fiyat:** 130 milyon lira, iki kişi 150 milyon lira **Tel:** (0242) 244 54 65

Adahan Otel
Yer: Bodrum Yalıkavak. Eski bir kervansaray restore edilerek yapılan Adahan Otel'in 26 odası bulunuyor. Şaraphane ve kitap odası da bulunan otele çocuklu aileler alınmıyor. Otelin Osmanlı, Ermeni, Rum ve Ege mutfaklarından değişik lezzetleri tadabileceğiniz mutfağı bulunuyor. **Fiyat:** 75 dolar, iki kişi 95 dolar. **Tel:** (0252) 385 47 59

Polka Country Otel
Yer: Polonezköy. Otel aslına uygun olarak restore edilmiş. 19 yatak kapasiteli otel ev yemekleri ve vişne mikörü ile ünlü. Kış aylarında gelenleri için şöminesi de bulunan Polka'da kütüphane, yüzme havuzu ve havuz başı da bulunuyor. **Fiyat:** 100 milyon haftasonu 125 milyon **Tel:** (0216) 432 32 20

Olympos Lodge
Yer: Kemer. 12 odalı otelin içerisinde şömine bulunan kış bahçesi bulunuyor. Portakal ağaçları ve çiçeklerle çevreli otelde ayrıca 40 ve 50'li yıllardan kalma iki 'old times' otomobil de turistler için düşünülmüş. **Fiyat:** 150 euro iki kişilik odada tek kişi, deniz manzaralı odalar 180 euro **Tel:** (0242) 825 71 71

Golden Key Hotel
Yer: Bodrum, Bördübet, Hisarönü. 3 önemli tatil merkezde bulunan Golden Key misafirlerin deniz bisikleti gibi motorsuz araçları ücretsiz karşılıyor. **Fiyat:** Bördübet tek kişi 75 euro, Hisarönü 60 euro, Bodrum 60 euro **Not:** İki kişilik odalarda ikinci kişi farkı yüzde 40 **Tel:** (0252) 466 66 20

Ada Oteli
Yer: Bodrum Türkbükü. Her biri farklı özelliklerde 14 farklı odadan oluşan otel klasik hamam mimarisini içinde barındırıyor. Suit odalarda teras bulunurken penthouse odalarda yüzme havuzu, jakuzi bulunuyor. Akdeniz mutfaklarından lezzetleri tadabileceğiniz menüsü, home theatre've çocuklarıyla gelenler içinse play station'ı var. **Fiyat:** Normal odalarda 245 dolar, Penthouse'lar 475 dolar **Tel:** 0252 377 59 15

Medusa House
Yer: Didim. Antik özellikte 6 oda ve 2 apart evden oluşan Medusa evleri Fransız turistlerin yoğun olarak geldiği bir mekan. Planet Guide ve ünlü Alman tur operatörü TUI'nin Türk sahillerindeki oteller kitaplarında yer alan otelin milletvekilleri ve sanatçılardan oluşan misafirleri bulunuyor. Evlerdeki herşey tarihe ve eskiye bağlı kalınarak yapılmış. Otel sahibi 'konuklar burayı müze zannediyor' diyor. **Fiyat:** 40 dolar **Tel:** 0256 811 00 63

Antik Tiyatro Oteli
Yer: Bodrum. Antik Tiyatro karşısında bulunan otel Bodrum evi kavramına mimarisi ile farklı bir boyut kazandırıyor. **Fiyat:** 2 kişilik oda 85 - 90 milyon lira **Tel:** (0252) 316 60 53

Mountain Lodge
Yer: Fethiye Yaka. Dağ yamacında bulunan otel, sakin ve denizden uzak bir tatil geçirmek isteyenler için ideal. Türkiye'de yaşayan yabancı ailelerin de sık sık kaldığı mekanda her bütçeye göre farklı özelliklerde ve fiyatlarda odalar bulunuyor. **Fiyat:** 17 ile 28 euro arasında **Tel:** (0252) 638 25 15

Let it be small, as long as it's mine: *Boutique hotels have outdone the large holiday centres. Together with tourism experts we visited 10 boutique hotels which have their own wine cellars and art centres*

decided to thus widen the small space in which we lived, to turn this island, which everybody was so familiar with, into an area of freedom. If we ran into each other, we would smile slightly and continue on our ways without talking. [Tomris Uyar, "Ölen Otelin Müşterileri", *Yaza Yolculuk*, 1986, Can Publications, p. 89]

Room number 606 was a typical three star hotel room – so typical that it wasn't possible to either like or dislike it. On the walls there were scenes from a partly phantasy harem, women lying on velvety cushions behind latticed windows, careless mass production drawings for careless tourists. [Elif Şafak, *Araf*, 2004, Metis Publications, p. 321-322]

(The announcement begins with a song in English) … Yes, dear guests, good morning to all of you. A new day is beginning at Club Mega Saray. And of course we expect all of you at our activities throughout the day. You can obtain detailed information about each activity at our Animation Office. We hope you all have great fun at Club Mega Saray… (The announcement continues with the German, English and Russian versions of the same information) [The morning wake-up announcement which includes information on the daily animation programme, at the Antalya Club Mega Saray Holiday Village, 2005]

modifications of the environment. It also indicated that the public sphere was being increasingly sectorized and transformed into a top-to-bottom predesigned *consumption space*. This should be kept in mind when interpreting different tourism trends and the differences in class identity and status that accompany them.

Take *holiday villages*. Their growing numbers in the 1980s introduced a *new vacation concept*. Through advertisements and press coverage they were popularized as the symbols of an innovative type of luxury vacation. Although at first they targeted foreign visitors, in time, these resorts also came to represent the ideal holiday solution for "local tourists" – particularly the well-off and young middle classes. In recent years, holiday villages have started to take into consideration this local target market and are developing new strategies to attract customers; among these the *all-inclusive* resort vacation deal is the best known. This "dream vacation" offers gift stores, pool halls, bars, cafes, various restaurants, private beaches, live shows and just about anything else that might come to mind in an all-inclusive package. With everything included in a single upfront price, you can presumably "forget your cash" and "put your plastic away" during the length of your stay. Many of these resorts feature *themed* architecture, interior design, landscaping, accessories, and even staff outfits. Sea, sand and sun is no longer enough, now, images and symbols are marketed to prod desires, fantasies and dreams: "live in a palace," "set sail with the pirates," "discover the seven wonders of the world," are only some of the themes used to create the perfect holiday experience. For a long time now, tourism activities have heavily relied on the appeal of exotic visual imagery. The interesting thing here is seeing constructed realities based on *simulation* – such as those that amusement parks, shopping centers, fairs and of course Disneyland have accustomed us to – offered under one roof with the standard activities of mass tourism. In these resorts, areas like eating, shopping, accomodation and entertainment, which used to be considered relatively independent from each other in terms of space and time, have been brought together and interrelated in a *miniature* fantasy world. From the moment holiday makers get up in the morning, and during every hour of day or night, these villages or clubs organize their recreation activities according to a specific *order*.

right: **Holidays for millionaires in Bodrum. Holidays for millionaires in Foça… In Club Soytaş Holiday Villages.**

below: **All dreams included**

August 1980

Hürriyet
August 2002

Kentten indik "tatil köyüne"...

"Ultra, mega, maksimum her şey dahil" tatil köyleri, "dinlenmek" dışında her şeyi abartarak sunarlar...

Türkiye tatil köylerinden, kano üzerinde kalma yarışı ve "full monty" manzaraları. Sağdaki de, turistler için bonjur çiçekleriyle süslenmiş süt banyosu.

Radikal
17 February 2005

Kışın bomboş duran yazlık siteler şimdi insanla dolup taşıyor

Hürriyet
29 June 1980

BALKON SEFASI: Yazlıkçıların kent yaşamında bulamadıkları keyiflerden biri de mangalı, ya da kömür ocağı yakıp ızgara yapmaktır. Muratsuyu Sahil Sitesi'nin ehl-i keyf tiplerinden Feridun Çakarel yazın tadını en iyi çıkaranlardandır.

YAZLIKÇILAR

- Anadolu insanının yaylaya çıkışı gibi, büyük kentlilerin bir bölümü de 3-4 aylığına yazlığa göçer.
- 30-40 metrekarelik bir dairenin mevsimlik kirası 50 bin lira, satış fiyatı ise 1 milyon. Kamplarda bir çadırlık yerin kirası da 15 bin liradan başlıyor.
- Eskiden "yazlık" olarak Adalar bilinirdi. Şimdi Marmara'dan Akdeniz kıyılarına kadar birçok yörede yazlık kentler oluştu. B.Çekmece-Silivri arasındaki 30 kilometrede 116 tane yazlık yerleşim merkezi var.

above: **Migrating from cities to holiday villages:** *"Ultra, mega, maximum everything" holiday villages present everything in excess but "relaxation".*

left: **Summer resort residents:** *Empty all winter long, summer residences are now teeming with people.*

The world of lavish fantasy they offer, interestingly enough coexists with traces of a disciplinary regime.

Today, vacation villages and alternative forms of tourism have dethroned the once fashionable cheap summer housing developments (*yazlık*). For middle class families, owning a summer home had been both a way to escape the city during the summer months and a means to boost status. While not as popular as they used to be, these housing developments are still very much a part of the architectural texture of touristic regions today. Totally deserted in the winter months they turn into ghost settlements. Depending on their owner's budget they range from the more prosperous villa with garden and swimming pool complexes to the identical highrise developments aligned close together in rows. In the beginning, an obvious incentive to owning a summer getaway was the sense of control and independence that it gave. For those who couldn't afford to buy on their own there were timeshares. All these options addressed the desire for ownership and autonomy in individuals making them for a time more sought after then vacationing in a small hotel or pension. But nowadays, the summer home practice has lost much of its appeal. Savvy holiday makers today, whether they be conventional or avant-garde, want to discover new places that suit them. In this period of accelerated change, destinations just as rapidly go in and out of fashion. Meanwhile, for a large segment of society, vacationing somewhere else is not an option; they can only follow trends from a distance. As even the beaches become privatized in large cities like Istanbul, the underprivileged seek ways to find their own "place in the sun." Unheeding warnings of above acceptable levels of E. coli in the seawater, Istanbul youths and children leap into the sea in their underwear at every occasion, adding fuel to the endlessly ongoing controversy about *civilized behavior*.

In this isolated town at a distant point of the bay, this girl could only be a first for the local people who created shady areas in front of their houses and shops with vine pergolas and who found happiness with cage birds. With her very short hair, her silver ankle bracelet and the saddlebag which she obviously used as a purse, she was a real sight.

And for the summer residents, who climbed the ramp to the boarding house almost out of breath, who collapsed together with all their belongings in front of the door, who filled the balconies and terraces with laundry immediately after their arrivals and who cracked seeds in the moonlit evenings, she was an object of curiosity.
[Şükran Farımaz, "Süsen Pansiyon," *Bir Ağaç Bir Kadın*, 2002, Can Publications, p. 30]

Adab (comportment) brand swimming suit for the religious conservatives

Hürriyet
3 July 1984

Milliyet
11 June 2005

above: **The middle class on vacation**

right: **Private beaches all over Istanbul:** *Private beaches stretch from Büyükçekmece to Tuzla, from Sarıyer to the Islands.*

Vatan 34
30 June 2004

left: **We don't mind the bacillus coli:** *This is the Bosphorus… No one minds that the sea is polluted and full of germs. And it's not just the adults who swim in it, but their children too.*

below: **The summer resorts of the Islamist high society:** *The Islamist communities have chosen Esenköy, near Yalova, as their summer resort.*

Aktüel
4 August 1994

Buy now and pay later

Turkey entered the new millennium with new credit cards. The number of people using credit cards began to increase rapidly towards the end of the 1990s, reaching 15 million in 2005. Over the same period, credit card use spread to very diverse areas. It has now become possible to use plastic to charge every kind of purchase, and pay taxes, bills and even traffic tickets. Instead of postponing their dreams, consumers are encouraged to buy what they wish using credit cards offering extended payment terms on the purchase of goods and services. During this period, the number of people incurring credit card debts also increased dramatically. Police officers, state employees and retirees committing suicide because of cards they were unable to pay off have made newspaper headlines. Finally, as personal debt reached unprecedented heights, the government introduced new legislation at the beginning of 2006 to help individuals pay off their balance according to a debt repayment plan. Over the past 25 years people grew accustomed to hearing about the country's debt payments negotiations with the IMF; now, they are the ones that will have to discuss their personal debt repayment plans with their banks. Moreover, in the years ahead, it is estimated that an even greater number of people will turn to plastic. In this sense, the credit card industry in Turkey seems to be an ever-expanding market. All these developments have made debt one of the major concerns of our everyday life. How did this happen? How can this situation be related to other ongoing cultural and economic processes?

In Turkey, as in the rest of the world, the financial sector grew rapidly during the 1980s. Going back a little further and taking a look at what was happening in the world at the time can help us understand this expansion better: the 1970s world recession brought major structural transformations to the economy. Recession hit profit rates and rechanneled an important part

Examples of bank cards for children, produced by Garanti Bank

KARTLASIYORUZ

Düne kadar para ile yaptığımız ödemeleri bugün küçük bir kart kısa sürede hallediyor

Sabah **12 March 1992**

above: **We are really into cards:** *Payments which till recent were made with money are now quickly made with little credit cards.*

below: **Dad, I want a bank card:** *Children have become the favourite clients of banks. Yapı-Kredi and İş Bank have reached 185,000 active clients in their new "banking for youth" programme for 12-18 year-olds.*

Baba, banka kartı istiyorum!

Çocuklar, bankaların en gözde müşterileri oldu. Yapı Kredi ve İş Bankası'nın 12 - 18 yaş çocuklar için başlattığı 'gençlik bankacılığında' 185 bin aktif müşteri sayısına ulaşıldı

Tüketici kredilerinde yüzde 56'lık artış

Milliyet **30 July 2002**

right: **If you want to win, come along and bring a bag**

below: **As easy as pulling a hair strand from butter:** *You can get your money back whenever you wish, together with its accumulated interests.*

Günaydın
November 1981

Günaydın
January 1980

of global capital from industrial production to financial investments. In turn, this played an important role in the propagation of new technologies aimed at making international financial transactions quicker and easier. Parallel to these developments, when Turkey and other peripheral countries entered a debt crisis in the 1980s, the IMF and World Bank imposed structural adjustment policies which also transformed national economies. Liberalized capital markets were hurriedly constituted, facilitating the rapid transfer of money and all forms of capital from one country to another. According to some, the outstanding feature of the *new world economic order* was the crucial role of the *financial sector* in determining the stable functioning of other sectors. Within this economic restructuring – sometimes called globalization – it became more advantageous to "make money from money" than to invest in production.

Bankers were the first harbingers of the new "make money from money" era in Turkey. Their sudden appearance on the scene in the beginning of the 1980s, followed by their successive bankruptcies and the trail of "victims" left in their wake, were early warnings that this period would not roll by "like water off a duck's back," without difficulties or crises. Adopting free floating exchange rate policies, deregulating the interest rates on savings accounts, and opening the capital and money markets to foreign investors linked the financial sector to world markets and rendered it vulnerable to global fluctuations. The rise and fall of shares, mutual funds, government bonds and bills began to concern of a number of people, whether they were or not directly involved in the stock exchange, and keeping the markets happy became a top government priority. Susan Strange writes that, due to its inherent instability and unpredictability, the financial system makes a gambler out of everyone from worker, to storekeeper and farmer – whether they like it or not (Strange, 1998). In this period, when the state's control over the economy had lessened, *unpredictability* and *risk* became a part of everyday life. Fluctuations in foreign exchange rates and banks' interest rates and price volatility in the marketplace had a direct impact on people's earning power, savings and plans for the future. Under these unstable and uncontrolled economic conditions, the risk of losing money on money increased – in particular for the salaried segments of

1 US Dollar

We will get the stock exchange and market opening figures from C-NBCE in a little while. As for the figures, shares yesterday made an average loss of 2.6 %; the index closed the day at 30766 points. We see that treasury bonds interests are at the 14.80 combined level and that there are no changes in the interest percentage, which carries on at the 14.5 – 15.5 level. Yesterday at closing time the Dollar/TL parity was at the level of 1.3695, while the Euro/YTL parity was at 1.6390. The Cumhuriyet gold traded for 138 YTL. When we look abroad, yesterday the euro-dollar parity dropped below 1.19 for a while. It went down to 1.1876 but closed the day at the level of 1.1985. As for international markets, yesterday Wall Street rose and Dow Jones closed the day at 10414, with a rise of 1.25 %. In Brasil there was a slight upward movement and Bovespa closed with a rise of 0.79 %. While gold traded for 466 dollars an ounce, activity continued in oil prices at over 63 dollars: the day closed with a small reduction, at the level of 63 dollars 5 cents. Let's quickly move to expectations, the expectations that C-NBCE gets from brokering firms. Koç Investment believes that foreign markets picking up will support the ISE but that the delay in the social security law will cause concern on the stock exchange, and that while in the Dollar/YTL parity the YTL will gain value at the

opening, news from the IMF can push the foreign exchange up. In the bond market Koç Investment expects the 14.80-14.90 movement of combined interests to continue. According to Finansbank, in the Dollar/TL parity, influenced by the interest reduction of the Brasilian Central Bank and the parity, Dollar quotations can move around the 1.36-1.37 level; as for the bond market, the bond market is expected not to be affected by the global liquidity tension and to continue its horizontal movement...
[An excerpt from the economy news programme, broadcast after nine o'clock every morning on weekdays, on NTV Radio, 20 October 2005]

...
The glasses wil be collected soon
We will go dutch on the bill
Sweaty fingers will reach out for the credit cards
We'll squeeze into a taxi at night rate
Somehow your tongue will look for mine
We'll be caught in a safe house
All in front of a camera, with a three day beard
... [Metin Celâl, "Aids'e Şans Tanıma", *Çağdaş Türk Şiiri Antolojisi*, 1998, Papirüs Publications]

society. The crises experienced in the past decades in Turkey, Latin America and Far Eastern countries have amply proven how real these risks are and how disastrous their consequences can be for individuals.

If the focal point of the new economy is the financial sector, the key players of the sector are *banks*. In recent years, competition between banks to sell money has become fierce. The most common way for banks to make money is by charging interest on loans. From that perspective, it becomes easier to explain how we have become "card addicts." Through ad campaigns, promotions and the possibility of extending payment for products over time, banks attempt to make their own card the most attractive to consumers. Obviously, the way to make people use their credit cards more is to get them to *spend more and consume more*. Banks today have become institutions that encourage *consuming more than saving*; they no longer bring to mind piggy banks but credit cards. For a while now, money has become "virtual," plastic and invisible. Instead of putting money in the piggy bank, consumers now try to save *bonus* points, earn *points* for air miles or redeem points for gift cards. Each month in the mail, an assortment of colorful ads, free extra card offers, and "special day" promotions come in the credit card statement all with only one goal in mind: getting consumers to take on more debt in the coming period. At a time when the real buying power of salaried and state employees has decreased, creating a *virtual* buying power is obviously crucial to keeping the consumer economy thriving. As money goes "digital", all traces of labor and value also vanish. This in turn, completely *conceals* the aberrations and inequalities of production relationships.

Consumer loans have led to an even closer relationship between banks and the various consumer sectors. For instance, recently banks have started to offer residential mortgage credit. As a result, all over Turkey and more specifically in large cities, prices in the real estate market have soared. Similarly, as auto loans became widespread, car sales flourished. In other words, banks play a central role in shaping, regulating and transforming not only production but consumption as well. Meanwhile, with "interest-free banking" and other "Islamically correct" forms of investment,

right: **Victims of the banker:** *In Ankara, the street of the office of Banker Atalay, who is unable to pay his debts and has announced his bankruptcy, was completely full with his creditors.*

below: **We are in debt up to our necks:** *During the three years Özal was in power, foreign debts increased by 60 %, from USD 18,400,000,000 to USD 29,400,000,000.*

Günaydın
26 December 1981

Gırtlağımıza kadar borca gömüldük !

Sabah
25 January 1987

Sabah
27 October 2005

Türkiye
28 February 2004

above: **Traffic fines to be paid with credit cards:** *The Police Commissioner is bringing a change to the Traffic Regulations, in accordance with the European Union and in order to solve certain problems. According to the new regulations fines now can also be paid by credit card.*

below: **We have become card-a-holics:** *19,000,863 people in Turkey make use of the many different credit cards of close to 50 banks.*

the banking sector today indisputably attracts players of every creed and color.

While the relationship between a bank and the customer it has issued a credit card to may suggest reciprocity, it is certainly not based on equality. The relationship seems to imply give-and-take because banks need consumers to take out loans and want them to use their credit cards. One look at credit costs and interest rates makes it clear that lending is a very lucrative business for banks. In an age where consumerism is continually spurred, the "virtual" buying power that banks provide is essential to consumers. Assuming that consumption brings happiness, then credit cards are the sponsors of happiness. Today, living with credit has becomes widespread through the miracle of virtual buying power. By giving people the possibility to spend more than they earn, credit cards support an existence based on buying and consuming. But letting yourself be seduced by the lure of this illusory buying power also carries the risk of losing control over a situation which may at any moment topple into a downward spiral of big financial trouble, insecurity and bankruptcy. The alarming magnitude of personal debt in Turkey attests to the gravity of the situation. But a similar state of affairs can also be seen elsewhere. In the US, for example, the number of people unable to pay off their debts and filing for bankruptcy has risen sharply in recent years.

Credit cards allowing consumers to pay for their purchases *on installment* hit the market in the 2000s, considerably accelerating the prevalence of credit card use. In fact, paying on installment, as a means to boost sales, had been around for a while. In her study on the emergence of a white goods market in Turkey in the 1960s, Ayşe Buğra (1998) points out that even in an age where credit mechanisms like those in Europe or America had not yet appeared, the Turkish company Arçelik was already using a nationwide supplier network and offering retail installment sales. The primary feature of installment sales was their reliance on face-to-face social encounters and mutual trust. Nowadays, many businesses are opting for retail installment through credit cards instead of the installment campaigns they used to organize themselves. The contract based on mutual trust has turned into a more "rational" and formal relationship. The starting point for

I'll go shopping before boarding the plane: I sway my ass lightly to the rhythm of the simple pop songs coming from the loud speakers, I smell perfumes, I test blushers, I keep trying on sunglasses and removing them. Third rate love novels fall out of my bag; while looking for my credit card I scatter around the contents of my bag, I enjoy my irresponsibility... I decide to buy a Gucci pair of sunglasses. While I hold out my credit card, telling them in English to put the old sunglasses which are on my head into the box becuse I want to wear the new ones, a face is reflected in the mirror in front of me. [Oray Eğin, -Kal!, 2004, Grikedi Publications, p. 168-169]

Vada (mascot of Yapı Kredi Bank) keyring, generally sold by street vendors

… We were called to the reception hall of the company for an irregular meeting. The general manager told us that we would not be affected by the crisis and that there was a high probability that none of us would lose our jobs. That's when I discovered that there was a crisis. At times like this I was embarrassed not to watch TV or to read the papers and I was afraid of somebody noticing. "Of course you had your invalid to take care of in that period" said one of my friends, "you weren't aware of what was going on…" In the '94 crisis I had a debt of 2,000 dollars, We had generated this debt by buying a computer in installations. After I bought that computer its value dropped to 600 dollars and the dollar's value doubled. At least in this crisis I only have debts in Turkish Liras. As the Turkish Lira has lost so much value, this must mean my debt is worth less than it was before, should I be happy about this? [Serazer Pekerman, *Kolay Bir Aşk*, 2004, İletişim, p. 165]

all of this is, of course, the credit card agreement. However much effort credit card companies make to draw customers to their cards and appear user-friendly with colorful logos, mascots and amusing commercials, the fact remains that card contracts establish a relationship that implies strict regulations, threats and sanctions. As retailing relationships grow more anonymous, *official sanctions* increase as well. This is also an indicator that the market and *commercialization* have become more firmly entrenched. Commercialization has not only expanded to health, education and a number of other domains, through credit cards it now also has a much more radical impact on our everyday life. Certain purchases today can only be made by credit card. For instance, a card is required to shop online, benefit from sales or retail installment "opportunities," and make reservations. Under a cover of proffered *opportunities*, this process is also another technique of social exclusion; it isn't hard to anticipate that with the upsurge in the "privileges" cards offer, an increasingly large segment of society will be excluded. Credit cards may offer the luxury of spending tomorrow's resources today, but the price of this credit is an increasingly steeper mortgage on our future.

left: **A Bonus Miracle:** *How did I manage to accumulate this much bonus points?*

below: **Interest is forbidden by religion, but is the commission on credit cards permissible?** *Kuveyt Türk, which works with an interest free banking system, has begun requesting a 4.7 % commission from clients who make payments with credit cards, on account of the economic crisis.*

June 2005

Hürriyet
5 August 2001

Faiz haram, kartın komisyonu helal mi?

Faizsiz bankacılık sistemiyle çalışan finans kuruluşlarından Kuveyt Türk, krizi gerekçe göstererek, ödemelerini kredi kartıyla yapan müşterilerinden yüzde 4.7 oranında komisyon talep etmeye başladı. Oysa, kredi kartından komisyon talep etme hakkı, sadece benzin istasyonlarına tanınıyor.

Güneş
28 April 1984

Ses
4 April 1981

above: **Customers are questioned like aspiring son-in-laws:** *While almost all firms are steering towards sales on installment basis because of the shortage of cash sales, they are also trying to get to know better their customers, in order not to make a loss.*

right: *–We are a low income family, our son can only marry your daughter if you can give her in installments.*

Kredi kartı çarpıyor

ATO Başkanı Sinan Aygün, kredi kartı kullanım kriterleri hakkındaki raporu açıkladı. Aygün, "Kredi kartı milletvekilini de vurduysa, Mike Tyson olsa ayakta kalamaz" dedi

Kredi kartı borcunu ödeyemeyenlerin sayısı her geçen gün artıyor. 2004'te kara listeye girenlerin sayısı 130 bini buldu

Birgün **22 January 2005**

above: **Credit cards knock out:** *Sinan Aygün, Head of ATO, has revealed the report on the criteria for the use of credit cards. Aygün said: "If credit cards can knock out a member of parliament, even Myke Tyson wouldn't have withstood this."*

below: **Is there a crisis on the horizon?** *According to some economists, the debt of people who can't control themselves when making payments with credit cards, is a sign of major trouble concerning credit cards.*

Ufukta bir kriz mi var?

Radikal **3 September 2005**

Kredi kartıyla harcama yaparken elinin ayarını kaçıran vatandaşın bankalara olan borcu, kimi ekonomi yazarlarına göre büyük bir kredi kartı batağının habercisi. Bankalar cephesine göre ise ortada bir sorun yok. Kart mağdurlarından, banka yöneticileri ve tüketici derneklerine kadar herkesin bu konuda söyleyecek bir sözü var

What if we get lucky?

Doritos brand crisp packages with promotional goods

Mrs Esma was in a pitiful condition. Three years after she started collecting coupons she suddenly became weird. The moment she heard the words " for a shocking number of coupons" on the radio or TV, whether at home, on the street or wherever she was, she would start writhing, moaning, her body would tremble and quiver in various ways, she would run out of breath and then she would finally relax, sweaty, sighing and moaning and her eyes rolling. [Ayşe Kulin, "Sadece 1457 kupona", *Foto Sabah Resimleri*, 1996, Sel Publications, p. 129]

Is spending to win money a dream? Looking for game pieces and a chance to win a car under soda or beer bottle caps; saving newspaper coupons to get a TV set, tableware or an encyclopedia; saving credit card cash points to shop for "free"... All of the above are indicators of the daily expectation that made chance games the fastest growing sector in the 1980s: *winning*. Not by working or producing, but by consuming. Chance games, while providing ample food for thought on the mechanisms of our modern consumer society, are also a reference to a certain *way of living*. In this context, more questions arise: what changes has the "gambler" archetype – which traditionally figures in novels and other works – undergone? How are chance games related to broader economic processes and how are they a part of the culture industry?

The *gambler* personae in literature go back quite a long way. They are portrayed as individuals who refuse to conform to the drabness of the social order or the logic underlying it, and instead of reasonably reconciling ends and means, "bet big" and pin all their hopes on chance. The risks gamblers take mean they are also gambling with life; they are daredevils walking the line between reality and fantasy. Their approach to life does not coincide with that of others. Since it topples all principles of the work ethic that declare money should be earned through work, this perception of life puts them at the center of society's *moral* concerns. In literature, the other face of gambling is its depiction as a vice that can lead an individual to squander an entire fortune, ruining him/her and destroying his/her family. With the widespread popularity of chance games, today, everyone is a potential gambler. No longer a reckless adventure, gambling is almost considered a form of "rational" investment. Despite obvious

TALIH KUŞU BELKİ SİZİN DE BAŞINIZA KONAR

Ya... çıkarsa

Bilet satışlarından elde edilen gelirin yüzde 70'e yakını ikramiye olarak halka geri veriliyor.

Enflasyonla birlikte Millî Piyango'nun da gelirlerinden büyük artışlar oluyor.

Yıllardır zengin olma umudu ile aldığımız piyangonun gelirleri ile 8 yılda "Türk Hava Kuvvetleri Vakfı"na 4,5 milyar lira bağışta bulunuldu.

What if we get lucky?

Milliyet
22 June 1980

Her gün köşebaşlarında, vapurlarda sık sık rastladığımız ve "size de çıkabilir" diye uzattığı Piyango biletleri ile sizlere umut kapıları açan seyyar bayiler, piyango İdaresi'ne topladıkları paraları yatırıyorlar.

MİLLÎ PİYANGO'NUN NET BİLET SATIŞLARI VE NET KARLARI

YIL	BİLET SATIŞ GELİRLERİ	VAKFA DEVREDİLEN NET KAR
1971	183 MİLYON	65 MİLYON
1972	226 MİLYON	77 MİLYON
1973	284 MİLYON	99 MİLYON
1974	355 MİLYON	115 MİLYON
1975	534 MİLYON	168 MİLYON
1976	908 MİLYON	306 MİLYON
1977	1 MİLYAR 207 MİLYON	381 MİLYON
1978	1 MİLYAR 864 MİLYON	474 MİLYON
1979	3 MİLYAR 400 MİLYON	750 MİLYON
1980 (tahmini)	8 MİLYAR	2 MİLYAR

Günaydın
5 November 1981

Spor-Toto milyonerini ilk kutlayanlar bankerler oldu

Milyoner bakkal çırağı, henüz parasını almadığı halde dün gece en lüks gazinolara giderek kredi ile eğlendi

Hayaller de değişti

Eskiden "Büyük ikramiye bana çıksa bir ev alır, hayır işleri yaparım" denirdi
Şimdi yerli televizyon dizilerindeki gibi şatafatlı yaşam tarzı arzulanıyor

Vatan
10 December 2004

above: **Bankers were the first to congratulate the pools millionaire:** *Although he hasn't collected his money yet, the millionaire grocer boy enjoyed himself in the most expensive gazino with money on loan.*

left: **Dreams have changed:** *Once people used to say "If only I win the jackpot, I'll buy a house and give the rest to charity", but now they wish for a flamboyant life style, as seen in local TV series.*

inherent differences, playing the stock market or playing the national lottery and other lottery games like *spor toto* and lotto, all have the same result: they make life itself gambling.

In the 1980s, it was *state support* that first gave its impetus to chance games. Branding casinos and other gambling houses detrimental to the "morality" of society, the state brought restrictions against these "gambling machines" but gave free license to lotteries and other chance games. A large part of the income obtained from the lottery was donated to the army; thus, militarism indirectly contributed to the dream of becoming rich overnight. In a society where economic inequalities keep growing, the probability (or improbability) of winning the special New Year's draw of the National Lottery or becoming the next *spor toto* millionaire actually evens out socioeconomic differences. Yet, aspirations remain largely determined by "upper class," consumer patterns. "Getting lucky" means buying a house, a color TV or a car. Tragicomic stories on the moneyless "ordinary" National Lottery grand prize winners have appeared in the papers and inspired authors and filmmakers. Instead of improving the lives of the poor, this sudden access to phenomenal wealth is shown to destroy them through the jealousy and hate it engenders. In record time, lottery-made fortunes are inexplicably consumed. Yet, these cautionary stories only make those whom "lady Luck" has not yet "smiled on" more determined to win.

The causes underlying this booming demand for chance games can be related to more general economic processes. In their attempts to identify the attributes of the social dynamics generated by global capitalism, both sociologists and anthropologist agree on one point: in the economic sphere, production has moved back stage and become secondary, while the financial sector has gained ascendancy and the consumer-driven market has expanded and acquired greater visibility. (Camaroff&Camaroff, 2000) Thus, the crucial point in the changes experienced is not that labor-based production has disappeared, but that the contribution of labor to society's wealth has become invisible. In such a world, the notion that wealth can be acquired in the stock market or the marketplace by totally intangible means gains prevalence. This situation also triggers an increase in the tendency toward speculation. All over

He strained to reach the edge of the bed, leaned over, put his hand to his back pocket, took out his wallet and pulled out a coloured piece of paper… He unfolded the paper and held it close to my eyes. It was a lottery ticket. Then he immediately put the ticket away.

What is there in that ticket, I said. Continuing to smile proudly, he settled again on the bed. The jackpot, he said. I couldn't help screaming: Then why are you still cleaning those shitty toilets, you idiot? [Murat Uyurkulak, *Tol*, 2003, Metis Publications, p. 119]

the world, the rising dominance and proliferation of various forms of gambling, from playing the stock market to playing the lottery, have turned the planet – to quote Fidel Castro – into one big *casino*. With the blessing of the state and state institutions, gambling has gone from social sickness to *social policy*.

Under these circumstances, it is hardly surprising that chance games should have become so popular. At the same time, they also began to diversify. At the start there was only the national lottery, *spor toto*, and horse betting; now these have been joined by *spor loto*, numbers betting (*sayısal loto*), scratch-off games, and so forth... At this point, it might be relevant to look at who these habitués of chance games are. What kind of gamblers are these people? In our society, where labor is taken for granted, unemployment and poverty rise daily and the state's "protective" role has decreased, the single key to all services and security has become money. Yet, it is obvious that for many, making enough money from their paycheck to "ensure" a good future is unfeasible. Today, everyone in Turkey realizes that workers or state employees cannot hope to buy a house with their retirement bonus. In the general anxiety to survive, people no longer harbor any concrete plans for the future; money primarily qualifies the future they hope to win in chance games. Their dreams focus on a sudden, unexpected surge in income which will help them move up a class. But it would be misleading to consider the interest in chance games to be merely instrumental. Just as the motives of the classic gambler archetype cannot be reduced to a craving for wealth, the people who today latch onto chance games are not only in it for the money. Maybe it should be thought of simply as a desire to win. The risk and adventure elements intrinsic to gambling are still applicable today. Winning the lottery jackpot is a special event that suspends for a while the monotonous, routine flow of life. Modern societies tend to make people feel *insignificant* and *expendable*; games that call on chance are a way for us to feel unique and powerful. We may not be able to turn our lives around through our own efforts, but if luck has chosen us there might still be a way.

There is a growing *disillusionment* in society with certain values and ideals, such as the importance of a good education, striving

Book containing formulas for winning the Lotto

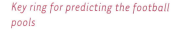

Key ring for predicting the football pools

Türkiye
7 February 1988

Sabah
15 September 2004

Milliyet
8 September 1989

top right: **Gambling machines blocked:** *The ANAP Members of Parliament are determined to prevent Turks from entering casinos.*

above: **Who is going to stop the lotto?**

right: **Pockets scratched clean:** *Enthusiasts queued up in front of National Lottery booths from the early morning and little heaps of blank tickets quickly piled up on the streets.*

Gençlik 'şans'a teslim!

YÜZDE 74'Ü ŞANS OYUNLARI OYNUYOR

Üniversite öğrencileri arasında yapılan bir araştırma, gençlerin çok büyük kısmının şans oyunu oynadığını ortaya koydu. En çok ilgi gören oyun ise "At yarışları"...

DÜŞÜK GELİRLİLER OYNUYOR- Ankete katılan vatandaşlardan şans oyunu oynayanlarının yüzde 73.3'ünün aylık 400 milyon lira ve altında gelire sahip olduğunun tespit edildiğini anlatan Aşan, "Deneklerin yüzde 28.6'sının her gün oyun oynadığı, yüzde 32.1'inin haftada bir, yüzde 17'sinin ayda bir, yüzde 22.3'ünün ise daha az oynadığı belirlendi" dedi.

Vakit
9 April 2004

Yeni Gündem
28 December 1986

above: **Youth surrenders itself to luck:** According to a research carried out among students, the majority of young people play fortune games.

right: –Just think Ayten, what if we had won?

for a successful career and working to make a living. The helplessness felt at not possessing the means to direct one's life or find a purpose to it may also explain the growing appeal of horoscopes, fortune telling and mediums. When existing permutations of ends and means are insufficient to explain or provide a solution to a situation, mystical interpretations bring exactly the same sense of empowerment that belief in luck does. In newspapers and magazines, we read our horoscopes to find out about ourselves and, by singling us out from the rest of the signs, they make us feel unique. We build our dreams according to these predictions and explain our failures through them. These are techniques to escape from *cruel realities* and approach them with a more *hopeful* logic than the "rational" world provides.

But this flight from reality is not the most striking aspect of chance games, fortune telling or horoscopes. In fact what they all do is *impose* reality on us. The sphere of chance games and fortune telling in large part merges with the *boundaries* of today's world. In this day and age, believing in chance and finding inspiration in supernatural powers both belong to a *planned industry*. In their work on the culture industry, Adorno and Horkheimer argue that *chance* and *planning* have become one and the same concept. In a society where culture brands every area with an identical stamp, ideology conceals itself under a mask of *probabilities*. Chance is actually the other face of planning. Chance offers the planners an alibi by making it seem that in life's system of negotiations and norms there still remains room for direct and spontaneous relations between individuals (Adorno & Horkheimer, 1979: 146). The conclusion to draw from all this is that our relationship with "lady luck" is not personal but *collective*.

Television game shows perfectly illustrate the connections between chance games and the *culture industry*. These shows, in which "knowledge" and luck combine, display all of the aspects we have discussed up to now; dreams of becoming special and famous, of making a lot of money and changing one's life later vanish faced with the *inevitability* – shared with thousands of past contestants – of being rapidly forgotten and tossed back into the routine of everyday life. As Adorno and Horkheimer have pointed

She had been holding very close the saucer covered by the coffee cup for the last ten, fifteen minutes. Then she turned her blue eyes onto us and we felt wrapped by a load of wet and dirty rags:

-There is an evil eye on you, my son...

She was looking at the coffee grounds on the edge of the saucer as if looking at infinity and with a kind of sorrow which she seemed to want us to imitate.

Neither of us moved. Is there anybody who hasn't experienced the ease of talking about the indefinite or the unknown? But the fortune teller was right. Once you believe in fortune telling, why not believe in evil eye too? They were a series within the same rosary
[Ahmet Hamdi Tanpınar, "Fal," *Bütün Öyküleri*, 1983/2003, Yapı Kredi Publications]

Scene from the popular TV show "Who Wants to be a Millionaire" [Kanal D, 2004]

out the "lucky person" on screen reflects the powerlessness of millions of people yearning for the same thing. Although the participants of chance games appear to be competing with each other, at times using their intuition then their knowledge, they nonetheless never stop being members of the same *unlucky society*.

While chance games in general interest women as much as men, bets on the outcome of a sport like football usually draw men more. The passion for football in particular has created a number of identities, starting with the masculine. Football betting based on guessing the outcome of a football game offers enthusiasts an activity based on the prolongation of football. In addition, to be successful in games like *iddaa* [betting], watching Turkish leagues is not enough, you have to follow world leagues as well. Those who add meaning to their lives through this game have formed a *virtual* community joined by their interest and knowledge. For many, *online games* and *online betting* sites are simply another extension of the game. It has become common today to show the commercials of betting sites before a match. Betting games played online from internet cafes, home or the office or those played in virtual gaming houses, offer excitement as well as the hope of winning, and, through the use of technology, the new possibility – however *limited* – of meeting other people and discovering other worlds.

In today's new online chance games, much as with the stock market and credit cards, the determining axis is *virtuality*. Spending without actually having earned or winning through spending creates the *illusion of boundless possibilities*. Endlessly repeated lottery draws lull people with the hope that maybe the next time will be their lucky time. Bad luck may turn to good. However, just as personal bankruptcies and, on a broader scale, the rapid depletion of the world's resources have currently unsettled the consumer craze and its implicit illusion of unlimited possibilities, the dreams that drive chance games can also run out. Some people now say they have "given up on chance." The "reality" offered in response echoes society's *collective logic*: who wouldn't want to get rich overnight?

Hürriyet
20 December 1980

right: **Fill up your football pools, draw your lottery:** *Hoping for luck.*

below: **This week somebody will get extremely rich:** *The National Lottery, the Lotto and Number Ten have all rolled over to next week. This weekend the grand prizes amount to close to 4 billion. Good luck and try to keep sane.*

Vatan
18 September 2003

Bu hafta birileri fena halde zengin olacak

Milli Piyango, Sayısal Loto ve On Numara devretti. Bu haftasonu 4 trilyona yakın ikramiye var. Şansınız açık, aklınız yerinde olsun

Yeni Şafak
22 December 2003

Güneş
15 December 1988

above: **Don't let the lottery knock you out:** *Thousands of people dreaming of winning the National Lottery's Grand Prize of 10 billion have queued in front of the lottery booths.*

left: **Penniless because of a 10 billion dream:** *The dream of starting the new year as a millionaire is dominating the whole country. People are making savings on their food and clothes and rushing off to National Lottery booths.*

right: **Ready to bet?**

Var mısın iddaaya?

SPORTOTO

iddaa

Var mısın?

Lig Kısaltmaları

- AVK: Avusturya Kupası
- BEK: Belçika Kupası
- DAN: Danimarka 1. Ligi
- HOL: Hollanda 1. Ligi
- İN1: İngiltere 1. Ligi
- İNCL: İngiltere Championship League
- İKP: İskoçya Premier Ligi
- İSV: İsviçre 1. Ligi
- İSÇ: İsveç 1. Ligi
- LKU: Libertadores Kupası
- ROL: İskandinav Royal Ligi
- ŞMP: Şampiyonlar Ligi
- UEFA: UEFA Kupası
- YUK: Yunanistan Kupası

Program 12 - 14 Nisan 2005 MAÇ SKORU OYUNU

- 113 NOTTINGHAM F - SHEFFIELD UTD
- 122 B.MÜNİH - CHELSEA
- 123 INTER - AC MILAN
- 124 BOLIVAR - DANUBIO
- 125 ALIANZA LIMA - BANFIELD
- 126 ONCE CALDAS - GUADALAJARA
- 213 DEN BOSCH - FEYENOORD
- 214 GERMINAL BA - GENK
- 222 JUVENTUS - LIVERPOOL
- 223 PSV EINDHOVEN - LYON
- 224 THE STRONGEST - UNIV. DE ŞİLİ
- 225 CARACAS - TIGRES
- 226 SAO PAULO - QUILMES
- 313 ALKMAAR - VILLARREAL
- 314 GÖTEBORG - VALERENGA
- 315 ROSENBORG - FC KOPENHAG
- 316 AUXERRE - CSKA MOSKOVA
- 321 PARMA - AVUSTURYA VIENNA
- 322 SPORTING LİZBON - NEWCASTLE UTD
- 333 ATLETICO PR - AMERICA DE CALI

Milliyet
April 2005

Almost everybody today complains about the accelerated pace of life. But in modern societies this so-called accelerated pace concept actually integrates a number of different processes. First of all, with globalized capitalism, time has become disconnected from people's lives and organized through various procedures and technologies on a much broader scale. As Marx foresaw a long time ago, capital has overcome every local obstacle in its effort to minimize the time needed to move from one place to another. On the one hand, this focus on time has a restricting effect on people's lives, on the other, it generates the desire to keep up with the frantic pace that defines modern societies. One way to achieve this is by keeping up with the latest technologies. In this section we look at three aspects of life in post-1980s Turkey not only from a functional viewpoint but also with respect to the "modernizing" meanings invested in them: fast food as a new way of eating; passion for cars as the symbol of speed and freedom; and the latest time-saving household appliances. In a world where time has become organized on a mass level, we are faced with the issue of free time with all the conflicts and tensions it implies.

seize the times

Fast food comes to Turkey

The sandwich shop was packed. Toast with mustard, sausage, cheese or sucuk and ayran, no one ever tired of eating these foods which were presented at every sandwich shop without the need to bring about any change, any innovation. For most, having a sandwich was a novelty in itself. It was low cost, even though this didn't sound very convincing to those who were used to prepare their meals at low cost, and for people who were sick and tired of potato dishes with lots of onions and little mince meat, which cooked for hours, sandwiches were still a novelty. When did the first sandwiches appear? The first sandwich shop opened in the narrow arcade next to the Grand Cinema. Its owner put up a sign saying "Hot Dog" on the sidewalk. As soon as it opened, it was immediately crammed with girls and boys from the Yenişehir College. At first, the sandwich shop was a place where college kids stopped by, being as they were more open to novelties, while most other people regarded it with suspicion. It was a source of worry for families who were angry with their children for ruining their appetites with these sandwiches, while wonderful food waited for them at home. Then, suddenly, sandwiches became widespread throughout the city…
[Sevgi Soysal, *Yenişehir'de Bir Öğle Vakti*, 1973/1988, Bilgi Publications, p. 17-18]

Actually, the concept of "food on the go" was never alien to Turkey, where the tradition of street food has long included everything from *balık ekmek* [charcoaled fish sandwiched in a slab of bread] and *ekmek arası köfte* [grilled meatballs, tomatoes and peppers tucked into bread], to *kokoreç* [lamb tripe grilled on charcoal] and various grilled sandwiches. In recent years, however, this traditional type of Turkish "fast food" has become the subject of much controversy: "Do *lahmacun* [flatbread coated with spicy ground lamb and herbs] and whisky go together?" "Can you serve *ekmek arası* [a sort of kebab sandwich] at a dinner party?" In the new millennium, there are those who staunchly defend the *sefertası* [Turkish lidded metal lunch or dinner pail] against fast food, and those who are ready to give up EU membership rather than go without *balık ekmek* or *kokoreç*. When did fast food (in the original American sense of the term) enter Turkey? What *new forms* have quick meals and snacks taken today and how should we interpret the *new meanings* they carry?

In the 1980s, certain types of food began to be associated with the concept of *fast food*. The internationalization of the Turkish economy and the market entry of foreign companies played a major part in this process. It was only when international food chain giants like *McDonald's*, *Burger King*, and *Pizza Hut* opened stores in Turkey, that quick meals really became *fast food*. But the spread of fast food in Turkey took a rather different course than it did in the US. Let's take McDonald's for instance. This fast food chain became popular in American society in the 1950s, and until the 1980s, continued to appeal mostly to middle class families; over this period it remained a food industry aimed at mass consumption and had a somewhat homogenizing effect on the eating out market. In the 1980s, as the middle class began to shrink and poverty increased, new tendencies toward healthy and natural nutrition emerged among the new strata of the middle classes especially and *fast food* significantly lost status. As a high-calorie and cholesterol-rich food, it began to be associated with

Gün
3 November 1993

Milliyet
12 February 2001

above: **Turkish style fast food**

right: **It will be ages before Turkey gets into the EU:** *The owner of Şampiyon Kokoreç says: "We'll sell lots of kokoreç, before Turkey gets into the EU."*

left: **Welcome to Istanbul, McDonald's:** *Turkey's first McDonald's hamburger restaurant has opened in Taksim.*

below: –Where to?
–You to the office, me home.

October 1986

2005

obesity and *poverty*. In other words, when McDonald's hamburgers were beginning to lose their popularity in America – at least among the upper middle classes – the same product hit the market in Turkey as a food indicating *high status*.

In those years, McDonald's rapidly established itself among Turkey's young population as one of the favorite spots to meet, gather and generally have a good time; *international fast food* corporations tend to open their restaurants in the most populated parts of the city and especially in affluent neighborhoods. In Turkey, as in many other parts of the world, *hamburgers* were associated with an *American lifestyle*, the west, modernity and youth, which no doubt played an important part in their popularization. Again in those years, McDonald's also became popular with another group in society: middle class families with young children. The special *Happy Meal* tailored specifically for children included a little toy and, like in America, restaurants offered play areas for kids that positioned McDonald's as a *family brand* in the food industry. In later years, with the increase in and diversification of this type of restaurant and their pricing policies, the food that McDonald's and similar fast food chains offered became more *common-place* and frequently consumed.

"Before the McDonald's, the Burger Kings and the Wendy's came into our lives, the first thing that came to mind in Istanbul when talking about hamburgers was Kristal Büfe. Here they would put a meat patty with garlic and lots of spices and a thinly sliced gherkin between two slices of round bread, buttered and pressed in a grill, and they would spread the slices of bread with diluted tomato sauce. The kingdom of the Kristal Büfe, in front of which people queued up after the cinema, in the pre-Tarlabaşı-demolition-Taksim Square, was first shaken by the hamburger chains which are the favourites of the new generation, and it was completely destroyed in time. [Ayfer Tunç, Bir Maniniz Yoksa Annemler Size Gelecek: 70'li Yıllarda Hayatımız, Yapı Kredi Publications, 2001, p. 302]

Another development of the past 20 years is that, as the fast food concept became more familiar and entered everyday usage, a number of local foods also embarked on a process of *McDonaldization*. As the number of foreign and local foods labeling and marketing themselves as fast food increased, fast food evolved into a domain that increasingly displayed *social differences* and *conflicts*. In the process, certain foods became a symbol of "otherness" and acquired a new identity in the consumer economy. In their gradual pursuit of "branding," *döner*, *kokoreç* and *dürüm* [a Turkish wrap] retailers attempted a variety of packaging, at times linked to authentic and *traditional* imagery, at others, emphasizing *modernity* and the west. The impact of class differentiation on locality is also significant. In recent years, expensive cafés in select

Toys given as presents with children's menus in fast food chains

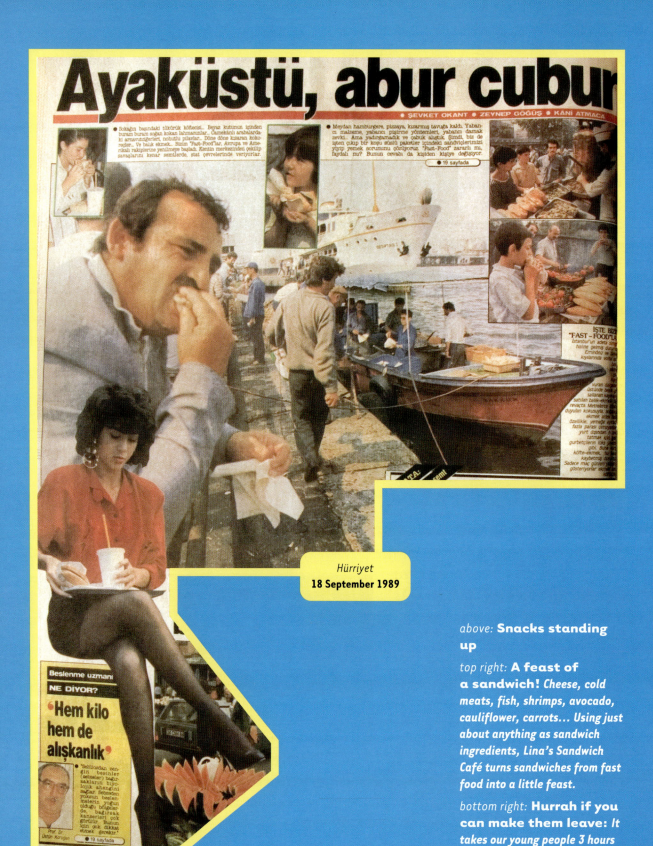

Hürriyet
18 September 1989

above: **Snacks standing up**

top right: **A feast of a sandwich!** *Cheese, cold meats, fish, shrimps, avocado, cauliflower, carrots… Using just about anything as sandwich ingredients, Lina's Sandwich Café turns sandwiches from fast food into a little feast.*

bottom right: **Hurrah if you can make them leave:** *It takes our young people 3 hours to digest the hamburgers prepared in 2 minutes.*

GÜLAY FIRAT

NİŞANTAŞI'NDAKİ LINA'S SANDWICH CAFE'DE, KOCA BİR SOFRA KURACAK KADAR ÇEŞİT VAR

Ekmek arası ziyafet

Peynir, soğuk et, balık, karides, avokado, karnıbahar, havuç... Hemen her türlü yiyeceği sandviç malzemesi yapan Lina's Sandwich Cafe, sandviçi fast food olmaktan çıkarıp küçük bir ziyafete dönüştürüyor. Nişantaşı'nda bir ay önce açılan cafe, Singapur, Monaco ve Belçika dahil pekçok ülkede şubeleri olan Fransız restoranlar zinciri "Lina's Sandwich Cafe"nin son halkası. Merkezi ise Paris.

Aktüel
January 1997

"FAST FOOD"U KENDİMİZE BENZETTİK...

Kaldırabilene aşkolsun !

Tempo
November 1988

İşte batılı bir mekân! Üstelik Türkiye'de... Her yaştan insanın, özellikle gençlerin ve Arapların uğrak yeri... Ama her toplumun kendine özgü kuralları var öte yandan... Ve ihtiyaçları tabii... Sözgelimi Türkiye'de gençlerin oturup laflayacakları mekânlara ihtiyaçları var. Şöyle oturup üç-dört saat sürecek gibi. Ama "fast food" denilen şey iki dakikada hazır oluyor. Yemesi de hiç uzun sürecek cinsten bir şey değil. Wimpy'nin Restaurant Müdürü Mahmut Recevik ise "fast food"un yanlış anlaşılmasından yakınıyor.

At lunch time we go to the same hamburger joint. We talk about school while we munch our cheeseburgers. We talk about the stale hamburger bread and about the passage of time. Those never ending nights of the past are very far now, for both of us. We are so tired that we fall asleep easily and we get up early, in the first hours of the morning. [Cahide Birgül, *Gölgeler Çekildiğinde*, 2002, Türkiye İş Bankası Kültür Publications, p. 172]

Bibs given to children in McDonald's restaurants

neighborhoods that generally target high-income groups have also started to include *hamburgers*, *cheeseburgers*, or different forms of sandwiches in their menus. Conversely, in sites close to Istanbul's trendy entertainment spaces, street stands offering *köfte* [meatballs] different types of kebabs or *kokoreç* can acquire fame overnight and figure in the society pages of newspapers and magazines.

When considering *lahmacun* – at the top of the list of local foods that have recently adopted fast food characteristics – it is possible to retrace this typical duplication and re-creation of social differences in the fast food sphere. The opening of *lahmacun* restaurants one after the other in the 1980s was closely related to the rise in rural urban migration during those years (and later), from southeastern Anatolia in particular. From the second half of the 1980s on, violence in the east, the disintegration of the agrarian economy and forced migration policies were among the chief factors that forced considerable numbers of people to *migrate* with their families to large urban areas. Arriving at the cities at a time when employment in the formal economy had narrowed, the majority of newcomers started to work in the service sector or as undocumented workers. For instance, today, many of the street vendors who sell *midye dolma* [mussels cooked in their own broth then stuffed with pilaf rice] originally migrated from the Southeast, more specifically from Mardin. Kurdish women, who had never seen the sea before much less tasted midye dolma, are now the ones preparing them. Again in those years, *lahmacun* was identified with new urban populations who were looked down on because of their *arabesk* lifestyle [a culture associated with the *gecekondu* or squatter towns on the fringes of large cities]. A newspaper headline at that time complaining that "Beyoğlu has been invaded by beer joints and cheap *lahmacun* eateries" and the district was "no longer an elegant promenading area" but "a showcase for *arabesk* culture," clearly expressed the link that had developed between *lahmacun* and the culture of *arabesk*. The "nouveau riche" Easterners are the other side of the *lahmacun* debate. The query "Do *lahmacun* and whisky go together?" with its implications that a beverage symbolizing modernity and wealth and the regional food of the East do not mix, rapidly gained popularity and often turned up in newspaper and magazine

İstanbul Life
June 1988

Havada ızgara kokusu var

above: **Smell of grilled meat in the air**

below: **The road from Mardin to clams:** *The stuffed clams, which are the main livelihood of people who have emigrated from Mardin to Istanbul, are a proof of the creativity and of the determination of Turks to fight poverty.*

Hürriyet
7 February 1999

Mardin-midye hattı

Güneş **2 Hovember 1983**

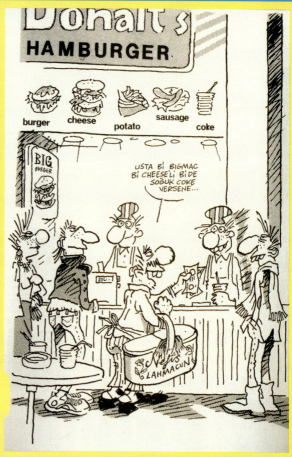

Latif Demirci, Nostalcisi Kandilli **1990**

above: **Beerhouses and lahmacun shops have spread throughout Beyoğlu:** *In the beerhouses, where arabesque music to make people cry, moan and feel sorry for themselves never lacks, it is possible to "get pissed" for 300-500 Lira.*

right: *-Chef, give us a bigmac, a cheese and a cold coke*

features. A closer look at these stories shows how the garlic, onion and spice-rich *lahmacun*, representing all that was "Eastern," backward and usually Kurdish, was being articulated as the symbol of "provincialism" in metropolitan areas.

Still, it didn't take long for *lahmacun* to turn into a *Turkish version of fast food*, with the emphasis on its inexpensive, practical and "authentic" features. *Lahmacun chains* like Hacıoğlu and Tatlıses Lahmacun appeared on the scene, embracing the marketing and production techniques of the McDonald's type international fast food chain and rapidly expanded their client base. Adopting basic principles like *standardization*, *efficiency*, *control* and *discipline*, they increased the number of their stores through *franchising*. Soon, other local and traditional foods joined the fast food caravan. New regional flavors like Izmir's *kumru* sandwich and Ayvalık's grilled sandwich revamped their identities in the big urban fast food markets, while certain popular *kokoreç*, sandwich and *köfte* joints opened new branches in various parts of the city. During this period, in which even the traditional *simit* [Turkish bagel] was revised and adapted to the standardized, automated, mass production model of fast food, those convinced that Turkish "national culinary culture" was in danger of dying out emphasized the harm this would cause to "our national identity." Actually, in its concern over the threat *fast food* poses to a country's culture, Turkey is not alone. The preservation of local culture is a theme common to a number of other countries engaged in the *fast food* controversy. A growing international movement joining India, France and other countries, who fear their "culinary culture is vanishing," has emerged to challenge McDonald's worldwide hegemony of hamburgers and the American lifestyle it symbolizes. The *sefertası* movement in Turkey or the movement in favor of slowness and "slow food" in Europe are good examples of this trend.

Still, it is impossible to ignore the *class* element inherent in these reactions. For example, "slow food" or meals featuring the entire rich array of traditional Turkish cuisine – soups, olive oil dishes and meat dishes – is taxing both time- *and* money-wise. Maybe one of the reasons fast food has become so popular in recent years is the upsurge in the number of people with neither time nor

ÜST: ... Last June we organised a street food festival in Sultanahmet...
That is, I had been to a meeting regarding fast food at the Istanbul Chamber of Commerce. There was a representative of international fast food chains there who got up and said that they don't do fast food but they do fast services. He said restaurants also serve food fast, you should fall in step with us, Turkish cuisine can also be served fast and so on. And we said "so you want us to serve fast, do you, we'll show you fast service!", and we presented in the Sultanahmet Square sucuk sandwiches, kokoreç, (sound of laughter) all those traditional foods which you can think of, which can be eaten standing up. Thanks to the Eminönü Municipality which let us have the square for two days.

Presenter: Were the foods only presented?

ÜST: They were eaten of course! People rushed to the food. Our movement integrated with the people for the first time. We were able to give people a good message. We told them that this meant that "You work and you don't have time to eat, so these increase in number." Man, there are also döner sandwiches and meatball sandwiches... You could eat those instead of condemning yourselves to the same taste everyday. It was a beautiful event...
[An excerpt from "Açık Dergi", with Ümit Sinan Topçuoğlu of *Sefertası* Movement, Açık Radio, 8 August 2001]

Sabah
5 June 1986

above: **Emperor of lahmacuns:** *İbrahim Tatlıses has opened his 11th lahmacun restaurant.*

below: **Whisky can go with lahmacun**

Aktüel
January 1994

Hızlı yemeye alışıyoruz

● İstanbul'da Mc Donald's'la başlayan hızlı yemek hizmeti veren işletmeler zinciri, dünya çapında isimlerle giderek büyüyor. Türkiye'de halen Wendy's, Pizza Hut, Kentucky Fried Chicken, Fuudruckers, Jiimmi's'ın şubeleri bulunuyor.

● Hepsi de adeta birer küçük fabrika niteliğindeki bu milyarlık fast-food işletmelerinde yüzlerce kişi çalışıyor. Bu restoranları, dışarıda eğitim görmüş yöneticiler işletiyor. Bu işletmelerin en gözde müşterileri ise çalışanlar ve gençler.

Sinan ÖZBALKAN

Hızlı yemekte, hızlı rekabet
Özellikle gençler ve vakti sınırlı olan çalışan kesimin ilgi gösterdiği fast food (hızlı yemek) restorant zincirleri, büyük şehirler başta olmak üzere giderek yayılıyor.

Hürriyet
7 December 1990

Getting used to eating fast: *The fast food chains, which started in Istanbul with McDonald's, are growing with the addition of new worldwide names.*

Straws of the Simit Sarayı, whose slogan is "Traditional Fast Food"

What's happening to us? Why is it becoming more and more difficult in restaurants to find a simple olive oil dish which doesn't even require much effort or time? For some reason, in a country like ours where fresh fruit and vegetables are found in abundance, we prefer imported tinned foods.

At the most ten years ago, we used to carefully determine when to light the brazier in the garden/balcony so as not to disturb people in the surroundings with its smoke or not to arouse their appetite with its smell. Nowadays, when I see the "free standing-up eaters" who spoon the runny substance stuffed into potatoes while walking the streets and roads, who don't mind spattering the clothes of other people they pass by, I think that that tradition which I once thought of as a little bigoted does not derive from being Muslim but from being civilised. [Tomris Uyar, *Yüzleşmeler*, 2000, Can Publications, p. 54]

money to spare. Large-scale *economic changes*, such as the increasing significance of the underground or informal economy, a workforce in transformation and the expansion of the service sector, have altered people's daily work routines; instead of restricting themselves to a single work environment, they are adopting more flexible or alternate work arrangements that don't restrict them to one place. Since this also means they are continually on the run, quick meals or snacks during breaks have become commonplace. Seen from this perspective, fast food seems to be answering a "need" created not only by a more hectic pace but by *fragmented time*. Attempts to revive the image of the *sefertası*, the lunch pail with which housewives would bring home-cooked meals to the workplace, and the growing number of restaurants featuring "home cooking" on their menu illustrate the new ways in which different social segments are trying to resist this fragmentation.

The *catering* sector, a fast-growing industry in recent years, has also significantly contributed to the prevalence of fast food. Not limited to local *catering* firms like Kurdoğlu and Sofra, the rapidly expanding sector includes global giants like *Sodexho* and the world leaders in voucher systems, *Accor Services* and *Cheque Dejeuner*. In return for a portion of their paycheck, employees receive meal vouchers which they can then use to pay for meals in restaurants. This, in turn, gives further impetus to the eating out market and popularizes the fast food concept.

It seems clear that, with the conversion to fast food, both the production and the consumption of food eaten outside the home has gradually severed all bonds with regional locations and practices. *Midye dolması* have turned Kurdish, *kumru* sandwiches have moved to Istanbul and McDonald's has "gone native." Nonetheless, the social meanings invested in these different foods and the controversies they generate carry heavy regional references. There is tension in any attempt to redefine a national identity that integrates diverse regional elements. So apparently, with fast food so widespread and the debates on identity it provokes still so heated, neither "loving it" nor "leaving it" is easy to do!

Milliyet **25 April 2004**

above: **My fellow townsman McDonald's:** *The world adventure of the fast food giant, resurrected by the general manager who died last week, had its ups and downs.*

below: **Lunch boxes vs fastfood:** *Gourmets, chefs, Turkish cuisine restaurants and nutritional experts have joined together to protest fast food, emphasising its negative effects.*

bottom: **Sour meatballs: 1 Hamburger: 0** *The McDonald's that opened across Ismet Pasha's statue closed down because of the Malatyalı Restaurant. Burger King went bankrupt too.*

Hürriyet **26 October 2000**

Milliyet **31 August 2003**

Leziz Türk dönerinin adı ve tadı, 72 milletin dilinde...

"KES BİİR!.."

Lüks lokanta menülerinde baş sıralarda yer aldığı gibi seyyar tezgâhlarda ekmek arasında da satılan döner kebap, yurt dışında da seviliyor.

En leziz türü, kömür ateşinde pişmiş yaprak döner...

Bir döner ustasının kazancı 50 ile 100 bin lira arasında değişiyor.

● Uğur CEBECİ

ARTIK tüm dünya Türk dönerini tanıyor.

Bazı ülkelerde Türk dönerine biraz da politika karıştırıp adını "Yunan döneri" "Hint döneri"ne çıkaranlara rağmen bu kebabın Türkler'den geldiğini herkes biliyor.

Cut us one portion! *Tasty Turkish döner is renowned in hundreds of countries.*

Hürriyet
29 November 1981

NAR GİBİ KIZARMIŞ: Öğle vakti İstanbul'u baştan başa saran dönerin iştah açıcı kokusu. Keskin bıçakları ve o kendilerine has ustalıklarıyla dönerciler, lokantaların vitrinlerinde ve büfelerde icrayı sanat eylemeye başlar, müşteri çekerler.

right: **Burgers replaced by simits:** *Once hamburger joints were fashionable, now it's the turn of the simit palaces which have opened at every street corner.*

below: **Either you eat or you go away**

Vatan 34
29 June 2004

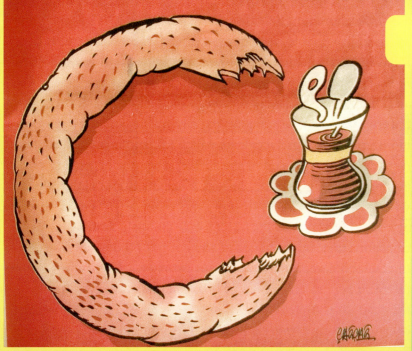

Leman
28 July 2001

Instrument of modernity: the automobile

The etymology of the word "automobile," from the Greek *auto* [self] and the French *mobile*, indicates a self-propelled vehicle. Historically, the car was considered the symbol of modernity. Contrary to bicycles or horse-drawn carriages, cars appear to move without manifest need of an exterior propelling force. This technological feature, separating them from the natural world and humanity, placed cars at the focal point of both aspirations and preoccupations concerning modernity. The automobile, it goes without saying, was a creation of the industrial age; at that time, production had become largely industrialized and human *labor* increasingly automated, making workers an *extension of machinery*. The cogs and wheels of social *mechanisms* relentlessly carrying individuals along have provided ample material for social critics and artists alike. The car as the center of the machine-human relationship has survived as a crucial theme to our day.

Yet the meaning of the automobile in people's lives extends far beyond that of a basic transportation need. Several aspects of society's perception and use of the automobile stand out: it has a *status*-determining function; it is an integral part of *family* life as the indispensable element of vacation, leisure and free time; it has implications for *gender representations*; and it symbolizes *individualization* and personal freedom. At the same time, automobiles call up some very negative sentiments: they pollute the environment, they clog up the city traffic, and they are "road monsters" that cause accidents which kill and maim thousands. Already toward the end of the 1930s, when the hegemony of the automobile hadn't yet reached such heights, Refik Halid Karay was warning his readers to stay away from cars: "The civilized age does not resort to the automobile uniquely as a means of transportation; in the hands of some it has become an instrument of ruse and deception, a perfidious machine... Naturally, I am not referring here to an ordinary Ford, Chevrolet or Citroen: the worst they can do is run over three chickens, two dogs and a man, or overturn, precipitating their occupants into blood and carnage...

A car passenger almost joins in the car's movement, simulating many of its movements. At high speeds almost all of us simulate the car. We lean right and left together with the car, we take stances against dangers together with her.
[Ahmet Hamdi Tanpınar, *Yaşadığım Gibi*, 1970/1996, Türkiye Kültür Enstitüsü/Dergâh Publications, p. 227]

The Volvo was a gift to him from the city which he watched every day with a profound sense of shortcoming and the houses on the coast of which he secretly admired, likening them to wet boxes of matches. It is the greeting of a technology which can dominate tremendous powers with a little movement of the foot, which can control vehicles of several tonnes with a turn of the steering wheel.
[Latife Tekin, *Buzdan Kılıçlar*, 1997, Metis Publications, p. 15]

Sabah
12 February 1987

above: **"We killed him to get a BMW":** Ahmet Tantur, lucky winner of the New Year National Lottery Prize was killed by Mustafa Tosun, son of his business partner and his friend Dursun Özen.

below: **No solution yet for traffic:** The new law draft gives no hope.

Milliyet
24 January 1988

January 1990

Zaman
26 January 2003

above: **The dream no one can give up: a car**

below: **Do cars contribute to the social status?**

But the danger of luxury cars goes beyond even that. They seduce you and capture your heart." (1939: 28)

Automobiles began to spread in Turkey in the 1950s. In those years cars were the symbols of *wealth* and *privilege*. Various car makes and models – in particular American cars – became the objects of an overriding *desire for modernity*. Many of the movies produced by the Yeşilçam film industry were adaptations of American feature films in which rich kids drove open-top convertibles and businessmen or fashionably dressed women were chauffeured around town in their expensive cars. Meanwhile, automobiles also entered the life of the less privileged who drove their taxis or *dolmuş* (collective taxis) for a living, making cars one of the key actors of modern urban life. At the same time, they constituted the basis for a number of social issues, such as oil shortages, soaring gasoline prices and congested city traffic.

A scene from a traffic accident as seen on a news programme [NTV, 2005]

We mentioned that when it entered *everyday usage*, the automobile set off a debate on modernity, whose most arresting examples would turn up in literature. Discussing the "love affair with cars" theme in the Turkish novel, Jale Parla explains that from the *Tanzimat* on, the automobile was always a passionate love object; the car theme – which brought to the fore the *man-machine* relationship – was a metaphor expressing the desires, fears, fragmentations, conflicts, and feelings of inadequacy or recklessness related to strivings for modernity and *westernization* (2003). According to Parla, from the early years of the Republic to the present, various writings have personified the car so that it is perceived as an *extension of the body*, yet, at the same time, it has become uncontrollably *objectified*. The car emerges as a fetish and rules over its worshippers. The paradox in the metaphoric meanings of the automobile only makes sense when considered in the broader context of Turkey's process of modernization. "In the process of modernization and industrialization, cars have come to form a central domain in Turkish everyday life. For a culture which has difficulty entering the public sphere and confronting its requirements, the car offers a space that is half public and half private." (Parla, 2003: 162)

The Black Cadillac is lit faintly from time to time with a phosphorous light, the source of which is not clear. I am going to approach it slowly, with fear and with respect, as if asking the Crusader-like guards standing next to it for permission. I'm going to force the door handles of the Cadillac, but this vehicle completely covered with clams and sea urchins will not let me pass – the squashed and greenish curtains will not budge. Then, I'm going to take my ballpoint pen out of my pocket and with its butt I'm going to slowly scrape off the pistachio green layer of moss. At midnight, when I light my matches in this frightening and magical darkness, I'm going to see in the front seat the skeletons of the gangster and his lover, kissing and embracing each other with their thin arms adorned with bracelets and their beringed fingers. It won't be just their chin bones that are interlocking, their skulls will also fuse with that immortal kiss.
[Orhan Pamuk, Kara Kitap, 1990, Can Publications, p. 23-24]

"Turkey's love affair with cars," and all its complex connotations, experienced a *boom* in the 1980s. During this period, there was a

greater commitment to the local production of cars and an increase in the number and models of imported cars. Japanese cars in particular started competing with the formerly favored European or American models. Considered a *status* symbol in the 1970s, the Mercedes that Turkish workers in Germany devoted considerable effort to bringing to Turkey became just another *foreign* car. As for the once greatly admired Chevrolet, it had long become the property of *dolmuş* drivers, or, in the best-case scenario, part of the collection of a classic car fan. The new diversity in brands also established a basis for the *personalization* of cars. Just as in the beginning of the 1900s, when the introduction of annual models to the automobile industry served to associate cars with notions of *style*, the increasingly wide variety of car brands available in our age has given a much more personal dimension to this quest for style. But in the 1980s, the rapid growth of the automotive sector, the expansion of the automobile manufacturing and assembly industry, and the upsurge in imports turned cars into *mass* products. Now, there was a car for every wallet and taste: "Wouldn't you also like one of your own?"

This Mercedes is for him like a lover, a spouse, a passion, the magical chastity, the intactness of which is ruined, which is not his anymore. It is impossible for him to be by her side again, to feel that first pure love he felt, knowing of a stranger's bite, of marks on its honey coloured body, of the bruises left by others, of the cuts and tears caused by others. To forget what has happened... To act as if nothing has happened... [Adalet Ağaoğlu, *Fikrimin İnce Gülü*, 1976/1996, Remzi Publications/Oğlak Publications, p. 227]

During those same years, Turkey made major investments in road construction. Özal, who was prime minister then, came up with the formula for defining individualization and collectivism. According to him, railroads were the first choice of communist regimes whereas, highways stood for *freedom*. As a result, modes of mass transportation like railroads and maritime lines were entirely neglected and highways and cars pushed to the fore as the crucial elements of transportation systems. In the city, the spread of the private car forced mass transportation into the background; cities were designed to give priority to the automobile. Parking lots started cropping up on every corner; to clear room for them, fires were sometimes deliberately set to older buildings. A parking lot mafia emerged, which, not content to simply administer formal parking lots, converted every open space into one. Whenever a new shopping mall or culture center opened, the first priority was a parking lot or garage. By making the car a *vital necessity*, demand naturally increased steadily.

Toy dogs that shake their heads parallel to the car's movement

Toy model of a Hummer brand jeep

SEIZE THE TIMES   INSTRUMENT OF MODERNITY: THE AUTOMOBILE   **149**

Sokak
8 October 1989

left: **Turgut Özal:** *Motorways represent independence. Left-wing extremists wish for and defend railways. With a railway system it's easier to control people. Even Hitler built highways.*

below: **Support for private cars and not for mass transportation:** *Instead of an underwater railway tunnel, three bridges are in plan for Istanbul. The underground is considered expensive, but according to experts new highways are even more expensive and the cost of these will be paid for by those using mass transportation and not by car owners.*

Nokta
December 1987

Yerlisi, yabancısı, eskisi, yenisi her markadan araba kıymete bindi

"Otomobil delisi" olduk!

★ Sürekli zamlara ve karaborsaya rağmen, araba almak isteyenler kuyrukta bekliyor. Ancak otomobile olan bu talebin "Refah işareti" olmadığı, enflasyondan korunmak amacıyla arabaya para yatırıldığı bildiriliyor

✓ Türkiye'deki otomobil pazarından pay kapmaya çalışan 21 yabancı firma, kıyasıya bir rekabete girdi. Bu amansız rekabete rağmen, araba fiyatları hâlâ çok yüksek ve dar gelirlinin otomobil sahibi olabilmesi yine hayal.

■ Şahin ve Doğan için Ocak 1991'e, Renault Station 12 için Şubat 1991'e gün verilirken, Jaguar, BMW, Mercedes ve Mazda gibi lüks otolarda da sıralar üç ay ile bir yıl arasında değişiyor.

Bugün
11 May 1990

Tempo
May 1990

OTOMOTİV SEKTÖRÜ PATLAMA HAZIRLIĞINDA

Herkese bir araba

above: **Crazy about cars:** *In spite of the continuous raises and the blackmarket, people who want a car are queuing up for their turn.*

left: **The automotive sector is soaring:** *A car for everybody*

And then, as we are an upper middle class family, it is probably expected "to do what's best", and my father is not very keen anyway; that moment finally comes. A light green Doğan, the most recent model (1983), and metallic too! Right in front of our door. We applied for it and we waited for our turn, for close to six months. We had already paid fully for it, in advance. They said "We'll call you" and they called us! But what luxury, what splendour! It's my Mercedes, my Cadillac; I can sleep in it, I can polish it, I can adjust the mirrors continuously. The first car of a family which missed the "Get your Ford, become a Lord" cyclone, in the Turkey of the early '80s. Having waited for it for years, having dreamt of it. Having always moved by taxi, with the belief that "once you have paid for it, all the cars on the street are yours", it hasn't been possible to set aside enough money for "four wheels", but "only just"…

There wasn't any taking cuts or making savings, any special bank loans or payments by installations with low interests then. Life was still simple. Everybody was nicer, and sillier. Ours was a brand new car, a car like a "girl", a Doğan. "Doğan-like Şahins" hadn't appeared yet. Ours was a genuine Doğan, the best possible for us, right in front of the door. If only someone knew how to use it, god knows how we would have cruised around with it…

[Fatih Türkmenoğlu, *Üç Kuruş Fazla Olsun Kırmızı Olsun*, 2003, Epsilon Publications, p. 26]

Today, the number of cars on the road is escalating sharply; in Istanbul, hundreds of new cars hit the streets every day. The increase in auto fairs, car advertising and magazines and, of course, car loans has further fuelled automobile demand. No one questions the desire of the majority to own a car, and the wealthy may have more than one. The consequences are there for everyone to see: endless traffic jams, more accidents, city air fouled by gasoline fumes and the cacophony of car horns adding to the general noise of the city. The complaints about traffic congestion never stop. New roads, upper level highways and highway bridges are continually being built. But as long as the number of private cars keeps increasing, it seeems nothing will prevent congestion in urban areas. In Istanbul, for instance, the bridges over the Bosphorus were constructed with car transportation in mind and, as a result, they are severely auto-clogged today.

Traffic is the one area that best illustrates the automobile's half-way position between the public and private spheres. The driver, insulated inside his or her car, tends to perceive car travel as a personal experience to be shared – at the very most – with the other occupants of the car. Automobile advertising also insistently plays up the limitless individual freedom myth. Most car ads picture the driver exhilaratingly pushing his/her car as fast as it will go on a deserted country highway; the car is the instrument enabling its owner to discover hitherto unknown facets of freedom. Naturally, the reality of bumper to bumper rush hour city traffic wastes no time in unpleasantly dispelling this illusion. Strangely enough, the traffic issue is always approached as if the number of cars and their owners' illusions of individual freedom were irrelevant. A "traffic monster" is evoked almost as if a supernatural power ruled over the cities.

Designating the car a symbol of *individual* freedom also carries with it a specific image of society. To individuals traveling in their private cars, insulated from the city's crowds, noise and filth, the city is reduced to a décor, a landscape usually set to the background music of the car's stereo radio or cassette deck. Pedestrians shoving and pushing each other along narrow sidewalks in rain or snow seem part of a different world. By providing a space essentially shielded from the exterior, the car

left: **It's more agressive now:** *The Peugeot 206 is a favourite of modification devotees.*

below: **Set your own route**

Hürriyet
12 January 2005

January 1999

HAYATA GÜCÜNÜ GÖSTER!

January 2005

NISSAN NAVARA PICK-UP
Pick-Up kategorisinin yıldızı! 144 ve 174hp'lik motor; manuel ve otomatik şanzıman seçenekleri, üstün performansı ve mükemmel arazi uyumuyla, ticari araçta maksimum konfor yaşatacak gerçek bir efsane... Bir Nissan Yetkili Satıcısı'na gelin, Pick-Up dünyasının yeni standartlarıyla tanışın.
www.nissan.com.tr

Oto Haber
23 May 2005

"Erkek gibi otomobil kullanırım"

"KURTLAR VADİSİ"NİN HIRÇIN KIZI İPEK TENOLCAY, SPOR OTOMOBİLLERİ SEVMESİNE RAĞMEN, KENDİSİNİ DAHA GÜVENDE VE RAHAT HİSSETTİĞİ İÇİN BÜYÜK OTOMOBİLLERİ TERCİH EDİYOR. BU YÜZDEN SEÇİMİ DE LAND ROVER DISCOVERY. ERKEK GİBİ OTOMOBİL KULLANDIĞINI SÖYLEYEN TENOLCAY, KADIN KULLANICILARA BAZEN ÇOK KIZIYOR.

above: **Show off your power**

left: **I drive like a man:** Although she likes sports cars, İpek Tenolcay, the cranky girl of the "Valley of Wolves", prefers big cars because she feels more secure and comfortable.

offers its occupants the experience of a "privileged" form of modernity.

At first introduced as the ultimate time-saving device and a way to adapt to changing times, the automobile soon became a means to acquire *status* as well. From this standpoint, the brand, model and color take on heavy symbolic meanings; they become the means of *differentiation* by which people set themselves apart from others. An automobile's features become the most obvious indicator of its owner's wealth, distinction and social status. The car is inextricably entwined with its owner's personality; it becomes the driver. But again there is a paradox involved here. As automobiles grow increasingly varied in model, color and accessories, a reversal of roles occurs: instead of the car being an extension of its owner, the owner now becomes an extension of the car. Thus, cars become individualized and acquire a distinctive *personality*. In this sense, the *fetish car* image Jale Parla evokes is arresting. By becoming dependent on a machine – an object – people are face to face with the danger of losing their souls. The lyrics from a hit song in the 1990s expressed this perfectly: "Onun arabası var ama ruhu yok!" [She has a car, but she has no soul.] Personified cars become increasingly "aggressive," but their "hearts belong to no one." By the time we reach the new millennium, everybody wants bigger, more *powerful* and *faster* cars…

The conversion of *jeeps*, originally restricted to military use, into fashionable city vehicles adds another dimension to the use of the car to bolster its owner's ego: owning an SUV is the surest way to "assert your domination over life." The oversized *jeeps* or SUVs charging down narrow roads and obstructing traffic, literally looking down at more modest motorists as they carve themselves a path through traffic, have become symbols of a *virile*, *militarist* power. As a result, the traditional feminine traits assigned to cars have also undergone a transformation. Right from the start, cars were not just related to status, they also had implications for *gender representations*. Since men usually drove cars, this made the car a

Two enemies
Came out of the ambush
Jaguar – Ford Cobra (A tiger – A snake)
A Rolls Royce Phantom hit the snake from behind
unpityingly
The snake died
The cars started to howl
Two sheepdogs
Big ones
Chevrolet Cadillacs
desperately dashed onto the street
To revenge the Ford Cobra
Of the snake Opel Coupe X (cropped ears) (one of the sons of Hadji Ömer)
Of the snake Opel Concorde (one of the sons of Hadji Ömer) Dashed onto the street
loudly
barking and howling
They started chasing the Rolls Royce Phantom
Of the snake's sons, overcoming incredible obstacles
Ferrari 365 GT
and
Maserati
sounds of brakes (They are always the same)
leaning to one side [Sevim Burak, Ford Mach 1, 2003, Yapı Kredi Publications, p. 13]

Stickers for cars

male area of interest while conferring a *female identity* on the car itself. Auto shows hiring seductive models to market their ware, female sexuality flaunted in car ads, and certain expressions commonly used for cars all contribute to positioning the *car as a woman*. Representations of cars in literature or the movies also follow this trend. Since the automobile is pictured as his extension, the male affirms his sexual potency by possessing the "female" car. At the same time, as weekend and vacation activities gain significance, the car also becomes part of the nuclear family framework. Although these representations stress the *family man* gender stereotype, the man still retains his *power* as head of the family. Nowadays, however, women increasingly own and drive cars, a situation that has produced endless disputes about the motoring capabilities of *female drivers*. Just as the "Easterner" migrants to big cities, who take up collective minibus driving as a profession, are looked down on as coarse "louts" [*maganda*], women car owners in this male-dominated sphere are branded as "inept female drivers" and "safety hazards." Both characterizations reflect a male-dominated culture's claims to "superiority" and privilege based on gender and ethnic origin. Interestingly, the increase in female motorists and the number of women from high income groups showing interest in "masculine" vehicles like jeeps and SUVs have affected the gender representations of automobiles and inescapably re-defined masculinity and male culture. Obviously, in a culture that belittles and harasses women drivers, "driving like a man" and preferably an aggressively large vehicle is a quality. While gender stereotypes associated with female drivers are increasingly challenged, the common myth about the "freedom" the automobile promised individuals and its time-saving benefits remains its greatest paradox. With chronic traffic congestion and limited parking space, cars now appear less a necessity in adapting to the frantic tempo of modern life and more a way to waste time and energy.

Examples of deodorant products for cars

- I'm thinking of marrying a Jaguar! said the girl.

When she saw the boy's eyes grow large, she burst out laughing.

Really weird things were passing through her mind, and naughty things too. But what she was dreaming of was very pleasant: she would get into the car whenever she wanted, and the minute she pressed the accelerator, she would go wherever she wanted to… The brakes would be in her control, there would be no moustaches or beards, no dirty looks, it would be brand new. It has no need for bread, no need for food. What inconvenience could the dear little thing ever cause? And she wouldn't end up underneath, as she did with men. She would always be on top, on its back. And she would command it to go wherever she wanted to.

She couldn't stop laughing, and she was trying to talk at the same time:

- Hehe… Hehe… Hehe, a husband with a nice sounding horn, strong brakes and a soft lap. Nice, isn't it?

The boy was laughing too.
[Peride Celâl, *Jaguar*, Can Publications, p. 31]

Zaman
14 February 1999

Hürriyet
3 December 1995

above: **Great design but no feelings**

below: **Unable to fly to the horizon:** *I have the colourful insert in front of me. It's Hürriyet's Sunday insert, dedicated to the Automobile Fair which has opened in Istanbul.*

Hürriyet
15 November 1981

Hürriyet
8 May 2000

above: **Life ceases, journeys endure:** *In Turkey there are 117 square metres of roads per square kilometre.*

right: *-Your licence and your permit... You have exceeded the speed limit, sir.*
-What? Speed? No way brother, how could it be?

Vakit
26 September 2004

The happy minority's frightening consumption: *The wild consumption of luxury goods makes the imports soar and cuts down the foreign exchange reserves of the country.*

Homes leap into the new age

"Leaping into the future" [*Çağ atlamak*] was one of the most popular expressions of the 1980s; all the period's politicians – starting with Özal – and newspaper columnists used it abundantly. "Leaping into the future" can be considered a revised articulation of the early Republican period's goal of "closing the gap with civilized countries." There has always been a tendency in Turkish society to view modernity in relation to the West, and a perception of "backwardness" has invariably resulted from such comparisons. In Turkish, the expression *çağ atlamak* [literally "skipping an age"] also carries connotations of closing a gap and "accelerated" progress. The conflictual pull between the *fear* of "being left behind" or "being late" and the *desire* to move forward has shaped dominant discourses and had a deep impact on the way modernity has been conceived and experienced. But as expressed in the 1980s, the "leaping into the future" goal incorporated certain deviations and breaks – related to the period's general socio-cultural climate – from the earlier ideal. "Closing the gap with civilized countries" had been an aspiration encompassing the population as a whole; when the intellectuals seeking to find a balance between desired "westernization" and national values imagined their ideal society, they also strived to dominate the public's imagination. In contrast, when the "leap into the future" goal was first expressed, "realistic" strategies were adopted instead of projects and ideologies aiming to transform society. During the 1980s, the emphasis was on the individual and "making it big." As new values such as sudden gain, individual initiative and advancing through consumption became the cornerstones of the ideological context, the expression "leaping into the future" also took on new meanings even while retaining earlier fears and desires with respect to modernity. In the 1980s and subsequent years, one of the areas that best displayed both the *continuity* of discourse on *modernization* and its breaks with previous articulations was the "home."

Modernization of the house and home life was one of the prevailing themes of the Republican period. In his study on

Ev kadınlarının her iş için "elektrikli bir yardımcısı" var:
Mutfaklar çağ atladı!

İthal mutfak âletleri, hem zamandan hem enerjiden tasarruf sağlıyor. Marifetli âletler, çayınızı, kahvenizi, kızarmış ekmeğinizi hazırlarken, düdüklü tencere gibi alıştığımız kolaylıkların yanında artık mutfak robotları ve soğan makineleri gibi yenilikler var

"Ortadirek seyrediyor"

Mutfaktaki yaşamı kolaylaştıran ve hızlandıran ithal mutfak araçları bir yandan albenileri ve hünerleriyle hanımların ilgisini çekerken, bir yandan da astronomik fiyatlarıyla el yakıyor. Müşterilerinin genellikle üst gelir grubundakilerden oluştuğunu belirten ithal malları mağazası yetkilileri, **"Ortadirek sadece seyretmekle yetiniyor"** dediler.

Markaları yabancı, fiyatları pahalı

CİNSİ	FİYATI
Fissler düdüklü tencere	260.000-320.000
Moulinex mutfak robotu	169.100
Kenwood Cuisine mutfak robotu	166.000-330.000
Moulinex fritöz	215.000
Seb ekmek kızartıcısı	129.000
Magic Line ekmek kızartıcısı	112.000
Seb katı meyve sıkacağı	195.000
Melita Trend çay ve kahve makinesi	190.000
Krups kahve öğütücüsü	86.750
Krups yumurta makinesi	69.500
Krups mutfak terazisi	38.500-59.900
Oster kıyma makinesi	138.000
Tefal su ısıtıcısı	138.500
Moulinex değirmenli blender	138.000
Moulinex soğan makinesi	124.500

Tercüman
24 January 1989

İthal yardımcıların marifetleri

- **DÜDÜKLÜ TENCERE:** Normalde 45-60 dakika arasında pişen bir yemeği en fazla 15 dakikada hazır hale getirebiliyor. Böylece zamandan yüzde 70, enerjiden yüzde 50 oranında tasarruf sağlıyor.
- **MUTFAK ROBOTU:** Hamur ve köfte yoğuruyor. Pasta ve kek hamuru karıştırıyor. Bütün bir eti küçük parçalara ayırıyor. İstenirse kıyma çekiyor. Patates püresi, salata, mayonez hazırlıyor. Katı meyve sıkıyor.
- **FRİTÖZ:** Etrafa koku yaymadan ve yağ sıçratmadan 3-5 dakika arasında tavuk, patates, et, sebze kızartıyor.
- **EKMEK KIZARTICISI:** En fazla 5 dilim ekmeği 1-2 dakikada kızartıyor. Kızartma işlemi bittiği zaman ekmeği otomatik olarak atıyor.
- **KATI MEYVE SIKACAĞI:** Havuç, elma vb. sebze ve meyvelerin suyunu çıkarıyor.
- **ÇAY VE KAHVE MAKİNESİ:** 3-5 dakika içerisinde 1 litre çay veya nescafeyi pişiriyor.
- **YUMURTA MAKİNESİ:** 7 yumurtayı aynı anda 1 dakikada rafadan pişiriyor. 3 dakikada ise tamamen haşlıyor.
- **MUTFAK TERAZİSİ:** En az 2 kilo, en fazla 5 kilo ağırlığındaki bir ürünü çok hassas bir şekilde tartıyor.
- **SU ISITICISI:** 3 litre suyu 2-3 dakikada kaynatabiliyor.
- **DEĞİRMENLİ BLENDER:** Hem sert meyve ve sebzeyi çok kısa sürede parçalıyor, hem de çekirdek kahveyi öğütüyor.
- **SOĞAN MAKİNESİ:** Soğana karşı alerjisi olanlar için oldukça kullanışlı olan bu âlet, soğanı isteğe bağlı olarak hem doğruyor, hem de rendeliyor.

İthalâtın serbest bırakılmasıyla mağaza vitrinlerini dolduran mutfak araçları, ev hanımlarına sınırsız olanaklar sunuyor.

Kitchens leap into the new age

Kadınca
July 1990

left: **Men say: women should leave work 2 hours early:** *Whether they are working women or not, women do house chores and take care of the children on their own*

below: *–Oh my poor long-suffering mother, she used to wash the laundry by hand and make it snow white and then she put it in this basket.*

Radikal
15 November 2005

vocational schools for girls between 1928 and 1940 and their attempts to rationalize housework, Yael Navaro Yaşın explains that the home was at the heart of those cultural spheres requiring "modernization."(2000:51) In other words, in the 1930s and 1940s, the "modernization" of mundane chores like the dishes, everyday housework and child care was considered to be an important goal of the ideal new nation. To this end, the vocational schools for girls and a number of other educational institutions made it their mission to inform and *instruct* women on the *modern techniques* for doing housework. Textbooks on home economics, columns devoted to women in popular magazines and the publications of the Ministry of Education frequently expounded the benefits of mechanized and modern housework techniques versus "primitive" and traditional methods. (Op. cit.) Since the family was the nucleus of society, the increasing *rationality* and productivity that women displayed in their housework was thought to be essential not only for family life but also for raising healthy generations and thus *advancing* as a society. At this point in the debate on family life, housework and their social consequences, the use of *kitchen appliances* also acquired significance. Until the 1970s for instance, almost every school textbook included a chapter on modern electric household appliances. In these books, the *refrigerator*, the *washing machine*, the *vacuum cleaner* and similar household appliances were presented as labor saving-devices that enhanced the productivity of routine housework, improved hygienic conditions in the home and, by saving time and money, also contributed to the welfare of society. With this new technological equipment, household tasks could be accomplished more competently and faster; families possessing these appliances – or rather the women assigned these tasks through the gendered division of labor – would thus have more time on their hands that they could dedicate to more useful activities and to developing their personalities. As households grew more modern, so would women. In short, for a long while already, the introduction of modern technology into the home has been considered one of the conditions necessary for the modernization of households and women, and, through them, of society as a whole.

As the impact and scope of the written and visual press expanded and advertising grew in the 1980s, messages praising the benefits

Bedri scorned the brazier. Cooking food in a brazier makes one's face as black as handpicked charcoal. Black or white, the brazier days were long in the past. Since she was married she always cooked with gas. But the sparks which were flung around in twilight in front of the kitchen door during childhood leave a lasting impression. Everything leaves an impression on her. According to Bedri she hadn't even managed to learn how to use a cupboard yet. "You don't know either how to wash the laundry, or how to dress to go out, or to go shopping!" Always the same talk.

- Our women work like labourers for twelve hours a day in their homes, they sweat and they barely have time to prepare a couple of dishes. Whereas European women know how to be very productive with little effort. And the circumstances are right too. The reasons are obvious.

Filiz repeated "The reasons are obvious". She clenched her teeth, shut her eyes firmly and hung on. She tried to blot out the grandiose dreams she had, she stood there motionless for a few seconds which seemed endless, thinking of nothing, hearing nothing.
[Oktay Rıfat, *Bir Kadının Penceresinden*, 1976/1992, Adam Publications, p. 13-14]

A scene from the "best börek making" contest in the "Joy of Cooking" programme [STV, 5 June 2003]

She took the younger daughter-in-law her tea. She went down to the kitchen and peeled Hanife Hanım's aubergines, picked the beans and chopped the onions. She washed once again the courtyard which was baking in the heat. She collected the laundry from the ropes, took it in in basketfuls. She prepared a coffee with little sugar for the middle daughter-in-law and a well-cooked coffee for the Mistress of the house. She prepared the table for lunch, served the ladies of the house. When the meal business was over, she took the bowl which the Mistress filled with her own hands and transferred leftovers from her plate to and pushing aside the leftovers of the old woman she ate her lunch. She washed the dishes. She cleaned the kitchen. She washed the courtyard once again.
[Ayşe Kulin, "Taş duvardır benim sevdam", *Foto Sabah Resimleri*, Ekim 1996, Sel Publications, p. 23]

Toy, automatic coffee machine

of household appliances in women's magazines also increased. *Popular media* and *advertisements* took on the *educating* role formerly held by school textbooks. During this period, *automatic washing machines, electric stoves, kitchen robots* and other small electric appliances were just starting to spread. Newspapers and magazines frequently ran ads presenting new technological devices and gadgets and reminding housewives that the washing machine was not a "laundry tub," the refrigerator not a screened cupboard, and that the stove was very different from a *mangal* [traditional Turkish barbecue]. At the same time, these ads promoted the image of the perfectly content housewife who had purchased and was using this new equipment. Another theme often resorted to was the emphasis on the *time-saving* benefits the technological changes in household appliances would provide both housewives and working women: in a washing machine ad from those years, Leyla convinces her husband to buy on installment the fully automatic washing machine she saw and admired in her neighbor's apartment and now her Saturdays are free for other activities. The female stereotype constructed and articulated here is that of the "modern" working woman who appreciates the value of time and realizes she needs to take time for herself, but who will never neglect her housework duties in the process. She thus becomes a role model to numerous other women struggling to balance office and housework. And to lighten this *double burden* weighing on women's shoulders, technology is there.

Much as in Turkey, the time-saving benefits of electric household appliances had also given rise to controversy in the West when these devices first appeared on the market. The notion that new household technologies would save women time and energy giving them more spare time for themselves and other activities was the most frequently reiterated theme in texts or advertisements marketing new household equipment. Another way of looking at this small-scale domestic revolution, however, is the argument that electric appliances didn't actually reduce the amount of household tasks, they simply redefined it. Ruth Schwartz Cowan writes that the "mechanization" of the American household in those early years actually established *higher standards* of cleanliness and general hygiene in the home. In America during the first half of the 20th century, most women's magazines and advertising campaigns

March 1985

How did Leyla manage to get her Saturdays back?

EV HANIMLARI HAYATLARINDAN MEMNUN

Hürriyet
27 April 1980

AYSEL ÇETİN
Yıllardır merdaneli çamaşır makinesi kullanıyorum. Makinemden son derece memnunum. Ancak tam otomatik çamaşır makinelerinin rahatlığını aradığım za-

EMEL İMER
Çamaşır makinem tam otomatik ve son derece memnunum. Yorulmadan yığınla çamaşırı kısa sürede yıkayabiliyorum. Toz deterjan kullanıyorum. Bulaşıkta sıvı deterjan kullanıyorum

MUKADDES DİKMEN
Otomatik çamaşır makinesi kullanıyorum. Çamaşırda büyük rahatlık sağlıyor. Çamaşırlarımı çamaşır tozuyla yıkıyorum. Krem deterjanı bulaşıkta kullanıyorum

SABİHA TOKATLIOĞLU
Çamaşır makinem kollu. Memnun olduğumu söyleyemeyeceğim. Tam otomatik çamaşır makinem olsun isterdim. Çünkü tam otomatikler çamaşırı kendisi yıkıyor.

Hürriyet
25 May 1985

"Buzdolabı ve çamaşır makinesini kullanmayı öğrenin"

Buzdolabına "Teldolap" gibi davranmayın

BUZDOLABINIZIN ısı yayan kafesi duvardan en az 5 cm. uzakta olmalıdır.

● Buzdolabının içindeki raflara örtü, naylon sermeyin, çünkü içindeki hava akımının dolaşmasını önler, dolabın verimini düşürürsünüz.

● Buzdolabının buzluğunda biriken **"buzu"** 1 santim kalınlığa ulaşınca, kesici aletlerle kazmadan **"eritme"** düğmesine basıp, kapısını açık bırakın. Temiz hava alırken, dolabı fişe takmayın.

Çamaşır makinesi "leğen" değildir

KULLANMA kılavuzunda belirtilenden fazla çamaşırı makineye koymayın. Yorulur ve verimi düşer.

● Çok kirli çamaşırlarınızı en son yıkayın.

● Çamaşırı atmadan önce, örneğin gömlekse cebine bakın, metal parçaları makinenin başına büyük dert açar.

● Çamaşır makinesini ıslak bırakmayın. Yıkama bitince kazanı yumuşak bir bezle kurulayın.

Fırın başka, "mangal" başkadır

FIRINI kuru ve toz temizleyicisiyle değil, emayeli kısımları sabunlu su ile silip kurulayın.

● Fırının tepsisi dışında tepsi kullanmayın ve fırını boşken çalıştırmayın.

● Isıtıcılarınızı (Termosifon) tamamen dolu iken çalıştırın. Sıcak su musluğundan su geliyorsa ısıtıcı dolu demektir.

● Elektrikle oyun olmayacağı için, sıcak su ısıtıcılarının elektrik bağlantısını mutlaka topraklı prizle yaptırın. Isıtıcıyı temizlerken, fişi prizden çıkarın.

October 2005

top left: **Housewives are content with their lives**

bottom left: **Learn to use the refridgerator and the washing machine:** *Don't use the refridgerator like a common cupboard. The washing machine is not a washing bowl. The oven is more than a brazier.*

above: **From the world of wonders of Arçelik**

Günün büyük bölümü temizlik yapmakla geçiyor

- Ev kadınları mutfak faaliyetlerine günde 140.1 dakika (2 saati aşkın) harcıyor.
- Ev kadının ev temizliği için harcadığı zaman 217.8 dakika (3.6 saati aşıyor).
- Çamaşır yıkama için 117.6 dakika (yaklaşık 2 saat), çocuk bakımı için 85.8 dakika (yaklaşık 1.5 saat) harcanıyor.
- Diğer aile bireylerin bakımına 30 dakika ayrılıyor.
- Alışveriş, bir ev kadınının ortalama 45 dakikasını alıyor.
- Ev kadının, işlerden sonra kalan serbest zamanı; 402 dakika (7 saate ulaşıyor)
- Çalışan kadınların ev işlerine harcadıkları toplam süre ise 5 saat 53 dakika.

Ev kadını ağır işçi gibi çalışıyor

Ankara'da yaşayan 142 evli kadın üzerinde yapılan araştırma kadınların ev işlerine bir günde ortalama 8 saat 32 dakika zaman harcadıklarını ortaya koydu

Hürriyet
1 May 2000

Housewives work like labourers: *A research carried out on 142 married women in Ankara has shown that women spend an average of 8 hours 32 minutes a day doing house chores.*

suggested that women would have more time to spend with their families by purchasing the new devices, and be better mothers and wives. According to Cowan, the notion that household technology has made women's lives easier and liberated them is a *myth*, and time studies on this topic corroborate her thesis. While women may have "saved time" through mechanization of the household labor, the total amount of time they spend on housework has remained constant because "new jobs" have been created. Now that housewives have refrigerators, ovens and electric or gas stoves at their disposal, they can more easily prepare and store a number of different foods at once. In turn, this has led to the expectation that the "skilled" housewife should produce a greater variety of dishes. Similarly, gradually more complex household equipment may require reading up on *complementary technologies* to ensure the right choice of purchase. All of which just means more time spent on (different) domestic matters. To competently use a washing machine implies acquiring knowledge about the various detergents, fabric softeners and lime and calcium buildup removers and how to use them correctly. Consequently, instead of liberating women from housework, new technologies have simply made the work they do *less visible*. As electronic household appliances grow increasingly sophisticated, they take over most tasks around the home and become the new "household servants:" the laundry and dishes go through their cycles automatically at the twist of a dial; meals and cookies are cooked by simply pressing a multifunction button; and the vacuum cleaner sucks up all the dirt around the house. To top it all, ovens now clean up after themselves and houses have become "intelligent." Smart home installations using networked technology "can run your household for you." Even though recent research indicates that the housewife remains "the only unspecialized worker left" in society today, the widely held view in the new millennium seems to be that home technology is making women's lives easier.

From a different perspective, it is interesting that the persuasive advertising used to promote the household devices purported as the means to *modernize* women and their homes should so frequently be associated with the image of a man. Such advertising protagonists as Mr. Muscle, the powerful male figure who does all your hard work for you ("loves the jobs you hate!"); "Çelik", the

If I was married to a prison guard… I wouldn't get up early especially on winter mornings, I would not lit the stove with a few bright red chips of wood, as soon as I heard the water bubbling in the teapot I would not slowly lift the quilt and put my cheek against his, in the evenings I would not turn inside out the socks which he throws here and there, I would not wash his vest which had turned yellow from being worn for ten days, his panties, his shirt and his trousers, I would not arrange them in order on a chair, I would lie under the quilt my mother sent from the village, smelling the warm air underneath it, moving my ass from right to left from left to right, I would open slightly one eye and watch my husband as if he was a stranger. [Hatice Meryem, *Sinek Kadar Kocam Olsun, Başımda Bulunsun*, 2002, İletişim Publications, p. 26]

Automatic sink plunger

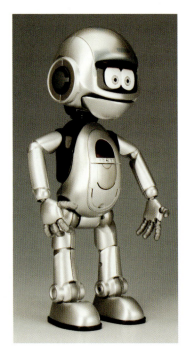

A model of the character Robot Çelik, used in the Arçelik advertising and promotion campaigns in the 2000s

- *I'm feeling depressed Leman. I was wondering whether we should rent out this house and move to a ground floor. I'm not so strong anymore. There is dust everywhere. The kitchen is downstairs. I'm sick and tired of going up and down. My back can't...*

- *Mom, my head is bursting...*

- *Wouldn't I want to work in a tiled kitchen? A well-built one... With its cupboards and everything... And we would get a refridgerator. As long as it's in installments...* [İnci Aral, "Ağda Zamanı", *Ağda Zamanı*, 1999, Can Publications, p. 28]

character popularized by the ad campaign for Arçelik, Turkey's leader in the white goods market; and even the toy bear and substitute male figure Yumoş, try to add a playful dimension to the drudgery and *routine* of housework while stressing the "masculinity" of technology.

An increasing concern with style and aesthetic value has started to determine both the designers of large domestic electric appliances and consumer choices. As some put it, "white goods are no longer 'white'." The bathrooms and kitchens of upper middle class homes have become spaces designed to express a lifestyle; the trend away from simple utility to aesthetics now advances *built-in* appliances – imported or manufactured locally – that look good, take up less room and make less noise. The reliance on electric household appliances is now shared by the entire population. But socio-economic factors largely decide which new technologies enter people's homes to simplify everyday household tasks and how they spend the extra leisure time this has given them. In a survey of cleaning women, Özyeğin notes that, though these women live in the slum neighborhoods [*gecekondu*] of Istanbul, they all have washing machines and refrigerators in their homes and own several small electric kitchen appliances, like toasters and hand mixers. However, "Most families own outdated washing machine models they either bought from their employers or "inherited" and which require that they manually put the clothes through the wringer." (Özyeğin, 2005:197) In the 1960s and 1970s, when households were just starting to be mechanized, owning a refrigerator or a washing machine was a *status symbol* in itself; today, the brand and model of the equipment establish *class* differences. Homes look to the future and smart electronic devices do all the household chores, but if that is really the case, why do so many women still complain they have no free time for themselves?

ZAMANLA YARIŞ!

İş hayatı, ev işleri ve çocuklar gibi pekçok sorumluluğun üstesinden aynı ada gelemiyorsanız, biraz bencil olun ve başkalarının zamanından çalın...

Practica
March 1994

left: **Racing against time:** *If you aren't able to cope simultaneously with numerous responsibilities such as a working life, house chores and children, be a little selfish and steal time from others.*

below: **Don't manage your home, let your home manage you:** *Living in intelligent houses.*

YAŞAM AKILLI EVLERE TAŞINIYOR

Filmlerde gördüğümüz, Avrupa ve Amerika'da yaygınlaşan ve birkaç yıl önce ülkemizde de uygulanmaya başlanan "akıllı ev"ler, oturanları şehir hayatının stresinden uzaklaştırıyor

Teknolojik evlerin yanında otel gibi hizmet veren residence'lar, zen felsefesine göre yapılan evler ve "konsept evler" gündemde.

Siz evinizi yönetmeyin bırakın o sizi yönetsin

Vatan
19 September 2004

2005

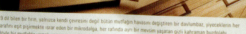

Have you ever thought why some people prefer cooking to eating?

Beyaz eşya beyaz olmaktan çıkıyor

Makio Hasuike (66), Ariston'un 36 yıllık tasarımcısı. 1963 yılında "Makio Hasuike & Co" adıyla kurduğu endüstri dizayn firmasından sonra İtalya'da yaşamaya başlayan tasarımcı, şu ana kadar ambalaj, perakende tasarım, fuar tasarım ve mimarlık alanlarında birçok tasarıma imzasını atmış. Bil's'in koleksiyonlarından hatırlayacağınız My Way markalı çantaların tasarımcısı Hasuike'den endüstri tasarımıyla ilgili tüyolar aldık. Öğrendik ki artık beyaz eşyalar beyaz olmaktan çıkıyor. Bundan böyle mutfaklarımızda mümkün olduğu kadar renkli tasarımlar olacak.

Fotoğraflar: Levent ARSLAN
Tuğçe ERDEMLİ

Makio Hasuike, ülkesi Japonya'da eğitimini tamamladıktan sonra İtalya'nın ilk endüstriyel tasarım firmalarından birini kuran, hayatının 41 yılını tasarıma vermiş bir sanatçı.

TÜRKLER ALIŞKANLIKLARINDAN VAZGEÇEMİYOR

Tüketici alışkanlıkları bizim ürün tasarlamamızdaki temel noktalardan biri. Alışkanlıklar zamanla farklılaşıyor, takip etmek zorundayız. Mesela, yurtdışında sebze yeme alışkanlığı çok fazla yoktur ama Türkiye'de çok fazla. Bu nedenle Türkiye için geniş sebzelikler tasarlanmaya başlandı. Avrupa'da büyük buzdolapları insanlara gereksiz geliyor ama Türkiye'de tam tersi. Dondurulmuş gıda tüketimi yaygınlaşmadığı için buzlukları geniş buzdolaplarına talep yok. Aynı durum çamaşır makinelerinde de geçerli. Standart beş kiloyken altı kilo oldu. Fakat Türkiye'de makinenin ne kadar fonksiyonu olursa olsun tek bir program kullanılır. Narin çamaşırları yıkayabilen çamaşır makinesi programları var. Her ne kadar tüketici bu programı kullanmak için bu makineyi almış olsa bile makineye hiç güvenmiyor. Çamaşırı elde yıkamaya devam ediyor. Bazı tüketiciler tüm fonksiyonları kullanıyor ama yüzde oranına bakarsak bu çok az.

Hürriyet
24 April 2004

Beyaz eşyalar artık duygusal ihtiyaçlara göre şekillendiriliyor

Vatan
3 October 2004

above: **White durable goods are not white anymore**

right: **White durable goods designed according to emotional needs:** The Electrolux Design Laboratuary in Italy, that researches white durable goods for the future, has begun a new project to create home appliances for the future.

Got any spare time?

Rubicube, a once popular pastime

monday: bruised streets, tuesday: a revolution which drowns in liquor, wednesday: the fingerprints of a former lover found in the house, thursday: standing suddenly in front of the mirror, friday: the evening of heterosexuals under compulsion, combined with lutes, clarinet and kettledrums, saturday: the proud repetition of resistance, of boycott, of opposition, sunday: the history of poverty assembling in front of betting shops.
[Küçük İskender, *The Kırmızı Başlıklı İstasyon Şefi*, 1996, Parantez Publications, p. 54]

We keep hearing how valuable time is: *time is money*. In our day, almost everyone complains they have no free time; the frantic tempo of city life, longer and longer working hours, never-ending housework, the rush to get somewhere on time, all make *free time* even more precious. Just comparing present conceptions of time with those of the past reveals the extent of the change. First of all, it is well established that life in a modern capitalist society has turned time into an increasingly *abstract* notion. Instead of different perceptions of time related to personal experience and defined by it, time has become a collectively owned construct measured by watches and calendars. Whereas in a farmer's life sunrise, sunset and the turn of the seasons all have their time-defining purpose, today's urban population resorts to general and abstract criteria to evaluate time. A number of factors led to this abstraction of time: the segregation of the home from the workplace brought about by industrialization; the imposition of synchronic forms of time on labor by the capitalist work discipline; and initiatives to create a national economy, social unity and conformity with the international order.

In the 19th century, when a capitalist conception of economy had become widespread and institutionalized, *long working hours* were what factory workers opposed most passionately. Their refusal to submit to the tyranny of time and an enforced work discipline erupted into strikes and disputes over the impossibly long and arbitrary working hours. After a long struggle, European workers won their legal right to an eight-hour work day. In the process, the distinction between workdays and weekends and holidays was also established, the latter being considered a time for workers to replete their energy reserves. Stuart Ewen (1976) explains that when the concept of the *weekend* was introduced at the beginning of the 20th century in America in order to get workers to accept new measures of standard time, advertisements began to market new consumer goods alongside leisure activities suggested for the weekend. Similarly, in its Republican period Turkey accepted the

Haber: BİR GÜNÜN GERİYE SAYIMI

Hiç gün nasıl geçip gitti" diye endişelendiğiniz oldu mu? Normal bir kadının günde altmış altı dakikası ev temizliğiyle geçiyor. Bu süreye çamaşır yıkama ve halı süpürme, çocukların oyuncaklarını toplama, eşinin çoraplarını, çamaşırlarını toplayıp çamaşır sepetine doldurma gibi ekstra işler de dahil. Diğer istatistiki bilgiler şöyle:
- 7 saat 25 dakikayı uyuyarak ve 7 buçuk saati de çalışarak geçiriyoruz.
- 49 dakikayı kendimize çekidüzen vermekle, giyinmekle vs. geçiriyoruz.
- Yemek pişirmek 64 dakikamızı alıyor.
- Çocuklarımızla bire bir geçirdiğimiz zaman ancak 25 dakikayı buluyor.

Options
March 1997

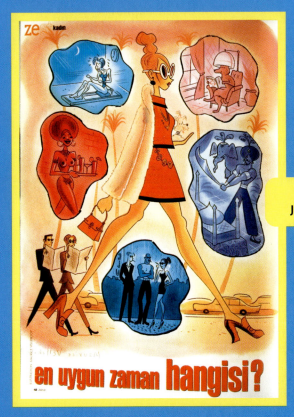

Zest
January 1999

above: **Countdown of a day:** *Have you ever worried about how the day has passed by? An ordinary woman spends sixty six minutes a day cleaning house... Seven hours and twenty five minutes sleeping...*

left: **When is the best time?**

established time standards of the western system; the state declared the Gregorian calendar the official *national* calendar and time measurement and calendars were readjusted accordingly. Sunday became the day off, replacing Friday, the day of rest and worship according to Islam. Nonetheless, the conflict between the azan, which calls for prayer following the course of the sun, and national time, which regulates the workplace, school and many other daily activities, has endured to this day.

It did not take long for an entire culture, generated by radio, TV and advertising, to develop around Sunday, the official day of rest. Soon after, when Saturday joined Sunday, the weekend established itself as a unit of free time. People worked through the week out of *necessity* and the weekend became the *special free* time dedicated to themselves and their family. What they did with this slice of time, however, remained largely shaped by the *images* proposed in movies, advertisements, magazines and books. Enjoying the fresh air, spending time with your family, going on a picnic or to the movies and seeing friends were represented as activities to *look forward to* and value. Reality was somewhat different though. Families usually spent their Sundays *at home*, the men watching sports on television, the women doing little odd jobs around the house and the children busy with their homework. Sunday was a *dull*, uninspiring day, devoted mainly to preparing for the week ahead. This image will appear familiar to most and in fact appears in literature as the *Sunday blues* theme. In her study, *Pazaröğledensonralar* [Sundayafternoons], Nurdan Gürbilek examines the relationship between the meaning invested in Sundays and desire, which, though sourced in the home, is impossible to satisfy: "The desire invested in Sunday all through the week and drawn out over a late morning breakfast still craves gratification as the table is cleared, and we finally realize that it will, in fact, never be satisfied. What happens to this desire then?" (1999: 70)

The unquenchable desire concentrated on Sundays, or, more generally speaking, on the entire weekend, is correlated to the broader concept of "free time," which itself connects directly to working life. The notion that free time is *granted* to people is just the flip side of the argument that work *steals* time away from

Sundays... Nowadays... Passing through the streets... if I see fathers in their pyjamas, if I see smoking chimneys in rainy and grey days... if the windows of houses are misted over... if I see laundry hanging inside rooms... if the clouds are close to wet tiles, if it's drizzling, if a football match is broadcast live on the radio, if the voice of people having arguments can be heard from the street, to leave, to leave....that's what I always want. [Tezer Özlü, Çocukluğun Soğuk Geceleri, 1980/2003, Yapı Kredi Publications, p. 16]

Grassman: a popular pastime and accessory of the '90s. Grass grows from its head when watered.

Piyale Madra,
Ademler ve Havvalar 4
2005

left: **–This week I'm terribly busy again. On Monday and Friday, exhausted and all, I'll go to the gym.**
–On Tuesday I have an appointment at the hairdresser. Manicure, pedicure, etc…
–On Wednesday I've got a salsa class.

below: **Put to good use your free time:** We are making a work space at home and a cupboard with colourful drawers.

Ev
March 1982

Boş Zamanları Değerlendirme Eğitimi

FATMA KARABIYIK

Boş zamanlarını nasıl değerlendirdikleri konusunda insanlara sorular yönelttiğimizde aldığımız cevaplar aşağı yukarı aynıdır. Boş zamanları değerlendirme faaliyetleri olarak televizyon seyretmek, müzik dinlemek, sinemaya gitmek, kitap okumak vs. zikredilir. Zamanı değerlendirme genellikle bir birinin aynısı gözükmekle birlikte, kişinin yetiştiriliş tarzındaki eğitim ve zevk anlayışı bakımından seçilen türün kalitesi farklılıklar gösterir. Kitap okumanın dışında, televizyon seyretmek sinema ve tiyatroya gitmek, müzik dinlemek gibi boş zamanları değerlendirme unsurları, kişi kendinden bir şey katmadığı için "pasif vakit geçirme" usulleri olarak nitelendiriliyor.

Başkalarından vakit geçirme usulleri beklemeğe alışan bir halk bunun hemen arkasından başkalarından emir beklemeğe de başlamaktadır.

Kadın ve Aile
May 1987

left: **Training to manage free time:** *People who get used to hear from others about ways to occupy themselves, can also quickly get used to expect orders from others.*

below: **What are you doing this weekend?** *You can provide support so that a magazine survives, you can look through the pages of another, newer, magazine, or you can run to Parkorman and listen to a beautiful concert.*

Radikal
13 July 2005

Bu hafta sonu ne yapacaksınız?

Bir derginin hayatta kalması için destek verebilir, yeni çıkan bir başka derginin sayfalarını karıştırabilir ya da Parkorman'a koşup güzel bir konser izleyebilirsiniz

them. This is actually rather different from the "right to laziness" formulated by philosophical anarchism, which rejects the work ethic and discipline as a form of enslavement and proposes that life be founded on other principles. In one of her writings, Perihan Mağden implies that housewives also have a right to laziness: "The house is a mistress that never stops complaining. She's never happy however much you struggle. She's always hungry and never satisfied." (1997: 225) The real issue here is redefining work and our relationship with it. Funny enough, suggestions about what to do with our *free time* sometimes sound like more work.

After the 1980s, an emerging discourse on the importance of using free time wisely became pervasive. A number of initiatives specifically targeting housewives tried to teach them to use their free time *wisely*. As feminists have repeatedly pointed out, in our society, though housework is never really considered work, in fact it is a form of "invisible labor." Closely linked to this idea is the widespread belief that housewives *waste* their time and do nothing constructive. Consequently, to fill the emptiness in their lives and the psychological problems that go with it, they should devote themselves to *useful occupations*. Put differently, they should *fill* their free time with *useful crafts* or *hobbies*, such as learning macramé or flower arranging, decorative wood painting, fabric painting and so forth... Craft and hobby centers guided women in these *wise* endeavors and the press freely dispensed "useful" knowledge on these topics. In a different vein, charities and fundraiser associations and the *kermesse*, exhibitions and various other events they organized also served to fill women's spare time, with the added benefits of providing an occasion for a different kind of social interaction and redefining *social roles*. This concurrently created a platform for differentiation among women; those from higher-income groups with time to spare for such activities, took on the function of *assisting* and *instructing* the less-privileged, "ignorant" and "uneducated" women. This gave the former a sense of superiority and at the same time bestowed on them the stature of edifying models for the rest of society.

Likewise, *children* were also *taught* to make the most of their spare time; on weekends, and especially during the long summer vacations, they were encouraged to spend their time reading,

Two hours later it was as if somebody else had come out of the cinema onto the street, amidst the crowd. He was thinking: "A short-lived creature lives in our era, that past centuries knew nothing about. It's the man who comes out of the cinema. The film he has watched has affected him. He is not a man who thinks only of his own good. He is in peace with others. It is hoped that he will do great things. But five or ten minutes later he dies. The street is full of people not coming out of the cinema; with their sullen faces, their indifference, and their insidious walk they surround him and make him dissolve." He looked at his watch. It was twenty five past four. "I could go home and read." He walked to the bus stop. "I know how to save them. Big cinema halls must be built. One day everybody living on the earth must be crammed into these. Let them see good films. Let them go out onto the street all together..." He laughed at his own thoughts. The people waiting at the bus stop turned to look at him. A woman frowned. Everybody knew that one must not laugh out loudly to himself in the middle of the street. "God, what people! So what if I laughed?" He walked away. He wasn't going home. They have killed "the man who came out of the cinema". The part of him that is left alive is troubled, angry. Is it necessary to behave always in a measured and prudent manner? Says who? While others think that he is going home, he will go to a tavern, to drink. He crossed the street where there was no crossing. The cars flowing by stopped hesitantly. A driver swore at him. He didn't hear it. [Yusuf Atılgan, *Aylak Adam*, 1959/2005, Yapı Kredi Publications, p. 18]

right: –*Cemal, do you remember, on the May 1st of '77? If we hadn't left that corner shop at the right moment, would we be able to picnic here!? Those were the days...*

below: **A sunday in the country**

Yeni Gündem
3 May 1987

Life+
July 2000

Kırda bir pazar

Heidi'yi hatırlar mısınız? Alpler'de dedesiyle yaşayan, hiperaktif, pembe yanaklı çizgi film kahramanını. Eski günleri yad etmeye ne dersiniz? Heidi'nin köyü size sadece yarım saat uzaklıkta! Polonezköy'deki Saklıköy Country Club, İstanbullular'a gerçek bir kır hayatı sunuyor.

improving their test skills, or learning a new sport at summer camp. Organizing such activities for their children was, of course, another *responsibility* their mothers were expected to fulfill. As for the men, having worked hard all week, they were *entitled* to do as they pleased on weekends: sitting in a café, doing crosswords, watching sports on TV, fiddling around in the yard (if there was one), or simply lazing around the house was considered acceptable in their case. Meanwhile, retirement brought with it a whole different set of problems. It was generally accepted that when people stopped working and retired, they also grew apart from society and their lives became empty and without purpose. The empty time facing *retirees* was just more proof of the essentially life-defining function of work.

From the 1980s on, free time stops being a family issue and simply becomes an individual's property to organize according to his or her own preferences or means. Leisure industries developed rapidly, offering people enhanced opportunities for enjoying their spare time. In big cities, certain new themes associated with weekends have appeared. Sunday breakfast is one of them; people now take pleasure in a prolonged Sunday breakfast at one of the city's many *cafes. Brunch* is all the rage, and cafes, restaurants and hotels compete fiercely to draw customers. Meeting friends, closing a deal, or simply leafing through one of the now requisite *Sunday supplements* over *brunch* has become a widespread weekend activity. A varied range of cultural events, including movies, theaters, performances, exhibitions, concerts, festivals and fairs, vie for our leisure time with special programs and shows on weekends. When sports activities like jogging, swimming, horseback riding and golf or simply shopping are also considered, it seems inevitable now that weekends must be planned for ahead of time. Today, the media and the internet categorize weekend activities and offer long lists of recreational choices. These lists are not restricted to city limits and include short trips and weekend "getaways" as well. The "how to spend your weekend" issue thus acquires major significance, especially

BEKO presents "Axis of the City". BEKO is a world brand:

Hello everybody, this is the "Axis of the City." The first event of the day is Spanish DJ Paco de la Cruz's performance at Roxy. The captivating music of Paco de la Cruz, who once played with David Bowie, is a combination of funk, disco and deep house. The performance will start at 23.00 at Roxy. ... The video programme "Desire and Boredom" first screened within the frame of the 25th International Rotterdam Festival and curated by Jan Schuijren can be seen till 20.00 at the Platform Garanti Contemporary Art Centre. "The Censorer," an unusual play which tells the story of an unhappy man and his life in the dark office on a basement floor of the Films Censorship Board, is staged this evening from 20.30 onwards at Dot in Beyoğlu. Those wishing to spend an evening at home, can watch the film the box-office film "Jungle Fever" on CNBC-E...

["Axis of the City" programme, covering the day's arts, culture and music events, Radio Eksen, March 2006]

The FRP handbook and examples of various puzzle books popular in the 2000s

"If you have read the inserts can I have them Nermin?" Selim, my son, the Sunday ritual of the little bourgeoisie is divided into three parts, the "Sunday Papers" - divided into three, the daily news, the articles and the puzzles – the "Grand Breakfast" and the problem of "Who shall we go to this afternoon?" This class law is carried out every Sunday, with great care. If you are bored, as you are today, you take a look at the inserts and you hold them out to your wife saying "You do the puzzle this time" with a great show of renunciation. Nermin's eyes were full of happiness and she said "Really?", reaching out.

I'm troubled Nermin. If I had come to you with smaller worries, I wouldn't find this so difficult now. My dear, you know how some nights the men gather together in a corner of the sitting room and talk about subjects for men only which the women appear not to care about? Let this be one of those times. But it is not. He got up, sat next to his wife on the settee. He put his arm around her and his head lightly on her shoulder. Nermin smiled without changing her position and immediately asked: "Tell me an animal with a seven letter name that ends with an "n"." He said "chicken", trying to suppress the worry inside him. [Oğuz Atay, *Tutunamayanlar*, 1972/2000, İletişim Publications, p. 87]

for high-middle income groups. Wasting away the weekend at home without a specific program almost creates a *feeling of guilt*.

Does this careful *organization* of our free time into well-determined leisure activities do away with the earlier mentioned "Sunday blues?" Quite the contrary, we may even assume that it actually magnifies the desires invested in the weekend. It is now imperative to do even more, go more places, have more fun... The fact that most of our weekend recreational activities take place outside the home simply fast-forwards everything, leaving us less time to get "blue" in. The profusion of choices creates the *illusion* that *consuming* can satisfy these desires. We no longer have time on weekends to focus on feelings of emptiness. The increasingly frantic pace of our free time seems to have more in common with work. A weekend spent *chasing* after special leisure programs and activities is more conducive to severe *exhaustion* than the blues!

While the upper and middle classes in big cities attempt to satisfy their desires through the consumption of *organized weekend activities*, the remaining less affluent majority also find themselves motivated by similar aspirations. Getting out on weekends is such a common trend that certain parts of the city are now highly overcrowded on those days. This is the case for the waterfront public park and promenade areas in Istanbul during the summer, and for districts like Taksim, Kadıköy and Bakırköy the whole year around. Weekend leisure time and how one uses it has become a crucial *cultural identity* matter. Some picnic on the side of the road, others head for the newest "in" café in own. The *accelerated* pace of time and minute planning of weekends has turned them into replicas of working days: free time has becomes drudgery. Spending your time well becomes an obligation. "Take a Sunday drive up the Bosphorus or else try the seafood at..." We're in fact being told what to do... And always, there remains the same lingering anxiety: wasted time, no time... Whose time is free time anyway?

Akşam
16 July 2005

left: **Traditional picnic battles at Zeytinburnu**

below: **If not to the Bosphorus, then to teras:** *Now that there are few days of good weather left, you can put such limited time to best use in outdoor venues.*

bottom: **People and... people**

Radikal
13 August 2005

Star
19 July 2005

This section is organized around four headings corresponding to some of the essential activities in people's lives: language, sex, weddings and popular entertainment. In any society, language makes communication possible; sex is its life force; weddings count among its most important rituals; and entertainment, by bringing individuals together and appealing to their sense of fun, generates a form of creative energy. Because of their centrality in the lives of individuals, these areas have always been the chief targets of morality and social norms. At the core of the present chapter lies the premise that the unifying characteristics these activities once shared are noticeably fewer. In the two and a half decade span from the 1980s to 2005, each of these areas has witnessed an unprecedented and "boundary-breaking" exorbitance. On the one hand, these areas have become platforms for the emergence of new market-based power strategies and for defenders of moral values to denounce these "excesses." On the other, they have become stages for fierce struggles and quests for identity.

i was like, whoa, you know?

Where is the Turkish language headed?

Too straingerz
In ze darqness of ze nite
Handz klaspd togeder
In ze darq-ness of ze nite
Heartz beet togeder
Too straingers
Haf met zus
Ze starz witnessd zis luv
Ze moonlite said
Luv at nite iz somezing else
And to trick ze straingerz
Ze moon dizappeard
And to trick ze straingerz
Ze moon dizappeard
Lost among ze cloudz
For luverz, hand in hand, look for darq-ness
Why do zey always chooz ze nite?
The straingerz, hand in hand, make luv

Too straingerz
Eyez lokd togeder
Too straingerz
Heartz beet togeder

Too straingerz
Hidden among ze shadowz
The straingerz make luv hand in hand, in ze dark

Luv is blind
The luverz hide in ze darq-ness
Zey mite be seen
Becos at nite
Ze sinz are hidden [Sevim Burak, *Palyaço Ruşen*, 1993, Nisan Publications, p. 117- 118]

From the first years of the Republic onwards, the matter of *correct Turkish* has always been on the agenda. Whether or not to use Ottoman Turkish words – and, if not, deciding what their new equivalents should be – and whether to match "western" concepts and terms with their Turkish substitutes, when translating from foreign languages, are issues that have always preoccupied both state institutions and the wider intellectual coterie. Although shifts in emphasis may have occurred, these continue to be current issues. Historically, the function of the Turkish Language Association (Türk Dil Kurumu) was to re-engineer Turkish into a written language and establish its position as a spoken language by adopting the Latin alphabet. This rapid transformation met with several major difficulties. Ottoman Turkish was the main language of science, philosophy and literature in Ottoman society. Thus, the first problem was to find new equivalents to Ottoman words. The new language formed partly with words already in colloquial usage and through the creation of new terms appeared rather *alien* even to those involved in the process. The second difficulty was more technical: how to write these new words using the Latin alphabet. In addition, it has always been the case that while certain new terms catch on, others are immediately rejected, and controversies over *correct spellings* have lasted to our day.

Another issue concerns the infiltration of borrowed *foreign words* in the language. The Republican period brought with it the hegemony of the partisans of a "purified" Turkish, free of either Ottoman or foreign terms and presented as the people's "genuine" language. The Sun Language (*Güneş-Dil*) theory – which attempted to find in language the essential roots of the nation and, by proving that all languages were descended from a primal Central Asian tongue, demonstrate the prevalence of Turkish and the Turks – was at the same time a *nationalist* theory of *race*. Interestingly enough, certain foreign words that entered the language to replace banned Ottoman terms gradually caught on.

DİL YARESİ BİLEN VARSA BERİ GELSİN

NECE KONUŞUYORUZ BİZ?

Günlük yaşamda son derece kısıtlı sayıda kelimeyle konuşuyoruz; ortalama 500 kelime.. Bu, elbette yazılarımıza da yansıyor. Kullandığımız kelimelerin hepsi Türkçe, ya da bizim tercihimizle dilimize yerleşmiş yabancı kökenli kelimeler olsa yine iyi, ancak öyle değil. Osmanlıca'yı Türkçeyle haşlayıp, üstüne bozuk İngilizce sosu döküyoruz. Buna mide mi dayanır?

Tempo
20 August 1997

Vay Türkçenin haline

"Türkçe nasıl kurtulur?" sorusuna yanıt arayan milletvekilleri ve dilbilimciler, "bye bye, müşahhas, dejenerasyon" gibi onlarca yabancı kelimeyi kullanırken, durumun ciddiyetini de ortaya koydu!

Milliyet
5 June 2005

above: **What language are we speaking?** *In our daily lives we speak with a very limited number of words, an average of 500.*

below: **Poor old Turkish:** *Members of parliament and linguists who are looking for an answer to the question of "How to Save Turkish", and also using foreign words such as "bye bye, müşahhas, dejenerasyon" are demonstrating the gravity of the situation*

left: **Kiss the kids for me**

below: **Law drafted to protect the Turkish language:** *According to the draft law presented to the Council of Ministers, firms are not allowed to take foreign names and products will be given Turkish names. People wishing to become radio or TV presenters will have to pass an exam.*

KISS ÇOLUK ÇOCUK FOR ME

"Bal tutan parmağını yalar" dedikleri bu olsa gerek. Mesut Yılmaz iktidardayken, oğlu Yavuz, Coca-Cola'nın İstanbul Anadolu Yakası distribütörlüğünü almıştı... Recep Tayyip Erdoğan'ın Başbakanlığı'nda ise, oğlu Burak, Ülker'in yeni ürünü Cola Turka'nın Anadolu Yakası dağıtım işini kaptı...

■ Başbakan, oğlunun dağıttığı Cola Turca'yı içiyor. Ne diyelim: İnsana bu kıyağı babası yapmaz!

■ İşte o çoluk çocuk, yani Burak Erdoğan...

■ Yavuz Yılmaz da iktidardaki babası sayesinde Cola işine girmiş; genç yaşında iş güç sahibi olmuştu.

Star
15 July 2003

Türkçe'yi korumak için yasa hazırlığı

Bakanlar Kurulu'nda imzaya açılan yasa taslağına göre, işyerlerine yabancı isim verilemeyecek, ürünlerin markaları Türkçe olacak. Radyo ve TV'de spikerlik yapmak isteyenler sınavdan geçecek.

Dilimiz bozuluyor

Yasa taslağı Atatürk, Kültür, Dil ve Tarih Yüksek Kurumu'nun bağlı olduğu Devlet Bakanı Işılay Saygın tarafından hazırlandı. Saygın, "Toplumun aydın kesimi, Türkçe'nin yanlış kullanımından rahatsız. Yasal düzenleme kaçınılmaz oldu" dedi. **Sayfa 12'de**

Sabah
2 January 1997

This was the case with *konservatuar* [conservatory] for instance, introduced as the equivalent of *darul elhan*.

Although a *technical* aspect to the linguistic polemic does exist, it has, since it first emerged, usually carried heavy *political* connotations. With "new" Turkish officially proclaimed the national language, another crucial political issue began to take shape: a number of other languages spoken in the population were *de facto* ejected from the public sphere and even *banned*. Although, as official minorities, Jews, Armenians and Greeks retained the right to worship and receive education in their mother tongue, this was never enough to actually bring these languages right out into the public sphere. Quite the contrary, from the 1920s on, various state-sanctioned initiatives, notably the *Vatandaş Türkçe Konuş* [Citizen Talk Turkish] campaign, posed a threat to *minority groups* and their native languages by attempting to *marginalize* them within the community. As for those ethno-linguistic groups who did not possess official minority status, they were from the start considered *non-existent*. The dominant nationalist discourse viewed in ethno-linguistic diversity a threat to nationhood and consequently did not recognize the Arabic, Syriac, Kurdish, Laz, or Circassian tongues.

The post-1980 decades simultaneously witnessed two different, even conflicting tendencies. The first was Turkism, or a form of Turkish nationalism promoted by the military coup, and the *Turkification* policies that went with it. These brought about an increase in the oppression exercised against Kurds and the systematic elimination of any vestiges of non-Muslim "cultural heritage." As a result, numerous churches in Anatolia were burnt down or converted to mosques, the names of villages and streets changed, and books, publications or radio broadcasts that could be considered a threat to Turkish nationhood were prohibited. At the opposite end of the spectrum, the liberalization of the economy and the ensuing market boom during the Özal period introduced, first, various foreign product names and subsequently a flood of foreign terms into the language. As *foreign brands* entered common usage, Turkish products were also outfitted with brand names borrowing foreign words. In a remarkably short time, boutiques, restaurants, bars and magazines acquired names with

They'r drawng a wld rectngle… The commndr, trtured, tvrn, rapd… Excutng youths cght… They draggd to the sqre Esmr, Sle, Kmam, Brc and the othrs… trn to pces… undrssd them… beat them reptdly, for hrs… til blod came from btwn th legs… their brests torn…

Şr drags hrslf out of the trture plce… sombdy taks her arm… Salih, the truck is nearby… Come on… com'n… Şr looks… Esm… blod cmes from her mth… her eyes are snow white… hr eies are snw whte…

Aaaaaaaaaaaaaaaaaaaaaaaaaa……
[Murat Uyurkulak, *Tol*, 2003, Metis Publications, p. 191]

Examples of resources for correct spelling and grammar rules

That day, before all the stars of the night sky over the Tigris disappeared and before the rays of the sun in the country of Cizira Botan shone from the summit of Mount Cudi, I woke up to Ape Xelef's voice. It was never clear when Ape Xelef would go to sleep or when he would wake up, but the new day had already started for him. He was wandering slowly within the house which consisted of three rooms and a dark and narrow stable adjacent to it, which was full of lambs, kids, billy goats and sheep, all too sick and too tired to follow Ape Xelef's shepherd's pipe and go to pasture. He was murmuring slowly to himself the song of the city of Cizre. [Mehmed Uzun, *Dicle'nin Yakarışı*, 2003, Gendaş, p. 46]

FCUK brand t-shirt with printing in English

The language pollution, which first started in the parliament, spread to the society through the television channels. In dubbing for films or TV series, "alright" became "tamam", "OK" became "oldu" - in accordance with the lip movement — and "peki" and "evet" was forgotten. Then our main streets started filling up with Dallas bars and Flamingo shops, all names snatched from those TV series. In this Young and the Restless everybody was really Bold and Beautiful. Because making people forget their knowledge of Turkish wasn't a simple message.
[Tomris Uyar, *Gündökümü*, 2003, Yapı Kredi Publications, p. 287]

Examples of books on the correct use of Turkish, which have been increasing over the last few years

words lifted from other languages. The names of favorite characters in *foreign television series* produced lexical inventions such as *Ceyarlaşmak*, (an expression obtained by adapting to Turkish spelling and phonics the name of the infamous JR in the hit American TV series Dallas). Nowadays, it has become increasingly common to merge Turkish with foreign languages, leading to such inspired "Turkishisms" as *Kebab's*, for a restaurant name, and *The Türkler*, for a book title. Another fashionable linguistic practice consists in resorting to an English-like spelling for a Turkish term, as witnessed in *Mydonose*, the first tent show center in Istanbul.

In recent years, arguments have generally centered on the so-called total *degeneration* of the language. Some adopted terms have so completely naturalized into Turkish that hardly anyone remembers they were not native products at the start; this is true of *restoran*, *sandviç*, *şov* and *kafe*, to name only a few. People tend to use less familiar foreign words in an effort to *individualize* their speech. This *hybridization* of the language is increasingly alarming to supporters of "pure" Turkish, who must now also contend with another inevitable deviation from linguistic norms: *slang*. Essentially the *informal* vernacular of youth, slang uses standard words in nonstandard ways, makes up new words or transforms the meanings of terms and phrases. Partisans of "correct" Turkish view these alterations of standard speech as indicators of its "deterioration." Yet, the new slang-sprinkled hybrid Turkish also incorporates the *reactions and values* of different segments of the population, especially of its youth. The once phenomenally popular neologism, *herild yani*, (a sort of Turkish "well, duh...") involved a rather amusing "double" corruption of the English name "Harold" and the Turkish *her halde* ("obviously"). The phony English inflections given to the expression clearly represented a misuse of Turkish but at the same time implied a *parody* of this misuse. We may see here a form of linguistic criticism, aimed not only against the invasion of Turkish by foreign words (or phonics) but also against the rapid admittance of foreign lifestyles into the

Türkçe konuşun please!

Ahmet Hakan Coşkun'un sunduğu İskele Sancak, medyada yıllardır tartışılan, ancak yine en fazla medya tarafından kuralları ihlal edilen 'Türkçe' ve 'dilin korunması'nı ele alıyor.

Yeni Şafak
6 July 2001

Ahmet Hakan Coşkun

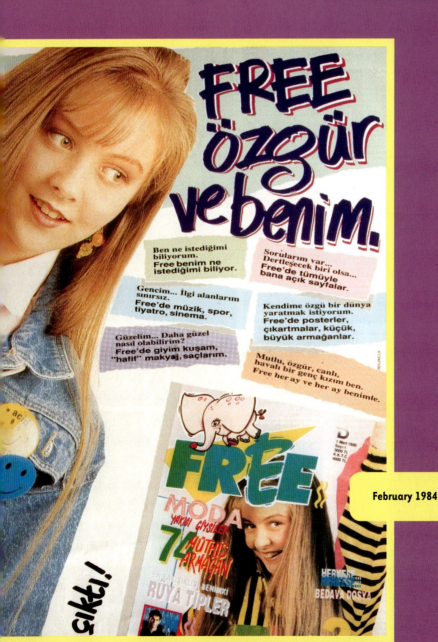

February 1984

above: **Speak Turkish lütfen!** *İskele Sancak, presented by Ahmet Hakan Coşkun, deals with Turkish and the "protection of a language", subjects which have been discussed for years in the media, which is actually most responsible for violating its rules.*

left: **Free is independent and mine:** *I know what I want. Free knows what I want. I have problems... If only there was somebody to confide to... Pages on Free are completely open to me.*

Examples of albums confiscated at various times: Aynur, Keçe Kurdan; Knar, Knar and Anatolian Armenian Folk Music

country and their adoption, as status indicators, by the upper classes. In any case, can we not consider this new "slangy" informal speech an offshoot of *humor magazines* which emphasize and ridicule certain established values? Isn't slang particularly appropriate for the caricature genre anyway? In an age where central cultural policies have become less unifying and protectionist and the *fragmentation* of society has acquired greater visibility, the new colloquial language offers fertile ground for the formation of *new identities*.

There has always been a tendency for different youth groups to adopt *invented* fad words and create new forms of *social slang*. Among Turkish youth, *concon ağzı* ("concon slang") is one of these. But reducing slang or colloquial jargons to simply a verbal expression of youth culture would be misleading. There are also numerous examples of its use to reinforce social bias and abuse related to sexual and ethno-religious identities; it can become a strong means of social and political expression spurring *nationalism*, *racism*, *sexism* and other ideologies. Conversely, the use of language in the struggle of certain minority groups to assert *suppressed* and *ignored* identities endures. Within Turkey's framework of *multiculturalism*, a certain linguistic diversity has emerged, especially in the field of music; albums in Laz, Greek, Armenian and Kurdish are recorded and released. But this does not imply that the social controversy surrounding these ethnic identities has ended. Quite the opposite, as diverse languages and identities have acquired greater visibility, the debate has also become more *vehement*. The Kurdish and Armenian mother tongues, in particular, are considered *dangerous* and TV or radio broadcasting in these languages is as *suppressed* today as it was in the past. Along with the statistics of the many taken into custody or, worse, subjected to torture because of their use of Kurdish, it is hard to forget the *violence* displayed toward singer Ahmet Kaya during one of his concerts after he expressed a desire to sing in that language.

A scene from Ahmet Kaya's speech during the Celebrity Journalists Association's award ceremony, where he announced he would sing and make video clips in Kurdish, which drew strong reactions
[Show TV, 11 February 1999]

Gırgır Nostalji
1993

left: –Where is the Sultanahmet mister?
–Wot you sayin' man, spik Turkish,...

below: –The new generation is heedless of good manners.
–Well, like, shur thing.

Milliyet Aktüalite
17 July 1988

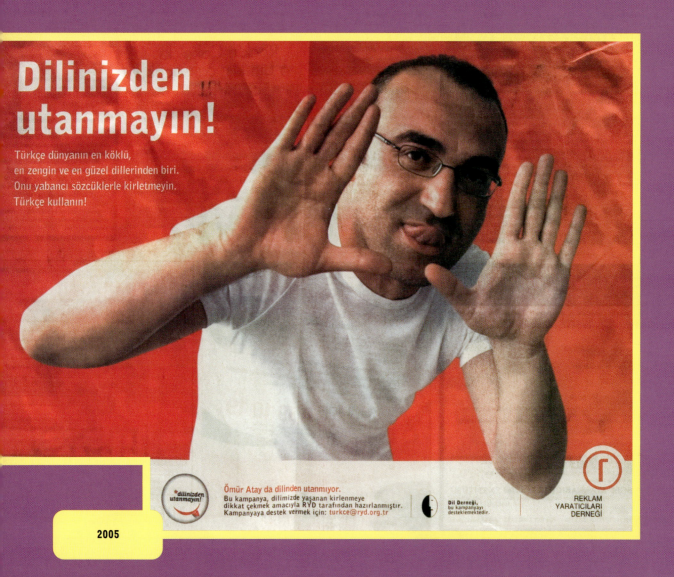

2005

above: **Don't be ashamed of your language:** *Turkish is one of the oldest, richest and most beautiful languages in the world. Don't pollute it with foreign words. Speak Turkish!*

right: *–My son, don't you know, there is a generation gap between us. But we can still talk, can't we? Hey dude, are you listening? Come on, man, take it easy, chill out...*

Joker
14 December 1992

Radikal
12 September 2004

'Concon ağzı' öğrenilebilir mi?

NUR ÇİNTAY A.
nur.cintay@radikal.com.tr

'Muck' yaptı

"Ölürüm Sana" adlı albümmü ile müzik piyasasını alt üst eden Tarkan, İnönü Stadyumu'nda fırtına gibi esti

Sabah
18 August 1997

"SİZİ YERİM"
İki saat boyunca kıvrak dansları ile stadı dold... coşturan Tarkan, sevenlerine "Sizi yerim" de... kızlar dansları ve seksi kıyafetleriyle göz doldu...

above: **Can one learn the "preppy slang"?**

right: **He went "smack, smack":** Tarkan, who turned the music charts upside down with his album "I'll die for you", rocked the İnönü Stadium like a hurricane.

Faced with its growing inadequacy to handle the complexity of social experimentation taking place in the nation, Turkish continues to borrow foreign terms and invent new ones. *Cultural industrialization* is just another dimension of this issue; in this case, industrialization has generated a fragmented cultural sphere. Weekly news magazines were the first indicators of the growing professionalism in the media; they offered a *new approach* and *idiom to news coverage*. Ahmet Oktay draws attention to the changed structure of press jargon – and particularly news headlines – in the 1980s. According to Oktay, one of the aims in leaving out the verbs in such "teaser" headlines as *Adalet Sancılı* [Justice Pains] and *Memura Bir Parmak Bal* [Only Tidbits for State Employees] was to engage the reader's interest (quoted from Gürbilek, 1992: 45). In the 1990s, the growing number of private television networks offering news and entertainment programs also contributed *sensationalism* and *provocation* to the new idiom. In an attempt to catch the public's eye, commercials resorted to a variant form of Turkish liberally sprinkled with foreign words. As for the *pop music* industry, one of the clearest cultural expressions of recent years, some of its songs render language totally incomprehensible and *automatic*.

Meanwhile, severe reactions to the deterioration of language continue; authors, column writers and politicians give vent to their *anxieties* on the subject. Campaigns are organized against the encroachment of foreign words, exhorting us to "take pride" in our native tongue. State institutions pursue legislations and restrictions. However, the fact that a wide range of individuals in high places, from the prime minister to politicians, have adopted a style of speech highly colored with slang, renders the issue even more problematic. *Hıyar* [jerk, schmuck] and *dangalak* [pompous ass] are commonly hurled invectives in the Grand National Assembly and the term *ulan* [a ubiquitous term that embraces a number of meanings from the relatively mild "hey buster!" to more serious insult] routinely figures in nearly every politician's vocabulary. In this context, those attempting to resist outrages to the mother tongue don't stand much of a chance. Like it or not, the use of globalized technology, mainly cell phones and the internet, is rapidly altering language. thx tr :)

Gıli and Tina started making love at the crack of dawn and kept at it till the hammer sounds and lathe counters were silenced. While the kettledrum, violin and clarinet trio were making the street weep, the faces of the Kolera Street residents wrinkled with happiness. Tina looked towards the sounds coming from the street and noticed the dude, the chicks and the old biddies. The raven chicks were wearing their clogs so their hips would look more attractive while dancing. The chick who danced looking at the sky noticed Tina looking at her full of admiration and said "Why don't cha come down, an' shake your ass like us." When Tina hesitated and said "I'm very tired, we've been tussling all day long", the raven chick insisted, saying "Then why don't cha come to Çitiki this evenin', ther'll be a nice wedding. Ye can both shake your ass and go to ala turca so it'll be a nice gesture for the dude who's getting hitched." Tina sent the raven chick a kiss meaning I accept and lay down next to Gıli.
[Metin Kaçan, *Ağır Roman*, 1990/2002, Metis Publications, p. 101]

Cumhuriyet
8 June 1995

above: *–Come on, dear, take the child to bed… Live from the parliament is about to start, I don't want her to learn bad manners."*

below: **Voices from the parliament: prick… blockhead!**

Günaydın
4 September 1986

Seviye iyice düştü!

Erdoğan'ın, 'Oraya üç nokta koyuyorum' sözüne Baykal'dan yanıt: Üç nokta yakasına uygun. Ama uygun görüyorsa, başka bir yerine koysun

Radikal
30 December 2005

CHP lideri Baykal, Çubuk ilçesinde hayvan pazarını ziyaret ederek, besici ve üreticilerle görüştü. Besici ve üreticilerin sorunlarını dinleyen Baykal, destek sözü verdi. FOTOĞRAF: FIRAT YURDAKUL / AA

tsk tr :-)

December 2000

Her gün ortalama 500 bin kişi e-kolay'ın işe yarayan internet sayfalarında aradığını buluyor.
Bu, Türkçe internet dünyasında bir rekor. Türkiye'nin internetçilerine gösterdikleri büyük ilgi için tsk eder. Şeker Bayramınızı ve yeni yılınızı kutlarız.

above: **Manners sure have declined!** *When Erdoğan said: "followed by three dots", Baykal replied: "Three dots are fine as a badge on his collar. But if he finds it suitable, he can also put them somewhere else."*

left: **Thnx tr:)** *We would like to give our thnx to the internet surfers of Turkey and present them our best wishes for the Şeker Bayram and the New Year.*

Sex is everywhere

She always remembered that smell of strawberries, like soft red clouds that cradled them and hid them from view. While they were kissing, Cem kept pressing his body against Aylin's and then pulling it away, he wanted her to feel moving over her legs, her loins and her thighs, the hardness which made her so excited. [Ahmet Altan, *Aldatmak*, Eylül 2002, Can Publications, p. 88]

The medication Viagra, used in the treatment of "erectile dysfunction"

Sex and *sex related issues* crop up in every corner of contemporary society. Sexual orientations that deviate from the *norm*, such as homosexuality, transsexuality and transvestism, now possess almost as wide social *visibility* as heterosexuality. These matters are treated by the media, particularly the mainstream channels, as material for public debate or the opposition politics of specific social groups. For those with a more conservative standpoint on moral issues, the current situation primarily represents a "breaking of all boundaries." The most persuasive evidence in support of the social degeneracy and moral turpitude arguments can be found in the sphere of "unrestrained" sexuality. Meanwhile, the market remains unaffected by this debate and adheres to a predominantly *liberal* discourse that tends to emphasize the *breaking of taboos* and restrictions. This is clearly illustrated by the fact that sex is the main element of advertisements for as varied a range of products as credit cards, chocolate bars, clothes irons and cars. Erotic images meant to kindle desire have *besieged* television channels. How then are all these incompatible discourses and practices interrelated?

It is impossible to isolate the issue of sexuality and evaluate it independently from discourses related to socially defined and ascribed gender roles. Contemporary discourses redefine male and female gender roles within a society's sex system as a polarization based on an opposition of terms. This polarization at the same time reveals gender stratification. Men, considered to symbolize reason and fortitude, traditionally take center stage in the grand narratives of nation, politics and history, whereas women, by virtue of their deficiencies with respect to men, are from the start relegated to the more mundane, routine activities within the domestic sphere. In contemporary discourses, however, this feminine sphere is at the same time one of *fragmented* subjectivity. There are several aspects to this fragmentation. On the one hand, female roles are identified with the "sacred" duties of motherhood and exalted in the public sphere. On the other, "female" brings to

Aktüel
27 January 1994

above: **Sexuality is everywhere:** *Hidden behind the closed doors of bedrooms till only one or two generations ago, sexuality hasn't only got out of the room, it has become dominant in every field of our lives. Sexuality rules everywhere, whether to a higher or lesser degree, it is visible everywhere.*

below: *–Kerim and I have made love everywhere… In the lift, in the car, in the jacuzzi, in the kitchen, in the tent, in the sea, in the woods.*
–Oh no, this man doesn't love you my dear. He didn't allow you into his bed.

Radikal
28 April 2004

Eşinizle SEKS'i konuşurken dikkatli olun

Erkekler çokbilmiş kadını sevmez

Haftanın Sesi
2 December 1983

● ÇOK BİLİN AMA, AZ ANLATIN Yapılan araştırmalar, erkeklerin, seks konusunda çok konuşan kadınlardan hoşlanmadıklarını ortaya koyuyor. Bu yüzden, eşinizle konuyla ilgili olarak konuşurken, dikkatli davranmakta yarar var... Ve, çok bilip, az anlatmak en güzel yol...

● Cinsel konularla ilgili olarak basında çıkan haberler genellikle kadınları etkilemektedir... Ancak erkekler, kadınların bu bilgilerini yatak odasına taşımalarından sık sık yakınmaktadırlar. Bu yüzden, eşinizle konuşurken asla bilgiçlik taslamayın...

above: **Men don't like pedantic women:** Press articles regarding sexual subjects generally influence women... But men frequently complain that women carry this knowledge into the bedroom. You must therefore never act pedantic when talking to your husband

below: **Sexual terror is getting out of control:** According to experts: "artificial objects on sale in stores are like traps for young people. The state should take serious precautions on this subject."

Tercüman
6 October 1992

Kutsal bir değer olan aile mefhumumuzu yıkmaya çalışıyorlar

"Cinsel terör azdı"

Uzmanlar: "Mağazalarda satılan sun'î objeler gençler için bir tuzaktır. Bu hususta devletin ciddi tedbir alması şarttır"

PROF. DR. GÖZEN GÜREL PROF. DR. CAHİDE AYDIN DOÇ. DR. ÖMER SÜDEKAN DR. BEKİR GREBENE

right: **Is virginity a certificate of virtue?** *There are different opinions regarding the fact that virginity is considered a standard of virtue in Turkish society*

below: **Sexual explosion among the Islamists:** *Young women with covered heads hold hands and kiss with their boyfriends. The colourful scarves are a symbol of the bubbling sexuality. Religious women expect romance from their husbands. They wear G-strings, nail varnish and make-up. Most watch celebrity programmes and can't disengage themselves from TV series.*

Milliyet
3 April 1988

Tempo
9 August 2005

above: **Turkishfetish:** *The second biggest attempt to "attract God's anger" in Turkey since Zeki Müren.*

left: **How to seduce a man:** *Five stratagems that lead to a happy end.*

mind unrestrained sensuality, passions and lust. The "mother" identity, totally cleansed of erotic connotations, is presented in contrast to a *dangerous* female sexuality. As a result, woman's existence in the public sphere has always been the focal point of heated debate. Unable to reconcile modernity with the Islamic decree that women should cover up outside the private sphere, the secular Republican regime advanced the "virtuous" female stereotype; without resorting to the veil, modern women would display their modesty through their personal choice of clothing and body language. Clearly, the fragmentation of feminine role depictions has always been most obvious along the axis of sexuality.

The boundaries determined by family, community and nation establish the acceptable, in other words, controlled forms of female sexuality. At the same time, this defines the border between "good" women and "bad" women, or viewed from a different perspective, between "our" women and the "others." The new female figures displayed in the showcase of Turkish modernity, symbolizing Westernization and progress, are those "self-denying" women who have succeeded in restraining their sexual identities within *socially acceptable* norms. In vivid contrast are the "femme fatale" or "seductive" female stereotypes depicted in popular literature or the movies, who, through their *unbridled* sexuality, bring about the downfall of both the men they seduce and themselves. These women are sometimes portrayed as the cause of catastrophes threatening *an entire nation*.

As for men, they were also expected to confine their sexuality to within family bounds and fulfill their obligations as good husbands and fathers. Extramarital, or worse, homosexual relationships were thus outside social norms. But in practice, men could conduct extramarital relationships without the threat of fragmentation to their identities faced by women. Male infidelity has always existed on the institutional margins of family and marriage; cheating is literally "dirt on a man's hand" that can easily wash off, whereas the adulterous woman is marked for all times. At this point we may well ask ourselves how moral judgments and political interventions of a sexual order, institutionalized and articulated around sexual mores, fit in

Then he said that we could always continue seeing each other, that we would remain friends. Yes, but friends don't make love... Whereas I was a little girl who had discovered everything with him. He had scraped off from my psyche my previous lousy sexual experiences. I now enjoyed sexuality. One Sunday we went to his house. We made love again. And that week I discovered that I was pregnant. The last time we made love I had told him that I didn't feel well, that I might be pregnant. He covered his thick penis with a plastic armour all the same and entered me.

I told him on the phone that I was pregnant. At first he was saddened. And the next day he told me in anger that he was disgusted with me, that he never wanted to see me again. And I went and had an abortion, but it was very difficult.
[Şebnem İşigüzel, *Hanene Ay Doğacak*, 1993/2001, Everest Publications, p. 94]

Türk kadınları, gizlice Viagra kullanan kocaları yüzünden depresyona giriyor

Kocam 50'sinden sonra iyice azdı doktor bey

Hürriyet
18 July 1999

CİNSEL SUÇLAR
5 yılda 2 kat arttı

Nokta
12 May 1985

Akbank'ın "Gençlik Yılı" nedeniyle düzenlediği konferansların üçüncüsünde Prof. Dr. Özcan Köknel gençlik döneminde kız-erkek arkadaşlığı konusunda konuştu

FLÖRT... EN DOĞAL İLİŞKİ

Hey
25 March 1985

top: **Doctor, my husband is in his fifties and has completely gotten out of hand:** *Turkish women are having depression because of their husband's secret use of viagra.*

above: **Sexual crimes have increased two-fold in 5 years**

left: **Flirting is the most natural relationship:** *In the third of the conferences organised by Akbank to celebrate the "Year of Youth", Prof Dr Özcan Köknel talked about friendship between teenage boys and girls.*

Cosmopolitan
April 2005

SEKS Tarzınız Ne?

Cinsel hayatı sıkıcılıktan kurtarmak herkes için önemlidir. Her seferinde aynı ritüelleri uygulayıp aynı sonuçlara varmaktan sıkıldıysanız bu rutinden kurtulmanız için birkaç seçenek sunuyoruz. Sizin tarzınız hangisi?

Kadınca
1 April 1982

Cinsel organ nasıl olur

S.Y.

"Ben 24 yaşında nişanlı bir kızım. Bazı sorunlarım nedeniyle evlenmeye çekiniyorum. Duyduğuma göre kadın cinsel organı, bacaklar bitişik durduğu zaman çizgi şeklindeymiş. Büyük dudaklar küçük dudakları kapatırmış. Fakat benim küçük dudaklarım, büyük dudaklarımın arasından, et parçası şeklinde aşağıya doğru sarkıyor. Bu durum beni çok üzüyor. İkincisi, benden devamlı beyaz akıntı geliyor. Hemen hergün külotumu değiştiriyorum, neden? Üçüncüsü, birkaç yıldır mastürbasyon yapıyorum. Hayal kurup bacaklarımın arasına birşeyler sıkıştırıyorum. Dölyolumda kasılmalar oluyor ve su geliyor. Bu konuda beni aydınlatır mısınız? Ayrıca kadın orgazmını tarif eder misiniz? Bir de çok kıllıyım. Bunlardan nasıl kurtulabilirim?"

"Kadın cinsel organı genellikle sizin tarif ettiğiniz gibi olur. Ama pekçok kadında da şekil değişiklikleri görülür. Nasıl herkesin burnu birbirine benzemezse, her kadının cinsel organı da birbirine benzemez. Bazen küçük dudakların, büyük dudaklardan daha fazla geliştiği görülür. Bu hiç de endişe edilecek bir durum değildir, normaldir. Akıntılarınız normal olabilir ama çoksa nedeni iltihap olabilir. Ama size bir ilaç ismi öneremeyiz. Doktora gitmelisiniz. Bunda utanacak hiçbir şey yok. Üstelik nişanlı bir genç kız olduğunuzu yazıyorsunuz. Zaten evlenmeden önce doktora gitmeniz gerekir. Mastürbasyon konusuna gelince, suçluluk duymanıza gerek yok. Zevk aldığınız zaman dölyolunuzun kasılması da normaldir. Zevk alındığı zaman vajina ıslanır. Belki de akıntınız fazla olduğu için siz su geldiğini sanıyorsunuz. Kadın orgazmı tarif edilemez. Bir duyguyu tarif edebilir misiniz? Ederseniz belki ama bu tarif birçoklarından değişik olur. Orgazm da onun gibi herkese göre değişik bir duygudur. Yüzünüzdeki tüylerden kurtulmanın en iyi yolu, epilasyon. Biraz uzun sürebilir ama sabrederseniz epilasyonla onları bir daha çıkmamak üzere yokedebilirsiniz."

above: **What's your sexual style?** Rescuing one's sex life from boredom is important for everybody. If you are bored of carrying out the same rituals and reaching the same results, we offer you a few alternatives to avoid this routine. Which one is your style?

right: **What does a sexual organ look like?** I am 24 years old and I am engaged, but I'm afraid of getting married because of certain problems. I hear that a woman's sexual organ should look like a line when the legs are held together. The outer lips should cover the inner lips. But my inner lips hang down like a piece of meat in between my outer lips...

An encyclopedia from the 1980s, aiming to provide scientific information on sex and sexual health

While they are trying to save their marriage and their worn out love, his wife makes a contradictory sounding proposal: Let's have relationships with others for a while. Not sentimentally, just plain sexual relationships. Let's miss each other, let's try to understand what our love means to each other. Let's see how strongly we come out of this. If we can jazz up our enthusiasm, let's continue, otherwise let's split up.
[İnci Aral, *Taş ve Ten*, 2005, Epsilon Publications, p. 184]

Examples of lingerie intended for sexual fantasies

with today's atmosphere of ostensible sexual liberation. In other words, how can we explain the *contiguity* of discourses restricting sexual conduct and messages vehemently promoting its outward expression, provoking discussion on the subject and encouraging the pursuit of new sexual experiences?

The post-1980s were a period of sexual *liberation*. In opposition to the conservative attitude that condemned female sexuality as taboo, the opinion that flirting was natural emerged. Sexual rhetoric in newspapers and magazines counseled women on the techniques for attaining sexual bliss. Women were advised to "slip into something a little sexy" around the house. The new sexual discourse, disseminated through the mass media in particular, encouraged *liberation* from traditional mores. By the 2000s, almost all magazines, but especially those for women, offered a wide array of sex articles and quizzes, most of them translations of the original versions in Western publications. "Discover your erotic style," "How to seduce a man," and similarly edifying headlines are sufficient proof that sexual discourse has moved far *beyond* the boundaries and restrictions of previous decades. Going by the stories in these magazines, casual sex, gay sex, bisexuality and even sex changes are becoming commonplace. Women, just like men, and perhaps even more so, avidly pursue their sexual freedom. Seductive outfits, no longer reserved for the privacy of one's home, are flaunted on the streets. Mini skirts, micro shorts, cleavage-revealing tops and belly button-baring cropped T-shirts are by now familiar images in popular magazines. Some fashion spreads or brand ad campaigns use photographs so sexualized they verge on the pornographic. Models acquire fame in direct relationship to the amount of skin they display. Catwalk shows are regarded as *erotic shows*, much like Fashion TV is perceived as a sex channel. All these developments are said to be the natural consequences of new freedom and the breaking of taboos, but that is only one side of the picture.

In the first surging wave of new sexuality, new forms of *control* also began to take

Kavgaların ve boşanmaların önüne geçebilmek için:
Hanımların evde biraz seksi giysilerle dolaşmaları önerildi

Psikolog Dr. Kemal Keskinel, "Yaşam koşullarının sinirli yaptığı erkeği rahatlatmak eşinin elinde" dedi

Amaç rahatlatmak

Yaşam koşullarından sinirlenen kocanızı rahatlatmak için iç açıcı renklerden oluşan seksi kıyafetler giyinin.

Saklambaç
2 July 1980

left: **Women are advised to wear sexy clothes at home:** *Psychologist Dr Kemal Keskinel said: "Women have the power to relax men stressed out by daily living conditions."*

below: **Our sexiest outfit:** *In the most exclusive pharmacies.*

en **seksi** kıyafetimiz
en seçkin eczanelerde

March 2000

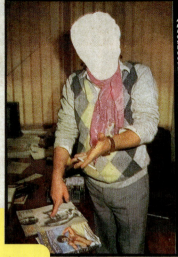

Milliyet
29 September 1985

Milliyet
11 December 1987

above: **I regret what I did... I am receiving treatment... I will be cured...:** *A penitent homosexual called out to mothers: "Raise your girls like girls and your boys like boys."*

left: **Obscenity fined with 800 million:** *The Bravo and Playboy magazines have been flooded with fines.*

shape. One of their manifestations was the medical approach to sex. Mentioning Ertürk Yöndem, one of the 1980s research-journalists who hosted the program "Chronic Depression," Nurdan Gürbilek stresses that sexuality was handed over to *the experts*. (Gürbilek, 1992: 40-41) This is the *contemporary* style the government adopts; using current knowledge and technologies, it tries to appear up to date and legitimize its discourse at the same time. In the emphasis on individual liberties, the public is challenged to talk and incited to accept specialized discourse as a means to attaining accurate information. In Yöndem's "Chronic Depression," and similar programs, an *issue* is identified and *solutions* advanced. From *Güzin Abla*'s column [the Turkish equivalent of "Dear Abby"] to the opinions of psychologists and doctors, "experts" have taken the leading roles. Discourses inviting discussion on sexuality at the same time define and describe its *deviant* forms. The main characteristics of an anomaly are thus established. Once homosexuality is classified as a *sickness* that can be cured and individuals have expressed their regrets and affirmed their beliefs in "cure" and "salvation," the basis for a new individualized conception of morality is set.

The continued debate over what does or does not constitute normal behavior has brought with it an inclination to discuss in public private problems and intimate matters, in short, a craze for *confession*. The recently created popular website "confessions" is full of such examples. These personal revelations both wield a highly erotic appeal and constitute an environment where norms are established and, in the light of "expert" opinion, right is separated from wrong. In a similar vein, newspapers and magazines run sex articles rife with intimate disclosures, and sexual issues are visual material for television channels. But these media have also become settings to *brand* and pass judgment on those who have transgressed and broken socially-defined boundaries. They have their own regulations, separate from state laws and institutions but at least as *violent*. To better understand the scope of this violence, one need only recall those individuals whose private lives once revealed and their

...
those with good voices sang,
those who could belly dance well, danced.
everybody would become more of a woman
everybody would become more of a man

There was no such thing as womanhood or manhood. Both womanhood and manhood were like a game. There were only successful or unsuccessful players.

The fags were the most successful epic players. [Murathan Mungan, "ÇC", *Son İstanbul*, 1985/1988, Remzi Publications, p. 149-150]

An erotic video tape on sale in shops in the early '90s.

A few issues of Erkekçe, a popular man's magazine in the '80s and '90s

Hello, if you know the code of the operator you would like to speak to, you can press it immediately. If you don't know it, you can press 3 for our passionate erotic stories which have been completely renewed. To talk face to face and live to our operators, press 1, if you want to participate in a group formed by a few people, that is in a conference call, press 2, if you want to listen to real phone jokes, press 5, if you want to hear all about your horoscope, press 4.
[A pre-recorded message from a sex and chat phone line, 0 546 321 66 66, December 2005]

Stimulants aiming to increase the sexual drive

Incense with Kama Sutra theme

"problems," "perversions" and "illnesses" made public, became *targets* to humiliate, attack and ultimately kill.

Consequently, *violence* often occurs at those points where the dominant sexual system and gender roles determined by national moral norms intersect with the forms of behavior sanctioned by current sexual discourses. As always, the most affected are those "secondary" or marginalized groups such as women, homosexuals, transsexuals or transvestites. Faced with the dangers of boundary-breaking, state institutions continually attempt to counteract excesses through restrictions. Alongside censorship laws and decency acts to control the media and supposedly protect minors (and adults) from harmful material, such controversial practices as forced virginity tests and adultery laws once again pose female sexuality as *dangerous*. On the one hand, state legislatures are accused of attempting to regulate "bedroom activities." On the other, a lot of what state institutions *fail to do* also has an impact on the sexual system. Some of the first shortcomings that come to mind are the state's blind eye to "honor killings," its failure to punish violence against women, and its inaction on preventing the rape or murder of countless female or transvestite prostitutes. On the eve of Turkey's bid for EU membership, these issues still remain unresolved. In fact, quite the opposite is occurring; the *violent controversy* over these matters, by merging the sexual sphere with chauvinist concerns, has fanned the flames of nationalism.

Where sex is concerned, fantasies and threats, restrictions and dreams of transcending boundaries always go *hand in hand*; the one almost seeming to summon the other. The free discussion of sexuality together with the shaping of sexual experimentation according to new norms and the growing prevalence of this experimentation has objectified and brought new forms of control to sexuality's apparently liberated *subjects*. Nonetheless, it cannot be ignored that there is an unceasing *political* struggle to name and brand the new sexual identities that emerge from the freely addressed and debated field of sexuality. Sex, today, is one vast battlefield.

Sabah
29 September 1986

right: **Screens flooded with nudity:** *Our hearts and eyes will feast… Films by the clothes-shedding women of Yeşilçam have passed the TRT Inspection Board.*

below: **Three cars had a pile-up accident because of me:** *Even my neighbors threaten to fire the doorman if he ever comes to my apartment.*

Güneş
18 December 1985

NASIL YERSEN ÖYLE sevişirsin!

İlk defa yemeğe çağırdınız geçenlerde tanıştığınız o yakışıklıyı! Bir sürü yemek hazırladınız özenerek, heyecanla... Fakat o da ne? Sürekli yemek seçiyor; 'Onu yemem, bunu yemem' diye yakınıyor. O klas erkek elleriyle yemek yiyor, ağzına burnuna bulaştırıyor sosları. İşte tüm bu yemek yeme şekilleri erkeğinizin yatak alışkanlıklarını ele veriyor! Yemek seçen pozisyon da seçiyor, obur olan yatakta bir şehvet düşkününe dönüşüveriyor... ▷

Marie Claire
1 December 2004

Tell me how you eat, I'll tell you how you make love: *You invited to dinner that handsome man you met recently. You prepared a variety of dishes with great care. But hey! He starts complaining that he won't eat this and he won't eat that. That refined man eats with his hands, he smears his face with sauce. Your man's eating style gives away his habits in bed.*

right: **The state is in the bedroom:** *Adultery: a crime dating to the Middle Ages.*

below: **Ultimatum from the EU and adultery is dropped:** *When party members' reactions were added to that of the EU, AKP came to an agreement with CHP and gave up the regulation regarding adultery.*

Yeni Gündem
9 November 1986

Sabah
15 September 2004

What a wedding!

Marriage ceremonies and weddings have always reflected the rituals of a given society. The act of two persons entering the covenant of marriage and a new phase of life directly concerns both their immediate families and more distant relatives. Obviously, marriage does not only stand for a union of souls, it also implicates the transfer of wealth, the formation and consolidation of political, social and economic ties, and, on a symbolic level, the perpetuation of traditions. The social significance of the rules applying to marriage – especially in those patriarchies that abide by dowry or "bride price" practice – is well-known. Weddings also testify to a family's standing and wealth. The wedding receptions of the rich in particular, with their showy abundance, extravagance and culinary delicacies dispensed to distinguished guests and the poor alike contribute considerably to sustaining existing social and cultural relationships. In modern societies where a marriage contract is entered under the supervision of the state, marriage is a registered, official procedure and its economic, political and social terms subject to state regulations. In Turkey, for example, the Ministry of Finance delivers marriage certificates. But the social function of weddings is not necessarily dependent on an officially contracted marriage; in the Republican period especially, although *imam* marriages were considered invalid, their meanings prevailed in weddings with heavily religious overtones in various segments of society.

Wedding candies adorned with toppers and flowers

Although present-day weddings cannot be said to have entirely lost their past significance, their meaning has largely been transformed. From the 1980s, when *ostentation* first became a social *norm*, to the present, three major changes have appeared in relation to weddings: the diffusion of upper class ideals and practices throughout society; the creation of a wedding industry; and the

Damadın ağabeyi, geline altın kemer taktı
...al ile Ceyda'nın muhteşem düğününde Diyarbakırlı davetliler gelini altınla do-...ttılar. Bilal'in ağabeyi Veysel Kadayıfçıoğlu da, Ceyda'ya altın kemer taktı.

İbrahim Tatlıses türkülerini, Erbakan'ın eşi ve kızları için söyledi
İbrahim Tatlıses, Tayyip Erdoğan'ın eşi Emine Hanım (sol başta) ile Nermin Erbakan ve kızlarının bulunduğu masaya giderek türkülerini burada okudu. Portakal suyu içen Nermin Hanım, Tatlıses'i bol bol alkışladı.

Geline dolar yağdı

...iyarbakırlılar'ın düğününe Nermin Erbakan ...e kızları da katıldı. Ünlüleri bir araya getiren ...ecede, yeni evlilere kilolarca altın takıldı

Akşam
10 January 1997

Sahneye saçılan doları otelin garsonları topladı.
Diyarbakırlı Kadıyıfçıoğlu ailesinin ortanca oğlu Bilal'in düğününde ilginç isimler bir araya gelirken, gelinle damada kilolarca altın takıldı. Sahnede halay çekenlerin üzerine saçılan doları ise garsonlar topladı.

Bride showered with dollars: *Nermin Erbakan and her daughters also took part in the wedding of the couple from Diyarbakır. During the event, which brought together many celebrities, the newly marrieds were adorned with heaps of gold.*

İstanbul bu düğünü konuşuyor

Kolları bilezikle doldu
...eşem düğünde, davetliler gelin Gül Kırbaç'ın ...rlıoğlu) kollarını bilezikle donattılar. Fotoğrafta, ...lıoğlu ailesinin yakın dostu olan Ayşe Öztürk ...lin hanıma bir bilezik takarken görülüyor.

Kuyrukta 1,5 saat beklediler
Yaklaşık 500 davetli gelin hanıma altın takabilmek için adeta birbirleriyle yarıştı. Altın takmak için kuyruğa giren davetliler, uzun süre sırada beklemek zorunda kaldılar. Düğünde, Gül Hayırlıoğlu'na milyonlarca lira değerinde altın takıldı. Güzel gelin düğün boyunca, takıları taşımakta bir hayli zorlandı.

Mutlulukları gözlerinden okunuyor
Gecenin geç saatlerine kadar neşe içinde devam eden düğün süresince Hayırlı... ailesine mensup hanımlar güzel gelini hiç yalnız bırakmadılar. Fotoğra... Hayırlıoğlu ailesinden İhsan, Selma, Pelin ve Dr. Gülser Hayırlıoğlu, gelin G... Kırbaç (Hayırlıoğlu) ile damat Taner Kırbaç'a mutluluk dilerken görülüyor...

Bugün
21 June 1990

Gelinin kardeşleri
Gecenin en mutlu kişileri gelinin kızkardeşleri Pelin Hayırlıoğlu ile, geçtiğimiz günlerde evlenen Meltem Domaniç kardeşlerdi.

İzzet Altınmeşe coşturdu
Türk Halk Müziği'nin sevilen sanatçılarından İz... Altınmeşe, türküleriyle davetlileri iyice coşturdu.

Gırgır
5 February 1989

above: **Istanbul is talking about this wedding:** Mechanical Engineer Taner Kırbaç and Gül, elder daughter of the famous businessman İhsan Hayırlıoğlu were married with a magnificent ceremony.

left: —The bride's uncle couldn't come from Germany, so he sent a special tape he had recorded.

(re)invention of traditions. There often seems to be a fairytale-like quality to the weddings of the rich. Among the bourgeoisie, attempts to emulate aristocracy by lavishly spending on wedding receptions worthy of kings or sultans are frequent. With such weddings, which become "the talk of the town," the aim is to show off and strengthen one's social status. Since the affairs of the wealthy endlessly fascinate the less privileged, those not included in such festivities keep informed through the press and dedicate a good deal of their time to discussing the bride's wedding gown and jewelry, the food and the wedding gifts. There is envy but also distance in this behavior. The weddings of other segments of society are suited to their incomes and values and distance themselves from the performances of the rich. After all, those weddings are *unattainable*. The royal nuptials of Prince Charles and Lady Diana in the beginning of the 1980s are recorded among the most magnificent. Large numbers in Turkey viewed the marriage on national TV, falling under the spell of a ceremony where everything, especially the 25 foot train of Lady Diana's wedding gown and the dresses of her bridesmaids, held the fairytale charm of an old-fashioned palace wedding. This grand moment in the life of far-off aristocrats, celebrated in a style reminiscent of period films, was discussed at length with worshipful admiration in Turkey as in the rest of the world. Still, it represented a very distant lifestyle. Shortly, however, these *distant lifestyles* would draw *closer* as the notion that styles and products indicating wealth were *accessible* gained prevalence. Media-propagated fashions and the wide range of products filling a rapidly expanding market introduced into people's lives objects which had once seemed impossibly remote ideals. As Roland Barthes points out, when bourgeois culture becomes the norm in a capitalist society, the bourgeois class loses its own name and becomes anonymous; in other words, bourgeois myths become those of the entire population. A secretary getting her first pay starts to daydream about a flashy wedding (1996: 206). *Identifying with* dreams of a grand bourgeois marriage involves rejecting inequalities as illusory. In the post-1980s Turkey, the growing ascendancy of market values erased the ideological basis of economic inequalities; undeniably, for the majority of society, the feeling that everything was *attainable* had become prevalent. At a time when privileged upper class values were accessible to

We are going to get married, I'm going to teach you a lesson for not wanting me, as if I was flawed. I'm going to teach you that lesson during the wedding; my dear father-in-law the doctor and his very respectable consort are going to learn a lesson they will never forget. I'm going to wear a magnificent wedding dress, they will never be able to forget it…

With the dowry money my father gave me, I got myself wonderful dresses, shoes, lingerie. And I got married with a wedding dress and a veil that came up to my ass.

"What a rebellion" said my sister, "you are kidding yourself, if you'd managed not to get married, that would have been the real rebellion, or at least if you hadn't worn the wedding dress, if you'd worn jeans, now that would have been a real rebellion, but a mini wedding dress, well…!

We are on our honeymoon, in the honeymoon suite of a real luxurious hotel, in a real hot city… Sweety has no money but he loves luxury.
[Duygu Asena, *Kadının Adı Yok*, 1987/2004, Doğan Publications, p. 57]

SHOW TV'DE YENİ BİR YARIŞMA PROGRAMI
EVCİLİK OYUNU

● Show TV "Çarkıfelek", "Süper Aile", "Saklambaç"ın başarısı üzerine ekranlara yeni bir yarışma programı daha getiriyor. Sunuculuğunu tiyatro ve sinema dünyamızın ünlü ismi Müjdat Gezen'in üstlendiği yarışma programının adı "Evcilik Oyunu".

Müjdat Gezen'in sunuculuğunu üstlendiği "Evcilik Oyunu" 2.5 yılını aşmamış evli çiftler arasında yapılıyor ve eşlerin birbirlerine ne kadar tanıdıklarını ortaya çıkarmayı amaçlıyor. Hedef ise çiftlere ikinci bir balayı yaşatmak.

Hürriyet
15 February 1993

BEKARLARIN GÖZÜNÜ KORKUTMAK İSTEMEYİZ AMA, ŞÖYLE SIRADAN BİR DÜĞÜN 450 BİN LİRAYA ÇIKIYOR

"EVET" demek için yürek gerek

ERHAN AKYILDIZ

Gelinlik, 8 bin lira ile 20 bin lira arasında değişiyor. Eğer bir moda evinden almak istiyorsanız 50 bin liradan 100 bine kadar gelinlik bulabilirsiniz.

Beyazıt'taki Abdullah Düğün Salonu'nda 300 konuklu bir düğün 18 - 20 bin liraya yapılırken, Sheraton Oteli'nde 300 konuk için 500 bin lira ödeniyor...

B İRİ erkek, biri dişi, iki kişinin dudaklarından dökülen iki "evet" sözcüğü ile gerçekleşen evlilik olayı, günümüz koşullarında çiftlerin yanına yaklaşabilmekten bir umacı gibi kaçındıkları korkulu bir rüya gibi...
Evlilik öncesinde, mutlu düşlerin, sıcak bir yuva özleminin getirdiği pembe hayaller, evlilik gerçeğine yaklaşınca en ucuzundan dörtyüz elli bin, biraz lüks düşünülürse üç milyon liraya kadar varan

Milliyet
8 March 1981

Star
1 July 2005

top left: **Wedding game:** *Following the success of "Çarkıfelek", "Super Family" and "Hide and Seek", Show TV brings a new contest to the screen.*

bottom left: **You need guts to say "yes":** *The cost of a wedding dress varies between 8,000 and 20,000 Lira. If you wish to get a wedding dress from a fashion designer, you can find one between 50,000 and 100,000 Liras.*

above: **Don't let your fame be tarnished:** *Nowadays, families wishing to show off their riches in weddings rent gold. They adorn their children with gold rented on a 10 % commission.*

right: **A show off with fire works costs 550 million a minute:** *The cost of adorning events like weddings and festivities with 5 minutes of fireworks varies between 550 million and 1.5 billion Lira.*

below: **Like an Oscar ceremony:** *The wedding finale of Yosun Mermerci and Olivier Reza was no different from Hollywood galas. Guests getting off luxury cars posed on the red carpet with a smile for the exploding flashes.*

Hürriyet
24 December 2000

Vatan
4 August 2003

society as a whole and the market blurred the jealously guarded cultural boundaries of upper crust society, the big bourgeois wedding also became a *norm*. As weddings competed with a growing passion for a place in the spotlight, it became imperative to *spend more* and be more "creative." Meanwhile, the concept of marriage as a ritual gradually left its place to that of a wedding ceremony as a sort of *spectacle* where society itself was the public. Today, new ways to achieve still more glamorous weddings continue to be a current issue. Through music blaring from megaspeakers and, of course, fireworks, summer weddings in five-star hotels or the "in" clubs of the city broadcast their festivities for miles around. Weddings are now the stage for every kind of extravagance: "fireworks at 55 million a minute," expensive jewels, money – sometimes even dollars – strewn on the ground, showy wedding gowns and luxurious buffets... Photo spreads of the event are splashed across the tabloids and the pages of society magazines. High society weddings are the *talk of the town*. Receptions "as fabulous as the Oscars" fascinate *outsiders*, and a spectacular wedding is hyped as top on *everyone's list of desires*.

But stirring up aspirations in people has also transferred to weddings some of the *violence* that comes from living with boundless, unfulfilled desires. The traditional firing of gunshots into the air is practiced in trendy clubs, and the explosive noise from fireworks going off in rapid succession lasts deep into the night. A chief source of violence is derived from the economic inequities concealed under the gloss of collective desires. The less fortunate mobilize all their assets to emulate the glamorous marriage ceremonies of the "beautiful people." Wedding gowns and jewels are rented to create an unsubstantiated impression of affluence. This *tendency for excess* and the inequalities that underlie it also make newspaper headlines. "Working class attitudes at upscale wedding" seems a caption for a social drama; the unconcealed struggle to get to the open buffet – closer in concept to an all-you-can-eat spread – betrays unconcern and vulgarity... At the same time, the sentimental values of an extravagant wedding also seem to be fading. In contemporary society, the focus is increasingly on marital troubles; divorces occur more frequently with the accompanying issues of property division and alimony suits while domestic violence and similar

Fireworks frequently used during weddings

My cake has nine tiers. Our cake, that is. Because now I'm married. So now I have become "we". Weren't we supposed to forget about saying "I"? There is no "I", there is "we". Bloody bourgeois girl! Can't you stop constantly saying "I"? I have already stopped, Gül. Give my regards to all my old friends who kept reproving me like this for freqently starting my sentences with "Listen, I..." Tell them Ayşen has become "we". That is, when you hear about this from your father. You can also hear about it if by chance you see one of those newspapers with lots of pictures which feature weddings, just to spite the ones featuring desolation. You will see how we cut the nine tier cake which my father couldn't see me cutting, how Ercan's hand was on mine, how we cut the cake together, yes, together, hand in hand, how we cut it. How I became "we"... [Adalet Ağaoğlu, *Bir Düğün Gecesi*, 1979/2004, Yapı Kredi Publications, p. 239-240]

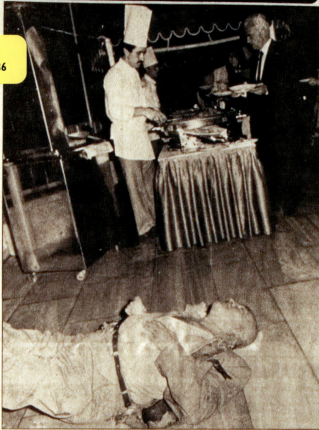

Hürriyet
28 August 1986

Drama at the Hilton: *A lower-middle class person had a heart attack waiting in line for the open buffet.*

topics are more often addressed by the feminist discourse and articulated from the vantage point of women. All the above are indicators that both in the economic and spiritual sense, the supposedly unassailable institution of marriage is being *undermined*. A number of reality TV "marriage" shows, using a competition-based format, attempt on-screen redefinitions of marriage, as do specialized discourses offering advice on how to "save your marriage."

Various wedding invitations

Another important perspective to the marriage issue is the development and *industrialization* of the wedding sector. Despite the efforts of celebrities to make their own marriages ever more sensational, wedding halls offering menus and programs suited to different budgets and social segments set the standards for the marriage industry. It is now possible to choose among different *wedding packages* which come ready with everything from the cake and wedding favors to standard lists of wedding gifts. Magazines entirely devoted to marriage planning and other wedding themes are part of the industry. The large variety of available publications – further enriched with the Turkish versions of foreign magazines – disseminate marriage fashions in all their details, thereby also contributing to their homogenization. The magazine *Bride*, for instance, offers expert advice on bridal hairstyles, wedding rings, gowns and bouquets and also suggestions for alternative wedding venues, services and products. Thus a ready menu is provided for even those with more unconventional tastes.

While Turkey receives new wedding fashions *at the same time as* the rest of the world, a new tendency to add *local values* to marriage receptions stands out today. In the 1980s, one of the most popular activities of Semra Özal and her *papatyas* [literally "daisies" – lady cohorts] was to arrange civil unions for couples who were joined only by an *imam* marriage. Countless civil marriages of young and old couples were held collectively as a form of charity campaign. This initiative was presented as a *modernizing* step towards a contemporary civilized society, especially since it liberated women from the clutches of a traditional order. Defenders of "civilization" still wage a campaign

The Marriage School begins, with the contribution of Psychiatrist Professor Doctor Nevzat Tarhan. Prepared and presented by Özlem Atik:

ÖA: ...Professor, we said that this is one of the most important decisions in life, what is the most important thing to consider in order to take a wise marriage decision?

NT: There are two important decisions, two important choices in one's life, one is the choice of profession, the other is marriage. To take this decision it is necessary to analyse properly the plusses and minuses. If this analysis is done properly, later on there won't be that much need for the words "if only". It isn't only feelings that must be used here, and it isn't only reasoning either. This is a decision which needs to be taken following an evaluation based on both feelings and reasoning. And, in a marriage, one must not get married with somebody one doesn't know well. What do we mean by "knowing somebody"? How necessary, sufficient or important is "knowing somebody"? For example there are many examples of people who flirted for years and who divorced 6 months after having married. How does this happen? How can people have flirted for this long without getting to know each other? And there are marriages which are very successful although the two didn't know each other. How does this happen? If we evaluate a marriage on a scale of 100 points, spouses knowing each other beforehand make up for 20-30 percent, the effort and care put into the marriage to make it work count for 70-80 percent. That is why love in marriage is not the beginning but the result of marriage. Love is generally considered a necessary part of a marriage... This view has to do with not knowing well the meaning of love... In marriages based on love, young people don't see each others' flaws, that is, their behaviour is based on erroneous perceptions. As a result of this, when the waves of the real sea of life come crashing, then they start saying "what have I done". That is why reasoning and feelings need to be used in a balanced way in marriage... ["Marriage School", AKRA FM, 31 December 2005]

Gelinli-damatlı pasta üstü süsü

against *imam* unions today. While a number of women's social groups and organizations rehash the legal and socio-economic pros and cons of legal matrimony, a civil marriage is still considered an indicator of modernity. Yet, present-day modern values also integrate a rather novel trend: the *revival of tradition*. The *imam* weddings, which had never lost their popularity among the Islamist segment of society, now take on new forms. A wide variety of bridal gowns with matching headscarves are designed according to the latest Islamist fashions and religious elements are grafted onto costly wedding ceremonies. Even those without an "Islamic" agenda are pursuing traditional values. The *modern* "henna nights" held in various locations – the most popular being the *hamam* – are the clearest illustration of this revivalist trend. The press runs stories of the henna nights of the rich and famous. Revisiting old customs has added a *new local meaning* to weddings that were rapidly losing their ritual value.

The *re-invention* of customs to suit contemporary norms can be evaluated on a wider scale as well. While globalizing capitalism circulates the same products and consumption patterns throughout world markets, it also generates local forms shaped by the same dynamics. Just as in the case of the global fast food chains that in Turkey offer *ayran* as well as coke, globalizing cultural practices assimilate the "traditional" to re-identify it. Another crucial dimension of this process is that just as capitalism turns values into merchandise, it presents merchandise as values; it stirs up desires but is incapable of providing lasting gratification. As John Berger puts it, images in advertisements and the media that continually aim to seduce are able to do so only by creating a sense of want in individuals. (Berger, 2005) The resulting state of unfulfilled desire both encourages violence and incites new quests for meaning. Attempting to find new significance in past customs, which appear removed from the current erosion of values in our society, is only another aspect of the escalation of desires. In the end, weddings are simply getting their share of these processes. They have become a pretext for showing off fame, wealth, the power derived from spending or misspending money, in short, the means to display every form of *excess*. And in each of these circumstances lies a clamorous manifestation of the collective search for new purpose.

Kına gecesi yapmayan yok

Son yıllarda yerini bekarlığa veda partilerine bırakan kına geceleri yeniden moda. En ünlüsünden en sadesine kadar artık herkes bu geleneği yaşatıyor

Sabah
24 July 2005

left: **No lack of henna nights:** *Henna nights are in again, after having been replaced by bachelor parties in the last few years. Everybody, famous or not, is reviving this tradition.*

below: **Weddings in five star hotels forge ahead:** *While many industrialists are making their personnel redundant, claiming that they are affected by the economic crisis due to the 5 April decisions, weddings worth billions continue to be hold in five star hotels.*

Beş yıldızlı otellerde düğünlere devam!

★ 5 Nisan ekonomik kararları dolayısıyla pek çok sanayici krize girdikleri iddiası ile personel çıkartma yoluna giderken, 5 yıldızlı otellerde yapılan milyarlık düğünler eski hızıyla sürüyor.

Pahalılık kimseyi etkilememiş

İstanbul'daki beş yıldızlı oteller arasında, 5 nisan ekonomik krizine rağmen son günlerde görülen rekabet artarken, düğün, sünnet, nişan ve mezuniyet törenleri de aynı hızla düzenlenmeye devam ediyor. Dolar bazındaki fiyatlar, bu büyük ve pahalı otellerde düğün yapanları hala etkilememiş görünüyor...

Günaydın
1 July 1994

right: **Competing with Mrs Özal's friends:** *The ladies of the Ege Apartment Block in Izmir organised an official marriage for the building caretakers Muzaffer and Meral, who were previously united in a religious ceremony only.*

below: **A modern Bridal Turkish Bath:** *The Bridal Turkish Bath, which is a kind of "bachelor party" for the girl-to-be-married, can be quite entertaining.*

Milliyet
24 October 1988

Akşam
9 July 2005

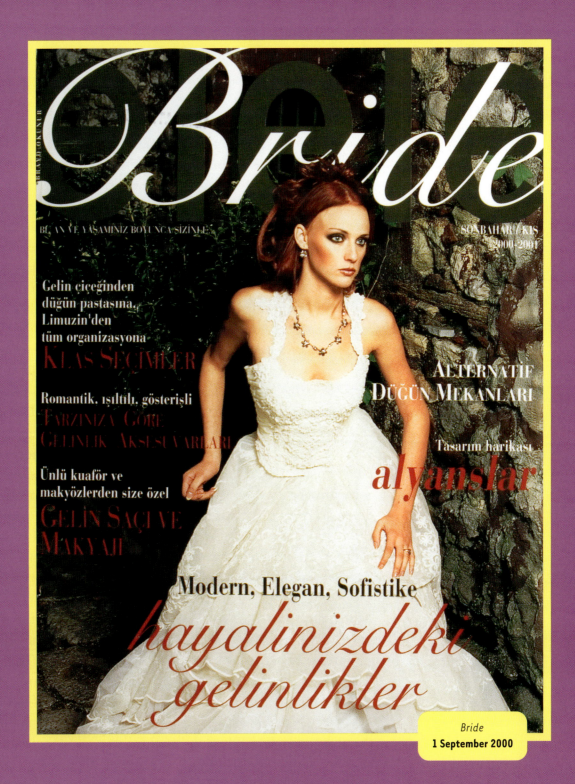

The wedding dresses of your dreams: *Modern, chique, sophisticated.*

A nation is partying!

"Now we disco just like they do in Europe," read the headline of a story on the once legendary Stüdyo 54, run by the magazine *Hey* in 1985. "Stüdyo 54 kids are delighted!" the story went on, "once they get Saturday night permission, they can disco the night away, safe under the watchful eye of the security guards..." By the time we reach 2003, the tone has changed: "How much does it cost?" queries one headline. And the article continues, "Revelers at Laila, one of Istanbul's hippest clubs, enjoy a night out in the spellbinding atmosphere of the Bosphorus. That is, if they can make it past the bouncers at the door who size up their clothes, looks and attitudes..." There are rather striking differences between these two articles on the "hot" spots of two distinct eras. First of all, the idiom of the 2000s is noticeably more self-assured and sophisticated in its terminology: "the *delighted kids* discoing *the night away, just like* their Western counterparts" has made way for "the *revelers* in one the city's *hippest clubs* enjoying *a night out* in the *spellbinding atmosphere of the Bosphorus*". Secondly, the emphasis is no longer on youth; Laila's trendy clientele covers every age category and obviously the younger crowd requires no permission to party. Finally, there is no need to wait for Saturday night to have fun anymore; "night out" can be any night of the week now.

At the same time, the feature on Laila is proof that in the 2000s only a privileged few get a taste of Istanbul's ultra-trendy nightlife. The article stresses the obstacles to enjoying a night at Laila. Clubs like these, reserved for an exclusive minority, have a highly selective door policy. Compared to the security staff of the 1980s discotheques that kept a "watchful eye" on kids dancing through the night, today's trendy clubs employ extremely competent, assertive and somewhat menacing doormen; they are professionals accustomed to judging a customer's "personality" from getup and attitude and deciding who will or will not get past the door. In more general terms, the differences in content and articulation of the Stüdyo 54 and Laila press coverage provide useful clues about

Hey — 25 March 1985

● BORA MERİÇ

"Burası müthiş bir yer. Arkadaşlarımla geldim. Bundan önce pek diskoteğe gitmezdim ama artık her hafta Stüdyo 54'e geleceğim. Öyle çok eğleniyorum ki..."

● ŞEHNAZ SAM

"Stüdyo 54, gerçekten süper bir diskotek. Müzik çok iyi. İçerisi rahat. Geçişler ve ışık düzeni müthiş. Kısacası tam bir Avrupai nitelikte Stüdyo 54."

● NADİ TURAN

"Stüdyo 54'ün en güzel yanı büyük olması... Herkes rahatça dans edebiliyor. İç düzenleme bir harika. Ses düzeni de olağanüstü."

"Stüdyo 54" gençliği konuşuyor:

"Artık Batılı yaşıtlarımız gibi eğleniyoruz..."

Stüdyo 54 gençliği mutlu... Artık ailelerine haber verip, hafta sonları Stüdyo 54'te soluğu alıyorlar... Koruma görevlisi ağabeylerinin sayesinde huzur içinde eğlenip, dansediyorlar...

"Enjoying ourselves like our Western contemporaries...": The youth of Stüdyo 54 are happy. On the weekends they inform their parents and they rush off to Stüdyo 54. Thanks to the friendly security, they enjoy themselves and dance in peace.

Lalia

Giriş Ücreti:	30 milyon (Yerli-Yabancı bir içki dahil)
İçki:	Yerli: 8 milyon Yabancı: 15 milyon

İstanbul'un gece alemi denildiğinde ilk akla gelen mekanlardan biri olan Laila'ya gidenler İstanbul Boğazı'nın büyülü atmosferinde keyifli bir gece geçiriyorlar. Ancak kapıdan girerken görevli beylere kılığınız, kıyafetiniz ve kişiliğinizle kendinizi mutlaka beğendirmeniz gerekiyor. Yoksa...

Bu eğlence kaça?

Laila ve Reina... İstanbul'un gece aleminde adları en çok geçen eğlence mekanları... Sizler için bu iki dev mekanı araştırdık. Ne yenir, ne içilir, nasıl eğlenilir ve HESAP NE GELİR?

Yarın
18 July 2003

Giriş Ücreti:	25 milyon (Bir içki dahil)
İçki:	Yerli: 8 milyon Yabancı: 15 milyon

Reina
Gecede 1000 kişiyi ağırlayabilen Reina'da hafta içi giriş ücreti alınmıyor. Yemeklerde Doluca ve Nevşehir şarapları ikram ediliyor konuklara.

The cost of entertainment: *Laila and Reina... The entertainment venues most referred to in the night world of Istanbul... We examined these two giant venues for you.*

the change in the conceptualization and practice of entertainment over the past decades in Turkey.

As we already pointed out, "partying" now includes all age groups and every night of the week, a clear indicator that the concept of "fun" has evolved. Nowadays, no matter what time of the day or day of the week, television channels bombard us with entertainment programs and images of people conspicuously enjoying themselves. One particularly striking example are the morning TV shows where members of the public spontaneously jump up to accompany the singer with a little belly dancing show of their own. Another is the large amount of coverage that the press gives to the entertainment issue: "Who was seen where," which new club is "totally hot," where to find the best "chill spots" and similar headlines frequently make front page news. We are continually fed stories about *celebrities* from the world of music, movies, television, fashion and business. With poverty rapidly rising and less money available for entertainment spending, why is there this exaggerated focus on having fun? What does this paradox tell us?

Although Turkey really began to "rock" in the 1990s, the first intimations of change came earlier. The Stüdyo 54 type *discotheques* that opened in most large cities were the earliest examples of entertainment spaces modeled on the West. In those years, new forms of music and dance hit the scene: *Heavy metal, lambada, reggae...* These were also the expansion times of *taverns*, music bars where "pianist-singers" performed. The best-selling tapes they later made were recorded with special conversation effects interspersed through the songs to recreate the *impression* of actually being in a tavern, making those listening to the tapes feel they were a part of the fun. When private TV channels emerged, the "live" entertainment effects were visual and broadcast to the entire nation. Under the tutelage of private channels, the traditional entertainment show format adopted by state television channels – which considered themselves the protectors of a "select" official culture – also began to change rapidly. Entertainment programs became available almost every day of the week. Live studio audiences, which had once clapped timidly during the entertainment shows of Cemile Kutgün – who

The time I passed in the night club wasn't like anything else I had experienced. The two glasses of gin I quikly downed probably played a role in this. Again, it could have been because of the drinks, but that music which I always found unbearable, was having a numbing effect on me this time. We were sitting close to the stage. People were dancing nearby. Among the crowd I caught glimpses of Deniz and Adnan from time to time. They kept repeating the same movements, without touching each other. Their slim bodies kept appearing and disappearing. I too wasn't feeling bad. It was as if everything had quietened down in my head. The noise had disappeared, the grand convention had ended. The leather armchairs were comfortable and being amongst all these people, but in a kind of distant numbness, had relaxed me. I lifted my empty glass towards the waiter and the smart boy noticed me immediately, in spite of the crowd. My drink was refreshened immediately.
[Cahide Birgül, *Gölgeler Çekildiğinde*, Aralık 2002, Türkiye İş Bankası Kültür Publications, p. 73]

Examples of music tapes of the taverna type

Çılgın geceler

Son dönemlerde İstanbul'da sayıları büyük bir hızla artmaya başlayan barlar, müşteri çekebilmek için çılgın partiler düzenlemeye başladı. İstanbul'un çılgın eğlence yerlerinden Moda'daki Time Club, her geçen gün çılgın eğlencelerine bir yenisini daha ekliyor.

Tersine dünya
Moda'daki Time Clup, geçtiğimiz günlerde "Tersine dünya" adlı çılgın ve uçuk bir parti düzenledi. Bu partiye katılan erkekler kadın, kadınlar ise erkek kılığına büründü...

Günaydın
7 July 1994

Tempo
11 March 2004

TÜRKİYE YIKILIYOR!

above: **Wild nights:** *Having increased greatly in number especially in recent times, bars have started to organise wild parties in order to attract customers.*

below: **Turkey is totally awesome!**

Kim nereye gidiyor?

İstanbul özellikle hafta sonları gece yaşamında hızlı bir trafiğe sahne oluyor. Meyhanesinden farklı müziklerin çaldığı gece kulüplerine kadar her mekanın ünlü müdavimleri var.

Milliyet
31 October 1999

Kadınlar matinesi Aydın'la YIKILIYOR

Akşam
23 March 2005

above: **Who is going where?** *Especially on weekends, Istanbul is scene to a busy night life. From tavernas to night clubs playing various types of music, every venue has their own regular customers.*

right: **Aydın rocks the women's matinee:** *The women's matinee, one of the most important elements of the "gazino" culture, has been revived...*

The audience enjoying itself with İbrahim Tatlıses' songs during an entertainment show on the new year's eve of 1991 [TRT, 31 December 1991]

hosted TRT's primetime Saturday music programs -- flocked to the stage to sing and dance with their favorite pop star or *türkü* [Turkish folk] singer. This form of "live show" soon became an unchanging feature of entertainment TV. Meanwhile, *having fun*, in its various forms, with all the *excesses* that this activity implied, became a *collectively shared desire*. Partying, watching others doing so on TV, or reading about them in the press became a normal way to "enjoy life" and "de-stress." In fact, not conforming to these general summons to "have fun" would have been considered "strange."

In addition to the simulated live performances provided by tapes or TV shows, for those who had the means, the growing number of entertainment spaces was another option. The last 15 to 20 years have witnessed a boom both in the number and diversity of new music night spots and similar venues, especially in the larger cities. Istanbul, for example, now has a wide variety of bars, music clubs or nightclubs offering *fasıl* [classical Turkish music], *Turkish pop*, *world music*, *türkü*, *hip hop*, *rock*, *club*, *jazz*, or *reggae*, to name only a few. Today, music clubs occupy central points on Istanbul's consumption map. The large, mainly "Turkish pop"-oriented nightclubs located on the shores of the Bosphorus or in affluent neighborhoods like Etiler and Levent get frequent media coverage which only adds to their appeal. Popularized through TV entertainment programs, the tabloids, and the magazine, or arts and culture supplements of dailies, these leisure spaces contribute to the visibility of certain districts and render them identifiable with specific segments of society. Private radio stations and advertisements make them directly accessible to a much larger portion of the population. As a result, they become directly linked to the functioning of a wide-ranging culture industry.

The neon sticks distributed at the entrance to night clubs

The entrance bracelet for RockIstanbul, a music festival with camping facilities

While Istanbul resonates to *local rhythms*, it also becomes integrated with *global cultural capital*; certain live music bars and clubs in Beyoğlu invest in costly *world-scale events* to draw leading musicians, bands and exponents of different music trends to their own venues. At first, large corporations began to sponsor these activities. The financial support of companies, banks and newspapers to the concerts, festivals and music performances held in these clubs gave even more impetus to the *industrialization* of

Tan
3 January 1990

KENDİLERİNDEN GEÇTİLER Samimi bir dans. Alkol sınırının belli bir noktasına gelmişler... Kendilerinden geçmiş bir halde, "lambada" yapıyorlar...

FIKIR FIKIR Pistte, birbirlerine kenetlenmiş bir çift. Coşkuyla "lambada" yapıyorlar. Kanları kaynıyor besbelli. Bunda, yeni yıl mutluluğu da var kuşkusuz...

Herkes, yeni dansı yapmaya çalışıyor...

"Lambada"cılar

■ Tüm dünya gençliğini etkisi altına alan "lambada", yılbaşı gecesinin gözde dansı oldu. 1990'ı, çeşitli eğlence yerlerinde karşılayanlar, adeta bir "lambada" yarışı içine girdiler.

■ Bazı açıkgöz çapkınların "lambada" teklifleri, bazı bayanlar tarafından reddedildi. Bunun gerekçesi de, "Dans etmek bahanesiyle, yakın olup, faydalanma düşüncesi"ydi...

Günaydın
25 November 1984

Heavy Metalci kızlar Ömür ve Sevgi...

"Heavy Metalcileri" görmek için İstanbul'a kaçtılar

above: **Doing the "lambada":** *The "lambada" which has influenced young people all over the world, was the favourite dance of New Year's Eve.*

left: **They ran away to Istanbul to see heavy metal bands:** *2 girls, fans of Heavy Metal, have made a habit of running away from home; they were caught wondering the streets of Istanbul by police making routine identity controls.*

The European Istanbul:
Our night life has reached a level where it can compete with world famous centres.

Hürriyet
5 January 1992

Casting their anchors in the Bosphorus: *The tavernas on the Bosphorus have been taking on the weight of the entertainment world for many years. The pianist/singers, who verify the mindset of the customers within the entertainment chain extending from Tarabya to Kuruçeşme, are much admired.*

Sabah
5 December 1991

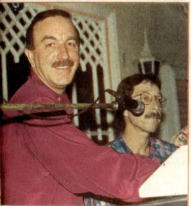

Like every night, tonight too Beyoğlu had become like a river of people, churning in its depths. So I let myself flow with the churning of the river, till I reached the Balo Street. Finding Baraka wasn't difficult at all. It was on the second floor of a majestic building at least one hundred years old, constructed by god knows which Italian architect, facing the street on a little island formed by the buildings wedged between the long Balo Street, which opened out on to Tarlabaşı and the short Solakzade Street. I ignored the antiquated lift for two and started climbing the wide marble staircase. I sort of heard faint sounds of jazz, but a mixture of folk songs and halay music suddenly overpowered everything. When I reached the floor where it said Baraka, I stopped in front of the door. The noise coming from the upper floor hadn't stopped but now I could hear the sounds of jazz again.

[Ahmet Ümit, *Beyoğlu Rapsodisi*, 2005, Doğan Publications, p. 96]

Red Bull brand energy drink, distributed as promotion at techno parties, the sale of which was forbidden at one point

entertainment. Live music spots began to enjoy the benefits of the strong relationship between capital and culture already apparent in such varied fields as literature, painting, photography and film. As capital increased its investments in leisure, an assortment of new night spots opened in close succession, driving the entertainment industry into accelerated growth. The sector has diversified not only into genres but into cultural segments. For instance, Beyoğlu – which has emerged in recent years as one of the most vibrant neighborhoods of the city's entertainment and cultural scene – perfectly illustrates this diversity. With its *pavyons* [cheap local nightclubs] and *türkü bars* sharing space with *after-hour clubs*, *performance centers*, *lounge bars*, and *underground clubs*, Beyoğlu has become a melting pot of seemingly conflicting cultures. The "dark" and more mysterious side of entertainment attracts its followers just as much as the chic, glitzy side does. The city is rewriting its cultural map to embrace every clash and paradox; party time in Istanbul – with every kind of song and dance, be it jazz, *türkü*, strutting to cutting-edge beats, belly dancing or linking hands for the halay [an Anatolian circle dance] – is *defining new boundaries* and *breaking others*.

Despite the media's exploitation of every *excess* and the buzz they generate in the public sphere, these venues nonetheless cater to a somewhat small portion of the urban population. However disparate their "identities" and customer profile, in the end it's always "money talks." The issue thus carries a very definite class dimension both in terms of economics and culture. Clothing – especially designer wear – or luxury cars can be *passports* to get in most of these places. This has created private *pleasure communities* isolated from the *rest of the world* behind the *closed doors* of exclusive clubs. But finally, these selective venues only further goad the desire for entertainment. And, once again, the media is here, serving up juicy celebrity news, gossip and scandals. As people increasingly aspire toward a captivating lifestyle defined by the wild and *unreserved* drive for pleasure, the *conflict* between desire and means grows even fiercer. What is more, while this general craving for amusement takes shape, it generates new perceptions of Istanbul as a model for urban living and the entertainment capital of Turkey. Alongside the urban landscape, the term "nation" is also redefined in terms of entertainment. For

Tempo
1 July 1998

The party-goers' summer route: *Now that the weather has warmed up and the summer is making itself felt, the centre of the night life has moved from the Nispetiye Street in Etiler to the Ortaköy - Kuruçeşme area.*

Milliyet
25 August 2001

above: **Entertainment bugs:** *Among the work they have realised there is a party attended by 5,000 people and a magazine with a circulation of 10,000. Urban Bug has already become a spokesman for urban people looking for alternative entertainment.*

right: **The official drink of this festival is ayran!** *Everything is fine in the "Rock to Peace Festival." Every kind of cola is forbidden at the festival, where many anti-globalisation groups have opened stands. The official drinks of the festival, which takes place in Sarıyer, are ayran, fruit juice and water.*

Radikal
7 September 2003

right: **High society tavernas:** Once there were traditional tavernas. Now there are also high society tavernas, where the entertainment consists of lots of belly dancing, popular music and little food.

below: **On the threshold of entertainment:** For reasons of work only, we have examined the chaos right outside entertainment venues such as Laila and Reina. And we saw that the outside is a real sight and several times more entertaining than the inside.

Milliyet
24 October 1999

Hürriyet
3 August 2002

On crowded nights time passes faster. I don't even notice when it becomes morning. When Osman plays the songs I like, and he knows what happens if he doesn't, I get up and dance. I never dance for two songs in a row. Otherwise I sweat and my clothes become a mess. I like one song at a time.

Be it trendy or not, he plays for me the Weather Girls' 'It's raining men', Eartha Kitt's 'Where is my man', 'Sleepless every night" the way Ajda Pekkan first sang it and sometimes 'Somebody completely different", and definitely a Grace Jones or RuPaul. I also dance if I like some of the latest hits.

The girls and also our clients use the dance floor as place for show off. Anybody who wants to exhibit themselves goes onto the floor and starts doing their best. If they get along with Osman, he will even turn a spotlight on them. And the show begins. [Mehmet Murat Somer, *Peygamber Cinayetleri*, 2003, İletişim Publications, p. 28]

Doll which sings and dances on the sound of clapping

instance, the expression "a nation is partying," simultaneously implies concern over the excesses of entertainment and authenticates the image of a nation partying. Furthermore, the evoked image conveniently overlooks the class dimension of late-night revelry.

Zygmunt Bauman uses the concept of *neo-tribalism* to define the new identity politics which have emerged in the postmodern world (1991: 248-9). This term refers to the insistent and often obsessive quest of individuals to either join an existing community or create one. Bauman claims that these *new tribes* chiefly strive to forge an identity around various concepts. These identities, however, are typically fleeting and fluid. Tribes express the symbolic characteristics that unite their members, and are also sustained by them. Consequently, they exert a *magnetic pull* towards both their members and the rest of society. These groupings provide an avenue for the affirmation of individual identity and at the same time serve to channel various desires. But the instant their magnetic force ebbs, they disband. The "pleasure communities" mentioned earlier may be considered neo-tribal groupings. These communities also offer their members a distinctive identity that is at the same time extremely ephemeral. They only exist from one night to the other, from festival to festival, from program to program. You may see them at a concert applauding an international jazz artist; next, they are exuberantly dancing in a night club while they listen to the songs of Ajda Pekkan or Orhan Gencebay. The diversity of the messages that these "pleasure communities" convey to *those outside* is as significant as their self-containing aspect. This fluidity spurs a still more universal search for pleasure. Enjoyment emerges as an ideal that can be pursued and attained. As the desire for "fun" becomes a generalized social concern, it brings with it the anxiety and fear of remaining on the outside while "a nation is partying." The issue of achieved or elusive enjoyment harbors traces of violence that we accept as a normal part of our imagery of pleasure and take in as just *another form of entertainment.*

Alternatif bir eğlence

● Cihangir'de çok yönlü bir şekilde hizmet veren Bilsak'ın en üst katında farklı bir dünya var. African Bar'da haftanın dört günü reggae ağırlıklı müzik yapılıyor. Açık olduğu diğer iki günde ise yani çarşamba ve perşembe günleri, Erkin Koray sahneye çıkıyor. Sevilen şarkılarını söyleyen Erkin Baba, hem coşuyor hem coşturuyor. African Bar'ın işletmecisi de İstanbul'da yaşayan bir Afrikalı öğrenci...

● Başta Bob Marley olmak üzere, Rasta akımını destekleyen ünlülerin posterleriyle süslenen duvarlar arasında alternatif bir eğlence biçimi var. Dileyen kafa sallıyor, dileyen göbek atıyor. Fiyatlarını da öğrencilerin gelebileceği şekilde ayarlayan Bilsak African Bar, özellikle Erkin Koray'ın sahneye çıktığı gecelerde tıka basa dolu oluyor.

Özgür ortam
Bilsak African Bar'ın müşterileri de çok özel. Üniversiteli Aslı Gürsoy, İlknur Gürsoy ve Kurtuluş Yağmurdereli tüm şarkılarını ezbere bildikleri Erkin Koray'ı dinlemeye birlikte gelmişler. Üç kızın rahatsız edilmeden, diledikleri gibi eğlenebilecekleri bir yer African Bar...

Dans etmek serbest
Sema, Ayla ve Gonca, Erkin Koray'lı bir African Bar gecesinde doyasıya eğleniyorlar. Oturduğu yerde eğlenmek yerine piste fırlayan üç genç kız, hem Erkin Baba'ya şarkılarında eşlik ettiler hem de doyasıya dans ettiler. Başkalarını rahatsız etmedikçe her türlü eğlence anlayışına gösterilen African Bar'ın belki de bu kadar ilgi görmesinin sebebi bu...

Hürriyet
17 February 1992

İşletmeci Afrikalı Osman
İstanbul'a öğrenci olarak gelen, kentimizde yaşayan Afrikalı öğrencilerle Türk öğrencileri kaynaştırmak için African Bar'ı açan Osman, yarattığı ortamla övünüyor. Osman'ın en büyük yardımcıları ise personelinden Bahadır, Emre ve Serhan...

Erkin Baba'dan baba şarkılar
Gitarı ve öve öve bitiremediği synthesizer'ıyla sahneye çıkan Erkin Koray, "Şaşkın", "Fesüphanallah", "Çöpçüler" gibi sadece bir kuşağa değil, kuşaklara mal olmuş şarkılarını seslendiriyor. Eski hayranları babayı yalnız bırakmıyorlar ama çoğunluk her zaman gençlerde oluyor.

Alternative entertainment

Yeni Gündem
25 October 1987

above: **Beyoğlu is a blood bath:** *Nights which end either in a police station or in a hospital.*

top right: **The worship of the techno computer generation!** *The dance of techno music, "robot".*

bottom right: **A nation which enjoys itself has a right to independence!...** *Beyoğlu now is hosting not only its regular customers but also celebrities from all over the country.*

Aktüel — **3 December 1992**

90'LARIN GENÇLİĞİ "SIFIR İLETKEN" BİR MÜZİKLE DÜNYADAN KOPUYOR

Techno
Computer kuşağı ayinde!

- Techno müziğin dansı, "robot." Dakikada 160 vuruşa ulaşan bir ritm ve buna uyarlanmış bir ışık düzeneği, dansedenler arasındaki her türlü iletişimi önlüyor. Herkes kalabalık içinde yapayalnız.
- Techno, anti-nostaljik bir müzik. Bütün eski klasik parçalar, DJ'ler tarafından techno'laştırılıyor. İnsan sesi çok az. aradabir şöyle sözler tekrarlanıyor: "Who is Elvis?"
- Techno, bütünüyle "yapma" bir müzik. DJ'ler tarafından mixer, kayıt cihazı ve ritm box'lar kullanılarak yaratılıyor. Yeni müzik starları artık DJ'ler, enstrümanlar ise makinalar.
- Techno çalarken duyulan elektronik efektler, kozmik gürültüler, bu müziğe değen herkesi yaşanan dünyadan "koparıyor."

Hakkıdır eğlenen milletimin İstiklal!

ETİLER "SAKİNLERİ" BİLE EĞLENCENİN ROTASINI BEYOĞLU'NA ÇEVİRDİ

Aktüel — **22 February 2001**

Safran ve Chan'ga ile başlayan değişim zirvede. Beyoğlu artık eski müdavimlerinin yanı sıra memleketin tüm ünlülerini ağırlıyor. "Bobo" dediğimiz bohem - burjuvalar da, tencere - tava çalanlar da İstiklal Caddesi'nde. İşte Beyoğlu'nun en yeni ve "in" mekânları...

Are evolving and continually improving technologies really making the world smaller? Do we now live in an age of communication where everyone can be instantly in touch with everyone else, and new ideas, trends and developments are rapidly disseminated throughout the world? In the early 1960s, McLuhan had claimed that electronic media (TV) would turn the world into a "global village." Today, digital technologies like the internet and cell phones have taken communication much further. Despite all these developments, it is clear that communication cannot be viewed independently from global economic processes. In a world where a new regime of capital accumulation is re-shaping the economy; intra- and inter-country income

inequalities are increasing rapidly,
and culture is merging with capital,
communication serves to divide and fragment
as much as it unites. While some are able to
connect, others are excluded. The topics
we look at in this section, television,
communication technologies, and issues
connected with the internationalization of
coffeehouses and urban transformation
provide important clues to the examination
of synchronized "globality."

connecting people!

Television watches the world for you

A regulator for black and white television sets

The television, which today has become one of the most important instruments in our relationship with the *world* and occupies a central position in the life of a great many people, entered Turkey relatively late. The state-run Turkish Radio and Television (TRT) station started broadcasting in the 1970s and began full-day broadcasting in 1984. During those same years the first color TVs appeared on the market, so there was no longer any need to place colored panels in front of black and white television screens to add color to them. Television met with great interest from the day it first entered the market and continues to do so today. How should we interpret its widespread acceptance in so short a time? Where does television, which in our age is equated with the term "media" and considered both an instrument of modernization and of corruption and degeneration, get this great strength?

… With the arrival of televisions, especially in smaller towns, the slow rhythm of life changed, old habits were abandoned. Gardens were deserted in the summer. There was a smaller number of people sitting in tea gardens and eating ice cream. The evening gatherings which made winter nights so much more pleasant were given up, the playing cards which were brought out when neighbours came together were left in drawers, cinemas closed down, girls started to do their embroidery during the day and fathers read their papers in the office. The changing images on a black and white screen started to determine a lifestyle which was slow but which had a flavour of its own.
[Ayfer Tunç, *Bir Maniniz Yoksa Annemler Size Gelecek*, 2004, Yapı Kredi Publications, p. 85]

In a way, it can be said that television replaced the radio. The chief feature of the radio, which could fit an entire "world" into a little box and transport it into homes, rooms and even – if it was carried by hand – right to the very person, was that it could create visual imagery through sounds. People could only make the atmosphere created by sound come alive through their imagination. Sometimes, as in the broadcasting of sporting events like football matches, the host had to possess special skills enabling him to carry on a rapid running commentary and analysis of the game and convey it to listeners. Nevertheless, the radio was a "blind" medium, which set the imagination free to a certain extent. Television, on the other hand, brought "reality" to the imaginary visual. In addition to hearing voices, it was now possible to see what was being told. The reality designed through television also gave the rational world another form. In modern societies, sight has pushed other senses into the background and come to the fore; that sight produces both *vision* and a *regime of surveillance* has often been discussed.

left: **Full day television broadcasting from the new year onwards:** *The "Women's World" programme broadcast two days a week will be broadcast every day. Then a new programme entitled "In The Afternoon" will go on air.*

below: **The most economical world tour:** *Sit back in your armchair and relax. We are going on a world tour! With Telefunken.*

Günaydın
31 January 1984

November 1987

November 1984

To buy a colour TV,
count till 12

As for television, it has created an order of *seeing* and *being seen* all of its own.

The extent to which TRT, Turkey's first TV broadcaster and, as we noted above, a state-run institution, was able to maintain its *autonomy* was always a subject open for debate. The first TRT legislation passed in 1964 defined the institution as an "autonomous public entity," but after the military coup of March 12, 1971, the clause on autonomy was annulled and replaced by "impartial public entity." According to Gülizar, this would render television "dependent on political power" (1995: 48). From then on, the government very strictly controlled what could or could not be shown on television. Furthermore, the appointment of TRT's general director was always an area of potential dispute. News bulletins presenting "the day's current events," were among the TV programs that showed this dependence on *political power* most clearly. But news programs were also presented with a backdrop and general atmosphere meant to convey *neutrality* and *objectivity*. A dramatically realistic effect was deliberately sought with the introductory music, the world map in the background and the presenter's serious bearing, voice and elocution. In those days, news related to activists of the opposition youth and people's movements, which had emerged in the 1970s and after the 1980 coup, invariably figured on the program. News bulletins always reported the executions, raids on "safe houses" and "capture of dead militants" (presumably killed in the struggle.) Programs also included extensive reports on the speeches, various activities and "contacts abroad" of political leaders – or rather of the generals who had seized power. In this sense, television news programs can be said to have constituted an effective area for open *political propaganda*. But the impact of news bulletins went beyond the open bias generated by propaganda. The "realism" of these programs was always deliberately scripted to provoke *fear* and *anxiety* and create in viewers the conviction that the world was a very unsafe place to be. Accordingly, the programs gave wide coverage not only to alarming political threats but also to epidemic outbreaks, terrible natural catastrophes, and gory traffic accidents, which increased unease as well. As a result, having brought "the world" to people's homes, television became a tool for them to *withdraw from* and *avoid* actual contact with the exterior world.

> ...sometimes, when I'm watching TV, when I'm watching certain programmes in particular, especially the news bulletins, I think that one day the TV and all the programmes it contains will stretch and stretch and the minute I press one of the buttons of the remote control it will either explode or go crazy, that it will create a visual hurricane which will take us all within, that it will burn and destroy everything, that it will first gobble up and then blow up everything. [Metin Üstündağ, "televizyondan korkuyorum", *imza: bir dost*, 1998, Parantez Publications, p. 44]

Cumhuriyet
5 July 1984

below: **Two epidemics of 1980: "Petroil" and Dallas:** *While we sang as a nation the song of Petroil, which shot up to 38 dollars a barrel, to find solace, sister-in-law Christine finally shot JR and appeased us…*

Ses
3 January 1981

Evlerde ikinci TELEVİZYON DÖNEMİ

MUTFAKTA Ev hanımlarına büyük kolaylık. HÜRRİYET'in ikinci televizyonuyla mutfakta daha rahat daha keyifli çalışacaksınız. Eşiniz ve çocuklarınız için yemek yaparken, bir yandan da gözünüz izlemek istediğiniz dizilerde olacak.

- Televizyonlarda kanallar arttı, programlar zenginleşti, evlerde tartışmalar başladı. Çocuklar bir kanaldaki programı izlemek isterken, evin büyükleri başka bir kanalı takip etmek istiyor. Tabii bu, evlerde tartışmalara hatta kavgalara yol açıyor...

Hürriyet
9 January 1992

PRATİK TAŞINIR HÜRRİYET'in okurlarına armağanı ikinci televizyon çok pratik. İstediğiniz yere taşıyabilirsiniz. Anteni üstünde. İster spor yaparken izleyin, isterseniz dilediğiniz yere yerleştirin. Uzaktan kumandanızla ekran seçimini yapın ve keyfinize bakın...

- Bu duruma son vermenin yolu evlere ikinci televizyondan geçiyor. İsteyen aile ferdi, istediği televizyon kanalını izlesin ve tartışmalar son bulsun...
- İşte gazeteniz HÜRRİYET şimdi evlere huzur getiriyor ve 150 okuruna televizyon veriyor. İkinci televizyonunuz HÜRRİYET'ten. Hem de 14 kupona...

The era of second TVs at home: *The number of TV channels has increased, there is a richer variety of programmes, arguments have started in homes. While children want to watch one programme, adults want to watch another channel. And this results in arguments, and even fights.*

KAVGA BİTER Evlerde televizyonun izlenmesi bakımından geceler en hassas dönem. Evin erkeğinin maçı olur, evin hanımının ise dizisi... İkinci televizyonunuz bu kavgaları sona erdirecek. İsteyen istediği kanalı izlerken evinizde huzur rüzgârları esecek.

Kaçırmayın... İlk kupon yarın...

The insulating effect of television is in itself a separate topic for discussion. By replacing visits with neighbors, communal fun, and the informal networks of communication and information that used to link people, the advent of television produced a new *public sphere*. Watching TV alone or, as was quite common when television broadcasting first began, with friends and neighbors, engenders a feeling of *togetherness*. In particular, the opportunity that TV provided of experiencing national and world events in real time played an important part in the emergence of *national civic* consciousness. For instance, the inauguration of the Bosphorus bridge in 1973, which drew huge crowds of people, was broadcast live both in Turkey and, through Eurovision, in Europe. In later years, the live transmission of events as diverse as the funeral ceremonies of politicians, football matches or Eurovision song contests continued to present occasions for shared excitement and sentiments. By the 1990s, V had started to give live news coverage of wars, creating the impression that a powerful connection existed with places outside Turkey and that the world had really gotten smaller. At the same time, it gave rise to the notion that reality on television was increasingly altered but that any reality outside of it was also losing credibility. It was to this simulation of reality that French philosopher Baudrillard alluded in his highly controversial formulation: "The Gulf War did not take place."

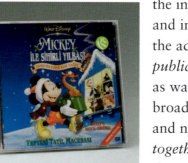

Mickey and Barbie animated film DVDs

... He turns on the TV; it is set to the video channel, the screen is still black. He sits in the armchair on the left. He is undecided as to put his feet up or not... undecided... He holds the remote control from a distance in a way that it can see the machine and he presses the PLAY button. The light emanating from the TV suddenly spreads to the whole sitting room.
[Yekta Kopan, *İçimde Kim Var*, 2004, Can Publications, p. 31]

VCR head cleaner

After the 1980s, television stations in Turkey started diversifying; a number of private stations opened successively, and with the addition of satellite and cable TV, television became an even more forceful communication medium. But this also modified in great part the relation that had been established with that medium. As both national and foreign TV stations increased in number and variety, zapping between channels became standard practice and brought with it the inevitable bickering over who held the remote and thus "controlled" programming; thus, watching television now led to *disputes*. Previously identified with the state and the nation, television now found expression in an expanding market. For some, this was a sign of pluralism and democratization. Certain

Çanak antenler pıtırak gibi çoğalırken, televizyona ilgi azalıyor

UYDU YAYINLARI TRT'Yİ UNUTTURDU

TRT göstereceği filmler üzerindeki denetimine istediği kadar özen göstersin, uydu yayınlar aracılığıyla porno filmler ve en sakıncalı yayınlar bile pek çok evde rahatlıkla izleniyor

Milliyet
15 May 1988

left: **Satellite broadcasts outshine TRT:** *While satellite dishes keep sprouting like mushrooms, interest in TV programmes is declining.*

below: **TVs become more of a problem every day:** *TVs are a cause of fights between husbands and wives. Watching TV continuosly makes one absentminded...*

bottom: **Remote-control maniacs!** *Series, films and programmes clash. TV viewers that miss one programme while watching another are dismayed.*

Günaydın
29 January 1980

UZMANLAR AÇIKLADI:

Televizyon her geçen gün biraz daha sorun oluyor

★ KARI KOCA ARASINDA TARTIŞMALARA NEDEN OLUYOR
★ SÜREKLİ TV SEYRETMEK İNSANI DALGIN YAPIYOR
★ TELEVİZYON KARŞISINDA SÜREKLİ OTURMAK AŞIRI ŞİŞMANLIĞA YOL AÇIYOR

Sabah
18 September 2004

Kumanda manyağı olduk!

Dizilerin, filmlerin, programların saatleri çakışıyor. Birini izlerken, diğerini kaçıran TV izleyicileri bunalımda.

TV izlemede şampiyonuz

Televizyon izlemede Türkiye, Avrupa'da birinciliği kimseye kaptırmadı. Dünya sıralamasında ise ABD'den sonra ikinci olduk.

Hürriyet
23 May 1996

left: **We are champions in TV viewing:** *Turkey comes first in Europe in TV viewing. In the world grading we come second, after the USA.*

below: **She cried for her TV:** *Selin Tunç, who was taken to court for her debts and whose furniture was confiscated, said in tears: "Take everything, but leave me my television."*

"Gitti can yoldaşım" dedi

Televizyonu için ağladı!

■ Borçları yüzünden icraya verilen ve eşyalarına el konulan Selin Tunç "Her şeyimi alın. Ama televizyonumu bana bırakın" diyerek gözyaşı döktü

"Cana gelmesin, mala gelsin"
Selin Hanım'ı teselli etmeye çalışan komşuları "Üzülme kardeş. Biz de ölü var sandık. Cana gelmesin mala gelsin" deyince, genç kadın "Size göre hava hoş. Giden sizin televizyonunuz değil ki?" diyerek ağlamaya devam etti.

Bugün
6 May 1990

musics, performers and controversial topics, which had formerly been *prohibited* – supposedly to protect the public's morals – under the monopoly of state-controlled programming, could now be viewed on screen. The ensuing *relentless competition* between the various channels to draw more viewers led, on the one hand, to the search for increasingly sensationalist and supposedly *innovative* material, and on the other – in order to minimize the risks – to programs which still addressed the most *conventional* emotions. This multiple aspect of programming in the 1990s and the 2000s – the reality shows and violent debates; the emphasis on sex and entertainment; the focus on "delicate" topics like poverty, conflicted identities, and private lives, which public television had always avoided, and their complacent "scrutiny" on screen – can be considered the product of the search for attention-grabbing subject matter.

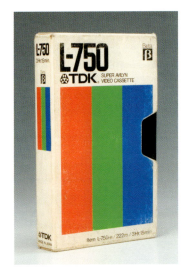

TDK L-750 Beta video tape

Raymond Williams, one of the pioneers in the field of cultural nd media studies, mentions two key features of television and the visual order it imposes. One is the logic of "planned flow." Williams suggests that since no TV program in itself holds any real significance, programming strategies are aimed at creating a continual flow of different programs. The crucial role of *sound* in this process is the second key feature of television transmission; it is an essential part of the hook for in-home TV viewing. Television broadcasting in Turkey after the 1990s unquestionably corroborates William's reasoning. The continuous flow from one program to the next includes frequent reminders and information about subsequent programs, advertised either as headlines crawling across the bottom of the screen or proclaimed loudly with "next on..." or similar phrases. This immediately carries the meaning of the various programs, whatever their content, to another level. In the logic of the flow, general structure is more relevant than actual subject matter. Frequent commercial breaks demonstrate the dependence of contemporary television on advertising. Commercials interrupt programs, but programs are instrumental for advertising. As indicators of the competition between channels, ratings are in fact messages to advertisers; the most watched channels or programs would draw the most advertising. In this sense, *advertisers* become *spokesmen* for the viewers.

Beta video tape rewinder

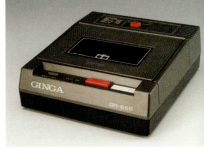

- The bitch is riveted to the TV news again... Like the contestants wearing headphones in the Turnstile Contest, she just sez yes or no, without understanding what I am saying... Girl, listen to yer mother, I'm telling ya something, ya think I'm just an old fart?

- No...

- Ya bitch... Watch the news carefully, cause yer going to save the world... As if it's up to ya... She still isn't listening... I hope rocks as big as TVs, no, I hope a communication satellite falls onto yer head...

- God, mother, why are you bugging me... This is the age of information... Of course I'm going to watch the news... Both the world and our country are in such a mess... Do I have to watch those idotic contests like you do, or The Young and the Restless...

- I'll impale ya with a number three knitting needle! So what's wrong with those contests and things? If they'd called ya you'd jump for joy and run... Ya little leftist...

[Atilla Atalay, "Sıdıka'nın İletişimi...", *Sıdıka: Öpücük Balığı; Fabrıga*, 1997, İletişim Publications, p. 51-52]

From the 1990s on, TV news programs also get their share of media marketing and sensationalism. The main aim of news stories now is to grab the attention of the viewers rather than appear objective. World news, in particular, is delivered in a package format on global news networks, turning it into just another merchandise. The credibility of television news derives not from its objectivity but from the sentimental bond and especially the feeling of trust established with the people delivering it. TV anchormen, who form the link between television viewers and the world, have become the personalities driving news programs and are frequently transferred from one station to another for huge sums. They filter world events and it is their interpretation that gives the events meaning for audiences. This has made television viewers even more *passive*; television is no longer a window to the world but a medium where viewers watch what TV sees for them. But at the same time, these images on the screen gradually become the viewer's life. And this in turn has political implications, which have led to major debates.

This tendency for television to be "life-like" becomes particularly salient in the 2000s, when TV actually begins to replace real life. Reality TV shows like *Biri Bizi Gözetliyor* [the Turkish *Big Brother*, literally "Someone is Watching Us"], which bring the private (!) lives of people to the screen, are the most astounding examples of the new voyeuristic trend in the medium. Meanwhile, popular weekly series have dramatically increased in number and captivate wide audiences by providing them with a means to escape into fantasy lives, histories and locations. The increase in Turkish series set in the East simultaneously creates an *Eastern* imagery people can relate to and shifts the focus away from past conflicts in the region. The chief characteristic of episodic series, of course, is that they break the well-defined beginning and end format of feature films, thereby creating a continuous narrative. This brings them closer to real life and viewers tune in out of curiosity and a sense of *identification* with the protagonists. Erecting a monument at the filming location of *Asmalı Konak* [The Porticoed Mansion], one of the most popular Turkish series of recent years, or placing an obituary in the newspaper when a character from the series dies, vividly indicates the extent to which the boundaries between fiction and reality have become *blurred*.

MODERN ZEHİR
TELEVİZYON

● Televizyon günlük yaşamımızın vazgeçilmezleri arasında. Sosyal ilişkilerinden uzaklaşarak, onsuz vakit geçiremez hale gelen çağdaş insan, uydu kanalları sayesinde Dünya'nın dört bir köşesiyle iletişime geçtikçe beyaz ekranın tiryakisi haline geldi. Ancak bazı uzmanlar, televizyonun yararlarından çok zararları olduğuna dikkatleri çekip, televizyonu modern bir zehir olarak tanımlıyorlar.

left: **The modern poison-television:** *Television has become an indispensable part of our daily lives.*

below: **Mummy, on TV it's not the storks that bring the babies:** *The films of sexual content, not suitable to children or even teenagers, broadcast by private TV channels early during the day in order to attract more viewers are meeting with severe reactions.*

Hürriyet
3 February 1994

Cinsel içerikli filmlerin erken saatlere yayılması uzmanlara göre son derece tehlikeli

"Anne, televizyonda bebekleri leylekler getirmiyor!"

✗ Özel kanalların daha çok izleyici toplama uğruna özellikle çocukların ve hatta gençlerin seyretmemesi gereken cinsel içerikli filmleri erken saatlerde yayınlamaları tepkiyle karşılanıyor. Ruh sağlığı uzmanları bu tip yayınların cinsel sorunları ve şiddeti artıracağını söylüyorlar.

Yeni Günaydın
22 August 1992

HERKES YAŞININ PROGRAMINI İZLEMELİ- Uzmanlar çocukların izlemesi gereken programların kesinlikle onlara hitap eden filmler olması gerektiğini söylüyorlar. Ne var ki özel kanallar sayesinde bu kural yıkılmaya başladı.

Today locally-made series have taken over the primetime slot which in the 1980s was occupied mostly by American imports – a fact that no doubt enhances their realistic impact. A new kind of public is being created that discovers its country's regions and problems – and the sentiments they inspire – through popular series. The nationalistic feelings thus disseminated produce an imagery that brings people from all backgrounds closer. At the same time, landing a part in a TV series is now high up on the list of dream jobs. Simply watching television is no longer enough, the desire to be *a part of it* is also growing. The decade of 2000 is characterized by hopefuls forming long lines to audition for parts in TV series or contests and busloads of people (mostly women) being carted to the studios every day to attend free tapings of morning shows.

Do not forget to turn off your TV: The warning message that used to appear at the end of the daily programming before TRT began to broadcast 24 hours a day in 1984.

As television becomes the mirror in which society watches itself, it emerges both as a powerful *object of desire* and a significant *threat*. Its harmful effects on morality, family life and children have been at the center of countless discussions and publications. Regardless of *generalizations* on the impact of television and the characteristics of viewers, it is extremely difficult to determine how TV programs are actually watched and interpreted by different social segments. In a society where television has invaded every aspect of life, has *taken over life* in fact, it may be time to remember "to turn off your TV."

Akşam
5 March 2005

left: **Tülin becomes a TV star:** *Tülin, who became famous after the contest programme "We're Getting Married" began her acting career in a new TV series.*

below: **Queueing up for fame:** *There was chaos in Bostancı for the Istanbul finals of the Türkstar programme, which has broken audience and participation records.*

Tempo
4 March 2004

above: **Aunty Adile is back:** Adile Naşit, who would send her little "lambs" to bed with the stories she narrated on TV, will be back on the screens thanks to computer animation.

right: **The "Asmalı Konak" series is now immortal:** The Ürgüp Municipality has erected a giant statue in honour of the Asmalı Konak series that made a major contribution to the region's tourism.

Zaman
11 April 2004

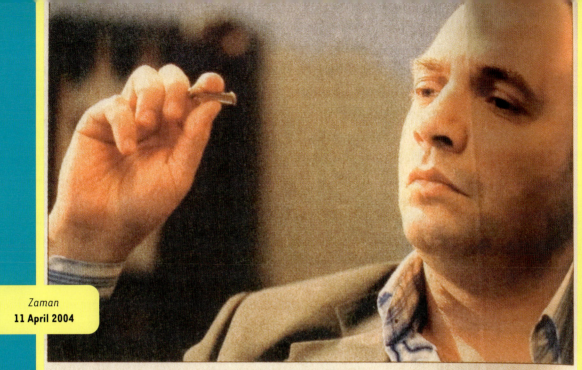

Hasmı tarafından vurulan 'Kurtlar Vadisi'nin Süleyman Çakır'ı (Oktay Kaynarca), dizinin son bölümünde ameliyat masasında hayatını kaybetti.

Çakır'ın ölümü üzerine sevenleri taziye ilanı verdi

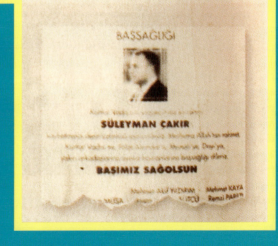

On Çakır's death his fans put an ad on the papers: *Upon the death of the Süleyman Çakır character, played by Oktay Kaynarca in the "Valley of the Wolves" series, a group of young men put a condolence add in their local paper.*

Reaching out to others

Kur'an in MP3 format

I heard a voice from the other end of the phone which reminded me of voices in my childhood coming from radios which had static and made squeaking sounds when the controls were pressed, a voice which came from deep down, as if from the depth of a well. It was a voice from before World War I, it made me shiver. My hair stood up.
[Nazlı Eray, *Sis Kelebekleri*, 2003, Can Publications, p. 53]

We are experiencing an all-encompassing communications "boom." New communications technologies, like cell phones, the internet, and email, complement each other to form a *communications network* of incredible scope. In fact, it is often said that we live in the communication age. How and when did communications get to be such a key concept? What are the local reflections of this development in Turkey?

Mass media such as radio and television emerged at the beginning of the 20th century and quickly acquired a highly influential social presence. For though they functioned as a one-way communication process – targeting very large numbers of people at the same time and from a single location – they nonetheless created a *communication model*. This model was based on a simulation of the two-way communication between individuals. Television has also resorted to a variety of techniques to simulate two-way communication. Faxes and letters from viewers supposedly received during the show, "ordinary" people invited to programs, phone conversations with spectators during transmission and the ubiquitous "canned laughter" not only suggest a communication model but establish it as a widespread practice. Indeed, John Durham Peters, a media theorist, notes that interpersonal communication, defined as the *mutual give-and-take of messages*, only became an area of study and reflection after mass media emerged. In the end, it is simulation that suggests a model for reality.

Before mass media technologies acquired today's prevalent purposes, they served other goals. Radio, for instance, evolved out of wireless transmission. It was, in a way, a fusion of the telephone, the instrument of personal communication, and the wireless. In point of fact, when radio first came out in Turkey, it was referred to as the "wireless telephone." As for the *internet*, a

Telsiz hayatımızın bir parçası oluyor

Bip...Bip..Bip..Sesimi duyuyor musun?..

- Dünyada telsizle hayat kurtarılıyor, oyuncak oynanıyor. Telsizi her an, her yerde görebiliyoruz.
- Bizde telsizi yasaklayan 1937 tarihli kanun yakında değişebilir ve telsiz en büyük yardımcımız olabilir.

Hürriyet
25 October 1981

Çarşaf
23 June 1982

above: **Beep... Beep... Beep... Can you hear me?** *Walkie-talkies are used all over the world both to save lives and to play. Walkie-talkies are now all over the place*

right: *-Why are you shouting so much, you idiot?*

-What can I do, I'm talking to Kars.

This is Bionic Man, are you there Plastic Duck:
Following the abolishment of the walkie-talkie ban, the use of walkie-talkies is spreading quickly.

Günaydın
13 December 1984

"Biyonik adam lâstik ördeği arıyor"

- Telsiz yasağının kaldırılmasından sonra halk arasında telsiz kullanımı hızla yayılıyor
- Telsizin, telefonun yükünü hafifleteceği kuşkusuz. Karı-kocalar, arkadaşlar, işadamları, amatör telsizcilere ayrılmış kanallardan rahatça haberleşiyor, telsiz aracılığıyla yeni dostlar ediniyorlar.
- Çifti 80-100 bin lira arası satılan telsizlerde telefondaki gibi çevir sesi beklemek, yüksek faturalara katlanmak, bağıra çağıra konuşmak yok. *(Yazısı sayfa 4, sütun 5'de)*

"Lastik Ördek, neredeydin?"
"Lastik ördek" aslında elektronikçi **Tuncer Bahçevan**'ın eşi Zülbiye hanım ev için gerekli malzemeyi telsizle "**Biyonik adama**" sipariş ediyor. "Ama" diyor, "**Biyonik**'ten habersiz adım bile atamıyorum **Lastik ördek neredeydin?**" diye hesap soruyor. Kızları Gökçe de "**Biber**" koduyla, geleceğin telsizcisi olma yolunda ...

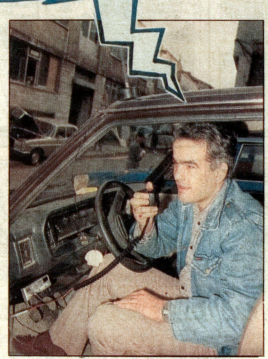

"Biyonik Adam" telsiz başında
Elektronik teknisyeni **Tuncer Bahçevan** el telsiziyle yetinmemiş, arabasına da güçlü bir telsiz yerleştirmiş. Yolda giderken eviyle ya da işiyle haberleşmek için telefon kulübesi aramıyor, açıyor telsizini ya **lastik ördekle**, ya da **Donkişot**'la dilediği kadar karşılıklı konuşabiliyor ...

product of more recent times, it was adapted to mass communication from a technology originally used for military purposes. The history of communication techniques and their spread to everyday life, which constitutes in its own right a major area of investigation, provides us a broader context for understanding the now conventionalized concept of communication and its related technologies. Going back to the Latin roots of the word, "communication," helps shed a different light on its current uses. In its Latin form, *communicare* applied not to verbal exchange but to the exchange of concrete objects; in other words it carried connotations of the marketplace and the trade associated with it. In numerous countries, the early uses of radio not only included the transmission of music but also news from selected markets. As for television, its link to the market through advertising is common knowledge. The connections, then, among these mediums, the concept of communication itself, and the market economy seems reasonably straightforward. Yet, the Latin term *communicare* also has another meaning: belonging to a society. Considered from this angle, the word also evokes the totally integrated society that is the ultimate aspiration of mass media tools.

In this respect, today's popular communication technologies seem more like instruments for individualization and individual message transmission. The telephone is a good starting point to discuss individualization and its boundaries. In the first place, the communication technologies of the telephone are dependent on very complex infrastructure and networks. When looking at the history of the telephone in Turkey, its course was clearly fraught with technical difficulties. For a long time, the telephone was the privilege of only a few city households and, for all its success, put users at the mercy of frequent breakdowns in the network, line noises and interference from other conversations, and hour-long delays when placing international calls. In addition, long waits were the rule when applying for a telephone. Özal's large investment drive in telecommunications in the 1980s was aimed at eliminating technical problems in the network, providing villages with telephone service, and encouraging widespread telephone use. As with many similar initiatives, the goal underlying this plunge toward technical modernity was to connect spaces to one another

Now he was spying on the mobile phone shop from his car. There were shops like this at every street corner, but the shop in front of which he had stopped had a special campaign which the others didn't. Mobile phones here were sold at half price, and here they had exactly the model he wanted. Only a third mobile phone could save Burak from the nightmarish jealousy he was experiencing in the last few days. Jealousy makes people more stupid than they are, and it hadn't been difficult to create this effect on Burak, reason why he hadn't thought of changing the batteries of his mobile phones. He kept coming up with silly advertising slogans in his head such as "A third mobile", "Why not?", "You can never have enough mobiles", "Before your lover doublecrosses you, triple your mobiles." [Doğu Yücel, *Hayalet Kitap*, 2002, Stüdyo İmge Publications, p. 212]

consider it's nighttime
killers feel uneasy
   robbers are edgy
     the wicked are jittery
their hands reach spontaneously for the phone
the night is a terrific grounds for treachery
   informants are like foxes
     jumping from one phone to another [Atillâ İlhan, "Tut ki Gecedir", *Çağdaş Türk Şiiri Antolojisi*, Memet Fuat (ed.), 1985, Adam Publications, p. 396]

Aktüel
27 January 1994

Sabah Melodi
10 January 1998

above: **Find some space in your pocket:** *GSM mobile phones will be in use from March onwards.*

below: **Women like mobile phones:** *This is the age of communications. And mobile phones are an indispensable part of communications. If used correctly, mobile phones can make life easy. And this contemporary and necessary tool of communication is used mostly by women.*

and, in doing so, simultaneously achieve economic and social *interconnectedness* and *dynamism*. The 1990s were the "golden years of communication" in Turkey. In 1994, the cell phone hit the market and spread rapidly. TÜBİTAK-BİLTEN's research on the "Turkish National Information Infrastructure Master Plan" shows a significant and rapid increase in the number of cell phone users. The rates of cell phone ownership per households increased from 10.1 per cent in 1997 to 50.2 per cent in 2000 (quoted by Suner, 2001:115). Of course, the same survey reveals that cell phone ownership varied significantly between income groups; while in high-income groups the ownership rate reached 79.7 per cent, in the lowest income groups it fell to 28.2 per cent. By the time we reach the 2000s, we can safely assume that cell phone usage has become much more widespread even if these variations remain. Today, there is a huge cell phone sector with aggressive advertising campaigns, new models appearing every minute offering special features like built-in cameras and internet access, and a growing second-hand market. The obstacles that once hindered communication through land-line phones seem to have vanished with cell phones. Yet, we may still wonder to what extent they really offer the individual freedom that advertisements promise us.

The greatest effect of all the new communication technologies, including cell phones, is their alteration of our *perception of space*. Whereas fixed-line telephones came to the home, they now come to the person. With cell phones, people have acquired greater *flexibility* and *speed* within their living space. As the number of cell phone users increases, the boundaries between *public* and *private* spheres have become blurred. By turning private and intimate space into public space, cell phones have rendered the private sphere meaningless. Loudly discussing the most intimate subjects on the street, in cafes and restaurants, or on public transport violates the boundaries of private space. At the same time, this situation creates what may be called as private breaches in public spaces, permitting different forms of interrelations to develop between people. But at this point, it becomes necessary to consider the kind of communication framework that encompasses the varied aims and forms of cell phone usage. In their research on cell phone use, Özcan and Koçak establish that the main

- Dad, how was I born...
- 900 900 907 my child... (the number of Hello Doctor, Pre-Natal Information line)
- My sister Sabiş said "a stork brought you"...
- 006 my child... these are 006... (the number of Tell Me a Tale line)
- I don't understand... I'll ask mom... Where is mom?...
- 011 my child... (the number of Phone Numbers Enquiry line)
[Atilla Atalay, "Alo Servisleri", Uyuyamadığım: *Düş Kovalayan*, 2000, İletişim Publications, p. 251-252]

A public phone token

The phone rang in the afternoon. It was really me who was calling. I called at lunch time too, but no one answered. So you were after the poultry seller too. The phone rang and rang and there wasn't a soul to answer it. Yes, it was me calling. I called you from my mobile. I kept calling you because I was lost in pitch-like darkness. I stayed there looking at you from a long distance: 37 53 54. [Müge İplikçi, "Telefon Yolculuğu", *Transit Yolcular*, 2002, Can Publications, p. 98]

CONNECTING PEOPLE! REACHING OUT TO OTHERS 271

Hürriyet
2 January 1992

Nokta
29 December 1992

above: **PTT's torture by phone:** *Phone calls are frequently interrupted and lines cross in Tuzla Aydıntepe, due to the antiquated numerical telephone exchange that about 100,000 subscribers are linked to.*

left: **The golden year of communications:** *1996 was the year when the new Türksat satellite was launched into space, when many new television channels were launched and when the use of mobile phones and computers soared.*

February 1988

Ardahan Münih 5 saniye!

TELETAŞ SAYESİNDE

Sadece Ardahan'ın köyünden değil, ülkemizin en ücra dağ köylerinden bile bütün dünya ile telefon bağlantısını sağlayan modern radyolink sistemlerini... kablosuz, kırsal haberleşme sistemlerini dev bir Türk şirketi üretiyor: **Teletaş**.

Şu anda Türkiye'de milyonlarca insanın haberleşmesini sağlayan modern teçhizatı da dev bir Türk şirketi üretiyor: **Teletaş**.

Ülkemizde ve kıtalar arasında anında yazılı haberleşmeyi gerçekleştiren en gelişmiş teleks cihazlarını da dev bir Türk şirketi üretiyor: **Teletaş**.

Haberleşmek istediğimiz her yerde, her anda bizi ülkenin ve dünyanın dört bir yanına ulaştırmaya hazır olan kumbaralı telefonların tümünü de dev bir Türk şirketi üretiyor: **Teletaş**.

Ülkemizdeki haberleşme sistemlerini dünya standartlarına çıkaran bu dev Türk şirketi **Teletaş** şimdi halkımızın ortaklığına açılıyor... Özelleştiriliyor.

Teletaş'a siz de ortak olabileceksiniz.

TELETAŞ
HABERLEŞMEDE **İLERİ** TEKNOLOJİ

BAŞBAKANLIK TOPLU KONUT VE KAMU ORTAKLIĞI İDARESİ BAŞKANLIĞI

Ardahan to Munich in 5 seconds: *The modern radiolink systems make it possible not just for Ardahan's villages, but even for our country's most distant mountain villages to communicate by phone with the rest of the world... The wireless, rural communication systems are produced by a giant Turkish company.*

While she was waiting for me to prepare another bad coffee in the kitchen, she got up as if she wanted to look out of the window. I let her pass. Then I took the cups from the coffee table and walked towards the door of the sitting room. I had barely passed the table when the mobile phone rang. Since we came here with the real estate agent to rent the flat, this was the first time that a mobile phone had rung inside the house, except for the ones on television. It had a very irritating buzzing sound. I stopped for a moment and looked over my shoulder. Muazzez Güler leaned towards her bag and easily took out her mobile. She looked at who was calling on the screen, the she put it to her ear and said "hello!" with a voice which was partly impatient and partly angry. [Celil Oker, *Son Ceset*, 2004, Doğan Publications, p. 35]

an attack of loneliness hit me last night. i called everybody and everywhere for which I had a number in my phone directory. only the phone numbers which had police, fire brigade, hospital and ferry to the islands written next to them answered... i was very moved by this... the police phone actually said that if I talked any longer and occupied their line in vain any longer, they would come suddenly one night for an extrajudicial execution... i was moved, i was loud of myself.... i was proud, I mean, that is, there was a loud cry of happiness from my rumbling stomach... i felt unnecessarily well... then I took two diazepam and I was fine... i felt healthy as an ox, just like before.
[Metin Üstündağ, "Kardeşim Günlük", *Denemeyenler*, 2000, Parantez Publications, p. 308-309]

motivations are increased social contact or connectedness, security, and convenience (quoted by Suner, 2001: 116). Adopting a different perspective, Geray (2001) takes up cell phone usage within the context of an unpredictable neo-liberal socio-economic restructuring; the growing significance of the informal sector and the increase in secondary jobs and night jobs, in other words an *employment structure* that calls for greater *flexibility* at every level, has resulted in a greater reliance on cell phones. In a totally different vein, Suner argues that the cell phone has a meaning that goes beyond such motivations as status enhancement or social convenience. For the teenagers or young adults that form the majority of Turkish cell phone users, the cell phone, she suggests, may be a device "symbolizing global culture," and a means to "get away" and "break loose" without actually going anywhere. Especially after the 2001 economic crisis, the desire to get away seems to have replaced the goal to "make it big" among the young, most of whom now view prosperity as an increasingly distant possibility. Through "text messaging, listening to music, conducting banking transactions, getting stock market updates and other interactive practices," cell phones – to a point – "activate" people and offer them ways to create "other worlds" without going anywhere (Suner, 2001: 126).

From all the arguments above, it emerges very clearly that, whether considered as a tool to *connect* or one to *break loose*, the usage of cell phones and similar new communication technologies incorporate a society-related imagery. On the one hand, due to the wide range of models and accessories, cell phones are coded as *status symbols*. On the other, by transcending spatial boundaries and transforming spaces, they produce fantasies of a new *community*. Interestingly, although many of these fantasies are built on a notion of *freedom*, cell phones have inevitably brought with them certain new forms of *control*. It is well known that for employers, spouses or parents, the cell phone has become a very useful supervising tool. In this respect, the internet, which is perceived as an unsupervised and unconfined environment, contributes more tangible meaning to fantasies of a new community. Internet technology can bring together users from very different locations who share similar interests and tendencies. While it provides a global platform to diasporas and political

CEP TELEFONU KADIN ERKEK İLİŞKİLERİNDE BİR SEMBOL OLDU
Erkeği 'cep'ten tanı

Cep telefonuyla hayatımıza giren davranış modellerini inceleyen bilim adamları 'Kadın cebini çantasına koyar, erkek ise masanın üstüne. Bu iktidar bende gösterisidir' diyor

Sabah
23 November 2001

above: **You can tell who a man is from his mobile:** *Scientists who are analysing the behaviour models which have emerged with mobile phones, say "Women put their mobiles in their purses, while men put them on the table. This is a show of power."*

below: *-Are you sending group e-mails? (Come, come, whoever you are, come... Whether you are a pagan or...)*

Leman
28 July 2001

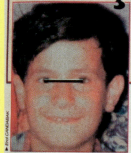

Hürriyet
1 January 1992

Hürriyet
3 July 2000

above: **This child can lose his mind:** The 11 year-old A., who used to leave home to go to school and used instead to go and play atari, has been expelled from school for absenteism.

below: **www.verboten.com:** Internet cafés are having to close down, following a directive of the Ministry of Interior. The restrictions brought in order to prevent pornographic broadcasts and separatist websites prohibit computer games and even legal CD films.

Siber âlemden dünyaya geçtiler

İnternetteki siteler aracılığıyla sosyalleşiyor, sosyalleşmekle kalmıyor internetteki görüntüleri aracılığıyla aşk yaşıyor ve yapıyorlar! İnternetteki romansı dünyada yaşayarak mutlu olup evlenenler de, hep aynı model kızla çıkmayı arzulayıp sonunda çıkan ama mutsuz olduğunu itiraf edip rahatlayanlar da, kulüplerde sabaha kadar takılıp, eğlence fotoğraflarını internetteki bir sitede yayınlatarak piyasa yapanlar da var! İnternet insanları, internetten kente taşıdıkları maceralarını Marie Claire'e anlattılar. AYŞEGÜL SÖNMEZ

Marie Claire
December 2004

above: **Moving from the cyberworld to the world**

below: **The virtual lonely hunters of the nights:** *While you are sleeping at night, about 100,000 people do not sleep. They try to find a solution to their loneliness, through the "lonely instrument", their computer.*

Gecelerin sanal yalnızlık avcıları

Star box
4 May 2002

Siz geceleri uyurken, bu ülkede yaklaşık 100 bin kişi uyumuyor. "Yalnızlık aleti" bilgisayarlarıyla, tekliflerine çözüm bulmaya çalışıyor. Arkadaş arıyor, dost arıyor. Sevgili arıyor. Partner arıyor

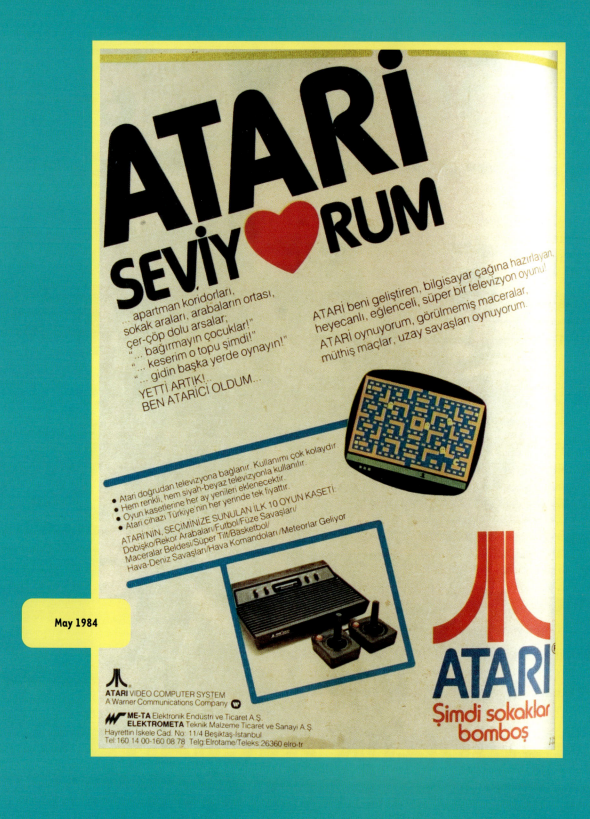

May 1984

I love Atari

movements, it also offers opportunities for a wide variety of pursuits and hobbies, for personal research projects, shopping or simply to make new friends. To illustrate the extraordinary range of possibilities the internet offers, one need only consider that at one extreme, alternative globalization movements are organized through the net, while at the other, friendships are struck in cyberspace and cyber love sometimes leads to marriage.

Yet, while contributing to the formation of diverse relationships and affiliations, new communication technologies, especially when applied to the sphere of games, are also denounced as promoting social alienation. The first PCs in Turkey were the Atari video game consoles; today, the internet offers a huge assortment of tempting video game sites (some people have even started playing Turkey's "national" backgammon online). The "game" aspect of communications is usually considered a deviation from real objectives and, because of the *addictive* potential of video games, perceived as a *threat*. There are those who have developed a taste for 900 lines, kids completely mesmerized by video games, teenagers who spend all their time in internet cafes. All are held up as examples of "cyber slaves" in a society where modernization has also spawned *degeneration*. Obsessive game playing, listening to (or downloading) music, visiting pornography sites, transforming the computer or cell phone into an electronic game room or displaying an excessive fondness for trivial accessories like the I-pod sock are all cases of *extra* meanings bestowed on new technologies that deviate from the inherent "logic" of communications. These extra meanings are frequently resorted to in an attempt to alleviate loneliness, a lack of purpose in life or simple boredom; still the majority of these quests remain confined to consumption-related communications. The current forms of individualization that new media technologies have produced, though defined by social norms, can at times push their limits and violate them. From the time mass media technologies first appeared to the present, there has been an ongoing conflict between the control they are seen to exercise on people and the new meanings these technologies have acquired and may still acquire. But in the communication age, to be or not to be [!] in the coverage area of your cell phone operator has become an existential issue in its own right.

In the field of mobile phones, users have been introduced for the first time this year to 2 megapixel resolution. Sony Ericsson was the first to do this with its K650i model. On the other hand, the ever changing trends in mobile music have made it possible for the fixed disc mobile phones to be realised. This trend started with Samsung's V5400 model and continued with Nokia announcing its N91 model. Besides its traditional phone field, Nokia also introduced a Linux based palm computer. Samsung took the whole thing a step further and presented a model with movement sensors. Thanks to this interesting feature, to dial a number it was enough to draw the number in the air with your phone, and the games within were also played in the same manner. For example if your character needed to jump you would jump too, if he needed to turn right you would turn right too. Of course one wonders what people watching you would think. [A section from Serdar Kuzuloğlu's "Virtual World" programme, NTV Radio, 28 December 2005]

An i-pod sock set

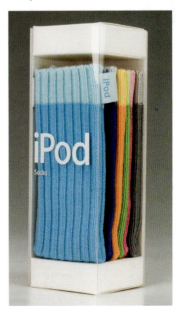

Hürriyet
15 November 1992

Telefon faturasında '900' kâbusuna son

Süleyman SARILAR / İSTANBUL (Hürriyet)

TELEFON abonelerini astronomik faturalarla şok eden 900'lü telefonlar, istenildiğinde bir dilekçeyle, on bin lira karşılığında görüşmeye kapatılabiliyor. PTT yetkilileri, isteyen abonelerin telefonlarını şehirlerarası ve milletlerarası görüşmelere kapatabildikleri gibi, sadece 900'lü görüşmelere de kapatabileceklerini söylediler.

■ Erotik fıkralar, tahrik edici seks anıları, falcılar, medyumlar, şarkıcılar, dansözler, seks doktorlarından sonra politikacıları da bünyesine alan "Alo Bilgi" ve "Alo Tel" gibi 900'lü özel telefonlar, yüksek faturalarla abonelere şok yaşatıyor.

■ Dakikası 5833 liradan Türkiye'nin her yerinden aranan bu telefonlar, özellikle çocuklu abonelerin faturalarını astronomik rakamlara ulaştırıyor. PTT ile aboneler arasında büyük sorunlar yaratan 900'lü telefon faturaları, itirazları artırdı.

■ PTT yetkilileri, isteyen abonenin telefonunu bir dilekçeyle 900'lü telefon görüşmelerine de kapatabileceğini bildirdiler. Yetkililer, başvuruda bulunan abonelere, ayda iki bin lira karşılığında ayrıntılı fatura da gönderildiğine dikkat çektiler.

İnternet aşkı

21 yaşındaki Yozgatlı Soner Akgül internette chat yaparken tanıştığı 57 yaşındaki Türk asıllı Amerikan vatandaşı Çiğdem Karasu ile evlendi

Sabah
15 November 2000

ARALARINDA 26 YAŞ FARK VAR
Soner ve Çiğdem Akgül, "Aramızdaki 26 yaş farkı hiç önemli değil. Biz Birbirimizi seviyoruz" dediler.

above: **An end to the "900" lines nightmare on the phone bill:** *The 900 lines that shock the telephone subscribers with their astronomical costs, can be blocked with a petition and a payment of 10,000 Lira.*

below: **Love on the internet:** *The 21 year old Soner Akgül from Yozgat has married Çiğdem Karasu, a 57 year old American of Turkish origin, whom he met while chatting on the internet.*

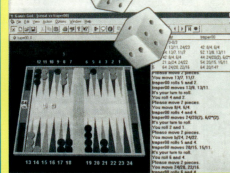

Milliyet
1 June 1997

Aktüel
18 May 2000

above: **Backgammon on the internet is something else**

below: **Virtual slaves:** One loses his fortune to an overseas lover he has never met, one is influenced by a transexual he has had an argument with and draws away from his wife, one becomes a gambler in one night... The increase in internet addiction has led experts to open a treatment website.

International coffeehouses

When Turkey first discovered *Nescafe* in 1984, it simultaneously learned how to obtain "the full flavor and rich aroma" of coffee in under a minute, and shared in a taste that the world enjoyed. A few years later, the ad slogan for Jacobs carried similar "global" references: "Trust your palate," and "offer your guests a taste of Europe." Gradually, both corner stores and supermarkets started to offer a wide variety of world-leading instant coffee brands. This perhaps explains why suddenly the need arose to label as "Turkish coffee" the cup of coffee that had been a part of the local culture for centuries.

The liberalization of the foreign trade regime and the deregulation of coffee imports in the 1980s put an end to TEKEL's monopoly as the sole buyer and seller of coffee. As newspaper headlines on coffee shortages became history, coffee as an *internationalized commodity* soon took its place in the market instead. It was not only imported "instant" coffees that became a brand but also the freshly ground coffee that had been sold for years in little shops alongside dried fruit and nuts, now vacuum packed under such names as *Kurukahveci Mehmet Efendi, Kocatepe, Tiryaki* and *Keyif*. Doubtlessly,

Packaged brown sugar used in cafes

concern about adapting to changing market conditions and consumption patterns was a major reason why numerous local coffee companies renewed their production and sales strategies in the 1990s. This change and diversification in coffee sales was also reflected in consumer practices. As the term Nescafe entered everyday usage, it also weakened "Turkish" coffee's centuries-old sovereignty. Because of its novelty and "Western" correlations, the demand for Nescafe increased, particularly in middle class households. In recent years, we have witnessed a constantly growing diversification of coffee consumption that instant coffees first triggered. *Filter coffee, French press, cappucino, espresso, cafe latte,* and *ice coffee,* all terms still unfamiliar to most a few years back, have now gradually entered common usage, especially in

April 1984

Bir fincan nefis kahveyi yarım dakikada nasıl yaparsınız?

1 Bir fincan, bir-iki çay kaşığı NESCAFÉ

2 Üstüne sıcak su...- Ve dilediğiniz kadar şeker -

3 İşte! NESCAFÉ'niz hazır. Sadece 26 saniyede.

Dünyanın ünlü çekirdek kahvelerinin lezzeti. Nescafé Gold. Nestlé'den. Bir Nescafé yapın, çabucak. Dünyanın tadını yudumlayın. Yavaş yavaş. Keyifle...

İçi kahve. İçimi kahve. NESCAFÉ GOLD — Nestlé

December 1990

Konuklarınıza Avrupa'yı ikram edin...

JACOBS
"damağınıza güvenin"

above: **How to make an exquisite cup of coffee in half a minute**

left: **Treat your guests to a bit of Europe**

Engin Akın: I believe that if we had gone through a little trouble and had roasted the coffee at home, we would have reached a special taste, just like we wanted, ideal for our taste buds. That's the way it was after all, an aroma of coffee used to emanate from every house, I'm sure your family used to do this too?

Binnur Hataylı: Of course I remember it, actually they used to cook coffee even on the stove or on a brazier. But if you wish I could send you some raw coffee, and you could roast it, if you have time.

EA: But there is the question of time, isn't there? It needs to be done slowly, with care, but it's a bit like if you like a rose you need to endure its thorns; if we want something to be good, and we want it to be characteristic to us, we need to roast it. Which coffees would you like to try apart from Brazilian coffee? What coffee would you like to use to make a Turkish cofee? Costarican, or maybe Guatemalan?

BH: They all have very different flavours, I think it's worth trying them all.

EA: Like wine, you mean?

BH: Yes, exactly. The interesting thing is that there was a time when there was no coffee in Turkey, when its import had stopped and we had to bring it from abroad, but we never could find the flavour of the coffee made in Turkey.

[A section from Engin Akın's "Flavoured Conversations" programme, Açık Radio, 30 November 2002]

certain segments of society. Consequently, people now have their personal coffee preferences.

In his work, "The rise of yuppie coffees and the reimagination of class in the United States", William Roseberry examined the growing diversification of the coffee market in America – which up to the 1980s was limited to one or two brands sold in tin containers – and its relationship to changes in class structure. He linked the market entry of a wide variety of coffee types in this period to the rise of a new middle class. The members of this new social segment set themselves apart from other groups in society through their *consumer choices*; they opted for more *stylized* consumer goods (Roseberry, 1996: 773-774). Roseberry writes that during this period, coffee – as it had been in a much earlier pre-industrial age – rose again as the symbol of a more aristocratic, cosmopolitan and refined lifestyle to acquire a "gourmet" beverage status. In other words, by discarding previous characterizations as the ordinary everyday beverage of the working classes, coffee moved up a class and became *yuppified*. We may observe a similar process in Turkey where coffee – particularly in the 2000s – also gradually became a more *gentrified* beverage. *Nescafe*'s part in this process was in fact very limited. In the beginning of the 1980s, consumption of *Nescafe* and other instant coffees spread rapidly and became *commonplace* – at least among the middle classes. Thus, clues to the "yuppification" of coffee in Turkey should be sought elsewhere. In recent years, there has been a sharp increase – especially in affluent neighborhoods – in the number of shops selling a variety of coffee beans as well as the standard *Arabica*. In the same way, supermarkets catering to higher income groups now have *specialized* coffee sections. As automatic coffee makers, and French press or espresso machines become available, the new middle classes have broadened their coffee *repertoire*. The new *cafes*, which started to appear in Turkey after the 1980s, are no doubt one of the most important drivers of this pseudo-American rise in specialized coffee consumption. Today, especially in big cities, one can observe a dramatic upsurge in the number of places called *cafe*.

Today, cafes – from the French "café" – which in that language refers both to coffee and the place one has it – has become

Bir yudum buzlu kahve ferahlatır

Sabah
11 June 2005

left: **Refreshening with a sip of ice coffee**

below: **100 types of coffee from the Barista**
The coffee shops, trendy meeting places of late, have brought about also a new profession: the Baristas offer cappuccino with lots of milk to angry customers and espresso to those who need to energise.

Baristadan 100 çeşit kahve

Son dönemin moda buluşma mekanları 'coffee shop'lar yeni bir meslek kavramını da beraberinde getirdi: Baristalar. Onlar, öfkeli müşteriye bol sütlü cappuccino, enerji isteyene de espresso sunuyor

Akşam
14 October 2004

İtalya'nın en büyük kahve üreticisi Segafredo Zanetti'nin Türkiye distribütörü Metropolitan Gıda, bugüne kadar profesyonellere ve kahveseverlere yönelik düzenlediği barista eğitimini bu kez basın mensuplarına verdi.

Aktüel
4 August 1994

Life +
July 2000

above: **The coffeehouse of the wealthy:** *The café-bar "Cafée Inn" inside Pasha Disco is really "in" this summer.*

right: **Let's eat, drink and socialise**

common usage in Turkish as the generic term that a number of patisserie/restaurant/bar hybrids opt for when wishing to define themselves and acquire visibility as a novel and different food and beverage space. Cafes became particularly popular with the younger generation and rapidly gained prevalence to become one of the most ubiquitous features of the busiest streets, entertainment districts and shopping centers in big cities. But cafes are not just food and beverage spaces; at the same time they are places where people go to socialize. In this respect, the fact that they are called "cafe" instead of their Turkish (and actually rather similar-sounding) equivalent *kahve* cannot be attributed simply to a fondness for foreign terms. It is through the naturalization of the term "café" that these spaces have given public visibility to class and income determined differentiations. Faced with this cafe invasion, the one or two remaining classic Turkish coffeehouses (*kahve*) are now the sphere of other social groups and practices. Traditional coffeehouses are associated with laziness and unemployment and considered to be frequented by patrons aiming only to *kill time*. For a very long time, going to the neighborhood kahve was a socially frowned upon practice. In his study on coffeehouses during the period of the Ottoman Empire, Cengiz Kırlı gives interesting clues about the historical roots that may have led to such an unfavorable view: "Coffeehouses were places that generally aroused repugnance – at least among the urban elites who owed their wealth and status to the state. This repugnance was, of course, closely related to one of the most powerful images of the West about the East and of 19th century 'westernized' Ottoman intellectuals vis-à-vis themselves: the notion that the neighborhood coffeehouse was the traditional gathering place of the masses and for this very reason the focus of the state's suspicions, who regarded it as a den of gossip mongering and 'seditious' conversations. For these hesitant social engineers, in whom coffeehouses and their patrons roused shame about their own origins, these were the places where the East took concrete form; the temples where sluggards whiled away time neither dead nor alive but simply static." (Kırlı 2004) This stance against coffeehouses continued well into the Republican period. Today, however, the new cafes carry exactly opposite connotations: they symbolize urbanity, modernity and the "West." Just as the word "cafe" implicitly excludes certain social segments,

> *He used to talk about his brother in the smoky coffeehouse at the top of the street. The smoke inside the coffeehouse was like the fog that formed over the city, when the weather began to warm up after the winter cold. Just as the fog would swallow up the bridges and houses and the tip of your nose, the smoke in the coffeehouse would destroy the time that passed by. Our lives, attached to the rear end of time, would pass by with a clang, like tins tied to a dog's tail. In the coffeehouse, as soon as our faces disappeared in the smoke, with a sigh that befitted the destitute Başparmak repeated what his brother had said when he visited him in jail: "I would have cut off both my arms rather than miss the smoke of the coffeehouse."*
> [Şebnem İşigüzel, *Eski Dostum Kertenkele*, 1996/1999, Can Publications, p. 10]

> *I would walk carefully in order not to collide with cigarettes coming from the park and gulping the damp nighttime air I would get to our usual coffeehouse. The front entrance of the coffeehouse was kept covered with a pull-down shutter and one would go in through the small door on the side. Leaving behind the darkness of the street and experiencing the coffeehouse's smoky, bright and noisy atmosphere was always surprising. I would take a step inside and immediately stop. I would see two pensioners at a corner playing backgammon, the coffeehouse boy searching the radio for Arab style tunes, and my poet friend smoking at the table at the very end. I would pull up a chair and listen to my friend's newest poems.*
> [Oktay Akbal, "Şehrin Işıkları Söndü", *Aşksız İnsanlar*, 1949/2003, Can Publications, p. 87]

24 saat nöbetçi kafe

Gece kuşlarına müjde, artık İstanbul'un 24 saat açık bir kafesi var. Dolmabahçe'de, Ritz Carlton'ın altında açılan Chocolate 95 çeşit yemek, 40 çeşit kahve seçeneğiyle şehrin yeni gece-gündüz konsepti

Okan Bayülgen ve Sinan Çetin de müdavimi...

Milliyet
1 September 2002

above: **Café on duty 24 hours:** *Good news for night owls; Istanbul now has a café open 24 hours a day. Chocolate, which has opened below the Ritz Carlton, in Dolmabahçe, offers 95 types of food and 40 types of coffee and has brought a new night and day concept to the city.*

right: **Come and have a coffee:** *If you have had a great dinner in the previous page, come and have a coffee on this page. Let us present you with the terrific flavours of Starbucks Coffee, which has been in Istanbul for two months now.*

Buyrun bir kahvemizi için

Yandaki sayfada güzel bir akşam yemeği yediyseniz, gelin bu sayfada kahvemizi için. Size, İstanbul'a 2 ay önce gelen Starbucks Coffee'nin müthiş lezzetlerini sunalım. Caffe Misto mu, Iced Caffe Latte mi, Mocha Frappuccino mu alırsınız?

Star box
6 July 2003

it has differentiated the kind of socializing it offers from earlier "Eastern" forms by asserting the new modern identity it sought through its own name and space.

Another major difference between today's cafes and traditional coffeehouses is that the former are no longer essentially male public spaces. The male/female socializing taking place in cafes thus contributes to representations of modernity and distances itself from an "Eastern lifestyle" and the traditional *haremlik-selamlık* [segregation of the women's quarters from the men's] it evokes. Cafes have replaced the once popular pastry shops as spaces where male and female teens and young adults go out on dates, flirt or simply hang out. But cafes, both decor- and fare-wise, offer their clients much more contemporary and "global" forms of socializing and "lifestyle" than their precursors ever did.

At the same time, cafes obviously differ among themselves in terms of location, interior design, menu variety and pricing policies. While certain less "trendy" cafes cater to a young or more "plebian" clientele, high-end spaces immediately set themselves apart with their "high-concept" decors, richly varied menus – including a wide range of beverages in addition to coffee – and, not least, their prices. These are, of course, the cafes that frequently grace the pages of glossy lifestyle magazines, feature in newspapers as part advertisement, part news stories, and figure in TV culinary shows. These are the cafes that boast "bilingual" menus, a well-educated staff mainly made up of college graduates, a tasteful and refined decor and designer tableware; they bring Vienna, Rome, Paris and New York to Istanbul.

Paralleling the rise of cafes and specialized coffee varieties, international coffee chains like *Gloria Jean's* and *Starbucks* also opened stores in Turkey. While in America these chains have provided an alternative for lower income social groups during the coffee *yuppification* process, the exact opposite has occurred – at least for the time being – in Turkey. Promoted as spaces that "open Turkey to the world," these "brand" cafes have rapidly caught on, especially among the affluent young, but due to their high price

As soon as Café Boulevard opens, it starts filling up from the morning on and it stays full till midnight. All kinds of things that can be used as internal decoration for places like cafés, restaurants or bars, have found their way here. The place is heated centrally, but porcelain stoves are present all the same amidst the crowd, amidst all that lack of space. The phone is in use all the time. Everybody invites their friends to the café. A little further away from the phone there is a mirror in front of which it is usually men who rearrange their hair and study themselves for a long time, ending up with their hair even more dishevelled than before. In the ladies' too, a lot of combing and make-up refreshening takes place. The loud speakers continuously bellow the most trendy songs. The noise of the coffeehouse and of the traffic suppresses the music, but the music is still played non-stop. The waiters, wearing shirts resembling Ottoman janissary-like embroidered jackets, carry tea and coffee on plastic trays. The tea is stale and even the ice cream has soured. But the customers don't mind. The confusion doesn't bother anybody. On the contrary, this seems to be what attracts people to this coffeehouse. [Tezer Özlü, "Cafe Boulevard", *Eski Bahçe-Eski Sevgi*, 1978/1998, Yapı Kredi Publications, p. 39-40]

Take-away coffee holders

Narghile *(hookah) mouth pieces*

When I finished drinking my tea, the night-timers' coffeehouse had filled up with sleepy men. It was as if I hadn't seen them coming in; however much I forced myself, I couldn't remember their arrival. But there they were, their empty tea glasses in front of them. Some were completely lost in thought, some, their heads on their chests, were dozing off, and some were sitting, fist under chin, staring into space. Although they were sitting at separate tables, they seemed to be burdened by the same weight and to be thinking of the same thing, they even seemed to be carrying the same heart, unaware of each other. Then some of them put their heads down on the tables and fell asleep. God knows what they are tired of, I thought to myself, god knows who they are tired of. On the other hand, I was stubbornly trying to remember when they had come through the door.
[Hasan Ali Toptaş, *Gölgesizler*, 1995, Can Publications, p. 171]

policies have remained out of bounds for the majority of the population. Yet today, the cafe trend continues to diversify and alongside international brands and fashionable "in" spots, cheaper-priced options have now appeared; traditional coffeehouses and pastry shops are morphing into cafes while *nargile* [hookah] and *falı* [fortune-reading] cafes fuse tradition and modernity.

Historically, coffeehouses have always been an arena for political debate both in Europe and the Ottoman Empire. It was common practice for the Ottoman ruling elite, for example, to try and control "political" discussion and "seditious" tendencies by either shutting down coffeehouses or stationing informers there to spy on their patrons. At a time when the impact of the press was very limited and modern communication technologies were inexistent, coffeehouses opened a space for public discourse and were sites where people could gather to exchange views and information on socio-political and economic issues. This feature placed them among the key elements that constituted and shaped public opinion. In our age, where the public sphere has become dependent on the consumer economy, one may well wonder what function the new cafes now hold, especially in view of the fact that two people sitting across from each other in one of these spots are often engaged in their own personal cell phone conversations with someone else...

Yeni Gündem
7 September 1986

—Dear voters, rather than keeping you busy with boring election speeches, our party is devoted to making you happy. Our party officers will play cards with two of you. Moreover, our MP candidate for Zonguldak will play backgammon with some of you. The drinks are on us.

Bıyıksızlar da nargile fokurdatır oldu

Türk kültüründe 500 yıllık bir geleneğe sahip olan nargile; marpucunu, lülesini, şişesini toplayıp geri döndü. Artık İstanbul'daki birçok kahve ve çay bahçesi her yaştan ve gelir grubundan nargile tiryakisini ağırlıyor

Nargile tiryakileri gibi kahveler de çeşitlilik gösteriyor. Laila'cılar Tarabya'daki Hayrola'ya, öğrenciler Tophane'ye gidiyor

Milliyet
26 August 2001

Narghiles gurgle even for people without moustaches: *The narghile, which has a past of 500 years in Turkish culture, has come back along with its pipe, bowl and base. Now many coffeehouses and tea houses in Istanbul host narghile enthusiasts of all ages and income groups.*

right: **Finally a café for bookies:** *A new type of entertainment has been dominating the side streets of Beyoğlu for a while now. Sitting side by side in the cafés and bars that have sprouted like mushrooms, joining in the conversation at the table next to you and feeling suffocated by the crowd has almost become a tradition in Beyoğlu.*

below: **Fortune telling cafe:** *A new trend has started in the last few months in the cafés of Beyoğlu. The custom of fortune telling, which has existed in our society for many years, is now practiced very commonly in cafés.*

Aktüel
22 January 1997

Gazete Metro
12 January 2004

Moving toward a global city

Şehzadebaşı... A famous street of the 1930s and '40s, an exclusive place of Istanbul. It seems almost erased from the map now. Where is the Çinili Bakery, where is the shop of the Chemist Asaf Bey, where are the billiard halls, the dancing halls from the years of the dancing madness? Where are the cinemas, Milli Hilâl, Ferah, where is Naşit's theatre, where are the pastry shops, the ice cream shops, where is Ali Bey's shop, where are the little wine shops? Where is that photographer in whose large shop window I would get lost in thought! Where are the people of those times?
[Oktay Akbal, "Yoksulluk Çirkindir", Lunapark, 1983/2003, Can Publications, p. 92]

In the 1980s and subsequent years, Istanbul in particular and other cities as well rapidly designed new projects and structures that would attract inflows of global capital and goods. The new heights this process has reached today can be observed in the most recent series of initiatives – from Galataport to Mashattan, and Beyoğlu's Fransız Sokak [faux French Street] to the Haydarpaşa project, to name only a few – all grouped under the generic heading "Urban Transformation Project." These projects have laid the ground for new disputes: their defenders – among them the prime minister and several mayors – claim that Istanbul is becoming a *global city*, and that new opportunities for tourism, shopping and business are being created. They talk about "marketing Turkey" and turning Istanbul into a "global brand." Meanwhile, detractors draw attention to the huge *social* and *human costs* these initiatives will have. Considering that similar kinds of polemics existed in the 1980s, there seems to be constancy not only in the inclination to transform the city at all costs but also in attempts to resist such endeavors. How can we explain this continuity of both prevailing and opposition approaches and relate it to national/global socio-economic processes? In attempting to answer this question it may be helpful to focus on Istanbul, the epicenter of controversy surrounding urban transformation and global city aspirations.

Miniature Leander's Tower, Hagia Sophia and Galata Tower, sold in souvenir shops

From the 1970s on, the world economy entered a new *regime of capital accumulation*, often referred to as *globalization*, which generated sectoral and institutional changes and geographical shifts that had a direct impact on cities. During this period, as the finance and service sectors acquired dominance with regard to manufacturing, *banking*, *insurance*, *real estate* investments, *tourism* and similar activities significantly increased their capacity to create economic value. The large-scale transformations undertaken over the past thirty years in the field of

left: **Living in Istanbul is a privilege:** *Governor Ayaz says that there should be a cost to this privilege.*

below: **From the Byzantines to the Ottomans, from Dalan to businessmen:** *For whom is Istanbul being re-designed?*

Günaydın
21 December 1984

Yeni Gündem
22 November 1987

right: **Museumcity Istanbul:** *The Ministry of Tourism will transform Sultanahmet into an open air museum, the Sirkeci Train Station into an art gallery, the Feshane into a Textile Museum and the Camialtı Dockyard into an art museum.*

below: **Galataport is coming:** *The Galataport project, which aims to attract luxury oceanliners and wealthy tourists to Istanbul, has received approval.*

Gazete Metro
10 May 2004

Radikal
18 April 2005

communications and telecommunications were among the most important factors accelerating and shaping this process. Within this socio-economic conjuncture, the strategic significance of cities also acquired a new magnitude. Metropolises like New York, Paris, and Amsterdam were pushed to the fore as *world cities* that could accommodate, manage, coordinate and facilitate the business activities of banks, multinationals and financial markets; which possessed advanced communications and transportation infrastructure; which were open to global capital inflows and which could provide all the necessary services to workers and international companies (Sassen 2000). These metropolises differed significantly from other cities within the same national boundaries in both income and investment levels. This differentiation among cities may also be viewed as a reflection of the growing regional inequalities experienced both nationally and globally in a period when the capacity of states to organize and regulate their national economies has diminished sharply and large capital has become increasingly flexible and fluid. This is the conjuncture, therefore, that should be considered when evaluating the position of the political and economic elite, who envision Istanbul as a global city and argue that it must improve the scope and quality of its services to attract global capital or at least transform it into a regional center.

Parallel to developments all over the world in the last 25 years, the financial and services sectors in Istanbul have become increasingly dominant. Relative to earlier periods, there has been a major upsurge in investment and employment opportunities in banking, marketing, advertising, accounting, consultancy, insurance, computers and computer software, engineering, real estate and communications. Numerous international companies have entered these areas either through direct investment, joint ventures or licensing agreements. Nonetheless, the inflow of foreign capital to Istanbul through diverse channels has remained below the desired target for a number of reasons, including shortcomings in Turkey's legal and physical infrastructure as well as political and economic uncertainty and instability (Keyder 1999). Still, the recent rise in privatization sales, "encouraging" developments in Turkey's accession negotiations with the EU, various legal reforms, and "optimistic" views concerning the country's economic stability

You were always there Istanbul. You existed in a time that had no before and no after. Your name was Constantinopolis. You were the capital of an empire, with your three rows of unsurmountable walls, your underwater loopholes, your flags and towers, your palaces, your stone houses facing the sea and your devout people, your churches, your monasteries, your sacred springs and the icons within, and your monks and angels. You were called Constantinopolis... And the Tower of Galata cast its shadow on the roofs of houses, on the narrow streets lined with Genoese taverns. With your lodos wind, your poyraz wind and the fish schools flowing from the Bosphorus to the Marmara Sea, you were unrivalled. You have always existed Istanbul!
[Nedim Gürsel, *Sevgilim İstanbul*, 1986/1997, Can Publications, p. 11]

An akbil, an electronic transit pass

Arnavutköy'de onarımı Türkiye Turing Otomobil Kurumu'nca gerçekleştirilen ev. Bu bir başlangıç. Bir kültür mirası olan bu evlerin kurtarılması geleceğin turizm yapısını da etkileyecek. Semt halkı Boğaziçi'nde korumacılığın ve pansiyonculuğun desteklenmesini istiyor. (Mustafa AKÖZ)

 Türkiye Turing Otomobil Kurumu onarım çalışmalarını Arnavutköy'de sürdürüyor

Güneş
7 December 1982

Eski evler yenileniyor

Arnavutköy'deki evin onarımdan önceki durumu

The renovation of old houses: *The Touring and Automobile Club Of Turkey continues unremittingly its restoration and protection work. We can see contributions of the Touring and Automotive Club of Turkey to the protection of the city in almost every part of Istanbul.*

TourIstanbul: *The silhouette of Istanbul is changing. Following Eminönü, the squares of Sultanahmet, Beyazıt, Üsküdar and the Fatih Fevzi Pasha Street has been cleared of street vendors. Mayor Topbaş says that the secret of his success is "to be determined and not to confer any privileges to anybody".*

Cumhuriyet
5 April 1984

Tarihi doku canlanacak

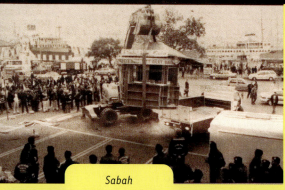

Üsküdar Meydanı ve çevresindeki gazete bayii ve halk ekmek büfesi belediye tarafından yıkıldı

Paşalimanı Caddesi'nde eskiden Zeynep Özal'a ait olan bir bar da dışarıya taştığı gerekçesiyle yerle bir edildi

Sabah
26 October 2005

above: –My dear friend, these housing projects are inhumane.
-Alas, the humane dimension of old houses is nowhere to be seen.
-We have to protect them, by moving all these people into other places. We should make this place suitable for arts and cultural activities.
-Unfortunately, those who live here treat them like trash.
-But in order to preserve these houses, we shall not do away with people, right?
-Yes, true. We have to move them into housing projects.

below: **Rejuvenating the historical environment**

have led to a resurgence in enthusiasm and the preparation of projects that aim to make Istanbul a global city. Among the many initiatives being discussed are the conversion of the historic peninsula into an open air museum; the creation of new opportunities for international tourism, shopping and business investments through the Galataport and Haydarpaşa projects; and the design of ambitious residential-business projects along the line of the Dubai Towers or Mashattan. All these projects form part of the "urban transformation project" devised for Istanbul, which has become the rationale for most of the new development and urban restructuring projects taking place in the city. The banning of street peddlers from Eminönü Square; the closure of small factories and workshops in the historic peninsula and their relocation to the outskirts of the city; the demolition of squatter housing in areas like Küçük Armutlu, Zeytinburnu and Küçük Çekmece are all undertakings that seek legitimization within the broader framework of the "urban transformation project."

Scene from "Siyaset Meydanı" programme, on the Municipality's "My City Istanbul Project"
[ATV, 25 April 2003]

When things reach this point, it becomes easier to understand the opposition and resistance these initiatives have encountered. In the first place, the transformations which have already taken place and those planned to take the process still further imply the social exclusion of a number of segments. From the examples given above, it is already possible to ascertain the short-term consequences of this transformation. It is not difficult to foresee that, as these projects impinge on the local environment the requisites of global capital, they will leave a great many people homeless, jobless, and face to face with material and psychological hardship. The restructuring of Istanbul means that a number of people's lives, their homes and the streets that constitute their everyday habitat will be directly affected and altered. In addition to its short-term impact, the long-term effects of this process must also be considered. The concept most frequently used in reference to the environmental changes experienced in Istanbul nowadays is *gentrification*. Over the past fifteen years, the increase in tourism, art and cultural activities in areas like Galata, Balat, Cihangir and Beyoğlu have pushed real estate prices and rent extremely high and rapidly transformed the social fabric. As more affluent social groups move into these districts, low income migrants, who arrived to the city a relatively short time ago, have been *forced out*

As soon as the warm weather becomes overwhelming, the city becomes deserted. The only ones left behind are the poor, the peasants and the bachelors. We usually go to the park. Immigrants from the villages and their city dwelling relatives crowd into the parks. Girls with waves in their hair like the sea, seasonal labourers and newly married women spread out among the tables. I act as if I'm not listening to them, but I listen very attentively. Their husbands talk about the congestion and the double-dealing in the cities and about the Russian prostitutes walking the streets.
[Suzan Samancı, *Suskunun Gölgesinde*, 2001, İletişim Publications, p. 26]

THE STREETS OF ISTANBUL BELONGED TO US

A flamboyant love affair
You and I had
The streets of Istanbul belonged to us
We used to show off, walking by the sea
We would even read poems
We used to wander around like festival fireworks
All day long
Among taxis, buildings, posters
Alas, those days now live
Only in the wounds of the two of us
[İsmail Uyaroğlu, *Şiirlerle İstanbul*, Kemal Özer (ed.), 1992, Yordam Publications, p. 85]

of their neighborhoods. On the one hand, these places have gained visibility on the city's consumer, culture, entertainment and tourism map. Yet, the same gentrification process that gave certain social groups access to many areas of the city simultaneously *closed them off* to others.

Fransız Sokağı, formerly known as *Cezayir Çıkmazı*, is one of the most striking examples of this *gentrification* process. A few years back, it was just another neglected street in Beyoğlu with no infrastructure to speak of and dilapidated historic buildings abandoned to their fate. A private company oversaw the "rehabilitation" and transformation of the street and its buildings, conferring upon it a brand new identity in the process. Today, entirely re-designed, the street merges shopping, recreational and cultural elements and has turned into a *consumption space*. With its cafes, restaurants, bars, art galleries and boutiques, it attracts people just passing through Beyoğlu or looking for entertainment. In addition to foreign tourists, it also draws a number of local visitors who wander like *tourists* in their native city.

Seen from one perspective, these all seem positive developments. Historic buildings are being restored, formerly neglected streets have acquired artistic and cultural vibrancy and new shopping and recreational facilities are created. Yet, if we remember that this process is shaped and functions within a framework in which the market rules and consumer economy prevails, its negative aspects also become more apparent. In the earlier example of *Fransız Sokağı*, an entire street has *de facto* renounced its identity as a *public space* and been taken over by *private capital*. The fact that a private company is in charge of enforcing security on the street is the most obvious indicator of the shift from public to private sphere. Clearly, with its high-end boutiques and trendy art galleries, the street is no longer a recreational option for many social groups. For the majority, then, their exclusion from *Fransız Sokağı* has occurred more by necessity than choice. Another point of interest here is the rapprochement between capital and culture. Nowadays, large banks and corporations open museums and exhibitions, and sponsor concerts. As Istanbul moves toward becoming a "global city," there is talk of more private sector bids for social control – through public art projects – over various public spaces of the city.

Nokta
8 May 1988

Milliyet
9 April 2005

above: **Bypass for the passage:** *The Çiçek Passage, which is approaching 100 years of age, is being restored from head to toe, in order to recreate its previous magnificent days. But will it be possible to revive its old regular customers such as Ahmet Haşim, Sait Faik, Münir Nurettin or any of the others?*

left: **Beyoğlu will rise in value through the "demolish & reconstruct" system:** *Beyoğlu Mayor Demircan has stated that they will renew the district and raise its value with the "demolish and reconstruct" model.*

Applying the logic Sharon Zukin used in her study of New York (1995), Istanbul may be considered another example of a city where there is a growing *symbolic economy*. As music, art, fashion, tourism, gourmet food and other forms of cultural consumption play increasingly important roles in the economy, the rising number of businesses and entrepreneurs in these areas generates the expansion of this symbolic economy. From this standpoint, it makes sense to argue that art serves the interest of the economy, which feeds off culture and relies on it. While culture plays a determining role in social differentiation, the distance between art and the market is reduced. The significance of the symbolic economy – the product of a blend of culture and consumerism – increases both in current representations of Istanbul and in conceiving and remembering its past.

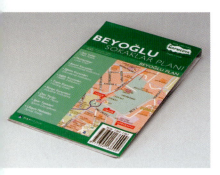

A map of Beyoğlu for local tourists

Getting off the bus in Taksim and walking towards Beyoğlu, Gülay quickened her pace in order to cross the square as soon as possible. She hadn't come to Taksim for years; she felt as if she was in a foreign country. As if she had taken a melancholy trip with an uncertain end to a distant country... When she had been with Yavuz they had steered clear of Taksim. Forbidden pavements, best to stay away from... This district was like an enemy. [Ayşegül Devecioğlu, *Kuş Diline Öykünen*, 2004, Metis Publications, p. 207]

We now know that globalization is an unequal and exclusionary process. During the past 30 years, inequalities in the income distribution of the great majority of countries in the world have grown. At the same time, economic inequalities between countries and regions have also increased. While globalizing capital rewards the groups who are able to *connect* with the inflow of goods and cash, it makes others even poorer. "Urban transformation" is the most obvious example of the complex and conflictive process of redesigning the built environment taking place in Turkey's big cities today. Apparently, for Istanbul now the sky's the limit, but at what cost?

Tempo
27 February 2004

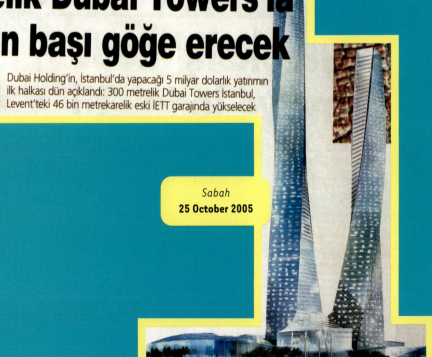

Sabah
25 October 2005

above: **Don't be a stranger to the French Street:** *In May, a French Street is opening in Beyoğlu, in Istanbul.*

below: **With the 300 metre Dubai Towers, Istanbul will touch the sky:** *Dubai Holding has unveiled the first phase of the 5 million dollar investmet it is making in Istanbul. The 300 metre high Dubai Towers Istanbul will rise in the 46,000 square metre former City Buses Garage in Levent.*

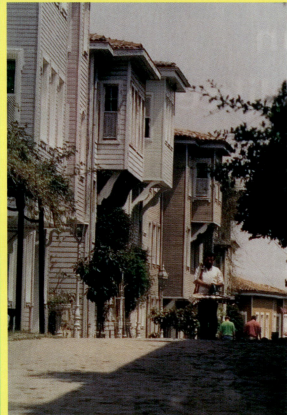

Fotoğraf: Gökhan ÖZAÇIKGÖZ

Soğukçeşme Sokağı... Üzerinde konuşulan, yazılan, hatta tuvallere yansıtılan bir sokak, bir tarih.. Bir esrar perdesinin açığa çıkarılan yüzü. Bu sokaktaki "Ayasofya Evleri" birbirinden şık ve ilginç odalarında misafirlerini ağırlıyor...

Orada bir eviniz var

İstanbul Life
June 1996

İki yüz yıl önce iplikçilere mekan olan sarnıç, bugün Antik Roma lokantası üslubunda...

Our home is there: *The Soğukçeşme Street... A street, a history that is talked about, that is written about, that is the subject of paintings... A mystery revealed. The Ayasofya Houses on this street host their guests in a variety of elegant and interesting rooms.*

Binalar ölüm TUZAĞI gibi

● Tarlabaşı'nda bulunan metruk vaziyetteki yüzlerce tarihi bina tehlike saçıyor. Depreme gerek kalmadan doğal şartlarla bile birer birer yıkılan bu binalar, önlerinden geçen binlerce insan için adeta ölüm tuzağı. Sık sık göçen binalar nedeniyle bugüne kadar çok sayıda kişi hayatını kaybetti. Onlarca kişinin de yaralanmasına neden olan tarihi yapılar, koruma altında bulunmaları nedeniyle yıkılamıyor. Yıkılmayı bekleyen yapıların bazılarında ise zor durumdaki insanların ikamet etmesi tehlikenin boyutunu daha da artırıyor.

Akşam
7 July 2005

TARLABAŞI yeni baştan

Beyoğlu Belediyesi, İstanbul'un merkezi olmasına rağmen en bakımsız semtlerinden biri olan Tarlabaşı'nı yok olmaktan kurtarmak için harekete geçti. Hazırlanan projeyle tarihi semt bambaşka bir görünüme bürünecek

Tarlabaşı all over again: *The Beyoğlu Municipality is taking action to rescue Tarlabaşı, which, although right in the centre of Istanbul, is one of the most neglected districts of the city. The project will change completely the appearance of the historical district.*

This section focuses on exclusion and violence, both by-products of the increasingly pronounced social polarization that emerged with the 1980s. Polarization showed up most clearly in urban centers. While the poor were driven off to the outer fringes of the cities, the middle classes fled from the undesirable exposure to the dangers of urban living and social pollution into gated communities that offered them a sheltered life in the company of others like themselves. A similar tendency can be observed in the area of social security. The state's retreat from social services has led to their privatization and to private insurance companies stepping into ensure health and social care. The difficulties experienced by those unable to afford such services have usually been ignored. Meanwhile, education is more than ever a rat-race strewn with numerous obstacles and ruled by merciless competition, yet nonetheless an institution tailored for the privileged. The key role that the 1980 military coup played in these developments becomes all the more evident when it is correlated to the upsurge of violence in society. Violence has become normalized and a part of everyday life, turning society into a sphere where fear rules.

no trespassers!

Sheltered lives

The apparent reason for their clash was the fact that while his brother wanted a modern, multistorey apartment, his sister, under the influence of her husband, insisted on a villa-style house. Two separate and contradictory tastes, in opposed directions? According to Kadir, rather than an East-West conflict in the background, this was more the tussle between two short-tempered people. Or maybe it was the struggle of a girl past her prime who discovered her womanhood only after covering her head and marrying a man trading in white durable goods in Sultanbeyli, and a despot who discovered his progressiveness after his sister got married and who thoughtlessly continued making use of this to cover up his professional failure.
[Mehmet Eroğlu, *Kusma Kulübü*, 2004, Agora Publications, p. 22]

Mustafa Kemal had changed the outward appearance of this nation. Or rather, he had taken each one of these people and given them a western appearance. Menderes on the other hand took this situation one step further. It wasn't enough for him to change the individuals, he changed the appearance of families as well. He put them inside apartment blocks. He took the traditional Turkish family from its wooden house and its vineyards and orchards and, following a brief period of coercion, turned it into an apartment block family.
[Demirtaş Ceyhun, *Apartman*, 1974/1981, Bilgi Publications/Sis Çanı Publications, p. 41]

From the 1950s on, Turkey's *housing problem* became a major issue and cause of conflict. In the growing tide of rural to urban migration, homeownership represented everyone's biggest dream, while simply "putting a roof over one's head" became a basic need. After the 1980s, the number of people migrating to the big cities for various reasons grew even more significant. The issue was often the topic of newspaper and magazine articles as well as of television programs. The division of urban space and the various modes of accommodation available within it directly impact the formation and configuration of socio-cultural hierarchies. This is illustrated by news headlines of the times such as – among countless similar examples – "Clash between big city slickers and provincials in apartment house," "Squatter wars," and "The whitest Turks come from the north," or advertisements for housing complexes carrying themes like "healthy, modern living," "modern living spaces," and so forth. Housing practices give rise to the images of urban/rural, modern/traditional, Western/Eastern, rich/poor and advanced/backward, in this way constituting and reflecting social and cultural hierarchies. The *conflicts* that emerge around these hierarchies are besieged on the one hand by more general economic and political processes, while on the other they contribute meaning to these processes through cultural and symbolic differentiation. The disputes experienced in the area of housing and their articulations over the past two and a half decades should be evaluated within this context.

The *migration* from villages to urban centers and the ensuing proliferation of *gecekondu* [literally, "built overnight" *squatter*] settlements are the crux of the controversy over urban space and housing. It may therefore be useful to briefly retrace the course of *squatterization* along its most general lines. Çağlar Keyder argues that the *gecekondu* phenomenon is very closely related to the political and economic processes that determine the commercialization of land in urban areas (1999). Since land policies in the Ottoman Empire upheld state and waqf ownership

"Yaşam farkı" komşuları birbirine düşürdü
Apartmanda, köylü ve şehirli kavgası!

■ Köyden gelen yeni komşularıyla mahkemelik olan apartman sakinleri "Bunlar yüzünden apartmanımızın kalitesi düştü" dedi

"Biz gavur muyuz?"
Komşularının kendilerine "Gavur eziyeti" yaptığını söyleyen Ayşe Göktay "Köylüysek insan değil miyiz. Biz de şehir adetlerini öğreneceğiz, ama biraz zaman ve yardım gerek" dedi.

"Ev alma, komşu al"
Şehirli komşularını anlayamadığını söyleyen Rafiye Göktay ise "Bizim oralarda (Ev alma komşu al) derler. Doğruymuş. Burada bizi hor görüyorlar. Keşke gelmeseydik" diye konuştu.

Bugün 2 June 1990

"Köylü köyüne"
Selda hanım "Allahın dağından gelip adam oluyorlar. Bunların şehirde ne işi var. Köylerine dönsünler" dedi.

Villagers and city dwellers fight in the apartment block: *The residents of an apartment block who sued their neighbours newly emigrated from the village, have said: "The quality of our apartment block has declined because of them."*

Hürriyet
15 October 1985

Cumhuriyet
28 April 1984

above: **Will they give us our deeds?** *There is only one question on the minds of the Yazar family that came all the way from the Palandöken Mountains to build a single-room shanty on the hills of Kartal.*

right: **A bulldozer instead of a title deed:** *200 shanties have been demolished in Ankara.*

below: **Shanty war:** *The municipality demolishes them, the residents rebuild them*

bottom: **We offer you modern living spaces:** *According to Emre Çamlıbel, General Manager of SOYAK, which realises housing projects in accordance with world trends, there is no stagnation in the construction sector, quite on the contrary, the projects they are developing are in great demand.*

Güneş
22 December 1988

Akşam
3 March 2005

Nokta
October 1985

Ali Gürbüz 8 katlı gökdelen konutunun hem mimarı hem müteahhiti hem ustası hem de sahibi

Ağır ağır çıkacaksın bu merdivenlerden.

KONUT /8 KATLI GECEKONDU

Ali Bey'in sağlam gökdelen kondusu

Kuştepe'de 8 katlı "genişleyen" gecekondunun sahibi Ali Gürbüz'ün en büyük endişesi bir gün belediyenin binasını yıkması.

Ali Bey's skyscraper shanty: *The biggest worry of Ali Gürbüz, owner of the 8-storey, "growing" shanty in Kuştepe, is that the municipality will one day demolish his building.*

rather than private property, this gave the state a determining role in shaping the *land commercialization process* of the Republican period. In the decades after the 1950s, the state's role became increasingly significant due to the surge in urban population and the growing demand for land suitable for residential development. Keyder considers that the chief driver of the "squatterization" process that emerged in this period should be sought in the *state*'s lack of either the will or the desire to institutionalize the regime of capitalist property relations. Owing to political calculations about legitimacy and political hegemony, the state has always maintained an *ambiguous* stance towards squatterization. In other words, central and local administrators have consciously avoided developing a clear-cut approach to the illegal squatter issue; quite the contrary, they have used this ambiguity as a means to expand their power base and political platform. For a long time now, squatter settlements have evoked memories of either the ceremonial granting of title deeds or melodramatic demolition scenes featuring bulldozer and municipal police forces; "Will they give us our title deed?" or "Will we get a legal title or the bulldozer?" frequently make the headlines. At the same time, we can observe that today, with the conversion of *gecekondus* into makeshift apartments, certain former squatter settlements have become formal neighborhoods possessing some sort of rudimentary infrastructure that links them to the urban center. In fact, these new urban "residents" have become a predominant component of the demographic and social fabric of rapidly expanding large cities – headed by Istanbul and Ankara – over the past fifty years.

But it wasn't only the squatter settlements that expanded after the 1950s; during this period the number of apartment buildings in big cities also increased. Owning an apartment with a spacious kitchen and bathroom, hardwood flooring and central heating, in a new building, became the dream of the middle classes. Those who could, acquired apartments built by independent contractors, while those who couldn't afford to became homeowners by joining building cooperatives. Ayşe Öncü notes that from the 1950s onward and in parallel to internal migration, apartment living – which almost from the very beginning of the century had stood for modernity and Westernization – became an even more

In the village, girls who went to milk the sheep grazing on mountain pastures in the summer and spending the night out in the open were called "Berci girls". The collection of the sheep milk and its transportation to the village by these girls was considered very valuable work. A girl's good manners was measured according to her behaviour while she was coming and going to collect milk. To show affection to girls that worked as berci one would stroke their hair and call them "my berci daughter!" In Çiçektepe only girls who picked and collected rubbish were given this title. Only such girls were affectionately called "my Berci daughter" and praised. A girl's good manners in Çiçektepe was measured according to whether she went to collect rubbish or not and according to her behaviour while she was coming and going to collect rubbish. [Latife Tekin, *Berci Kristin Çöp Masalları*, Adam Publications, p. 22]

Even if the governor gave them permission for three months, no, for three years, they would still not leave their shacks. They were clinging so tightly to these heaps of mud. They weren't looking for memories in these heaps of mud, but for a way to survive. Another three months would pass by... The governor would pardon them once again... But then, yes, then one day they would not be pardoned anymore. Then bulldozers would fill up the district, pickaxes would start to hit the mud brick walls...
[Muzaffer İzgü, *Gecekondu*, 1970/1981, Bilgi Publications, p. 53]

> *Soon we will run out of gunpowder. People will not have any money left to invest in housing. Banks will not be able to find clients capable of using housing credits. I am not making up a disaster scenario. I'm making calculations on the given data… It's obvious how much savings this nation has. It's obvious where the money is… The income of the majority of the nation doesn't increase, it cannot increase. It is impossible for the demand for housing to continue under such conditions… The demand is bound to start to fall soon… That's when the madness will end… The "soaring" prices will drop…*
>
> *I have a recommendation for those who wish to buy housing, who wish to invest in housing. If you have a lot of money, if the money you invest in housing doesn't disturb you, do as you please… But if your money was the fruit of a lot of work, if it was earned with difficulty, don't you be fooled by others… These prices are high, they are "soaring" prices. It is not wise to invest with such prices. It will be very difficult to turn this investment into cash quickly, in general. I have warned you… You can do as you wish.* [A section taken from Güngör Uras' column on *Milliyet*, broadcast on the "Among the Articles" programme, TGRT Radio, 10 October 2005]

decisive status symbol (1997: 65). In this period, a very marked cultural divide, one which directly affected the spatial structure of the city, emerged between the *urbanites* with residences in upscale neighborhoods and the so-called *villagers* living in the squatter settlements. This divide at the same time echoed the class differences between white collar professionals and the blue collar workers who did manual or semi-skilled work. After the 1980s, as big construction firms like ENKA and Doğuş began to undertake housing projects in the cities, certain sections of the middle class gradually shifted toward high rise apartment communities (*sites*). The Mass Housing Administration founded during those years actually accelerated this process with attractive credit and installment opportunities. Thus, the 1980s emerged as the decade in which the middle classes became more self-contained and the *spatial segregations* in the city's structure even more pronounced. While homeownership spread to a larger social base that also included first-generation *gecekondus*, living in a *site* became an indicator of prestige and a higher *quality* of life – at least for certain segments of the middle classes. Nonetheless, the decrease in the real income of public employees and other salaried groups over the same period, growing income inequalities, and the rise in real estate prices made *homeownership* progressively more *difficult* to attain. For though Özal claimed *there was no shortage of housing in Turkey*, the leitmotiv of those years – "who will give the *ortadirek* [lower middle class urban families] a cozy nest?" – vividly illustrated the unresolved housing issue. Meanwhile, those who could not afford to buy found themselves facing rapidly increasing rents; in some neighborhoods where real estate values had surged, dollar- and mark-indexed rents forced people to move.

When the newcomers to the cities in the 1980s began to acquire greater *visibility* through their publicly asserted musical preferences and lifestyles, this created heated controversy. Squatter districts were regarded as a source of cultural and architectural *pollution* and the *gecekondu* population branded "displaced peasants" unable to adapt to urban life. Sometimes condemned as the conveyors of the *arabesk* culture, at others labeled "invaders" or the "masses" that made the

A doormat with a welcome sign

Özal: "Türkiye'de konut açığı yoktur"

★ Başbakan Turgut Özal, Türkiye'de daha iyi konutta yaşama ihtiyacı bulunduğunu söyledi

Günaydın
1 November 1984

Nokta
October 1985

DOSYA
KONUT / HER DEVRİN SORUNU
Ortadireğin yuvasını kim yapar?
Dargelirlilerin konut sorununu çözmekte yetersiz kalan Toplu Konut Yasası'nda köklü değişiklikler yapılması isteniyor.

Ankara Batıkent, dar gelirliler için orası bile ulaşılmaz bir düş

above: **Özal: "There is no shortage of housing in Turkey"**: *Prime Minister Turgut Özal has said that there is need for better housing in Turkey.*

below: **Who will build homes for the middle class?** *Changes are needed in the Public Housing Law, which is inadequate in solving the housing problem of low-income families.*

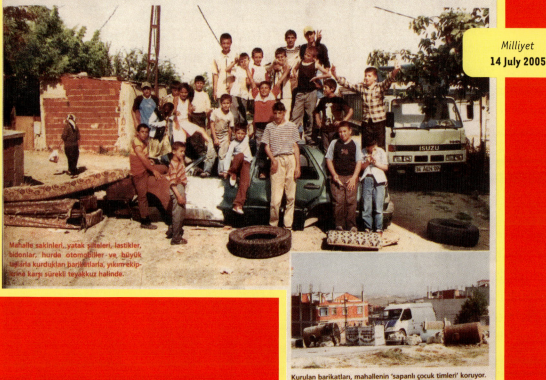

Milliyet
14 July 2005

above: **24 hour on guard against demolition:** *The residents of Bayramtepe in Küçükçekmece, who received an eviction notice, have built pseudo-Palestinian barricades on the streets. Full of the fear of demolition, the residents have entrusted the barricades in this unlawful operation to children with stones and slingshots.*

right: **Present-day villages:** *While shanty towns are demolished, luxury buildings are constructed in line with Istanbul Metropolitan Municipality's "Urban Transformation Project." "All inclusive" housing offers not only a home, but a lifestyle.*

İstanbul Life
September 2005

life of Turkish "citizens" more difficult, they drew frequent criticism in the mainstream press and other media. This disapproval essentially voiced the uneasy response of the relatively higher income city dwellers who defined themselves as Western and modern.

A few different types of door locks

Another development of the 1980s was the state's repudiation of national development policies and the resulting exacerbation of social *polarization* and conflict. Metropolitan areas now found themselves increasingly less able to accept the newcomers. While labor unions lost their clout, it also became harder for rural migrants to find work in factories, so newcomers found work at very low wages in the expanding *informal economy* fueled by the growing flexibility of production. One indication of the effect that rising poverty and deepened class differentiations had on culture was the term *varoş* which entered general usage around this time. Today, *gecekondus* not only signify "otherness" but also "threat." They are considered environments with "anti-secular" lifestyles and opinions, harboring "illegal, separatist political organizations" (Erman 2004:11). Squatter settlements are also viewed as the root of every form of violence and delinquency, from street gangs to glue-sniffing kids and pickpockets. The term "varoş" comes from the Hungarian and originally referred to settlements outside the city walls. It was adopted by the media, in particular, to indicate peripheral neighborhoods and acquired common usage at the time of the May 1, 1996 events when headlines proclaimed "The *Varoş* Hit the City" and "The *Varoş* Break Loose" and columnists wrote about the necessity of understanding how "millions of people flooding from their villages to the city outskirts" had been "pushed into the arms of radical Islam, terrorism or vandalism" (Bila 1996, quoting Erman 2004). The term "varoş" was thus associated with violence right from the start. As the squatterization process spread to the entire city and *gecekondus* themselves underwent certain transformations, the word lost its original meaning and "varoş" took its place to signify the political *threat* that the destitute rural migrants settled on the outskirts of the city now represented (op.cit).

Meanwhile, urban spaces began to alter as the upper middle classes fled, first to avoid what they perceived to be the threat that

It is good to be prudent around here. When they see an unfamiliar car in front of their doors, residents around here become even more uneasy. These people are always on tenterhooks. When they heard we were coming they must have felt uneasy anyway. It is difficult to be a leftist in the varoş. Being revolutionary around here is not a romantic adventure or a conscious choice of class, it's a life style, it's a fury. And it's dangerous.
[Oya Baydar, *Erguvan Kapısı*, 2004, Can Publications, p. 68]

Günaydın
29 July 1981

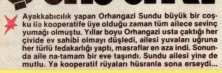

Hürriyet
10 January 1982

above: **The two ends of a stick:** *In order to own a home and a roof over their head, low income people have to rely either on the National Lottery or on joining a Cooperative.*

left: **The art of living in an apartment block:** *In an apartment block you don't have the freedom you would have in a detached house. You need to be careful in order not to distrub your neighbours and you need to follow all the rules and regulations of the apartment block lifestyle.*

Ortadireğe ev hayal oldu

Milliyet
9 June 1997

right: **Owning a house is a dream for the middle class:** *The rapidly increasing population of Turkey, the emigration from the rural areas towards the big cities and the fact that areas for housing are decreasing day by day has caused the real estate prices to reach astronomical heights.*

below: **To rent a house you need to pay in dollars, not Turkish Liras:** *-A mail carriage will sure pass by at some point… That's the only way I can pay you in dollars.*

Gırgır
27 August 1989

A security monitor and a camera

It wasn't often that one would see open or close the entrance to number five, Sevim Apartments. Almost no one ever entered the building, apart from the grocer's boy. The five inhabitants of number five, Sevim Apartments, who didn't even have any contact with each other, let alone with the outside, lived alone in their homes and never ever went out. They met all their needs via phone orders; they didn't even open the door completely to the grocer's boy bringing the orders, they would only half open it and in the darkness they would snatch whatever he was carrying, without deigning him with either a tip or a greeting, and they would retreat inside immediately. [Mine Söğüt, *Beş Sevim Apartmanı*, 2003, Yapı Kredi Publications, p. 8-9]

gecekondu settlements posed to their particular culture and later the imminent danger to "public order and safety" that the *varoş* – as they were now called – had come to represent. Today, this segment is concentrated in specific areas where it has chosen to reside within gated communities with the enhanced safety of "special security systems" and proximity of "others." In their search for "havens of peace and safety," these privileged *minorities* have thus gradually shifted to regions outside Istanbul where new types of settlement like Kemercountry, Zekeriyaköy and Alkent 2000 are situated today. In Istanbul, this is where the "whitest" Turks now reside, and similar developments have also taken place in Ankara. Over the past two decades, new gated communities have appeared in rapid succession on the Eskişehir Highway in districts like Bilkent, Korukent and Çay Yolu. Situated in a "natural environment" and offering a wide range of social facilities, the crucial characteristic distinguishing these residential complexes is the fact that they are enclosed in high walls and employ professional guards. Uğur Tanyeli speaks of a "fear of the metropolis" to explain the growing preference for these closed and guarded spaces (2004). Much more than any real desire to commune with nature, the decisive factor here is the possibility of forming the exclusive community that is no longer available in the metropolis. Ayşe Öncü uses a similar argument when she writes that the desire for the "dream home," fueled by images in foreign magazines and on TV channels, has shifted housing preferences in Istanbul from apartment houses to gated communities. But while the reason for this shift is usually expressed as a longing for more contact with "nature," she says the real cause is the wish to escape *social pollution* (1997). In the new millennium, when high walls isolate the rich from the dangers outside and protect them against the threat posed by the poor, the *varoş* youth form "Palestinian" barricades to stop bulldozers from demolishing their homes. Consequently, both concrete *and* symbolic *walls* segregate these different segments of the city from each other today.

left: **Happy and secure:** *Because they have decided to become partners in our cooperation with nature...*

below: **The whitest Turks are in the north:** *The jet set of Istanbul has escaped from the chaos of the city and has formed a "paradise of peace and security" on the Black Sea coast.*

May 2003

Tempo
1 March 2004

Piyasada para yoksa

Bunları kim alıyor?

DENİZE BAKMAK 5 MİLYON
Küçük Moda'daki bu yeni yapılmış apartmanın 260 metrekarelik, süper lüks dairelerinin fiyatı 25 ile 30 milyon lira. Müteahhitinin belirttiğine göre, üç tipe ayrılan dairelerde, fiyat denize bakış açısına göre değişiyor. Deniz az görünüyorsa 25 milyon, eğer daireden "deniz çok temaşa edilebiliyorsa" rakam 5 milyon daha pahalı.

❶ **Alan parayı nereden buluyor?**
❷ **Satan parayı ne yapıyor?**

● Nakit para sıkıntısından en fazla etkilenen emlâk piyasasında fiyatlar astronomik rakamlarda ve 50-100 milyona alıcı bekleyen konutlar var.

BEBEK'TEKİ DAİRE 85 MİLYON
Bebek'te ana cadde üzerindeki Münevver Apartmanının giriş katının üzerindeki 360 metrekarelik daire için sahibi "85 milyon peşin" diyor. 6 odası, 100 metrekarelik lambrili salonu, üç banyosu, bir tuvaleti, büyük mutfağı olan bu 85 milyonluk dairenin ayrıca, zemin katta 1 odalı, banyolu mutfaklı bir de müştemilatı var.

İSTANBUL'A TEPEDEN BAKAN DAİRE 75 MİLYON
Taşlık'ta İnönü Köşkü'nün sırasındaki Balıklı Apartmanının üçüncü katına 75 milyon isteniyor. Cephesi 10.5 metre olan, üç yatak odası, büyük bir salonu bulunan ve iç dekorasyonu için 18 milyon lira harcanan dairenin sahibi, yurt dışında tahsil gören çocuklarıyla birarada oturabileceği bir yer alabilmek için bu daireyi satışa çıkarmış.

"DEĞERLİ MÜLK" 80 MİLYON
Sahiplerinin "Başka özel işlerimiz var. Onlarla uğraşacağız" deyip satışa çıkardıkları bu 7 katlı işhanı İstiklal Caddesinin göbeğinde. Caddeye 8 metre cepheli, altında birahane ve dükkanı olan 159 metrekarelik işhanının her katında 5 odalı işyerleri var. "Değerli mülk" şeklinde değerlendirilen bu işhanına talep edilen fiyat peşin 80 milyon lira.

KALLAVİ'DE 14 MİLYONA HAN
Tepebaşı Kallavi Sokak'taki Akın Han da satılık. "Paraya ihtiyacım var" diyen sahibi, 5 katlı bu han için 14 milyon peşin istiyor.

15 MİLYONA VİLLA
Küçükçekmece gölü kenarındaki, sahibinin villa dediği bu iki katlı ev 800 metrekarelik alan üzerinde kurulu. 5 büyük odası olan, ancak içinde kimse oturmadığı için sahibi tarafından satılığa çıkarılan bu konut 15 milyon verende kalacak.

Who buys these? *Prices in the real estate market, which is affected the most by the shortage of cash, have reached astronomical heights and there are residences on sale for 50-100 million.*

Güneş
1 February 1983

Hürriyet
23 August 1986

November 1987

above: **Out of the bag came houses on installments:** When the 182 flats built in Ataköy by the Turkish Emlak and Kredi Bank were put on sale, there were 352 buyers and the new homeowners were determined by a draw.

right: **There is a gym in Alkent. For a modern and healthy life.**

Living, unregistered

One of the most frequently debated topics of recent years is the *social security system* and health care in particular. Actually, concern over the decrease in the number of minimum wage employees benefiting from some kind of social security, the long lines in front of state hospitals, the worsening living standard of retirees and similar issues have long been on the agenda. In addition, poverty is frequently a topic of discussion in newspaper and magazine stories or on TV programs. People foraging in the trash of garbage bins, living in tents and children selling kleenex have become the common street scenes of our urbanscapes. This in, turn, has led to an equal emphasis on the urgency for *social assistance* services as well as social security. Parallel to the deterioration in social security services, the past years have seen a surge in the promotion of private retirement and health insurance plans. Many banks and companies provide insurance services in a wide variety of areas. There has also been a marked increase in *private health* services. How should we interpret the overall picture that emerges from these developments? To give a meaningful answer to this question it might be helpful to first discuss two general developments: the transformation of the state's structure and functions and fundamental changes in employment.

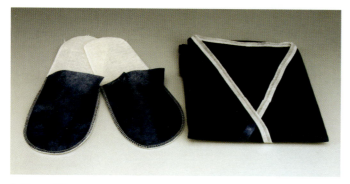

A disposable apron and galoshes provided for patients in private hospitals

In the 1980s many governments around the world began to *reduce* their social expenditures, essentially reversing the welfare policies that marked the post-World War II period. Buoyed by the wave of neoliberalism that engulfed the entire capitalist world, the proponents of less state involvement in the economy and less social spending – viewed as the cause of the budget deficit – won the ideological war. After 1980 most governments in Turkey defended similar views and, under pressure from the

Milliyet
15 May 1988

above: **4 out of 10 people have no insurance:** *While there is one pensioner per ten working people in European countries, here there are 4 pensioners per ten working people and this causes the social security resources to decrease rapidly.*

below: **All Turkey is being insured:** *According to the General Health Insurance law draft, all the citizens of the Turkish Republic will be covered by this insurance.*

Milliyet aktüalite — SAYI 36 SAYFA 3

15 MAYIS 1988 KAPAK

● Anayasa gereği herkes sosyal güvenlik hakkına sahip ama...

10 kişiden dördü güvencesiz

Batı ülkelerinde 10 çalışan sigortalıya bir emekli düşerken bizde 4 emekli düşüyor ve bu da SSK kaynaklarının hızla erimesine neden oluyor.

Bütün Türkiye sigortalanıyor

Genel Sağlık Sigortası Kanun Taslağı'na göre, Türkiye Cumhuriyeti'nin bütün vatandaşları sigorta kapsamına alınacak. Taslak, Başbakanlık'ta

SAĞLIK SİGORTASI ZORUNLU OLACAK

Genel Sağlık Sigortası'na katılmak zorunlu. Er-erbaşlar ile Türkiye'deki yabancılardan kendi ülkesinde sosyal sigortası olanların dışındaki tüm kişiler Genel Sağlık Sigortalı olacak. Sağlık sigortası için yüzde 5'i çalışan, yüzde 7.5'i ise işveren hissesi olmak üzere yüzde 12.5 oranında prim ödenecek. Emeklilerden sağlık hizmeti için prim alınmayacak.

EMEKLİLİK SİSTEMİ SİLBAŞTAN

Taslağa göre, emeklilik sistemi de silbaştan değiştiriliyor. Emeklilik yaşı 2035 yılına kadar kadınlarda 58, erkeklerde 60 olarak uygulanacak. 2036'dan itibaren emeklilik yaşlarında kademeli bir artış gerçekleştirilecek. İlk defa sigortalı olacaklarda en az 25 yıl (9 bin gün) prim ödenmiş olması şartıyla yaşlılık aylığı bağlanacak.

Yeni Şafak
4 March 2005

September 1982

Full Life Insurance: *You are the guarantee of your children, and we are the guarantee of the unknown world of tomorrow.*

IMF and World Bank in particular, implemented policies of this kind. Turkey, along with many other countries during this period, significantly decreased the budget for state expenditures in health, education, social assistance and similar social services. Another component of this policy trend was privatization. The private sector quickly filled the void left by the state's conscious retreat from certain economic fields, leaving areas like health, education and retirement subject to market forces. Under these conditions, it is no coincidence that private health services and the insurance sector in Turkey began to grow fast in the 1980s. Initially targeting high-income groups, private health and retirement plans are now becoming more widespread, especially among the new middle classes. For the large majority of society, however, an "insured" life is an increasingly distant prospect.

Any analysis of the social security issue requires a study of the transformation in employment. These days, parallel to the restructuring of the global economy and the new flexibility in production, important differentiations in blue collar employment have emerged. At the same time that organized labor's share in total employment has plunged, *employment security* has deteriorated and unregistered employment has increased. In Turkey, this process has led to the rapid *informalization* of labor markets and, especially in small-scale manufacturing, to the growing use of women and child labor. Consequently, concurrent with the sharp fall in workers' real income there has been a notable regression in their social rights. Undoubtedly, the repressive environment that followed the 1980 military *coup* was largely responsible for the relatively "calm" manner with which hundreds of thousands of people accepted the severe changes that would personally affect the conditions of their lives. One of the military regime's first measures was to halt the activities of *labor* unions and outlaw *strikes*. The 1982 Constitution guaranteed that the unions would never again return to their former, powerful days with numerous new prohibitions and limitations on the right to organize and union rights. Union officials were banned from participating in politics and supervision of the unions handed over to the state. Legislative changes led to the closure of relatively small unions. Today, the vast majority of workers in Turkey is employed on a *contract* basis and is

I said to myself how can she trust me, what have I got, she works in the ready-made clothing business all day long, making buttonholes and embroidering, what can she want from me. Look now, I'm taking it out, the way the poor girl struggles like a wounded baby bird, and her wanting to take refuge with me, her finding me important, made me feel weird, I was probably embarassed, that's what it was probably, I was embarassed. I don't treat anybody badly, either in the atelier or in the slums, but I didn't know I was prasied, I hadn't realised it at all. While Ayten was talking, out of breath, I must have enjoyed it, that's what it was...
[Adalet Ağaoğlu, "Dar Odanın Karanlığı", *Hadi Gidelim*, 1982, Remzi Publications, p. 24]

Başbakanın ilk mesajı sigortacılıkla ilgiliydi

«Mali kaynak yaratmada bankacılık, menkul değerler piyasası yanında sigorta sektörünün çok önemli olduğunu bilhassa belirtmek isterim. Bu sektör geliştirildiğinde, ekonomik kalkınmamızın ihtiyacı olan fonların bir kısmını yaratabileceği gibi, halkımızın ve iş hayatımızın beklenmedik tehlikelere karşı korunmasını sağlayabilecektir. Önümüzdeki dönemde Türk sigorta sektörünün, ülkemiz menfaatleri ve batı dünyası düzeyinde müessir olabilmesi için gerekli çalışmalar ve düzenlemeler yapılacaktır.»

Başbakan Turgut Özal

Sigorta Dünyası
1 December 1983

Umudumuz sağlık sigortası

SSK'dan umudunu kesen şirket yöneticileri, elemanlarını özel sigorta şirketlerine sigortalatma yoluna gidiyor. 1989 yılından bu yana grup sağlık sigortası yaptıran şirketlerin sayısı hızla artarak bu kapsamdaki sigortalıların sayısı bine yaklaştı.

Akşam
20 September 1994

above: **The prime minister's first message concerned the insurance sector.**

below: **Health insurance is our only hope:** *The company managers who give up on state's social security system prefer private insurance firms.*

deprived of its social rights. With unions as weak as they are, it is extremely difficult for these labor segments to demand their rights on a legal platform.

Changes in the structure of the state and its functions and the deep-rooted transformation of employment form the backdrop for the developments we are observing today in the area of social security. There is another point here to which we should immediately call attention: Turkey has never had a *welfare state* of the size or effectiveness of Western European countries. Turkey's welfare system is largely *informal* and mainly depends on family, relations and community ties. Alongside this system, the state social security institutions also filled certain useful functions, even if the quality of their services were not very high. Today, we see that the social security net provided by both systems has very much come unraveled. People are no longer able to keep up traditional relationships of mutual support in the changing economic and social structure of the cities. Growing unemployment, a narrowing of affordable residential areas in the cities and the decline in the assistance provided by relatives in the village as a result of falling agricultural income are gradually bringing family and relative-related support mechanisms to an end. We should add here, that the most affected have been Kurdish families forced to *migrate* to large cities by the state policy of vacating villages, the long-running conflict in the east, and declining agricultural revenues. Recent attempts to reform the state social security system hold little hope of meeting the growing demand for social security and health services. For example, most agree that the "green card" system for those segments of the population not covered by the social security system does not provide sufficient coverage of treatment and drug costs. With this overview we have tried to show that a very large segment of the population is *excluded* both socially and economically. At the forefront of these segments are children and the elderly.

At this point, it is important that we take note of an important demographic trend (Buğra, 2001: 27). As everyone agrees, Turkey is a young country. But at the same time two things are happening to change this: the birth rate is declining and the 65

A house ornament superstitiously believed to bring good health

These hands were snow white once. A far away, very far away sparkle of youth must have passed from this face, from this hair and these hands. Once she said: "I was young too once, my girl." She had said this when she was reproved by the girl's mother because she didn't have the energy to finish the house chores. She had finished her work and she was telling tales to the girl. When she was reproved her eyes filled with tears. She said it slowly. This was the only time she had spoken out against the mother. That's when the girl decided to protect her. If granny wasn't able to speak out, then she would.
[Ayla Kutlu, *Sen de Gitme Triyandafilis*, 2000, Bilgi Publications, p. 73]

and older population is growing in both absolute and percentage terms. In the near future this trend will create serious problems for the social security system. The rise in the number of elderly, the weakening of mutual support networks in communities and families, greater women participation in the workforce – all these factors mean that looking after the elderly is going to become a more visible problem in our society, whose gendered division of labor usually assigns women this task.

The critical problems in the social security system are naturally directly related to the process of growing poverty. Bu as the *social* extent of this poverty has conveniently been distanced from actual visibility, the lives of the poor only touch other segments of society as a form of *spectacle*. Representations of poverty have overtaken its concrete reality. Necmi Erdoğan points out that in recent years three among these have acquired prevalence: "phobic" representations, pathetic representations [*garibanizm* from the Turkish "gariban" meaning pitiful or pathetic] and romanticism (2001: 10-12).

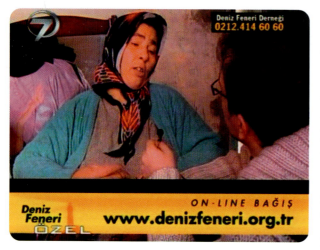

A scene from "Deniz Feneri" programme [Kanal 7, 13 April 2005]

"Phobic" representations accentuate the *threatening* aspect of the poor. Objectified in news stories as "glue sniffers," the "varoş," "street children" and "pickpockets," the poor emerge as an object of fear. One of the clearest expressions of the neoliberal ideology's approach to poverty, *garibanizm* has figured in certain newspaper columns. Defining *garibanizm* as "one level up from populism," Ertuğrul Özkök also says the following: "Income inequality is obviously bad. But looking at the issue solely through the lens of *garibanizm* only shows part of the reality. The other side to unequal *income distribution* is the availability of *cheap labor*. And this adds to the competitive power of a country's industry" (Özkök 2001). As Necmi Erdoğan puts it, this "technocrat" approach is typical of neoliberalism, which domesticates poverty and reduces it to an individual issue. Finally, "romanticism" appears essentially as part of the Islamist and nationalist discourses' quest for hegemony. It is best illustrated in television programs like *Deniz Feneri*, *Bam Teli*,

November 2003

Even though you can not be in this photo, your dreams for your loved ones are under guarantee.

Especially the fear of preventing the country from developing was a pressure not easy to endure. Our underdeveloped regions — and especially the East — were a compulsory source of inspiration for all writers and for all kinds of artists. And not only while creating... No, even during your daily activities you would feel this pressure on your back. While you wore your coat, you would think of the millions who didn't even have a scarf. While you read a book — or you wrote one — thousands of little eyes who hadn't attained equality in education followed you with anger — or hurt. While you sank your fork in the soft and well-cooked meat in your plate... I put the plate I was holding slowly onto the table, trying not to let anyone notice.
[Oğuz Atay, *Eylembilim*, 1999, İletişim Publications, p. 76]

Kimse Yok Mu?, which focus on very poor families. These shows emphasize various moral and religious values and convey the message that problems can be solved through *good wil*l and community solidarity.

A common feature to all these forms of representation is the *otherization*, *objectification* and *functionalization* of the poor. Needless to say, these representations thus stand in the way of any real *alleviation* of the economic and socio-political problems related to poverty. Some of the *measures* taken instead remain extremely superficial. Cases in point are news reports on how "hotels will distribute all 'surplus' food to the poor" and this way save 40 million dollars in wasteful expenditures and feed the hungry," and the Ministry of Health's recent decision to produce bread supplemented with vitamins to "reduce the high rate of iron-deficiency anemia and sicknesses caused by iodine or folic acid deficiencies." Social security is a *vital* necessity to assure both the present and the future. While some are able to purchase *health* or *life policies* or *personal pensions* to guarantee their futures and that of their children, friends or relatives, others remain completely excluded from the security these bring. It is no longer their labor that is unregistered, but their very lives.

Fakirlere portakallı ördek

Oteller, ihtiyaç fazlası tüm yiyecekleri yoksula dağıtacak. 40 milyon dolarlık israf önlenecek, aç vatandaş doyacak

Milliyet
8 September 2002

above: **Orange duck for the poor:** *By distributing all the surplus food to the poor, hotels will prevent a waste of 40 million dollars and the hungry will be fed.*

below: **Unregistered lives:** *It has been determined that 554 out of every 1,000 people living in Turkey are not covered by any social security system.*

KAYIT DIŞI HAYATLAR

Türkiye'de çalışan her bin kişiden 554'ünün herhangi bir sosyal güvenlik sistemine bağlı olmadığı saptandı

Birgün
18 January 2005

Education's hurdle race

Educational CDs for babies

- I only found out what will happen when you become a teacher. We would go wherever they appoint you, right?
- Are all the children admitted to this school from poor families, mom? Did you find out about that too?
- Well, of course, if they take exams for free boarding schools, they must come from poor families.
- Then I will pass the exam. Don't worry. I'll pass the exam with high grades. And then I'll make friends here. Two days a week you will leave the hospital and I'll leave school and we will go home together. And on visiting days I will get you grocery biscuits. [Füruzan, *Parasız Yatılı*, 1996, Yapı Kredi Publications, p. 100]

For the generals that engineered the September 12, 1980 military *coup*, the *young* were among the main perpetrators of the country's troubles and the "state of anarchy" it found itself in. University students, in particular, had fallen prey to the influence of "foreign" and "noxious" ideologies, and the institutions of higher education were incapable of fulfilling their duties. As soon as the generals seized power, they embarked on a series of measures aimed at regulating educational institutions and reaffirmed at every occasion their "resolve" in that matter. In Istanbul, the Court Martial Commandership made their intentions very clear in communiqué 52: "Any student who attempts to propagate anarchy in school will be expelled." Meanwhile Kenan Evren, in his messages stressing the need "to protect our children from corrupt ideologies," frequently reminded the public that certain modes of thinking were *prohibited*. To implement these proclamations, changes and new regulations were introduced at almost every level of the education system, and new institutions were founded. In other words, the generals' attempts to institutionalize the *authoritarian* mentality that could be felt very strongly in their discourse were aimed at *transforming* and *taming* the entire educational system from top to bottom. It is should come as no surprise, then, that over the past 25 years, *education* has been one of those areas where the traces of the 1980 military *coup* are still most felt. This also shows the *significance* of education for those in power as a means to achieve the desired conditions for production and establish ideological hegemony. From the 1980s on and in varying ways, education would continue to be an open arena for political regulation and power struggles.

During the 1980s, government policies sought to control and impose their discipline on almost every educational institution. The Higher Education Council (YÖK) is a product of those times

○ **23 Nisan Bayramı törenlerle kutlandı**

TBMM'deki törende Org. EVREN "Geçmişteki kâbus dolu günlere dönmemek için öğretmenlere büyük görevler düşmektedir,, DEDİ

67 il ve KTFD'den gelen ilkokul öğrencileri TBMM Genel Kurul Salonu'nda Org. Evren'le birlikte

EVREN 'Çocuklarımızı sapık ideolojilerden korumalıyız,

Tercüman
24 April 1981

Paşabahçe İlkokulu öğrencilerinden bir grup, dün 1. Ordu ve İstanbul Sıkıyönetim Komutanı Orgeneral Necdet Uruğ'u ziyaret etti. Uruğ, "Orgeneral" üniformalı bir öğrenciyi makamına oturtarak sohbet etti.
(MEHMET ÜNLÜ)

We must protect our children from perverted ideologies: *President General Evren addressed elementary school children from 67 provinces in the assembly hall of the Turkish Parliament.*

left: Students promoting anarchy in schools will be dismissed: *Communique number 52 of the Istanbul Martial Law Headquarters.*

below: **–Be a good kid and don't do any communist propaganda in school.**

İstanbul Sıkıyönetim Komutanlığı'nın 52 numaralı bildirisi:

Okullara anarşi sokmaya çalışan öğrencinin okulla ilişkisi kesilecek

Günaydın
1 October 1980

Gırgır
2 April 1989

and probably still its most debated and criticized institutional initiative. It seems highly indicative of the period's priorities that such an institution should have been founded even before a new constitution was drafted. The 1981 Law on Higher Education, aimed at centralizing the administration of universities and institutions of higher education, endowed YÖK with extensive authority. To quote Ahmet İnsel: "This law was molded to the political preferences of September 12. It reflected the reaction of the new regime's think tank to the university world, which it held directly responsible for the conflictual environment – the 'youth movements'– of the 1970s, and reflected the authoritarian and centralist aspirations of a technocrat mentality" (2003: 73). YÖK was given authority and *control* in a number of areas, from the appointment of university rectors and faculty members to curricular standardization and dress code. As the council began to use these powers, it initiated a number of measures that brought significant changes to university education. Courses in "history of Turkish revolution," Turkish and physical education were made compulsory. During those years, a great many faculty members resigned in protest of the "barracks discipline" imposed on universities. Although YÖK has been criticized on numerous platforms and subjected to more than 30 legislative changes since the day it was founded, the higher education law that underpins it is still largely valid. How YÖK has remained standing to this day, amidst all this criticism and controversy, is in itself a topic for investigation. Just the fact that it has endured demonstrates that the scars left by the September 12 military *coup* still run deep. This state of affairs is also a warning that the September 12 mindset is not restricted to the military but extends to a much wider social base. We should therefore discuss the topic on a broader level and in particular concentrate on two points: the general *militarization* of society in Turkey and the influence on education of *neoliberalism*, the dominant ideology of the post-1980 period.

According to Ayşegül Altınay, militarism is "the identification of an individual, a society or a non-military association with military values rather than with civil values" (2003). Militarization, then, is the process through which concepts embodied in the military spread to and are accepted by society as a whole. During this process, the militarist standpoint becomes dominant and the use

MONUMENT TO THE UNKNOWN STUDENT

Look here, here under this black slate of marble
Lies a child who would go to the blackboard
If only he had lived through one more recess
He was killed in a state school classroom

The incorrect question both the state and nature asked was:
Where does the Transoxiana pour into?
The only right answer came from a finger at the very back row:
To the heart of the revolution of a sallow nation's children!

Tying a purple hand-printed and emroidered kerchief to his neck
To ease his suffering, his father, the second-hand dealer, wrote:
I had convinced him that he had toys.

Wearing a soldier's coat and suckling a young deer secretly
From that day on, his mother, the washerwoman, wrote:
Oh, they have compensated my son for his labour.

His friends wove this poem with oleanders:
Never mind, 128! In the little free boarding schools of suicide
Every child has a child older than himself in his heart
All the class will send you birds free of envelopes on children's holidays. [Ece Ayhan, "Meçhul Öğrenci Anıtı", *Bütün Yort Savul'lar!*, 1999, Yapı Kredi Publications, p. 125]

Tempo
27 May 1990

right: **Determined to slaughter the system!:** *Özal is not keen on backtracking from the introduction of fees into the university education system.*

far right: **Enough is enough:** *SHP is going to bring the YÖK (the Higher Education Council) issue to the parliament in April.*

Nokta
23 March 1986

A toy Turkish soldier

That morning we picked up the teacher from the house of the head of the village and we went to school. The school had a single classroom and looked like anything but a school. In the garden of the school, surrounded by barbed wire, there was fresh cattle dung. ... When the rusty door of the school opened with a creak, the head of the village started coughing and rotating his prayer beads. "I'm going to oil it, don't worry!" The teacher bit his lips, took a deep breath and hunched his back, rose on his toes and with a voice that could barely be heard, said "this is impossible, a lot of work needs to be done, most of the windows are broken." At that point we all looked at each other. We immediately rolled up our sleeves. We worked till the evening, covering the windows with nylon sheets and repairing the cupboards. The daughter of the head of the village brought us tea and gözleme. The teacher had gone very red in the face; he mumbled, and there was a knot in his throat when he said "such a desolate village!" The head of the village patted the teacher's back and said "Don't, my son, we need your light..."
[Suzan Samancı, *Korkunun Irmağında*, 1996, Metis Publications, p. 55]

of force to solve issues is legitimized, to the point that "dying or killing for a particular cause" is glorified. Naturally, militarization is not a process limited to the post-1980 period only. Even the fact that there has been a "national security" class taught in schools since 1926 should give us an idea of how far back militarization efforts in Turkey reach. The content of the course and that a retired army officer teaches it rather than a teacher appointed by the Ministry of National Education reveal how children are exposed to military values and expected to assimilate them from a very young age (Altınay 2003). A number of other less obvious examples of militarization in education also come to mind: classroom layout and the arrangement of desks and working space; dress code; punitive discipline methods, in particular corporal punishment; and the content of history, literature and other textbooks – to name only a few. However, militarization is not bound to the educational sphere only; it infiltrates other areas and everyday social practices as well. Some instances include the send-off given by family and friends to new military recruits, the firing of gunshots into the air at weddings or after a match, and the soldier outfits sometimes worn by children at traditional circumcision ceremonies. In short, militarization emerged in the Republican period as almost an integral element of society and was compounded by the rising wave of *nationalism* that followed the 1980 military regime and the conflict in southeastern Anatolia. The September 12 military intervention, though meant to put an end to "anarchy," can actually be considered to have fueled and reinforced *violence*. Recent manifestations of violence, not limited just to universities but including high schools as well, may well be a hint to rethink events from this perspective.

The growing prevalence of *neoliberal ideology* is another development that may have assisted the spread of violence in society. Central to this ideology is the reduced role of the state. However, in Turkey and all over the world, the past 25 years have shown that the state's abdication of responsibility remained bound to the *economic* and *cultural* spheres; in the military field especially, state investments significantly increased. Actually, if we consider that policies to liberalize the economy and promote free-market rationality are largely dependent on institutional and political *regulations*, it might be more accurate to talk of a *revised*

Sınıfta dehşet

Psikolojik sorunları olan öğrenci, tabancayla sınıf bastı, öğretmeni rehin aldı, arkadaşlarına korkulu anlar yaşattı. İntihara kalkıştı, sonunda polise teslim oldu

Milliyet
19 October 1999

Öğrenim gördüğü okulda dehşet dolu dakikalar yaşatan S.U'nun (sağda) bir yıl önce ruh ve sinir hastalıkları hastanesinde tedavi gördüğü öğrenildi. S.U.'nun arkadaşları olayın şokunu uzun süre üzerlerinden atamadı (solda).

Horror in the classroom:
A student with psychological problems stormed the classroom with a gun, took his teacher as hostage and threatened his classmates. After an unsuccessful suicide attempt, he surrendered to the police.

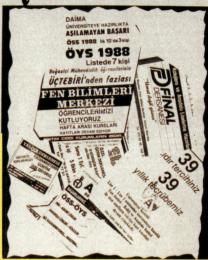

Son Havadis
3 October 1988

Star
19 July 2005

above: **Private tutoring schools compete ruthlessly:** *Some teachers wake up their students in the middle of the night to make them study.*

right: **Private schools have outdone state schools:** *The results were announced of the Highschool Entrance Exams, where 768,000 students worked hard to get into the best schools. While exactly 65,000 students scored 0 in the exam, all the winners came from private schools.*

left: **VIP medicine:** *In state universities there is 1 microscope per 15 students. Naturally education is difficult under such circumstances. But the situation is very different at the Yeditepe University. There, students have endless opportunities for education. The school charges a tuition fee, but if you are successful you can win a scholarship to study there.*

below: **1.3 million students will be privatised:** *If the law draft concerning private schools is ratified, the number of private schools will increase and costs will fall because of the competition. The number of students in private schools will climb from 260,000 to 1,3 million.*

Star box
2 March 2003

Sabah
19 October 2005

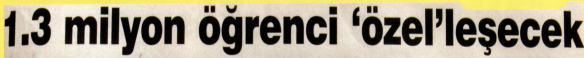

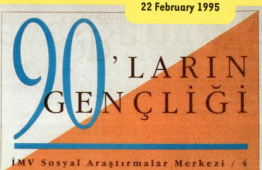

Yeni Yüzyıl
22 February 1995

Yeni Şafak
25 February 1998

above: **No tolerance for maganda, sharia supporters and snobs:** *The type of people the young feel hostile to are mainly based on subjective evaluations.*

left: **Secular madness:** *The oppressive regulations regarding clothes and appearance which started with the head scarf ban in the Religious Personnel Highschools is spreading quickly. At the Istanbul University students with headscarfs or beards were not admitted.*

role for the state rather than a reduced one. It is hard to maintain that neoliberalism is a liberal ideology on a political level. Its repercussions in the *educational* sphere seem obvious enough. However much the terminology used may have changed, the young are still viewed as a *threat*. For some today, this threat is embodied in headscarved students and radical Islamists. The 1990 regulation banning headscarved students from university campuses and classes was presented as a measure against this threat. In fact, regulations do not only target headscarves, any dissension or resistance is immediately and quite vigorously squelched. TV news often shows images of police officers dragging students along the ground or using pepper spray on them. Yet, while differing political opinions and tendencies are forcefully suppressed or banned, privatization sales have rapidly opened the educational sphere to market forces. The two sides of neoliberalism, political *repression* and *privatization*, are advancing neck to neck.

A scene from Ertürk Yöndem's "Perde Arkası", on student protests [TRT1, 14 January 1990]

Over the past two and a half decades, there has been a growing tendency toward *privatization* and *commercialization* in every area of education. The establishment of *private universities* and *private schools* are the most striking examples of this process. Whereas at the start of the 1980s there were only around two hundred private schools, today they number in the thousands. In addition there has been a sharp increase in the number of *dershane* [private tutoring schools] that coach students for the university entrance examination administered by the Examination and Placement Center, the common entrance exams for private schools giving instruction in a foreign language and the entrance exams for prestigious state-run high schools. Attending one of these *dershane* has become almost unavoidable for students preparing for these exams. Despite these efforts, hundreds of thousands of students are unable to get into the school of their choice or register at a university. Consequently, a fiercely *competitive* climate rules the educational sphere. As in the marketplace, however, it is an unequal competition. In this

"Listen professor, first, with an order from Ankara, you treated those intelligent, hard-working girls as if they didn't exist, and it took years to educate them, and they were are all the darlings of their parents, and all of them came top in their class. When they wrote their names in the roll-call, you erased them because their heads were covered. If seven students, one of which had her head covered, sat with their teacher, you ignored the covered one and got them only six teas from the tea man. The girls who were ignored cried because of you. And that was not enough for you either. With a new order from Ankara, first you refused to take them into the classrooms and threw them into the corridors, then you *kicked them out of the corridors too. When a handful of brave girls, who were defiant and didn't remove their scarves, who waited at the entrance to the school, trembling from the cold, in order to be heard, you picked up the phone and called the police." / "We didn't call the police." / "Professor, don't lie to me because you are afraid of the gun in my pocket. That day when the police dragged the girls away and arrested them, how could your conscience let you sleep that evening, that's what I would like to know.* [Orhan Pamuk, *Kar*, 2002, Iletişim Publications, p. 47]

day and age, when income distribution has become increasingly unequal and there is a dramatic surge in the number of children trying to contribute to their families' upkeep by peddling goods in the streets or working in unregistered workshops and small factories, obviously some children are "luckier" than others. Money is the first requirement in order not to "shun a brilliant future." In the end, education is only experiencing the class differentiations and inequalities that exist in almost every other sphere today. In addition, there are also significant *regional inequalities*. Newspapers continually remind us that education and instruction opportunities in the East, especially, are far below the standards in the western parts of Turkey. Considering that there have been major cuts in the share of the budget allocated to education in the past 25 years and that over the same period the trend towards commercialization has progressively gained strength, it seems safe to say that class differences will become even more marked in the long run, eventually *restricting* the privilege of an education to a privileged segment.

The impact of neoliberalism on schools and universities can also be traced in the changing quality of instruction. All through elementary school, children try to boost their *test-solving skills* in order to pass the entrance exams for a "good" high school. Later, they repeat the struggle to get into the universities of their choice. In the process, we are breeding generations of students who learn everything by rote, are incapable of critical thought, and reduce the world to a multiple choice test. The *decline* in the quality of instruction in schools and universities is another concern. After the 1980s, the sharp increase in the number of new universities was accompanied by complaints that their level of instruction was not up to par. Meanwhile, for many university graduates the fear of *unemployment* looms ominously over their future, since graduation no longer guarantees a career. Most university graduates – apart from those who hold degrees in management, economics or engineering from one of the "prestigious" universities in the large cities – are unable to secure employment in their field of study. In addition, many international companies make a master's degree a requisite for a

Liquid soap to be used at school

May 2003

Birgün
23 January 2005

above: **Don't let your child do without a brilliant future:** Applications for pre-registration for the year 2003-2004 at the Kemer Kid's Garden and Kemer College have started.

below: **They want to bury our daughters under ignorance**

Pencils with various types of toppers, erasers and a pencil sharpener

Our subject now is arithmetic.
Come on, together we will count.
Get up, Kerem who doesn't like to count, come and count.
Kerem stands up and counts: one, two, three, four, five, six, tens, twenties, thirties, forties, nineties, hundreds...
I tell Kerem to sit
I ask Alaaddin to come to the black board
I ask him to both count and write the numbers
He both counts and writes:
 1, 2, 3, 4, 5, 6, 7, 8, 9, 10, 101
Stop, I say. What is this?
Eleven.
Write twenty one, I say. He writes: 201.
Write thirty one. He writes: 301.
Write forty one. He writes: 401.
Stop, I say. I turn to the other children. Is this correct?
They shout in unison: Yeeees!
[Ferit Edgü, O/ Hakkari'de Bir Mevsim, 1977/1990, Yapı Kredi Yayınları, p. 105]

job application. As a result, a number of "distinguished" public universities have started offering MBA programs in an attempt to kill two birds with a stone: training the employees desired by the marketplace and generating revenues for their increasingly squeezed budgets. Concurrent to all these developments, universities are now institutions closely aligned with the market, equating knowledge with technology and training specialists for the market. In an environment where economics and management in particular have become increasingly *technical*, and where engineering has become totally isolated from the social sciences, opportunities to reflect on the *social meanings* of knowledge have diminished. With uniformity and restrictions imposed by state institutions on the one hand and markets on the other, the one who start the race first increasingly comes out ahead.

Joker fakülteler

GÜNÜMÜZDE her meslek dalında uzmanlaşmış elemanlara ihtiyaç duyuluyor. Uzmanlar, geleceğin alanında uzmanlaşmış kişilerin olduğunu ısrarla her fırsatta dile getiriyorlar. Ancak bazı fakülteler var ki tam bir joker görevini görüyor. Yani bu fakültelerden mezun olan öğrenciler pek çok alanda görev alabiliyor, meslek seçimi şanslarını genişletebiliyorlar. Adaylar arasında grafiğini yükselten joker fakültelerin başında, iktisat, işletme, uluslararası ilişkiler, endüstri mühendisliği, huhuk geliyor.

Milliyet
3 June 1997

Ayşa Babacan
İşletme

Ahmet Deniz
Uluslararası

Esra Baygın
Hukuk

Ersoy Gül
İktisat

Funda Gürgöse
Endüstri Müh.

Wild card universities

KAPAK 10 OCAK 1988

Liselilerin gelecek için en büyük korkusu:

SORUNLARINI YAZIYORLAR — Liseli gençler ankete büyük ilgi gösterdiler.

İşsizlik

Sait Seçkin: "Okul yöneticileri bize hammadde olarak bakıyor. Onlara göre okul bir fabrika. Eğitimin işlevi ise bu fabrikada toplumun değer yargıları doğrultusunda insan üretmek. Büyükler de siyasete karışmamamızı istiyor. Akıllı bir gençlik istemiyorlar"

işte liselilerin sorunları

BUGÜN İÇİN: En önemli sorun okul ilişkileri, ikinci sırada aileyle fikir çatışması geliyor
YARIN İÇİN: En büyük korkuları işsizlik, ikinci önemli sorun ise başarılı bir evlilik yapamamak.

Milliyet
10 January 1988

Unemployment: *The biggest fear of highschool students for the future.*

Piyale Madra, Ademler ve Havvalar 1 **2005**

-Teacher Ali comes everyday after school. He gives me tests. On weekends, I have private tutoring. After that, my mom and dad help me study. Then I do my homework.

- What do you plan to be when you grow up?

-A firefighter!

Violence rules

Violence is the most talked about and alarming issue of our time. In its most general form, violence has emerged as a global security problem, but it mainly affects lives through its personal and daily dimensions. The record of violence in recent years is disquieting: the outbreak of new wars in various parts of the world, "terrorist attacks" that threaten national and global security; unfinished massacres, lynching, torture, murder, rape… The most important promise of the *modern state* was that it would cleanse the society of violence and in this way provide its population a *secure* present and future. To achieve this, the state was to be given a *monopoly* on violence. To protect its population from internal and external "evils," the modern state would establish its own military and police forces and disarm the public. Additionally, it would treat all "violent" behavior that was not "legitimate" as unlawful. Various modernization concepts assert that it is a "rational" development for the public space to be freed of personal violence and forces of influence and forced to operate within a system of laws and rules that bind everyone. Today, the forms of violence that confront us indicate how fragile the limits of this conceptual framework are, making it essential that we develop new interpretations based on new conceptualizations.

Since the early years of the Turkish Republic, the relationship between the state and violence has been a salient political issue. On every occasion, state repression and the violence it has engendered has provoked furious long-term debate in certain segments of society, even if in the short run it has apparently legitimized its actions with justifications like "modernizing" society, protecting society from "internal and external" enemies or "reestablishing" an environment of security. In this sense, Turkey's main "unfinished business" of recent years is its military *coup*s between 1960 and 1980, which – if we add the "post-modern *coup*" of 1997 – have occurred cyclically about once every ten years. The violent "interventions" that these *coup*s have made in political and social life have occurred appropriately at important

The easy part is when the electric shock is burning my mouth and eyes and spilling my teeth. The worst is the one with the soft voice, who speaks like a human being. The hardest thing is the relationship which you establish with that voice.… To think that he will treat you well; to secretly expect this. To let him establish a relationship with you… To believe that there is a tiny bit of humanity left in him, to hope for help… Maybe he will take pity on you, maybe he will hurt you less… So easy to think like this when we actually hate each other.

My son, you know I'm a humanist, I'm against torture, but there are rules that I have to follow. Look, they are not going to torture you before the morning. I got out of my warm bed and came here to prevent them from torturing you. I left my wife's arms for this. If you really wanted to, you would be lying in your bed too… next to your wife.

Talk, my son; look, I have become a torturer because of you. It is you who makes me a bad man; talk!!!
[Ayşegül Devecioğlu, *Kuş Diline Öykünen*, 2004, Metis Edebiyat Publications, p. 32]

A paintball gun and bullets

Günaydın
23 May 1987

Özal has two pistols:
When carrying guns is legalised, Özal will go around like this, with two pistols.

Hürriyet
5 June 1994

American-type bodyguards for Çiller:
The team that is responsible for Prime Minister Çiller's personal security, carries out American-type practices never seen before in Turkey. The police officers, trained in the USA in personal security, have been selected by the Security Manager Resul Kalkan.

breaking points and moments of transformation in Turkey's history. One could argue that economic and institutional restructuring has always been accompanied by state violence. But even so, disagreement about whether these measures should be viewed as *legitimate* or not has created deep divisions in society. The 1980 military *coup* had this kind of two sided aspect as well: on the one hand it triggered a restructuring of the economy – economic "liberalization" for example – on the other, it used *force* to close various channels for expressing solidarity, criticism and opposition, this way creating a very repressive environment. The primary justification of the *coup* was bringing an end to the "anarchy and violence" prevailing in society.

However, the methods and institutions used to repress social opposition added new and dark dimensions to the unending debate about the legitimacy of "legal" state violence. In this manner, violence permeated into the very fiber of society. The ongoing conflict in the East against "separatist Kurdish organizations" that took place throughout the 1990s offers frightening examples of this process of permeation: the articulation in the region of state violence in the form of "civil police"; the effective creation of a violence-related economy and, during all of this, the unjust treatment – to put it lightly – of the regional population. Today, varied debates about the *long hands of the state* that are fuelled by diverse events, such as those recently in Şemdinli, continually refer back to this *dark aspect* of state violence.

It is possible to see the social and cultural reflections of the new network of illegal organizations that formed around and within the state after the 1980s but which hid themselves behind the rhetoric of the state and "buried themselves in." While the opposition organizations and movements were disarmed in the 1980s, overall ownership of personal arms increased. During the same period, *American style bodyguards* started to appear in the capital's political circles. The bodyguards that never left the prime minister's side were the first signs that the privatization of security had begun. Some time later, the use of *bodyguards* and *private security forces* spread from businessmen to the rich and famous and from cultural centers to the doors of bars, leading to the

… All kinds of resistance, demonstrations and behaviour against the Turkish Army, which has always been an integral part of the nation and at the service of the nation, and against the new government, will be crushed and punished most severely. In order not to spill any blood anywhere in the country, I ask all my citizens to stay calm and to behave in accordance with the communiqués to be made, without getting carried away by incitement, and not to go out onto the streets until a second communiqué. … I wish all a happy and bright future. [From the radio and television speech by General Kenan Evren on the day of the military *coup*, TRT, 12 September 1980]

"There is no one out there…" "So?" "There are tanks, and soldiers…" "So there is somebody after all. Come on, beat it!" "You don't understand, there is only them, they are all over the place, and there are so many.." "So, what do you mean?" "A coup. It's a coup!" That's how they met. They became friends through a kind of shared sense of destiny, a sense of adventure and exile. They listened to the announcements on the radio, they heard that there was a curfew for three days, they checked the amounts of spaghetti and chick peas they had and felt better, they crammed certain objectionable magazines, books and posters into the hot water heater, they took baths with the resulting hot water, they felt even better, they started conversing about the historical events that the songs of heroism, sang by a man with a deep voice in between the announcements, referred to, about the probable results of the coup, about the effects of the results and about the reactions to the effects. [Murat Uyurkulak, *Tol*, 2003, Metis Publications, p. 202]

The commanders told us that we were going to a nice place. I didn't sleep at all. A hundred of us were lying in a place which was formerly a sheepfold. We would get up morning and night and shout: We are heeeeere to protect the indivisible integrityyyy of the Turkish Republiiic, even under the mooost difficult conditioooons. I picked up lice. I was covered with sores from all the scratching. … We waited and waited. We waited because terrorists would arrive and we would kill them. They didn't come and we kept laying down and sleeping on rugs and then getting up. … Then they arrived. I ordered the soldiers to shoot. Ready, steady, aim, shoot! I don't know how many people died. I counted them then, but now I have forgotten. They made us put them side by side, in rows. Was it eight or nine? I remember fifteen ears. Either one of them was missing an ear, or it was lost or something in that confusion. I looked for it but I couldn't find it. I looked everywhere. I was looking for an ear. That evening the commander called me. What happened? I didn't understand. I looked him in the face. Don't look at me, he said. How many ears do you have, he asked. Two, I said. Fuck your mother, he said. Two, I said. I'll fuck your mother, he said, what did you do, why is one ear missing? I told him how I looked under the stones, among the bushes, under the trees, in the shadow or rocks, but he didn't listen. But he didn't cut my ear either.
[Gaye Boralıoğlu, *Meçhul*, 2004, İletişim Publications, p. 28-29]

A toy soldier crawling and shooting

expansion of the security sector providing these services. Gun shows were followed by "security fairs" featuring a variety of security technology. With the privatization of security, foreign security firms started to arrive so that today, many shopping centers and large chain stores work with multinational security firms. With the *privatization* of security, is the state's role diminishing? This debate can be linked to the reduction worldwide of the role of the national state or, as we say in Turkey, to the "shrinking of the state". According to Coronil, as national states withdraw their public support in this age of globalization, they reduce expenditures on education, social security and health and set aside the most for the defense budget. The state has taken on the responsibility of protecting international economic ventures and, because war is a constant threat, has focused on defense technologies, thereby transforming itself – from one point of view – into a "police state." (Coronil 2000) In this manner, the trend in education and the state's role in defense do not conflict; they *complete* one another.

The *need for security* and *fear* have turned into a self-perpetuating cycle. In our age especially there seems to be a lot of anxiety going around. Certain events have a worldwide impact that creates a sort of generalized mass anxiety. This was the case after the September 11 terrorist attacks on New York's twin towers, for example. As states organize and mobilize their "national security" need in response to such events, they also identify new *enemies* and set new goals, which in turn further fuels fears. Considering that the still ongoing, violent war in Iraq legitimized the increased need for security that followed September 11, the mobilization of American security forces targeting Islamic organizations and Muslims in general clearly shows the close link between fear and violence. Identifying Muslims as the enemy and *target* only kindles hostility and *racism* toward Muslim immigrants in Europe laying the groundwork for more violence and terrorism. On a different level, Michael Moore's startling documentary *Bowling for Columbine* exposed how the culture of fear that the media created in America spurred the gun industry, and the desire for firearms it provoked in American society engendered a violence so pervasive that it finally came to include its children. A similar trend can be observed in Turkey today as the wave of knife killings and assaults

Yeni Gündem
3 May 1987

left: **My gun kills better:** *The latest in the fair business: an Arms Fair.*

below: **Rush to arms:** *The interest in arms has reached a frightening level and it brings about various problems. People who own a gun but are not trained in the use of them damage either themselves or people around them.*

Akşam
23 September 1994

Akşam
28 June 1997

Security fair: *The Security Devices Fair where the latest protection, self-defence and anti-fire technology is exhibited, has opened in the TÜYAP Exhibition Hall in Beylikdüzü, Istanbul.*

Sabah
18 September 2004

Powers of police to bodyguards: *The Private Security Services Regulations,* which concern 2,500 private security firms, will be ratified next week. Bodyguards will receive 120 hours of training and they will given police powers.

among high school students demonstrates the increasingly common resort to violence as a means to settle scores, achieve recognition, and solve problems; yet, this trend is also a sign of the fear which rules society.

Social fears are always related to an *other*. Ideologies seeking to promote unity by creating internal or external enemies have always indicated "frightening" others. "They" are the ones trying to divide us; the one who have set their sights on our women, our jobs, our land. Immigrants, political groups, and religious and ethnic groups are all different faces of the "other." Their representation in centralized discourses is mythical; specific features are scripted as a *threat* and emphasized. As a result, the members of these groups are distanced from the general universe of human beings and become the objects of a destructive hatred. The history of modern societies abounds with dark instances –genocides first and foremost – where the objectification of this hatred has caused major breaks in modern dreams of humane democracies. Violent aggression perpetrated against groups considered the "other" in Turkey is never far from sight. A society that goes so far as to attempt lynching individuals branded "terrorists" due to their Kurdish origins is clearly demonstrating the extent to which some forms of *identitiy* are tied up with insecurity and *violence*.

Computer games of adventure and war, designed and manufactured in Turkey

Self-defence spray

As rising violence in the cities breeds new fears in people's lives, the urban landscape fills with spaces where fear rules. Certain neighborhoods, streets, houses, schools, stores, taxis, buses, and countless other places now need to be protected against potential dangers. As in all big cities of the world, fear is escalating: "Istanbul's residents are scared to go out." The media all too willingly fans the flames of this fear with news stories of horrific robberies and crimes. City dwellers are warned against pick pockets and thieves: "Watch out, don't tempt thieves!" As a preventive measure, there are steel doors and dead-bolt locks. Some suggest privatizing the security of neighborhoods against "robberies and pick pockets." Municipalities offer karate classes in public educational centers. Mace and other sprays to neutralize

Vatan 34
6 December 2004

left: **The people of Istanbul are afraid of the streets:** *This verdict came out of the "purse-snatching survey" realised on the website of the Vatan newspaper. All of the 3,927 Istanbul citizens who voted in the survey consider inadequate the present penalties.*

below: **The private guard debate:** *Ağar's proposal "for private security officers to protect all streets" to counteract the increasing number of robberies and purse-snatching, met with strong reactions.*

Sabah Bayram
21 January 2005

Rıza sees the knife that the blond boy is holding. He feels as if he recognizes the boy. His first reaction is that he is happy it isn't a gun. He can't help it, it's as if he holds a grudge against those black devils that spit gunpowder. But a knife, a knife is different, it's as if protecting yourself from a knife is easier. And the odds are equal. But the boy grasping his hand shifts the balance of the whole thing, he isn't even holding it tightly, but that much is enough. Before Rıza can pull back his hand, let alone touch the handle of his own knife, the knife enters his bowels. He still feels a silly consolation, oh what if it had been a gun, oh God what if it had been a gun, although he angrily tries to chase the thought away, it refuses to go. [Aziz Gökdemir, "Beyoğlu'nda Cinayet", İç İçe Geçmiş İstanbul Öyküleri, 1998, Gendaş Publications, p.162-163]

"You fucking whore," he screamed, " So you disgrace me, do you? You sent naked pictures to the papers, did you? You slut! You bitch, you fucking bitch, you whore... I'll break your bones... Let go of me, you bastards! What's it to you?"

Sitting on the floor and crying, Aysel really thought that her bones had broken. But when it seemed that her father was about to get away from those holding him, she jumped up with an agility she didn't expect from her hurting muscles and dashed out of the door among cries of "Don't Dündar Bey", "Stop Dündar Bey" and "You'll get a heart attack, Dündar Bey". [Pınar Kür, Yarın Yarın, 1976-1985, Can Publications, p. 81]

assailants are on the market. Despite its prevalence, this mass anxiety in urban areas is not totally abstract. Just as ideologies create a generalized fear of the "other," the upper and middle classes of the cities fear the "lower" classes, the *gecekondu* dwellers, the migrants, the vagabonds roaming the streets, the homeless, the street kids and the gypsies. They are the *eternal suspects*. This discrimination has led to a need for the insulation – in the name of security – of specific spaces against *trespassers*. Gated communities, now the first choice of urban upper classes; clubs and bars with highly selective door policies; private schools that only rich kids can attend – all illustrate attempts to carve out little *islands* of "safety" in an increasingly menacing cityscape. For those living or socializing in these "shut off" spaces, the "other" is never confronted and thus takes on an even more mythical quality.

Still, *television* is there to transport violence right into our homes. Action series with heavily violent overtones, particularly *mafia* stories are becoming all the time more popular. This popularity may be viewed as a reflection of the gangsterization of society. An offshoot of the growing informal sector, the mafia in Turkey, like everywhere else, is omnipresent... from the collection of overdue checks to parking your car or opening a bar [they will help you] "in the name of country...or behalf of nation..." Mafia heroes armed to the teeth have become role models for children, as in the case of Polat from the series *Kurtlar Vadisi* [Valley of the Wolves]. While seeking protection against violence and condemning its varied forms, one should also consider its broader significance. Violence does not necessarily require guns or knives. *Symbolic violence* can be expressed by a disparaging, condescending tone or behavior. Nor is it limited to the streets; domestic violence and the abusive acts of men against women are perhaps the most enduring forms of violence alongside violence against children. The most *invisible* form of violence is the one that is part of so-called "normal" social life, like the violence created by poverty. The severe conditions of *poverty* force a growing number of people to live with violence in every area of their lives. Today, resolving the problem of violence will clearly require more than prohibitions or well intentioned wishes!

Kapkaça halk çözümü

Bakırköy Halk Eğitim Merkezi, kapkaççılardan korunmak için uzman eğitmenlerin ders verdiği karate kursu açtı...

Sabah
23 November 2001

İstanbul'a gizli gözler

İstanbul Valiliği, "Mobil Elektronik Entegrasyon" yöntemiyle artık kentte uçan kuşu bile gözetleyecek. 52 bin cadde ve sokağın dijital haritaları çıkarılıp, kameralar yerleştirilecek

Milliyet
23 August 2003

above: **The people's solution to purse-snatching:** *Karate courses by expert trainers have started at the Bakırköy Community Centre, as a way of self-defence against purse-snatchers.*

below: **Hidden eyes over Istanbul:** *Istanbul Governorship will monitor the whole city through the "mobile electronic integration" system. 52.000 streets will be digitally mapped and cameras will be placed on every single one of them.*

right: **East-side story:** *New clues have been discovered concerning the murder of the young naval officer Hakan Eleldi, the subject most talked about over the last few weeks. The war among the youth gangs that have sprung up on the streets of Istanbul is intensifying.*

below: **The mafia in our lives:** *"The Mafia in Our Lives" report prepared by the Ankara Chamber of Commerce, has revealed the state of the mafia in Turkey. According to the report, the underground economy, which operates in about 100 areas, is worth 60 billion dollars.*

GENÇLİK / İSTANBUL'DA ÇETELER

"DOĞU YAKASININ HİKÂYESİ…"

Son haftaların en çok konuşulan konusu, genç bahriyeli Hakan Elaldı cinayetine ilişkin yeni ipuçları bulundu. İstanbul sokaklarında yeni türeyen gençlik çeteleri arasında giderek kızışan bir savaş yaşanıyor. **Nokta**, Kadıköy'den Pendik'e kadar uzanan bu savaşın iç yüzünü araştırdı.

Nokta
6 December 1987

HAYATIMIZ MAFYA

ATO'nun hazırladığı "Hayatımız Mafya Raporu", Türkiye'deki mafya gerçeğini gözler önüne serdi. Rapora göre, 100'e yakın alanda faaliyet gösteren yeraltı ekonomisinin büyüklüğü 60 milyar doları buluyor. Yani mafyanın geliri, 2 Koç Holding ve 2 Sabancı Holding cirolarının toplamının iki katı kadar

Star
7 June 2004

■ Polis verileri, Türkiye'de mafyanın yaygınlığını ortaya koyuyor. Verilere göre, 1998-2002 arasında 17 bin kişi çete üyesi oldukları gerekçesiyle gözaltına alındı, 4 bin 182 kişi tutuklandı.

Kurtlar Vadisi çocukları da yutuyor

Batman'da bayram harçlığı toplayan çocuklar, paralarını oyuncak silahlara yatırıp 'Mafyacılık' oynadılar. Birbirlerine taktıkları isimler ise Polat, Memati, Abdülhey ve Kılıç...

Birgün
22 January 2005

Çocuklar topladıkları bayram harçlıklarıyla silah almak için oyuncakçının yolunu tuttu.

The Valley of Wolves engulfs children too:
Children in Batman collecting pocket money in the Bayram invested their money in toy guns and played the "mafia game". The names they gave each other were Polat, Memati, Abdülhey and Kılıç...

In this last section, we examine how the various trends that have left their mark on the past 25 years — the pervasiveness of market values, cultural consumerism, simultaneous individualization and collectivization of desire, the rise in social polarization and fragmentation — and the conflicts they generate are intertwined with the problematic of belonging. Despite breaks and transformations, certain identification or belonging themes insistently return. Nostalgia, or put differently, the sentimental longing for the past, on the one hand seeks in the present traces of yesterday's lifestyles, on the other, attempts to create new "traditions" to add fresh color and vibrancy to the trends of our day. Thus we look at how nostalgia can become a driving force for designer brands in retro fashions; a longing for the past is commodified in ethnic cuisines; *religious rituals are rediscovered to forge social bonds in the nostalgia for bayrams [religious feast days] of yore; and finally, how, in the rising wave of nationalism, a redefined Turkism* has become an ever stronger basis for social identity. The meanings broached in this revisiting of traditions are either long gone or have been largely transformed. The quest for authenticity, though inevitable in a culture where consumerist ideologies have stolen the purpose of life, seems, just as inevitably, a cycle of disappointment.

everything old is new again

In fashion again

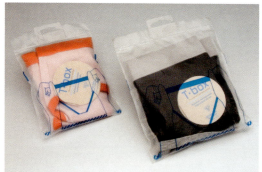

T-box retro products: retro briefs

... Actually I kept thinking of something all night long. I wonder what happened to bey baba's writing set? What did we do with it? Let's say the writing desk vanished, that it was sold... But what about the pens, the inkwells? And the writings from my grandfather, the calligrapher? What happened to them? And then there was a tiny Kuran, hand written... I must look among my bundles. But those are impossible to open. The safety pins must be rusty by now. The best thing to do today, my dear little Tarzan Bey, will be to tear off the pages of the calendar. The new year is approaching, but our calendar is still way behind time. Let's make an effort and tear away all the past pages. The best thing to do would be to burn all the calendars in the stove. Let there be just life. What use is it to know that time is passing by... [Melisa Gürpınar, *Yeni Zaman Eski Hayat* (play), 1992, Yapı Kredi Publications, p. 55-56]

The "leaping into the future" theme of the 1980s expressed a never-ending desire for renewal. The *new age* ushered in by the military *coup* was to be, first, a jolting *break* with the past – and all its negative meanings. The dominant discourse emphasized the need for people to forget the past and adapt to the new age by *renovating* themselves. During this period, expanding and enlivened markets also enhanced the impact of *fashion*. In the quest for new experiences, new concepts, new values, new products, brands, and new lifestyles emerged. Today, the scope of the fashion industry has long transcended just clothes or accessories to embrace a wide variety of areas including home decoration, music, buzzwords and slang – not to mention, every aspect of "high-tech." In the craze for diversity and change, fashion incessantly *renews* itself, pushing products and ideas forward in rapid succession and just as rapidly pronouncing them outdated. Yet, it seems that the sentimental power of *nostalgia* never wanes. How can we explain the *retro* appeal of past fashions? What does this paradox between fashion's unrelenting search for novelty and its partiality for nostalgia tell us?

Seen from this perspective the following topics appear relevant: the meaning of fashion and "new" in market economy; the quest for authenticity; and the contradictory messages nostalgic products convey. In the 1980s, Turkey was introduced to new consumer goods and the meanings and lifestyles associated with them. Advertising made possible the wider connotations incorporated in these products and, more often then not, ad slogans emphasized their "brand new" aspect. Marx talks about the fetishism of commodities in reference to objects that are produced in a capitalist economy for the purpose of exchange. His argument is that once commodities are offered for exchange, they are transformed; they create the *illusion* that they have magically appeared as consumer objects. While the reality of human labor

Options
1 March 1998

Leman
22 September 2001

above: **Defying the passing years**

below: **A man of feelings:** *A cartoon about the use of former taxis in TV series*

left: **The good old '60s**

below: **The spirit of the 1970s is back:** *Fake eyelashes, wide collar shirts, flared trousers... The '70s are back with the TV series "Çemberimde Gül Oya".*

Yeni Gündem
31 May 1987

Sabah
3 October 2004

disappears, objects acquire an added exchange or purchase "value." Fashions "animate" lifeless consumer objects by intertwining consumption practices with a sense of the present. Fashion represents a current *slice of time*. However, its power to symbolize what is current or new is obviously related to the social segments who define *current time*. In the beginning of the 20th century, Georg Simmel, one of the first theorists to write about fashion, suggested that fashions spread from the upper classes to the lower through *imitation*. The latest fashion is created for social elites but the desire to *emulate* them, moves the trend down to other social levels. Simmel argues that the aspiration to *belong* to a society by trying to resemble some of its members answers a psychological need. However, attempting to be like others through fashion is also a doomed practice. As fashion spreads to the larger masses, individuals, spurred by what Simmel calls "the need for distinction," start searching for new fashions to distinguish themselves from the rest of the people. In similar vein, Bourdieu pointed out that in a class society where individuality is defined by economic, cultural and social capital, the drive to separate from others is a necessity of class dynamics. Interestingly enough, even rejecting a current fashion means positioning yourself in relation to that fashion and thus expresses a dependency of sorts. At this point, fashion emerges as an interrelated and cyclical construct. Every new fashion, from the moment it first comes out, is doomed to become *outdated* and die. This is what makes fashions inevitably short-lived; even in their earliest stages they carry traces of their self-destruction. This aspect of fashion also sheds light on the meaning that "new" carries in a capitalist society. The drive to endlessly redefine the "new" deprives it of any real meaning and transforms "new" into just more of the same.

As a concept, fashion invites reflection on the social meaning of the relation created with the present. Walter Benjamin, another thinker who wrote on fashion, argued that in capitalist societies, the contemporary is a *mythic* time, based on repetition. Fashion continually reaches back in time to recreate the past, and as they say, "everything old is new again." Retro hit Turkey, concurrently with the rest of the world, in the 1990s. A craze for the "old" suddenly emerged in those years encompassing everything from

WHAT IS LEFT IS MELANCHOLY

*We used to converse once
in this solitude
we used to laugh often
the wings of the birds of laughter
  would flutter like stars*

*the coral like coals of the narghiles
  could utter such wisdom
time has changed
we have long parted
there is sadness today*

*alas, our youth is gone
like waves that carelessly hurl
  themselves onto the beach
like lofty poems ringing clearly
  throughout the world
what is left is melancholy*

*but can one forget the festive
  illumination of a town
the multicolour scattering from a
  fireworks pinwheel in the night
the strings head over heels in love
the raising of a goblet to the
  moonlight
almost like a wedding
life leaves no trace on time
you fall from one void into another
only to gather yourself and jump
  once again
what is left is melancholy*
[Atillâ İlhan, *Elde Var Hüzün*, 1982/1998, Adam Publications/ Bilgi Publications]

...what exists was once, what will be has happened in the past and one looks once again for what has passed. [Lâle Müldür, *Kuzey Defterleri*, 1992, Metis Publications, p. 19]

Son Havadis
14 September 1988

left: **The cloak is back:** *The cloak is back in fashion, but with no limitations. It's back with all of its gravity. It gives women a different air, an elegance, with day and night wear or with sports clothes.*

below: **Bergéres are fashionable again:** *The bergére has come back from centuries ago and has occupied the most important place in the sitting room.*

Yeni Yüzyıl
18 February 1995

home decoration and furnishings, to music and fashion: "Platform shoes" are "back again," "capes make their come-back," "the classic club chair" is "the season's 'new' must," and the list goes on... Today, the term "retro" is firmly entrenched in everyday usage, and provides us with fascinating insights both on fashion's cyclical character and the search for the "authentic." Present time, based on repetition and defined by its temporality, communicates a sense of emptiness to fashion. The "fashion victims" who blindly follow every new trend have always evoked scorn. An enduring theme that emerged during the *Tanzimat* and stretched into the Republican era is the contempt felt for those who, foolishly taken by a passing fashion – in particular Western fashion – deny their true "essence." On a somewhat different level, we frequently hear celebrities nowadays claim a kind of indifference to fashion. "Fashion means nothing to me, you should only wear what suits you," and similar statements indicate a quest for individuality and the "authentic," and point to the problematic relation between *belonging* and fashion. Retro fashion tries to add a so-called *enduring* and authentic quality – derived from the very fact that it is old and has stood the test of time – to the quick, fleeting aspect of consumer goods. Funny enough, retro does not have to go back centuries to create this impression. Even a few decades will do the trick. Sometimes a product will "quote" from its own history to create a "classic," as Coca Cola did when reintroducing its original contour bottle. This in turn has invented more recent pasts as modernity rapidly confers classic status on parts of its history.

While retro merges with the recent rising wave of *nostalgia*, nostalgic themes now make up a new *industry*. In many parts of the world, the past has become just another *commodity* as ceremonies and festivals commemorate events of long- and not-so-long- ago, and books, movies or memorabilia gifts look back to yesteryears. Lowenthal describes nostalgia as "memory with the pain removed" (1985). Turkey as well, especially in music, is experiencing the "winds" of nostalgia. Muazzez Ersoy's hit album *Nostalji*, which made it to the best selling record charts, is a good example of this trend. In the new millennium, clubs organize "nostalgic nights," featuring the music and decor of the 70s or 80s. Albums from those decades are reissued, and both television and radio offer "oldies but goldies" programs. While opportunities

Nida dear, apparently you have really made progress in your bridal trousseau business.

Yes. You remember Servet, my cousin, I set up a company with him.

... I saw your calendar.

Did you like it?

It's actually quite a good idea.

We worked hard on it.

It looks very nice, well done.

Thanks, said Nida. She was a little surprised. Then she immediately pulled herself together. Listen Siren dear, you and I are old friends. Since you have already heard a little of this calendar business, I can tell you this easily. I need a bergére armchair. I need it for the presentation of a new product... I hope you still have your bergéres, and they still retain their original beauty.

Oh, yes, said Siren. Turgut left them to me when he went. They are almost the only thing I still have. They are the only thing left from my past. [Müge İplikçi, "Berjer Koltuklarla Gelen", *Transit Yolcular*, 2002, Can Publications, p. 156-157]

Collector's item Coca Cola retro series, on sale at Nişantaşı Beymen

Cosmopolitan
1 February 2002

left: **Don't tell my mother I've gone to a cheap night club, she thinks I'm a clubber:** *Our recommendation for the Cosmo girls this month is the cheap night clubs that they cannot go to, because they would be underage.*

below: **We can't get rid of the '80s:** *This month's issue of the Elele magazine features the '80s which we can't seem to leave behind, in spite of entering the 2000s.*

Hürriyet
11 May 2000

for newcomers emerge in these fields, older names, like the well-known radio host Sezen Cumhur Önal, stand their ground by marketing their own image as a "nostalgic product."

In striving to add an authentic content to fashion and creating a longing for the past is retro merely replicating the capitalist logic of the production of commodities? It may be helpful at this point to examine in some detail the conflictive messages that nostalgia conveys. In the 2000s, the fad for the 80s is perhaps the best example of such contradictory messages in Turkey. The headline for a fashion feature in a newspaper claiming, "We still haven't gotten rid of the 80s" is food for thought. The 80s are very big today, not only in terms of fashion or music but also as a time frame for movies and TV series. It is difficult to explain this surge of nostalgic interest for those years uniquely with the profit-driven logic of consumer economy. No doubt, part of the interest does result from the drive to offer the past as "new material" to the culture industry. However, at the same time, a number of people feel an *actual* need to remember those years. Both the repressive environment that followed the 1980 military *coup* and the strict economic measures implemented immediately in its wake undoubtedly generated losses and grievances, which for a long time were never alluded to in the public sphere; memorabilia dating from those years may present specific groups with an opportunity to unite around common experiences and a shared social identity. The nostalgia industry packages the need for various memories and meanings from the past – "stealing" their significance and frequently sanitizing their painful content – and puts it on the market. In the growing wave of new products expressly designed to appeal to consumers' nostalgic feelings, it has really become impossible to escape the past ["get rid of the 80s"].

Brand names, because they individualize commodities and endow them with personality, capitalize on the same need for belonging. Naomi Klein writes that capitalism in the age of globalization is "the age of the brand" (2000). Products and services attempt to

Scene from a clip about Ajda Pekkan's music life in "Kent ve Yaşam" programme [TRT2, 5 December 2002]

It has been so many years, Nebalet. Thousands of students have passed through my life. I see some of them in the street from time to time, but I don't recognize them. They have all grown into big men with moustaches or women with children. I just cannot remember them. Most of the times I only act as if I remember them, so that they won't be hurt. But I haven't forgotten you at all. Especially as soon as I hear this song, you come straight back to my mind. This song has become fashionable again, I hear it a lot. I hear it so much and you come straight back to me so clearly that I can't stand it anymore... [İnci Aral, "Bir Şarkıda", *Ağda Zamanı*, 1999, Can Publications, p. 137-138]

Even if I knew that past fashions were sometimes revived, I would never believe that details would change radically. Because shoulder paddings which were fashionable till yesterday would disappear, maybe net stockings would be fashionable once again after so many years, but this time the diamond pattern would be either smaller or larger, shoulder paddings would reappear again, but the new padded shoulders would be defined as "space fashions"... That's why clothes from the past would never be revived.

As soon as a season passes, when summer is followed by autumn, or when winter blooms into spring, the fondness of the skin for summer clothes and for winter clothes will melt away, it will grow cold and they will all feel distant to the body. Anyway, wasn't it necessary to feel pity for clothes? How could the dresses, which exulted while they were designed, while they were dyed, while their pattern was cut out and finally when they found themselves in the hands of a tailor, guess that these bayram would only last a short time... [Selim İleri, *Mavi Kanatlarınla Yalnız Benim Olsaydın*, 1991, Can Publications, p. 33-34]

find their niche in the market by touting a brand. In fact, Klein claims that the brand-oriented consumer culture has turned people into "walking billboards." However, brands are not only about names or signature designs. They are laden with meanings *appropriated* from different lifestyles and social groups. Brands that target the young like Nike or Tommy Hilfiger play on the "cool" image of the black ghetto using ad campaigns that sell the black culture of America's inner cities to the white middle class. In similar fashion, styles associated with feminist, gay/lesbian, youth and music subcultures often constitute a basis to brand identities. Seen from this perspective, retro is just another message that sells. As brands identify with increasingly diverse cultural expressions, their products also appeal to a wider public. Fashions create a way to relate to the current and "new" but at the same time, they erode that novelty in their own cycle. Which past will be tomorrow's new trend?

Zest
1 January 1999

left: **Hippies again:** *Do you prefer nature, health and beauty to mechanical systems of the latest technology? Do you believe that only natural solutions can cure your physical, mental and spiritual problems? If your answer to these questions is "yes", you most probably are one of the new hippies.*

below: **The little ones are as good as the adults:** *This year Benetton's child wear has a nostalgic feel to it.*

Vatan 34
6 December 2004

In search of faraway flavors

Grandmother was tall and wiry. She used to chew her food so slowly that when she finally swallowed the food which had dissolved into threads in her toothless mouth and lost its taste, she had already forgotten what it was that she had eaten. And anyway, it didn't really matter. Being choosy with food was a kind of ingratitude. That's what she used to say. That's what she said and sometimes she would actually cook food badly on purpose. Sometimes she wouldn't add any salt, sometimes she would make it far too spicy, or she wouldn't use even a drop of oil. Children must get used to eat anything. Or even not to eat anything. [Elif Şafak, *Mahrem*, 2004, Metis Publications, p. 167]

The 1980s and subsequent years were a time to *discover* a wide variety of local, regional and national cuisines. During this period, as various *foreign* foods emerged in Istanbul and Ankara, some people were drawn to Chinese and learnt how to say *Mei Vei Ke Kou* ["yummy"], while others sampled coconut curry chicken in a newly opened Indian restaurant, and still others tasted Mexico's *guacamole* and *fajitas*. Another option for people seeking new culinary experiences, *regional* cuisine now offered its own tasty selections. Food aficionados experimented with the *yuvalama* of Gaziantep cuisine and the *mıhlama* of the Black Sea. In those years, *Ottoman cuisine* also (re)appeared on the scene and restaurants specializing in traditional Ottoman dishes joined the caravan of new places to eat out. Meanwhile for those gastronomes with fond memories of their grandmother's specialties, home cooking remained yet another alternative. The new diversity in cuisines and restaurants became material for both the printed press and television. "Taste experts" better known as *gourmets* now offered recipes in magazines or discussed foods at length on TV programs. Thus, food too turned into an area for *specialization*. Despite all these developments, a number of people remained cautious still voicing their longing for "old time" restaurants and their traditional fare and complaining that the new establishments served carelessly prepared, standardized food. Studies in the field of food culture have shown that restaurants are both commercial and *cultural* ventures. In other words, they do more than just serve meals, at the same time they address various images, values and desires. For both their patrons and their owners, these are spaces in which to display specific lifestyles. What does the growing interest in various cuisines tell us about our day and age? And how do the recent changes in food culture relate to the cultural practices of different social classes and groups?

For the middle-income group in Turkey, apart from the occasional cheap *kebap* or *pide* quick service place or the various

Milliyet
25 December 1987

left: **He has learned to say "very tasty" in Chinese, at the Dynasty Restaurant.**

below: **Foods with slanted eyes:** *The number of far Eastern restaurants in Turkey is on the rise.*

Yeni Gündem
19 July 1987

Yeni Yüzyıl
14 June 1998

Aktüel
15 January 1997

above: **A Black Sea restaurant in Istanbul: Pafuli**

below: **Master of yuvalama:** *Nezih offers the most delicious dishes & kebabs of the Southeastern kitchen. Yuvalama, şiveydiz, mumbar, frik pilav, kabaklama, olive börek, truffle kebab, aubergine pilav, peanut kebap and the rest...*

street stands, most restaurants put a serious dent in your budget. As a result, eating out appears before anything else directly related to financial means. That is just the most obvious aspect of the issue. Another series of considerations also arise, from which restaurant to chose to the choice of food eaten once there, which all reveal the extent to which the topic is related to both economic and *cultural capital*. Thus, the growing diversification of restaurants over recent years has provided a specific social segment with a new opportunity to distinguish itself from the rest, and assert its social and cultural *differences* in the public sphere. This is a relatively new development in Turkey. Up to 20 to 30 years ago, going to the restaurant was not a very common practice even for the middle classes. At that time, both the number and variety of restaurants was limited and in general, the practice of eating out did not carry positive connotations. For the middle classes of that period, who defined themselves more in terms of saving than consuming, eating out when there was "good wholesome food cooked at home" simply meant extravagance and wastefulness. In addition, apart from the hotel restaurants or luxury eating-places that the rich frequented, the great majority of other establishments were almost exclusively reserved for men. It was nearly impossible to see mixed company groups or families in either the eateries catering mainly to storekeepers and traders or the *meyhanes* [sort of tavern], which count among today's most popular eating-places. The only exceptions to these general eating out patterns were the *muhallebicis* [eateries serving a number of dairy-based or chicken dishes and puddings], pastry shops and ice cream parlors. Consequently, the growing visibility of eating out spaces in the public sphere can be directly related to a changing *cultural climate*. In our age, where every form of consumption has become more conspicuous and that consumer choices in all areas are interpreted as a sign of *status*, distinction or prestige, eating out choices have significantly contributed to the formation of cultural and culinary *hierarchies*. Discovering "new flavors," possessing a "developed" or "refined palate," being familiar with different ethnic cuisines, being a wine connoisseur, and showing a keen interest in restaurant trends, count among the distinguishing traits that determine the formation and articulation of social differentiation vis-a-vis the food practices.

... And it was that night that I discovered that Adnan Menderes, Prime Minister of the time, had been another famous guest of the Park Hotel. Every time Menderes came from Ankara to Istanbul, he insisted on staying here and many rooms on the first floor were reserved for him.

Now I could understand better the importance of the place where we were eating. (How important these things are during childhood...) Now I saw from a different point of view the little orchestra – or was it only one piano, only one pianist? – in a corner, in the distance, the elegant waiters running around, the clients trying to talk quietly and the women adorned with stoles.

[Selim İleri, *Evimizin Tek İstakozu*, 2002, Doğan Publications, p. 104-105]

Lezzet mütehassısları

Yemek yemenin saygın, önemli ve hayata renk katan bir iş olduğuna inanan gurmeler, Türkiye'de yemek kültürünün gelişememesinden yakınıyorlar

Nokta
3 May 1987

Ağzının tadını bilen işadamlarımızdan Ali Koçman az ama öz yiyor

left: **Taste experts:** *Gourmets, who believe that eating is a respectable, important and pleasant thing to do, complain that food culture is not developing in Turkey.*

below: **Food culture requires experience**

Sabah
16 June 2005

GURME
Yemek kültürü birikim ister

In this process, the fact that eating "well" has progressively become a matter of expertise, knowledge and culture is doubtlessly related to the increasingly accepted notion that a "refined palate" can be acquired by educating and broadening one's sense of taste with numerous and varied food experiences. Echoing this view is the relatively new upsurge in the number of food experts, gastronomes, gourmets and other food lovers who now freely dish out culinary advice in newspaper and magazine food sections. Atilla Dorsay's weekly column, *Ağız Tadıyla*, published in the daily *Cumhuriyet*, was perhaps one of the earliest examples of this trend. In his first contribution to the paper, Dorsay wrote: "Far be it from me to consider myself a food and taste expert or as the French would say a 'gastronome.' Obviously our country cannot hope to compete with France for example, where the degustation of food and wine, down to the most minute detail, is a part of everyday life, and books – every one of them a best seller – provide the recipes of local, regional and national cuisines or offer a comprehensive classification of the country's countless restaurants." (1993: 16) Dorsay notes that his weekly restaurant rating and review column provoked many indignant responses from readers. The most frequently voiced criticism was that it hardly "makes sense" in times "when life is so costly," to review restaurants serving shrimp, *escargot*, lobster and other delicacies at prices no "normal" citizen could afford. Interestingly, now that monthly food magazines, TV culinary shows, "gourmet" column writers, and frequent restaurant, cafe and bar reviews in the press have become the stuff of daily life, while a new cook or chef is acclaimed every day, this criticism – though the living standards of many have not really improved, in fact may have worsened – is no longer voiced. For most people, articles about food and restaurants have become "normal," if not in view of any actual consumption, at least out of a desire to stay informed. Thus certain foods, which carry very little chance of reaching the more general public, are nevertheless *coded* into the public sphere through cultural mechanisms both as concrete consumer objects and as codes in a socio-cultural space. These codes, norms and values organize desires and longings into defined hierarchies. That some should eat while others only *watch* is hardly a practice unfamiliar to historians. We know that in Europe, up to the mid-19th century,

Gökçen Adar: The Aegean cuisine is really one of the favourite cuisines of Anatolia. Why, you ask. I'll tell you. You know that there is a heavy emphasis on meat and grains in the Anatolian nutrition style. Anatolians don't know vegetables very well, they don't know artichokes, celery, etc, etc... The reason why the Aegean cuisine is privileged is because of the existence of various herbs, besides the main ingredients. There are about 70 types of herbs and there are about three or four hundred dishes made with these seventy herbs, so there are more applications of these herbs than of vegetables. Then there is a rich variety of sea foods. And of course there is a lot of olive oil. Wherever you go you find an olive orchard. Olive oil is used everywhere. From böreks to desserts, even baklava are made with olive oil. Pilav, börek, soups, whatever you can think of is cooked with olive oil. So when one talks about olive oil dishes, one would think of the cold vegetable dishes eaten after the main dish, but this is wrong: this doesn't exist in the Aegean, because olive oil is used everywhere. [A section from the "The Seeds of Tomatoes" programme prepared by Yücel Yemez and Zafer Yenal, Açık Radio, 15 July 2001]

left: **Your granny's cooking is at Ece**

Hürriyet
29 January 1992

below: **The classes of the kebab society:** *Clan chiefs that bribe with kebabs, arabesque singers that go courting, camouflaged members of a state within a state, coy women with children's voices. Here is the whole of the kebab world.*

Milliyet
23 October 2003

Tuğrul ŞAVKAY

MUTFAKTA SENTEZ DÖNEMİ

SON YILLARDA YERYÜZÜNÜN SİYASİ HARİTASI HALKLAR LEHİNE PARAMPARÇA OLURKEN KÜLTÜREL ALANDA TAM TERSİNE BİR YAKINLAŞMA KAYNAŞMA YAŞANIYOR. YEMEK KÜLTÜRÜNDE DE ULUSAL MUTFAKLAR YERİNE "BÖLGE MUTFAKLARI" ÖNE ÇIKTI. ÖRNEĞİN AKDENİZ MUTFAĞI...

Show
2 June 1992

Milliyet
17 August 2003

Modern meyhane

Kısa bir süre önce açılan ModaMar'da lezzetli mezeler, taze balıklar var. 1960-70'lerin şarkılarının çaldığı mekan modern bir meyhane havasında...

above: **The age of synthesis in kitchens:** *While the political map of the world is going to pieces in favour of the nations, on the contrary, in the cultural field there is a breaking of the ice and an integration.*

left: **A modern taverna:** *One can have tasty appetisers and fresh fish at the newly opened ModaMar.*

influential personalities would quite frequently eat in the presence of an audience and, in fact, even organize such "spectacles," which were a way for those in power to ascertain the symbolic allegiance of the viewers (Ferguson 2004: 152) Somewhat similarly, though on another level, today's "food media" may also be said to produce an *endorsement of power*. However, today's spectacles, unbound by either time or place, contribute to the creation and perpetuation of socio-cultural hierarchies whose topmost levels are occupied by "refined palates" and haute cuisine gurus.

I noticed the dish of stuffed leaves. Stuffed vine leaves and cabbage leaves in olive oil were arranged carefully on a long, boat shaped plate. Rows and rows of little people were set among the stuffed leaves, some holding a stalk of parsley, some with a round slice of carrot on their chest. Bodrum lemons divided into four wedges were arranged on the edges of the boat shaped plate. He was there too. He was lying between a stuffed cabbage leaf and a stuffed vine leaf and he was looking at me with eyes full of fear. [Nazlı Eray, *Ayışığı Sofrası*, 2000, Can Publications, p. 169]

This brings us the issue of authenticity. Usually, the "exotic" cuisines, considered to add depth and meaning to the various cultural practices seeking "authenticity," are usually, both at the time of their own configuration process, and when they enter different consumer environments, repeatedly fabricated. A lot of research shows that the notion of a national cuisine usually emerges concurrently with the *nation state building process*. French cuisine, for instance, considered one of the most refined and sophisticated in the world only began to acquire its national character in the mid-nineteenth century. The codification of a large national repertoire of local and regional dishes through cook books, magazines, newspapers, fairs and maps, played a major role in the emergence of a "French cuisine" (Ferguson 2004). Thus, just as occurred in the conception of the nation, the notion of a national cuisine was also an "invented" concept. Taking into account the social and ethnic diversity which may be contained within a country's frontiers, it seems obvious that a number of discrepancies or additional features not entirely congruent with the "national" appellation may also be present. In this sense, national cuisines are inventions possessing both a cultural and *political* content. On a different level, when national cuisines relocate, this adds a dimension to their specific character. Once outside of their own ethnic communities, these cuisines partially adapt to the flavors and preferences of their host countries, undergoing a small-scale transformation. Thus, Chinese food all over the

Corean ready-to-cook noodle soups with chicken, mushroom and hot flavors

YABANCI YEMEK BORSASINDA BİR TÜRK "BORSA"SI
Mutfağımız ağırlığını koydu

Ünlü Borsa Lokantası'nın Osmanbey şubesi, o yöredeki çeşit çeşit yabancı mutfağın arasında ulusal mutfağımızı temsil için yarışa katıldı

Başbakan Özal, açılışta
— Borsa ustaları, perhizi bozdurdu —

Milliyet
29 November 1987

BORSA USTALARI
"Yabancı mutfakların cirit attığı İstanbul'un Frengistan'ında Türk mutfağını biz temsil edeceğiz" diyen Borsa ustaları ve yarattıkları enfes tatlı türleri

Fotoğraflar: Bahattin Şenol

Our cuisine exerts its authority: *The Osmanbey branch of the famous Borsa restaurants has joined the race to represent our national cuisine among the variety of foreign restaurants in that district.*

Hürriyet
13 December 1981

Sabah
16 November 2001

above: **Turkish cuisine in Paris:** *7 Turkish restaurants introduce to the French the Turkish cuisine, unique for its raki and appetisers.*

right: **Sushi night:** *Rahmi Koç has treated his guests to Sushi.*

world is probably quite different in terms of the condiments and spices it uses from the same cuisine eaten on its native soil. Depending on where they have relocated, cuisines takes on American, English or Turkish traits. As cuisines become increasingly global, this actually leads to a transformation within their own environment as well. The "rediscovery" of Turkish cuisine in its native habitat is a case in point. As Turkish cuisine was revisited and packaged to introduce it to the world, it returned to its own context as a different creation. The Turkish cuisine internet sites which offer recipes for a wide variety of Turkish dishes are just as much a source of information for foreign food lovers as for their "native" counterparts.

The emergence of historical cuisines is also interesting. When looking at Ottoman cuisine the first question that comes to mind is "which Ottoman." From 1453, when Istanbul became the new Ottoman capital, and for close to five centuries, the Ottoman Empire contained within continually shifting boundaries a rich diversity of ethnic groups, religions, and classes. Even if by Ottoman cuisine we mean "palace cuisine," we know from a number of sources today, that in terms of the ingredients and quantities used, food cooked in the palace then differed significantly from today's so-called Ottoman dishes. The same arguments can be made for regional dishes. There are a number of reasons to assume that before they are put on the consumer market, ethnic cuisines go through a substantial transformation. Ethnic restaurants offering regional specialties in urban centers today, inevitably adapt their fare to their local clientele's tastes. Revising condiments and spices they strive to recreate specific flavors in a slightly more accessible form, while at the same time retaining a decor with an *authentic* effect.

Finally, frozen, pre-packaged regional dishes or their fast food versions take place at the extreme end of the urban food spectrum. Most supermarkets now offer Korean microwave noodle bowls, instant Kayseri mantı, Chinese rice stick noodles, a wide range of long-grain Indian or Thai rices,

That night we met up early in Beyoğlu. First we had dinner in an Italian restaurant. Good old Nesrin adores the Italians, as if they were very different from the Turks. Both her lovers in England were Italian, the two were actually very close friends, Nesrin had an affair first with one, then with the other. It is because of those boys that she developed this interest in Italian food. Anyway, the food at the Italian restaurant was wonderful, but there was no one there to find a remedy for Nesrin's suffering. From there we went to Babylon. Apparently it was Dynosaur's Night. Actually we were still young to be considered dynosaurs, but we both liked the music of the '70s and '80s. We didn't regret going there, and Nesrin managed to forget about her prolonged love affair for at least a few hours. [Ahmet Ümit, *Aşk Köpekliktir*, 2004, Doğan Publications, p. 113]

Knorr's "palace" soup mixes

Dardanel's authentic Kayseri manti

While we children bathed in the waters of Allaben or rode on the swings set up among the trees, the men would light the braziers, knead the raw groundmeat patties, prepare the bean salad with lots of parsley and onions and prepare the kebap. This could be pistachio kebap, onion kebap, garlic kebap, aubergine kebap, truffle kebap, lamb liver kebap, liver kebap, Japanese plum kebap, apple kebap or quince kebap, according to the time of the year.

Sunday was the day when men would prepare the food. This was valid not only when we went to Kavaklık but also when we stayed home. Whatever day it was, only men could prepare the kebaps. And the künefe of course. And they would be the ones to prepare and take to the bakery the ingredients for the lahmacun. [Ülkü Tamer, *Yaşamak Hatırlamaktır*, 2004, Yapı Kredi Publications, p. 31]

various far eastern soy, chilli, curry and oyster sauces, and an assortment of Italian ready made sauces. On a more national level, although the recent revival of Armenian, Greek, Jewish, Circassian, Kurdish and Syriac regional and ethnic cuisines, has added new traditions and foods to the culinary market, in fact this contribution remains extremely superficial, since it neglects to take into account the histories and significance of these diverse cultures. Thus though *forgotten* flavors are recovered, it is also the case that the lives they once shared remain lost. When we finally make up our minds to reclaim those losses, it will not be sanitized packages of "authentic" food experiences we are offered but an infinitely more complex, interrelated socio-cultural past.

Hürriyet
12 January 1997

Zaman
4 November 2004

above: **A chef with a master's degree:** *An Ottoman restaurant with a distinct style of service, cooking and ingredients*

below: **Our cuisine is not little known but completely unknown in the world**

Osmanlı lezzetleri ocakbaşında

Oba, Şamsa, Baca, Discorium, Çapari gibi mekânlarda başarılı işlere imza atan Cihan Oskay kısa bir süre önce ortak olduğu Biges Restaurant ile işletmecilik hayatına devam ediyor. Mekânda hem şıklık hem de salaş ocakbaşı keyfi bir arada yaşanıyor

Biges Restoran Levent'e farklı bir soluk yaşatıyor.

Akşam
1 March 2005

Usta getir bir LEHMECUN Halep işi olsun

Eskiden erkek kuzu etinden zırh ıyması çekilir, lahmacunun harcı evde hazırlanırdı. Fırına önderilen nar gibi kızarmış lahmacunun yanında da mutlaka ayran içilirdi

Sabah
12 February 2005

above: **Ottoman flavours at the fireside restaurants:** *Cihan Oskay, who has created successful clubs and restaurants like Oba, Şamsa, Baca, Discorium and Çapari, is continuing his career as an entrepreneur together with his new partner, Biges Restaurant. The venue presents both elegance and a relaxed fireside restaurant atmosphere.*

left: **Chef, bring us a lahmacun, Halep style**

left: **Broad beans with yoghurt is on the internet:** *The Kanaat Restaurant, famous for its types of broad beans, has started an online service.*

below: **Customers of global hotel chains prefer local foods**

Yeni Yüzyıl
7 June 1998

Zaman
26 January 2003

The good old *bayrams*

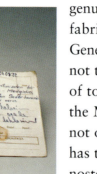

A few greeting cards for Bayram that used to be a popular tradition

Yusuf reached the fair ground set up during the Bayram. After having argued with his mother, he had worn his new shirt, which was a little small for him, the arms were a little short, about halfway between his wrists and his elbows, but the colour hadn't faded, it smelled mint-like, and he had some money in his pocket. Two liras. His father had thrust lots of change in the palm of his hand and master Arif had given him a white lira and he had even said "You aren't tired of looking in the mirror yet, are you, go on, go to the fair ground and look at them again and learn!"
[Hulki Aktunç, "Bayram Gömleği", *Gidenler Dönmeyenler*, 1976, Günebakan Publications, p. 132-133]

The older generations tell the young generations about those "good old days". Back then, everything was more authentic, more genuine...But the story of the past that *nostalgia* fabricates is usually one that never existed. Generally, the focus of fantasies about the past is not the past at all: it is the shortcomings and decay of today. The ways in which Turkey celebrates the Muslim *bayrams* [religious holidays] today not only demonstrate how a modernizing history has transformed religious rituals, but also how nostalgia has been an integral part of this process. During the religious holidays, all newspapers and magazines – not just the Islamic press – publish special *bayram*-related articles, and television and radio stations prepare special programs. All of these feature articles and programs evoke the past, the "old holiday times" with longing. The implication is that past holidays held more charm, were more magic, more genuine. Visits were paid to family elders, squabbles between family and friends were brought to an end and children were doted on... Over the last 25 years, however, *bayram*s have increasingly come to be seen as an opportunity for a *vacation*; hence the greater coverage by the media of travel and entertainment opportunities. Is there a *conflict* between this *longing* for the past and the needs and possibilities of the present? If there is, how should we interpret it?

In the process of modern nation building in Turkey, religion was distanced from the *public sphere*. By decree, Islamic principles and practices were abolished from most areas of public life, including the administration of the state, the legal system and education. At the same time that religious affairs were divorced from other state functions, however, they were also centralized; many religious orders and organizations were also dismantled. This new centralized religious establishment adopted the teachings of Sunni Islam. Conversely, "volk" Islam – as Şerif Mardin calls it – which wrapped itself in local beliefs and "superstitions", as well as

Baba bana bayramı anlat

Komşuların bütün kapıları kapalıydı. Hiçbir şey babalarının anlattığına benzemiyordu. Bayram yerlerinde atlı karıncaların ve cambazların yerine kaybolmuş bir çocukluğun betonlaşmış anıları vardı. Ne ipek mendiller kaldı ne de horoz şekerler

right: **Dad, tell me of the old bayrams:** *All the neighbours had their front doors closed. Nothing looked like what their dad had told them. The merry-go-rounds and the acrobats in the fairgrounds were replaced by the memories in cement of their childhood.*

below: **The good old bayrams:** *Citizens say "what's the use of a bayram for me" because of the cost of living and they are not even able to buy bayram clothes.*

Sabah
4 March 2001

Midilli'nin sefasını yapan son kuşak (1960). Hayat'taki bu fotoğraf Bülent Giz

Ne yeni giyecek alabiliyor, ne istedikleri gibi gezebiliyorlar

Nerede o eski bayramlar

■ Hayat pahalılığı nedeniyle "Bayram benim neyime" diyen vatandaşlar, bayramlık giyecek bile alamıyorlar.

Bugün
30 June 1990

Eminönü meydanı bomboş
Her bayram tıklım tıklım olan, işportacıların dolduğu, Eminönü meydanında bu bayramda işler kesat gidiyor.

Eskiden mutluyduk
Hasan Devamlı, eski bayramları anarak iç geçiriyor.

right: **Farewell, city of Ramadan:** *Minds cannot attain His essence, eyes cannot perceive Him in the world.*

below: **First it was the people that changed and then the Ramadans**

Sabah
9 August 1980

Nokta
4 February 1996

Hürriyet
11 February 1994

Güneş
10 May 1986

above: **Ramadan entertainment:** *A special "Another Night" programme for the sacred month.*

right: **Uğur Böcekleri** *duo on every night, throughout Ramadan*

A prayer mat with a compass

diverse Muslim ideologies and practices continued to fill symbolic functions for the common people (1997). These "superstitions" are the main target of modernization drives. As the central state establishes its hegemony it tries to break local knowledge and forms of belonging; at the same time, the state uses religion to win popularity and consolidate the hegemony of its rule. Throughout the history of the Republic, Islam and Islamic religious rituals have had a complex and contentious history both in state policies and within the social fabric. In recent years, the conflictual forms that have emerged between "secularism" and Pan-Islamicism have adopted this legacy, still not fully analyzed, and found new interpretations and meanings within current political movements. While the secularists violently oppose the extension of Islamic practices like the religious headscarf into the public sphere, organized Islamic groups that have redefined their modern forms are acquiring new "public faces" (Göle, 2000). This "Islamic ascendance," which a number of factions fear, may in one way – through the shape it has taken in the current government today – be a propelling force for more "modernization" in Turkey. So what meaning do religious *bayrams* take on in this complex political framework?

An electronic tasbee

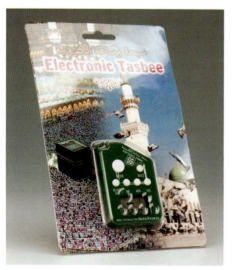

In the 1940s, in one of his programs on the state-run Ankara radio station, Galip Ataç focused his show on traditional *bayram* visits. Ataç wanted Turkish society to replace gloom with the optimism and cheerfulness of the West; and for Ataç, *bayram* visits were boring and glum. Instead of these visits, therefore, he recommended trips: "Freeing yourself of *bayram* visits will allow your mind to rest and can be a lot of fun... especially if you have a private car and save up a little gas beforehand" (1943:27) This attitude is a striking example of a modernist approach that essentially finds Turkish traditions to be unaesthetic, and thus wishes to be free of them all. However, a few years later when the Democratic

'Kurban tatili' böyle geçti

9 güne uzatılan Kurban Bayramı tatili kimileri için deniz ve güneşle kucaklaşma fırsatı olurken, büyük kentlerimizde de geleneksel bayram görüntüleri yaşandı...

Yeni Günaydın
15 May 1995

Modern kesim merkezleri
İstanbul'un birçok belediyesi, veteriner kontrolünde sağlıklı kesim yapılan modern merkezler kurdu. Bu uygulamadan memnun kalan vatandaşlar artık sokaklarda kurban kesmeye son vermek gerektiğini söyledi.

Güneşle kucaklaştılar
Bayram tatilini Güney ve Ege'ye giderek değerlendirenler, yazlarda merhaba dedi. Yeterince ısınmadığı için denize giremeyenler kendilerini güneşin yakıcılığına teslim edip, bronzlaşmayı tercih etti.

Mahkûmlarla yakınları kucaklaştı
Bayram dolayısıyla cezaevlerinde, oldukça duygusal sahnelerin yaşandığı açık görüş yapıldı. Mahkûmlar, sadece bayramlarda da olsa, sevdikleriyle bu kadar yakından görüşmenin, kucaklaşmanın keyfini yaşadı.

Çiller dua etti
Başbakan Çiller, Kurban Bayramı dolayısıyla, Zincirlikuyu'daki ana babasının mezarını ziyaret edip dua okudu...

Bayramda piknik keyfi
Tatile gidemeyenler, bayramı piknik yerlerini, parkları doldurarak değerlendirdi. Bayram süresince İstanbul'un piknik yerleri doldu, taştı. Mangalları yakan, getirdikleri yiyecekleri açık havada yiyen piknikçiler, çimenlerin üzerinde...

Bayram firarı!..

Otomatikman 10 güne çıkan bayram tatillerinde evinde oturana tuhaf bakıyorlar!

Bugün
28 May 1993

El öpmekten utanıyorlar!
Büyüklerine yarım kilo şekerleme almamak için dünyanın borcuna imza atıp tatile kaçan firariler, döndükten sonra da "Ay keşke gitmeseydik. Valla her yer öyle kalabalık ki!" diye yave yapıyorlar. (Ersin TURAN - BUGÜN Haber - OTOGAR)

above: **That's how we spent the Kurban Holiday:** *The Kurban Bayram holiday extended to 9 days was an opportunity for sea and sun for some, while traditional bayram festivities were held in our big cities.*

left: **Bayram fugitives:** *This bayram, which is automatically extended to 10 days, people staying at home are considered strange.*

Mustafa Toköz: Yes, today is the first day of the Bayram. People are at their happiest during the Bayram. ...Why are we celebrating this Bayram?

Osman Ünlü: Of course it's not because the Sacred Muslim Ramadan is over or because we are rid of our dues. God has commanded Muslim believers who worship him to fast during the Sacred Month of Ramadan. Believers who were honoured to receive this commandment are happy because they have fulfilled the commandment without any trouble, or because they were proud to receive this commandment and they have carried it out. That is why we feel this happiness... One can also involuntarily be happy because one can eat and drink freely, let's not kid ourselves. There are tea addicts, coffee addicts and oh I don't know, there are tobacco addicts. Are they happy too? Of course they can be happy, this is part of human nature. But they are not happy because they are rid of the Ramadan. People can be happy about this too, people can be happy about possessing material things too. That's something completely different. But a Muslim does not, cannot think that he is rid of it, this is not possible [A section from the "Islam and Society" programme, TGRT FM, 3 November 2005]

Candies offered to guests during bayram visits

Party was in power, religious *bayrams* were considered a major tool for generating social unity, and so were given wide use of the public sphere. In the 1980s, it was no surprise for deprecatory expressions about tradition such as "backward and coarse," to appear side by side with statements stressing how important religion and religious *bayrams* were. These examples can be interpreted as signs of the break between ongoing religious ideology and practices and "traditions." In this situation, new traditions are "invented" when current religious practices are transformed into traditions. But these new traditions will inevitably be shaped by the institutions of modern society, like the press, and by the dynamics of the capitalist economy. Television and radio play a crucial role in this process. In her analysis of the religious programs that the popular theologian Yaşar Nuri Öztürk hosted on television, and in particular, his religious discussions held during the month of Ramadan, Ayşe Öncü refers to a "fashionable packaging" of Islam (1995).

This longing for the past, or nostalgia, can now be understood as an attempt to authenticate newly created traditions. *Nostalgia* adds the missing feeling of *authenticity* to today's ways of living and thus creates continuity; despite its break with the past, the present thus remains *desirable*. The emergence of private Islamic radio and television stations in the 1990s revealed significant differences in the approaches to religious topics of "Islamist" and "secular" factions. Still, with the adoption of a standard radio and television format and idiom, these differences in content remain inconspicuous. Television often attempts to revive erstwhile themes using "special effects" in Ramadan programs and holiday *specials*, to integrate them into TV broadcasting idiom. This kind of television and radio programs always include the "bygone *bayram*" theme. As today draws its meaning from yesterday, it attempts to perpetuate the social identity dimension of religion.

All the same, one can also see entirely new themes in these broadcasts. With programs like *Televole iftar* (a gossip and celebrity show scheduled soon after the *iftar* meal that breaks the fast), Ramadan is adjoined to the existing world of television entertainment. Additionally, Ramadan and other religious *bayrams* have increasingly become associated with *consumption*, especially

left: **Sultanahmet shines brightly:** *Throughout Ramadan traditional Şehzadebaşı entertainment will be organised in the historical square.*

below: **30 days of rich flavours:** *The fast rhythm of the present days doesn't permit us to always cook traditional foods at home.*

Sabah
5 January 1998

Aktüel
15 January 1997

Milliyet **9 November 2002**

Milliyet **11 November 2002**

above: **Come and join us for iftar:** *Throughout the Ramadan month many restaurants and hotels are organising special events.*

right: **A Ramadan table that won't make you gain weight:** *Almost everybody complains of gaining weight during Ramadan in spite of fasting. Here are three proposals for iftar and sahur tables from the experts that, let alone making you gain weight, will let you lose weight.*

since the start of the 2000s. While from a religious perspective Ramadan is a time to withdraw from worldly desires and control one's "cravings of the flesh," in practice it is becoming a time when more consumption is encouraged, particularly consumption of food. Throughout the month of Ramadan, newspapers and magazines suggest *iftar* dishes and publish articles about the rich *iftar* menus being offered at select restaurants; food and beverage advertisements are also more prevalent than usual. Another frequent association is that of *iftar* meals with health and fitness. During Ramadan the preoccupation of many is the *iftar* dinner "that doesn't make you put on weight." *Shopping* is another aspect of holiday consumption. The shopping alternatives and opportunities presented during the holidays have grown more important than the religious meaning. Yet, as time goes by, the contradiction between nostalgia and consumption is gradually disappearing. *Nostalgia*, as a theme, promotes more consumption; special Ramadan and *bayram* products use nostalgia to advance their *brand*.

Furthermore, many who appear to have followed the advice that Ataç gave in the 1940s are now using the *bayram* as an opportunity to take a vacation. "Where are you going for *bayram*?" has become a *commonplace* question. Going to other places, traveling to other countries, going on vacation is now standard practice among the middle class, as evidenced by the growing number of *bayram package tours*. The number of people "getting away" during the *bayram*s is increasing; big cities empty out; and, as usual, *bayram*-related traffic accidents cause unnecessary deaths. Apart from those visit family and relatives in other cities, a large portion of the holiday travelers contributing to highway traffic are the ones going to holiday villages. The poorer segments, which have no other option, take advantage of the deserted streets to rediscover their cities.

The debate surrounding *Kurban Bayram* [the Feast of the Sacrifice] never seems to subside. The general view is that the "rivers of blood" that flow from sacrificed animals is not a scene becoming of a "modern" society. Sacrificing animals on the streets is a sign of "filth," "barbarity" and "coarse village behavior." The main desire is to make these scenes "history"; through the eyes of the

A tape by Nurhan Damcıoğlu, a popular singer who used to appear frequently on TV during bayrams.

He shut his eyes firmly. He remembered the large Ferris wheel, the popguns, the cotton shorts of his father, obtained from an old pair of trousers, and the rough and bulky shoes which were soled before the Bayram, and whose large surface was polished with a cheap polish that soiled everything else. What's the use of a bayram for poor people? What does the Bayram do for them, other than revealing the lack of things and the poverty which they struggle to hide honourably and meticulously. That's how it was, because he believed that the bayram was when some people realised even better how privileged they were. That's why the meat that arrived during the Kurban Bayram was difficult to swallow for him. Usually it was the most useless, the most fatty pieces that were distributed around. The tail fat that his mother heated and melted, continued for many months to be added to the food she cooked, and after every meal that bad, sour smell of goat meat would blend with the pain he felt because of his poverty and it would increase and intensify.
[İnci Aral, "Kirli Sarı", *Ağda Zamanı*, 1999, Can Publications, p. 45]

Clock with call to prayer

West, this spectacle hurts Turkey's *modern* image. For this reason, the people most opposed to this practice are the privileged "White Turks" of the large cities who have Western lifestyles and considerable cultural capital. From an environmental perspective, too, the sale and slaughter of sacrificial animals poses increasing problems. In short, carrying on with the old "traditions" of Kurban Bayram seems harder than producing new ones. At this point, when the needs of today come in *conflict* with the longing for the past, people turn to modern technology for a solution. For example, today it is increasingly acceptable to have your "sacrificial animal" slaughtered, packaged and delivered to your home.

The *urban poor* become more visible during Ramadan and other *bayrams*. Throughout the month of Ramadan city municipalities open tented soup kitchens serving free *iftar* meals and the state provides assistance to the poor, thereby reviving the tradition of *charity*. Although long lines form in front of the *iftar* tents in various districts of the city, how much of a contribution this practice – which might be considered some form of social assistance – makes to social peace and solidarity is open to question. In an environment where s*ocial polarization* in the cities is increasingly more acute and social and political problems are growing steadily, the *iftar* tents are little more than a show. So, the "peace of mind" that we expect from *bayrams* is overshadowed by the problems of society. In conclusion, the desire to establish a *continuity* between the past and the present and between generations, as represented by the request "Daddy, tell me about the *bayram*," is no longer enough to revive the past. *Even nostalgia doesn't taste the way it used to!*

Akşam
13 January 1997

Akşam
23 January 1997

above: **Free *iftar* in Usküdar:** *The Üsküdar Municipality is offering free iftar meals every day for 3,500 people in the huge tent in the district square.*

left: **If only it were allways Ramadan:** *Remembering citizens in need of help in Ramadan, municipalities have started competing to help the poor.*

left: Bayram clothes can be bought in supermarkets: *Everything is faster nowadays. We live fast, eat fast, shop fast. The minute we enter supermarkets, we want to finish everything we have to do and leave immediately.*

below: Alternative bayram shopping: *The prices of ready-made wear have caused the bayram shopping to move to other areas. Now everybody rushes to factory outlets, to end-of-season stores and to Merter, where export surplus is sold.*

Hürriyet
21 November 2003

Hürriyet
14 March 2000

Sabah
15 October 2004

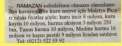

Akşam
30 January 2004

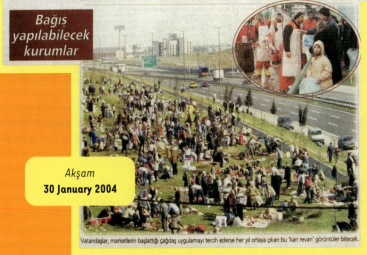

above: The most suitable addresses for Ramadan shopping: *Together with the approaching Ramadan, the pleasant panic of iftar and sahur shopping has started. In order to help you, we have checked out the stores where you can find suitable products at economical prices.*

below: Home-delivery kurban: *As an important step in the elimination of unpleasant sights during the slaughtering of sacrificial animals, meat cut in modern and hygienic establishments will be delivered from supermarkets to homes.*

NeoTurkism

A few VCDs recently on sale about "Turks and their enemies"

-The Tale of Our Cat-

When I was little I wondered
If the cat of our Greek neighbour
Was also Greek.

One day I asked my mother
apparently cats are Turkish
but dogs are Greek
and dogs attack the poor little cats.

Then one day
what should I see
but our cat
eating its very own kitten.

[Mehmet Yaşın, "-Bizim Kedinin Masalı-," *Sevgilim Ölü Asker*, 1984/1997, Adam Publications, p. 51]

Today, the concept of *identity* acquires meaning through the clash between the sense of *belonging* symbolized by identity and the increasingly *imagined* nature of identities. While on the one hand various identities linked to nationality, ethnicity, gender or sexuality gain visibility in the public sphere, on the other, the fact that these identities are growingly defined, displayed and lived through a "staging" process removes them from their "essential" and "genuine" meaning. Yet the fact that identities are imagined does not make them less important. Today, the rapid transformation of the feelings of belonging into identities creates a violent area of conflict. National identities rank first among conflicting identities.

National identity has always been an important and "delicate" matter for Turkey. During the first years of the Republic, a number of state institutions have been used to instill a sense of Turkishness, through the definition of Turkish culture and identity. In order to give some credibility to these definitions, particular stress was given to specific elements such as history, race, and language. At the same time, as Ziya Gökalp had advocated, a particular effort was made to ensure the development of a specifically Turkish "culture" even in the event of the adoption of "western civilization." The definition of national identity through Turkishness also brought the necessity to distinguish this identity from domestic and foreign others. Within the framework of modernization, Turkishness had therefore to differentiate itself not only from the West, which it took as a model, or from the multinational Ottoman past, but also from the "official minorities" that continued to live within the new national entity – Greeks, Jews, and Armenians – and from all other ethnic and religious communities that were not included in this definition. Despite the vagueness stemming from this painful differentiation needed to define identity, Turkishness as an *absolute* concept

Vatan 34
27 June 2004

Relive history at Miniaturk: *If you want to spend a day far from politics during the NATO summit, go immediately to Miniaturk.*

Aktüel
1994

Milliyet
13 October 1985

above: **The new Turks:**
The new Turkey rises upon the shoulders of these people who embrace both universal and traditional values

below: **We Turks:** *I am Turkish, I am honest, that's who I am.*

became the driving force behind the Turkification policies implemented in those years. Mustafa Kemal's famous aphorism of the early years of the Republic, "Happiness is to call oneself a Turk," was less related to a concept of Turkish origins than to the idea of presenting oneself as a Turk. Although different origins and feelings of belonging continued to bear importance in everyday conversations and in a variety of solidarity networks, *everybody* was expected to be a Turk in the public sphere. Alongside this absolute definition, based mostly on language and citizenship, more circumstantial definitions of Turkishness also existed. Those identities that opposed or threatened the power structure were openly viewed with suspicion. Those who allied around the idea of "national security and order" and opposed these identities were also defined as Turks. The oppression and exclusion applied against non-Muslim minorities, Kurds, Alevis, and Islamist groups throughout the history of the Republic, as well as their relationship to the rise to dominance of a modern Turkish identity are among today's controversial issues.

The postcolonial process following World War II in particular has witnessed the rise to the status of identity of histories and identifications that had formerly been suppressed and ignored. Following this period, the propagation of "third-world" nationalist movements, national revolutions and alternative resistances has brought yet another dimension to the war of identities. Today, postcolonial criticism has made it possible to reveal the nature of modernist inventions. Yet during the same period, we have witnessed the proliferation of national, ethnic, and religious currents and clashes based on "essential" identities. In a more recent past, the emergence of the European Union as a political body, the transformation of Europeanness into an identity aiming at defending its borders against aliens from within and from without, or the start of a war of the "Christian West" against the "Muslim world" after the attacks of 9/11, have all shown that identities are consciously manipulated for political purposes. All these recent examples point to a political *consciousness* about identities; they also show that these identities have long lost their natural meanings and are constantly organized and reorganized within a variety of strategies. Parallel to the rising *strategic* importance of identities and to the aggravation of

Güntaç Aktan's "Panaroma from Anatolia" programme, on a demonstration in a province in the Southeast region [TRT1, 18 April 1994]

A SHORT HISTORY OF TURKEY III

Since the surname law
hasn't been possible
To separate Turkey's name
From Atatürk's name:

In the 1930s
Etibank's Turkey;

In the 1940s
The atheist Turkey;

In the 1950s
The lute playing Turkey;

In the 1960s
The other Turkey;

In the 1970s
Atatürk's Turkey;

In the 1980s
Turkey in name only

And then there are the blue
   voyages,
And the greek
almost always:
Turkey the island. [Cemal Süreya, *Sevda Sözleri*, 1998, Yapı Kredi Publications, p. 221]

Bu da "Kokteyl Turka"...

Barmenlerimiz arasında, yerli malzemeleri kokteyllerde kullanma eğilimi nihayet baş gösterdi. Nar ekşisi, pekmez ve kuru incir kullanılarak yapılan ve NATO Zirvesi konuklarına sunulan The Turk kokteyli, bunlardan en ilginci...

Milliyet
25 July 2004

Sabah
2 March 1994

above: **And this is cocktail Turka:** *A tendency has emerged finally among our barmen to mix local imgredients in cocktails.*

right: **Change in a changing Turkey:** *A cartoon about the use of nationalist themes in fashion*

Ülker, colayı Türkleştirdi

Pepsi ve Coca Cola'nın hakim olduğu Cola pazarına Ülker, Cola Turka markasıyla girdi. 'Türkiye'nin Colası' olarak lanse edilen Cola Turka reklamlarında Hollywood'un ünlü komedyeni Chevy Chase oynuyor

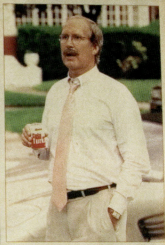

Hollywood'un Kemal Sunal'ı: Chevy Chase

Yarın Extra
8 July 2003

Ülker Tüketici Grubu Başkanı Karamollaoğlu, Başkan Yardımcısı Kuthan Erginbilgiç ve Ürün Grup Müdürü Şebnem Nasi'nin aralarında bulunduğu Ülker yöneticileri.

Türk gibi Amerikalılar

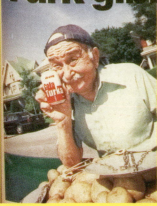

Ülker's Turkish version of Cola: *Ülker has entered the coke market dominated by Pepsi and Coca Cola with the Cola Turka brand.*

Aktüel
14 May 1992

above: **Euroturks and national louts**

left: **Hurrah for anybody who can get the colour of the Turks right:** *A subject of debate nowadays is the colour of Turks.*

Tempo
24 May 1995

conflicts, in Turkey, the issue of Turkishness is making a comeback as a *renewed problem*.

The 1980 military coup emphasized Turkishness on every possible occasion against foreign and domestic foes. During this period, *nationalism* formed a crucial axis of the new typology of the individual. However, during the political process that followed, Turkishness ended up losing its seemingly unshakable and absolute role. Discussions disseminated through the mass media played an important part in this process. According to Rıfat Bali, the journalist and author Çetin Altan was the first to initiate a discussion about the concepts of the "*maganda*" (urban yokel) and his opposite, the "Euro-Turk" (2002: 324). The "Euro-Turk," defined as a high-cultured and affluent individual having internalized western culture, is thus positioned against the rural migrants to the cities, characterized as uncouth yokels. Immediately after that, it was the turn for the "White Turks" issue to appear in the press, introducing it to a wider audience. A reference to the western discourse of racial segregation, the concept of the "White Turk" described the privileged status of a small minority of urban dwellers. The notion of the "White Turk" also voiced the accusations of Islamic milieus against the western affectation of this group. Interestingly, however, the term came also to be used by the very group that was targeted by the expression. Those strata who considered it a virtue to be western, modern and urban and those journalists, who spoke for them in the press, defiantly embraced this identity. Obviously, Turkishness no longer had to be read through national unity alone, but could also be defined in terms of "trends" acquired synchronically with the rest of the world. This led to a diversification of "types" of Turkishness. Adjectives preceding the term came to describe different identities: "Euro-Turks," "New Turks," "Red Turks," "Nigger" or "Black Turks," "national yokels"… While pointing to conflicting meanings in society, by complementing a worn-out identity, these attributes also contributed to revive it and to maintain it alive.

The fact that, from the 1990s on, Turkishness became a legitimate topic of research both in academic circles and in the press and that efforts were made to analyze the "social profile" of Turks reveals

İlhan started his words saying "My young friends… I wish all Turkish children were as patriotic as you. I wish they loved Turkey like you. I wish they were as morally upright as you. But alas… They are ready to sell their mothers and sisters to Moscow, they are wretches. My friends, I took an oath together with my very esteemed brothers who are prepared to risk their life for this cause. I gave them my word of honour. We are not going to let anybody live in this country who is not a Turk through and through. Look at yourselves, and then look at your other friends, whose private cars wait at their entrance and whose servants bring four tiers of lunch boxes at lunch time. Aren't you sons of this same country? Aren't you Turks, through and through? [Adalet Ağaoğlu, *Ölmeye Yatmak*, Kasım 1998/1973, Yapı Kredi Publications/ Remzi Publications, p. 174]

A key ring with an Ataturk portrait

A t-shirt with the Turkish flag

that the assumed identity had by then lost its natural character and was subjected to a process of reinvention to suit new social and political needs. The growing number of newspaper headlines such as "I'm a Turk, I'm honest, that's who I am" shows that this process was not devoid of an ironic self-perception. The fact that Turkishness acquired new meanings on the market added even more to this irony. Symbols of Turkishness entered the market as a process of commercialization. To give just one example, a regulation issued in 1980 during military rule made it a crime not to fly the flag on Republic Day. By the end of the 1990s, the flag could be found on a variety of artifacts, from tee-shirts to glasses, and from cushions to jewelry; one could even admire popular singers dressed in the national flag. "Red-and-White," "Crescent-and-Star," "Kemalizm," or "Secularism" became trendy. "The Tenth Anniversary" march (1933) became a pop tune. Turkishness invaded brand names: "Kolaturka," "Turkcell"... The trendiest bars and restaurants started adding a "turka" to their names, even boasting "cocktails-turka" on their menus. "*Alaturka*" (*alla turca*), an expression meaning "Turkish-style," which had acquired a derogative meaning of inferiority compared to "Western-style" (*alafranga, alla franca*) lost this negative meaning and entered pop culture. While this meant a growing *distance* from the age-old inferiority complex vis-à-vis the West, it also laid the ground for an *everyday* use of *nationalism*.

Buildings, buildings... As if these were not enough, they are building new ones. If a Turk has money, they say he'll spend it on buildings. Where else would he spend it? The same verse is on his mind: His song unfinished, a woman on his mind. And then his mind too is left behind. A man walking slowly crashed into him, he was a gentleman and he apologised. When does a Turk come back to his senses? He passed by the Monument of Confidence. He stopped, turned around, entered the park. There were no children, they were having their afternoon nap. The tramps were resting too. He looked at the statues: they didn't look like Turks, neither their posture nor their faces did. He remembered Kenan and smiled. They look like German Japanese people. One is proud, the other is confident and the other one works. [Oğuz Atay, *Tutunamayanlar*, 1972/2000 İletişim Publications/ Sinan Publications, p. 317-318]

One can safely say then that despite the increasingly visible speculative nature of Turkish identity, its strategic importance has not really decreased at all. At a time when the flag becomes part of pop culture, that same flag can also trigger mass hysteria. Against a single "flag burning" incident, "thousands of flags" are brandished. The Municipality of Şişli goes as far as to manufacture "the longest flag of the world." As in the case of several lynching attempts against "domestic foes," nationalist feelings can take a much more *violent* form. Even though the war in south-eastern Anatolia seems to be over, the least spark is sufficient to ignite it again. Despite all the reforms resulting from harmonization with the European Union and that are expected to trigger a process of pluralist democratization, nationalism, perhaps in reaction to these very reforms, is creating a growing anti-Kurdish sentiment. Triggered by increasingly "paranoid," harsh and excessive

Şimdi moda laiklik

Podyumlarda artık siyaset ağır basmaya başladı. Bir özel firmanın defilesinde "Türkiye laiktir laik kalacak" tişörtlerinin büyük beğeni toplamasından sonra, Kemer'deki Altın Nar Festivali'nde de Atatürklü tişörtler 'alkış yağmuruna' yolaçtı. Güzellik yarışması sırasında Türk bayraklı ve Atatürk resimli kıyafetlerle sahneye çıkan güzeller, Atatürk döneminin dünya güzeli Keriman Halis Ece'ye selam gönderir gibiydi.

Yeni Yüzyıl
27 June 1997

Secularism is trendy now: *Politics has started to dominate the catwalks.*

reactions, Turkishness has become a common feeling uniting a large section of the population. Throughout this process, one can observe the persistence of the question of westernization or Europeanization as a decisive factor. This issue had always been there, initially moving back and forth between the notion of "not being European enough" and the idea that "Europe doesn't want us, anyway"; it now dominates the agenda with slogans of the "Europe, Europe, hear our voice" type or fears that "Europe wants to partition us." In the past few years, the difficulties encountered in finalizing the process of European integration have led to an increasingly defensive state of mind. Turkey is experiencing a profound *crisis of identification*, characterized by an inability to establish a correspondence between globally consumed products and shared "world views," on the one hand, and locally assigned meanings, on the other.

A few examples of recently published books about Turks

A number of books about Turkishness that have recently flooded the market are seeking a solution to this identity crisis. Most striking among these works is Turgut Özakman's half documentary novel *Crazy Turks* (*Çılgın Türkler*), which, by referring to the War of Independence, tries to reactualize the meaning of the national struggle of the early 1920s. According to Sezgi Durgun, this novel "uses the expression 'crazy Turk' as an ironic response to western rationalism" (2006: 247). "Although the rebellion of the Turks against western imperialism is considered to be "foolish" in the eyes of the West, Westerners are really the crazy ones. Therefore, the expression "crazy Turk" inverts western values and defines our rationalism, thus locating the reaction to western rationalism at the center of the definition of a national self" (*ibid.*). Books like *Crazy Turks* that try to define "us" and to place Turkishness on the world scene attract much attention and go through hundreds of prints. Yet the fact that these books are sold in supermarkets, much like popular romantic novels some years ago, and side by side with mostly imported packaged goods is a crucial starting point to rethink the *trivial* but extremely *provocative* nature of nationalism today.

Vatan
24 March 2005

One flag is down, thousands are up: *A country-wide campaign has started, resulting from the Turkish flag being dragged on the ground by two children, while slogans were shouted in favour of the separatist organisation during the Newroz celebrations in Mersin.*

Ortak Pazar'a girmekle iş bitmiyor

'AVRUPALI DEĞİLİZ'

Fazla söze ne gerek — Avrupa'dan dönen Başbakan'a karşılama töreni.

Yeni Gündem
12 April 1987

We are not Europeans:
Becoming part of the common market is not sufficient.

Almanya! Duy sesimizi İşte bu Türklerin ayak sesleri

Yıllar önce sadece hayati ihtiyaçlarını karşılamak üzere Almanya'ya giden Türkler, bugün ülkenin uluslararası arenadaki yüzakı durumunda. Artık Almanlar'ı kendi gençleri değil, Türk evlatları temsil ediyor

Akşam
11 March 2005

Dubai kuleleri değil Kuleturka yapalım

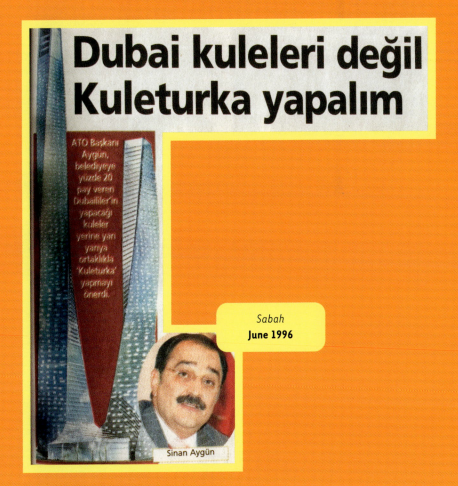

ATO Başkanı Aygün, belediyeye yüzde 20 pay veren Dubaililer'in yapacağı kuleler yerine yarı yarıya ortaklıkla 'Kuleturka' yapmayı önerdi.

Sinan Aygün

Sabah
June 1996

above: **Oh Germany, hear us, these are the footsteps of the Turks:** *The Turks who years ago went to Germany to earn a living, now are the pride of the country in the international arena.*

right: **Let's build Towerturka not Dubai Towers:** *Aygün, head of the Ankara Chamber of Commerce, has proposed to build a "TowerTurca" with half and half partnership, instead of the towers to be built by the Dubaians who will pay the municipality a 20 percent commission.*

Archives and Primary Sources

archives
Açık Radyo Archives
Ahmet Ekendiz Private Collection
The Archives of the Advertising Foundation and Association of Advertisers
Akra Radyo Archives
Best FM Archives
The Boğaziçi University Library
CNN Türk Archives
The Istanbul Metropolitan Municipality Atatürk Library, the Department of Periodicals
The Istanbul Municipality Caricature and Humor Museum
The Istanbul Bilgi University Library
The Istanbul University Library
The Library and Research Center of the Foundation for Women's Studies
The Ottoman Bank Museum Archives and Research Center Library
The Archives Department at Kanal 7
Naim Dilmener Private Collection
NTV Radyo Archives
NTV Televizyon Archives
Samanyolu TV Archives
The Turkish Journalists Association Press Museum
TRT (Turkish Radio and Television Association) Archives

newspapers
Akşam, *Birgün*, *Bugün*, *Bulvar*, *Cumhuriyet*, *Dünya*, *Gün*, *Günaydın*, *Güneş*, *Her Gün*, *Hürriyet*, *İlkhaber*, *Meydan*, *Milli Gazete*, *Milliyet*, *Radikal*, *Referans*, *Sabah*, *Saklambaç*, *Son Havadis*, *Star*, *Süper Tan*, *Tan*, *Tercüman*, *Türkiye*, *Yarın*, *Yeni Asır*, *Yeni Günaydın*, *Yeni Nesil*, *Yeni Şafak*, *Yeni Yüzyıl*, *Zaman*

periodicals
2000'e Doğru, *Airport Magazine*, *Ajanda*, *Aksiyon*, *Aktüel*, *Anne&Bebek*, *Arena*, *Baba*, *Bay*, *Beyoğlu*, *Biba*, *Bilim ve Teknik*, *Biz Bize*, *Bizden Haberler*, *Bizim Aile*, *Boom*, *Müzik*, *Bride*, *Bussiness Woman*, *Bussinessman*, *Capital*, *Car&Men*, *Cosmopolitan*, *Çağrı*, *Çarşaf*, *Domus M*, *Dünya Özel Ek*, *Ekonomik Panorama*, *Elele*, *Elle*, *Emekçi Kadınlar*, *Erkekçe*, *Esquire*, *Ev*, *For Men*, *Form Sante*, *Gazete Metro*, *Gırgır*, *Günaydın Gençlik*, *Haftalık*, *Haftanın Sesi*, *Haftasonu*, *Haftaya Bakış*, *Hanımeli*, *Harper's Bazaar*, *Hayat*, *Hey*, *Home Art*, *Hürriyet 8. Gün*, *Hürriyet Magazin*, *İstanbul Life*, *İş ve Yuva*, *Joker*, *Kadayıf*, *Kadın Kimliği*, *Kadın ve Aile*, *Kadın Vizyon*, *Kadınca*, *Kaktüs*, *Kapris*, *Kırmızı*, *Kim*, *Limon*, *Leman*, *Life +*, *Life Mydonose*, *Marie Claire*, *Maxi*, *Medyamarket*, *Milliyet Aktüalite*, *Milliyet Çocuk*, *Mutfak*, *Sağlıklı Yaşam*, *Nane Limon*, *Naturel*, *Nokta*, *Options*, *Oto Haber*, *Otomobil Magazin*, *Outdoor*, *Para*, *Pazartesi*, *Pirelli*, *Pişmiş Kelle*, *Rapor*, *Rapsodi*, *Sağlığınız*, *Sağlık Alemi*, *Sanat Çevresi*, *Ses*, *She + He*, *Show*, *Sigorta Dünyası*, *Sokak*, *Sporun Rengi*, *Star Weekly*, *Şebnem*, *Şehir*, *Şoför ve Trafik Dergisi*, *Tanıtım*, *Teleskop*, *Tempo*, *Turkish Airlines Skylife*, *Türkiye Turing ve Otomobil Kurumu Bülteni*, *Türkiye Yollar Mecmuası*, *Vatan 34*, *Vizon İstanbul*, *Vizyon*, *Vizyon Dekorasyon*, *Voyager*, *Yaşama Sanatı*, *Yeni Aktüel*, *Yeni Dünya*, *Yeni Gündem*, *Zaman Pazar*, *Zest*

books
Piyale Madra, *Ademler ve Havvalar 1*, İstanbul: Yapı Kredi Publications, 2005.
Piyale Madra, *Ademler ve Havvalar 4*, İstanbul: Yapı Kredi Publications, 2005.
Latif Demirci, *Nostalcisi Kandilli*, İstanbul: İletişim Publications, 1990.

Secondary Sources

Adorno Theodor ve Max Horkheimer (1979), *Dialectic of Enlightenment*, London: Verso.

Altay, Ekrem (1963), "Memleketimizde Aile Eğitimi," *Mesleki ve Teknik Öğretim*, v. 11, n. 128, p. 7.

Altınay, Ayşegül (2003), "Militarizm ve İnsan Hakları Ekseninde Milli Güvenlik Dersi", in *Ders Kitaplarında İnsan Hakları: Tarama Sonuçları*, Betül Çotuksöken, Ayşe Erzan ve Orhan Silier (eds.), p. 138-157, İstanbul: Türkiye Ekonomik ve Toplumsal Tarih Vakfı.

Arnheim, Rudolf (1936), *Radio: An Art Of Sound*, London: Faber & Faber Ltd.

Ataç, Galip (1943), *Radyoda Evin Saati*, İstanbul: Kenan Printing House.

Bali, Rıfat N. (2002), *Tarz-ı Hayat'tan Life Style'a: Yeni Seçkinler, Yeni Mekânlar, Yeni Yaşamlar*, İstanbul: İletişim Publications.

Barthes, Roland (1996), *Çağdaş Söylenler*, İstanbul: Metis.

Bauman, Zygmunt (1991), *Modernity and Ambivalence*, Ithaca, NY: Cornell University Press.

Berger, John (2005), *Görme Biçimleri*, İstanbul: Metis.

Berktay, Fatmagül (2002), "Doğu ile Batı'nın Birleştiği Yer: Kadın İmgesinin Kurgulanışı", in *Modern Türkiye'de Siyasi Düşünce: Modernleşme ve Batıcılık, Volume 3*, p. 275-285, İstanbul: İletişim Publications.

Bilgin, İhsan (2006), "Kent Üretiminin ve Kamu Yaşamının Örgütlenmesinde Güncel Eğilimler," *Toplum ve Bilim*, n. 105, p. 166-177.

Bordo, Susan (1995), *Unbearable Weight: Feminism, Western Culture, and the Body*, University of California Press.

Bourdieu, Pierre (1984), *Distinction: A Social Critique of the Judgement of Taste*. Cambridge: Harvard University Press.

Buğra, Ayşe (2001), "Kriz Karşısında Türkiye'nin Geleneksel Refah Rejimi," *Toplum ve Bilim*, Yaz, n. 89, p. 22-30.

-------------- (1998), "Non-market mechanisms of market formation: The development of the consumer durables industry in Turkey," *New Perspectives on Turkey*, Fall, 19, p. 1-28.

Camaroff, Jean and John Camaroff (2000), "Millennial capitalism and the culture of neoliberalism," *Public Culture*, 12, p. 291-343.

Carey, James (1988), *Communication as Culture: Essays on Media and Society*, Winchester, Mass.: Unwin Hyman.

Coronil, Fernando (2000), "Towards a Critique of Globalcentrism: Speculations on Capitalism's Nature," Public Culture, c. 12, n. 2, Spring, p. 351-374.

Cowan, Ruth Schwartz (1997), "The 'industrial revolution' in the home: Household technology and social change in the 20th century," in *Technology and the West*, T. S. Reynolds ve S. H. Cutcliffe (eds.), Chicago and London: The University of Chicago Press.

Deren, Seçil (2002), "Kültürel Batılılaşma", *Modern Türkiye'de Siyasi Düşünce: Modernleşme ve Batıcılık, Volume 3*, p. 382-402, İstanbul: İletişim Publications.

Dorsay, Atilla (1993), *Ağız Tadıyla*, İstanbul: Varlık Publications.

Durgun, Sezgi (2006), "Homo Balkanicus, Çılgın Türkler ve diğerleri," *Toplum ve Bilim*, n. 105, p. 245-264.

Erdoğan, Necmi (2001), "Garibanların Dünyası: Türkiye'de Yoksulların Kültürel Temsilleri Üzerine İlk Notlar," Toplum ve Bilim, Summer, n. 89, p. 22-30.

Erman, Fahire (2004), "Gecekondu Çalışmalarında 'Öteki' Olarak Gecekondulu Kurguları," *European Journal of Turkish Studies*, n. 1.

Ewen, Stuart (1976), *Captains of Consciousness: Advertising and the Social Roots of the Consumer Culture*, New York: McGraw Hill.

Ferguson, Priscilla Parkhurst (2004), *Accounting for Taste: The Triumph of French Cuisine*, Chicago and London: The University of Chicago Press.

Finkelstein, Joanne (1989), *Dining Out: A Sociology of Modern Manners*, Cambridge: Polity Press.

Geray, Haluk (2001), "Toplumsal Değişkenler ve Cep Telefonu," *Bilim ve Ütopya*, n. 83.

Gülizar, Jülide (1995), *TRT Meydan Savaşı*, Ankara: Ümit Publishing.

Gürbilek, Nurdan (1999), *Ev Ödevi*, İstanbul: Metis.

────────── (1992), *Vitrinde Yaşamak*, İstanbul: Metis.

İnsel, Ahmet (2003), "Bir Zihniyet Tarzı Olarak YÖK," *Toplum ve Bilim*, Fall, 97, p. 72-80.

Göle, Nilüfer (2000), *İslamın Yeni Kamusal Yüzleri*, İstanbul: Metis.

Karay, Refik Halid (1939), "Otomobilden Sakınınız!", *Bir Avuç Saçma*, İstanbul: Semih Lütfi Kitabevi.

Keyder, Çağlar (1999), "The setting" ve "The housing market from informal to global," in *Istanbul: Between the Global and the Local*, Ç. Keyder (ed.), Oxford: Rowman and Littlefield Publishers.

Kırlı, Cengiz (2004), "İstanbul: Bir Büyük Kahvehane," *Istanbul Dergisi*, 47, p. 75-78.

Klein, Naomi (2000), No Logo: Taking Aim at the Brand Bullies, Picador.

Lowenthal, David (1985), *The Past is a Foreign Country*, Cambridge: Cambridge University Press.

Kozanoğlu, Can (1992), *Cilalı İmaj Devri*, İstanbul: İletişim Publications.

Mağden, Perihan (1997), " 'Ev' Kadınlarının Tembellik Hakkı," *Cogito*, n. 12, p. 223-225.

Mardin, Şerif (1997), *Din ve İdeoloji, Toplu Eserleri 2*, İstanbul: İletişim Publications.

Navaro-Yaşın, Yael (2003), "Kimlik Piyasası: Metalar, İslamcılık, Laiklik", in *Kültür Fragmanları: Türkiye'de Gündelik Hayat*, Deniz Kandiyoti, Ayşe Saktanber (eds), p. 229-258, İstanbul: Metis.

────────── (2000), "'Evde Taylorizm': Türkiye Cumhuriyeti'nin İlk Yıllarında Evişinin Rasyonelleşmesi," *Toplum ve Bilim*, n. 84.

Öncü, Ayşe (2003), "1990'larda Küresel Tüketim, Cinselliğin Sergilenmesi ve İstanbul'un Kültürel Haritasının Yeniden Biçimlenmesi," in *Kültür Fragmanları: Türkiye'de Gündelik Hayat*, Deniz Kandiyoti, Ayşe Saktanber (eds), p. 183-200, İstanbul: Metis.

────────── (1997), "The myth of the 'ideal home' travels across the cultural borders to İstanbul," in *Space, Culture and Power: New Identities in Globalizing Cities*, A. Öncü ve P. Weyland (eds), London: Zed Books.

────────── (1995), "Packaging Islam: Cultural Politics on the Landscape of Turkish Commercial Television," *Public Culture*, n. 8.

Özkök, Ertuğrul (2001), "Garibanizm," *Hürriyet*, January 30.

Özyeğin, Gül (2005), *Başkalarının Kiri: Kapıcılar, Gündelikçiler ve Kadınlık Halleri*, İstanbul: İletişim Publications.

Parla, Jale (2003), "Makine Bedenler, Esir Ruhlar: Türk Romanında Araba Sevdası," *Toplum ve Bilim*, Spring, n. 96.

Peter, John Durham (1999) *Speaking into the Air: A History of the Idea of Communication*, Chicago: University of Chicago Press.

Roseberry, William (1996), "The rise of yuppie coffees and the reimagination of class in the United States," *American Anthropologist*, 98, n. 4, December, p. 762-775.

Rutherford, Jonathan (1988), "Who's That Man," in *Male Order: Unwrapping Masculinity*, Rowena Chapman and Jonathan Rutherford (eds), London: Lawrence and Wishart.

Sassen, Saskia (2000), *Cities in a World Economy*, Thousand Oaks, California: Pine Forge/Sage.

Strange, Susan (1998), *Casino Capitalism*, New York: St. Martin's Press.

Suner, Asuman (2001), "Bir Bağlantı Koparma Aracı Olarak Türkiye'de Cep Telefonu: Kriz, Göç ve Aidiyet," *Toplum ve Bilim*, n. 90, p. 114-130.

Tanyeli, Uğur (2004), *İstanbul 1900-2000: Konutu ve Modernleşmeyi Metropolden Okumak*, İstanbul: Akın Nalça Books

Uğur, Aydın (1991), "Bu Bir Kıl Olmayabilir", *Keşfedilmemiş Kıta: Günlük Yaşam ve Zihniyet Kalıplarımız*, İstanbul: İletişim Publications.

Urry, John (1995), *Consuming Places*, London: Routledge.

Zukin, Sharon (1997), *The Cultures of Cities*, Cambridge: Blackwell Publishers.

Index

1982 constitution, 329

1994 economic crisis, 66

1996 May 1 events, 319

2001 economic crisis, 66, 84, 274

A

Accor Services, 140

Adidas, 72

Adorno, Theodor, 121

ads, 106, 152, 156, 164

after hour clubs, 240

Ağar, Mehmet, 363

Akbal, Oktay, 287, 294

Akmerkez, 7-76, 83-84

AKP (Justice and Development Party), 66, 215

Aktunç, Hulki, 398

alafranga male, 3

Alkent 2000, 322

alla franca, 420

alla turca, 420

all-inclusive resort vacation, 96

Almancılar, 149

Altan, Çetin, 419

Altınay, Ayşegül, 339, 342

Altun, Selçuk, 62

anchormen, 260

apartment, 84, 164, 310, 315-316, 320, 322

arabesk culture, 134, 316, *see also* culture

Aral, İnci, 26, 81, 170, 208, 379, 407

Arçelik, 109, 167, 170

Armenian, 189, 192, 394, 412

Asena, Duygu, 18, 60, 219

Asmalı Konak (Porticoed Mansion), 260, 264

Assos, 94

Ataç, Galip, 402

Atalay, Atilla, 260, 271

Atatürk, Mustafa Kemal, 415, 419

Atay, Oğuz, 93, 182, 334, 420

Atılgan, Yusuf, 179

authentic, 6, 82, 93, 131, 137, 377, 379, 393-394, 398
  authenticity, 76, 369-370, 390, 404

automobile, 144, 147, 149, 152, 155-157, *see also* car as a fetish, 147
  as an extension of the body, 156
  as an indicator of status, 155
  as the center of machine-human relationship, 144
  as the symbol of modernity, 144

Avşar, Hülya, 56-57

Ayaz, Nevzat, 295

Ayvalık, 94, 137

B

backwardness, 33, 160

Bakırköy, 54, 75, 182

Bali, Rıfat, 6, 419

Bam Teli, 332

banking, 103, 106, 109, 274, 294, 297
  interest-free banking, 111

banks, 7, 66, 68, 102-103, 105-106, 108-109, 236, 297, 302, 316, 326

Barthes, Roland, 6, 219

Baudrillard, Jean, 256

Bauman, Zygmunt, 244

Baydar, Oya, 319

beauty, 10, 13, 18, 22, 26, 33, 57, 76, 377, 381
  beauty discourse, 22
  beauty industry, 33
  beauty salons, 33, 76
  ideal beauty, 18

belonging, 84, 269, 368, 377, 379, 402, 412, 415

Benjamin, Walter, 373

Berger, John, 226

Beyoğlu, 34, 134, 136, 181, 236, 240, 246, 293-294, 301-305, 307, 393

Bila, Fikret, 319

Bilgin, İhsan, 94

Bilkent, 322

BİLTEN, 271

Birgül, Cahide, 134, 233

Biri Bizi Gözetliyor, 260

bisexuality, 208

Black Turks, 419

Bodrum, 92, 94, 97, 390

body, 9-10, 12-14, 18-19, 22, 26, 28-29, 65, 147, 200, 205, 380
  body as capital, 18

body and social control mechanisms, 22
female body, 13, 22, 26, see also female body as an object of desire
the body as an indicator of social status, 18

Boğaziçi University, 62

Bourdieu, Pierre, 5, 373

Boyner, Cem, 66

brand, 6, 65, 72-73, 75, 79-82, 87-88, 99, 114, 121, 131, 149, 155, 170, 181, 189-190, 208, 240, 282, 284, 289-290, 294, 368, 370, 379-380, 407, 417, 420

Bride, 225, 229

Buğra, Ayşe, 109, 331

Burak, Sevim, 155, 186

Burger King, 128, 131, 148

Business Week, 65

C

cafe, 18, 82, 96, 131-132, 181-182, 271, 282, 284, 287-290, 293, 302, 387
from coffeehouse to cafe, 249

Camaroff, Jean, 117

Camaroff, John, 117

capital, 60, 66, 75, 88, 105, 126, 240, 248-249, 294, 297, 301-302, 304, 357,
cultural capital, 62, 236, 385, 408,
economic capital, 18, 62
relationship between capital and culture, 240, 302
social capital, 18, 373,

capitalism, 70, 93, 117, 126, 226, 379
capitalist, 60, 174, 219, 315, 326, 370, 373, 379, 404

car, 56, 75, 114, 117, 128, 144, 146-147, 149-152, 154-156, 179, 201, 222, 240, 269, 319, 364, 402, 419, *see also* passion for cars

career, 18, 62, 68-69, 121, 263, 348

Carrefour, 72

Castro, Fidel, 118

catering, 140, 284, 385

Çay Yolu, 322

Celal, Metin, 106

Celal, Peride, 256

cell phone, 197, 248, 266, 271, 274, 279, 290,
as status symbol, 274

Cezayir Çıkmazı, 302

Cheque Dejeuner, 140

Chevrolet, 144, 149, 155

child, 18, 22, 29, 31, 46, 60, 72-73, 76-77, 88, 99, 101-102, 104, 128, 131, 162-163, 171, 176, 179, 181, 198, 221, 255, 261-262, 266, 271, 276, 318, 326, 328, 331-332, 334, 336-340, 342, 348-350, 358, 367, 379, 381-382, 385, 388, 394, 398-399, 419-420, 423
child care, 46, 163
child labor, 329
children's education, 339
street children, 332
violence against children, 364

Chinese food, 383, 390, 393

Circassian, 189, 394

Citroen, 144

civilization, 225, 412

cleaning women, 170

class, 5, 14, 18, 31, 56, 62, 65-66, 72, 81-82, 84-85, 92-93, 96, 99-100, 117-118, 128, 131, 149, 152, 170, 182, 192, 216, 218219, 223-225, 236, 240, 244, 282, 284, 287, 308, 315, 317, 319, 321, 329, 342-343, 347-348, 364, 373, 380, 382, 385, 388, 407, *see also* middle, new middle class, upper class

class differences, 5, 131, 170, 316, 319, 348

Coca Cola, 377, 417

Çocuklar Duymasın (Don't Let the Kids Hear), 29

coffee, 76, 84, 94, 121, 164, 274, 282, 284-285, 288-289, 404
yuppification of coffee, 284, 289

coffeehouse, 249, 282, 286-291, 292
coffeehouses as an arena for political debate, 290

Cola Turka, 417, 420

commercialization, 110, 310, 315, 347-348, 420

commercials, 50, 110, 122, 197, 259, *see also* ads

communication, 184, 248-249, 253, 256, 260, 266, 269, 279, 290, 297, 301
age of communication, 266
communication boom, 266
communication devices, 256
communication network, 266
communication technologies, 266, 269
informal communication, 253

competition, 6, 61, 66, 106, 225, 259, 309, 345, 347

confession, 211

consumer, 75-76, 81, 84, 106, 109

consumerism, 18, 22, 31, 70, 72, 76, 81-82, 88, 109, 304, 368

consumption, 5, 7, 65, 71, 73, 75-76, 78, 81-82, 84, 93, 96, 106, 109, 128, 140, 159-160, 182, 226, 236, 279, 282, 284, 302, 304, 373, 385, 387, 404, 407
production of consumption, 81
consumer culture, 22, 302, 380
consumer society, 114

Coronil, Fernando, 358

Cosmetic, 13, 26-27, 33

Cosmopolitan, 10, 207, 378

Cowan, Ruth Schwartz, 164, 169

credit card, 71, 75, 102-103, 106, 108-111, 113-114, 122, 200

crisis, 40, 53, 60, 68, 84, 105, 110-111, 113, 227, 274, 422, *see also* debt crisis

culture, 5-7, 22, 93-94, 114, 121, 134, 137, 147, 149, 156, 176, 181, 192, 219, 233, 235-236, 240, 249, 274, 282, 292, 302, 304, 316, 319, 322, 358, 369, 379-380, 382, 386-387, 394, 412, 419-420, *see also* arabesk culture
   cultural fragmentation, 315
   culture industry, 114, 121, 236, 379
   popular culture, 6, 93

D

Dalan, Bedrettin, 295

debt crisis, 105

degeneration, 6, 190, 250, 279

Democratic Party, 402

Deniz Feneri, 332

depression, 45-47, 50, 52-54, 206, 211

Deren, Seçil, 34, 36

Desire, 5-7, 9, 22, 26, 31, 34, 70, 82, 96, 99, 118, 126, 147, 152, 160, 176, 181-182, 192, 200, 223, 226, 236, 240, 244, 262, 274, 297, 315, 322, 336, 350, 358, 368, 370, 373, 382, 387, 407-408
   female body as an object of desire, 26
   automobile as an object of desire, 147, 152
   television as an object of desire, 262
   desire and violence, 226, 358, 368
   desired Westernization, 160
   desired nation, 163
   control of desire, 22
   unfulfilled desires, 176, 182
   desire for entertainment 240, 244
   desire for progress, 160
   consumer desires, 109

Devecioğlu, Ayşegül, 40, 304, 354

diet, 13-16, 18, 20, 22, 29

dietician, 13-14

difference, 5-6, 93, 96, 117, 131, 134, 170, 316, 348, 385
   differentiation, 81, 93, 131, 155, 179, 287, 297, 304, 310, 319, 329, 348, 385, 412
   differentiated, 5, 50, 289

Disneyland, 96

diversification, 70, 93, 131, 282, 284, 385, 419

Doğuş, 316

Dorsay, Atilla, 387

Dr. Stress, 52

Dubai Towers, 301, 305, 425

Durgun, Sezgi, 422

E

East, 134, 260, 287, 310, 334
   Eastern, 5, 106, 134, 137, 156, 260, 289, 310, 383
   Easterner, 134, 156

Economist, 65

Eczacıbaşı, 66

Edgü, Ferit, 350

education, 46, 93, 110, 118, 163, 189, 309, 329, 334, 336, 339-340, 342, 345, 347-348, 358, 362, 398
   education and violence, 342, 347, 362
   privatization of education, 110, 309, 329, 347-348, 358

Elele, 10, 39, 378

Elites, 6, 287, 373

Elle, 10

end of line stores, 82

English, 96, 109, 190, 393

ENKA, 316

entel, 33

entertainment, 76, 82-83, 96, 134, 184, 197, 232-233, 236, 239-240, 242-245, 259, 287, 293, 302, 398, 401, 404-405

entrepreneurship, 61, 64

Eray, Nazlı, 266, 390

Erdoğan, Necmi, 332

Erman, Fahire, 319

Eroğlu, Mehmet, 310

Ersoy, Muazzez, 376-377

Euro-Turk, 419

Europe, 10, 20, 75, 77, 92, 109, 137, 230, 256, 258, 281, 283, 290, 358, 387, 422
   European, 34, 72, 75, 109, 149, 163, 174, 238, 327, 331, 422, 424
   European Union, 109, 415, 420

Eurovision, 256

everyday life, 6, 40, 52, 65, 93, 102, 105, 110, 121, 147, 269, 309, 387
   everyday life and belonging, 415, 420
   everyday life and militarization, 342

everyday language, 52

Evren, Kenan, 43, 336-337, 357

Ewen, Stuart, 174

excess, 13, 20, 24, 33, 60, 98, 185, 212, 223, 226, 236, 240, 244, 279, 420

exchange, 370, 373

exercise, 10, 12, 28, 34

explosion of words, 50

extravagance, 216, 223, 385

F

factory outlet, 82, 410

fashion, 12-13, 26, 31-34, 36, 40, 54, 65, 76, 82, 99, 208, 219, 221, 225-226, 233, 304, 368, 370, 373-374, 377, 379-380, 404, 416

Fashion TV, 208

fast food, 76, 127-129, 131-132, 134, 137, 139-141, 226, 393

Fatih, 76

fear of the metropolis, 322

female sexuality, 26, 156, 205, 208, 212

feminism, 380
    feminist movement, 10
    feminist writers, 179
    feminist policies, 225

Ferguson, Priscilla Parkhurst, 390

the fetishism of commodities, 370

finance sector, 70, 294

fitness, 10, 13-14, 18, 22, 76, 407

flexible production, 66, 140

food court, 75

football, 26, 33, 118, 122-123, 176, 250, 256

Ford, 144, 152, 155

franchising, 137

Fransız Sokağı (faux French Street), 294, 302

French cuisine, 390, 392

G

Galataport, 294, 296, 301

Galleria, 75, 84

gambler archetype, 114, 118

gambling, 114, 117-119
    gambling as rational investment, 114
    gambling as sickness, 118
    gambling as social policy, 118

game, 114, 121-122, 211, 221, 250, 279, 367
    chance games, 71, 114, 117-118, 120-122
    computer games, 276, 362

garibanizm, 332

gastropornographic, 18

gecekondu, 134, 170, 310, 315-316, 318-319, 322, 364, see also squatterization

Gencebay, Orhan, 244

gender, 22, 144, 155-156, 163, 200, 212, 332, 412

gentrification, 301-302

Geray, Haluk, 274

Givenchy, 72

global city, 294, 297, 301-302, see also world city

globalization, 105, 279, 294, 304, 358, 379

Gloria Jean's, 289

the glossy image age, 6

Gökalp, Ziya, 412

Göle, Nilüfer, 402

green card, 331

Gülizar, Jülide, 253

Günday, Hakan, 66, 72

Gürbilek, Nurdan, 6, 43, 50, 176, 197, 211

Gürpınar, Melisa, 370

Gürsel, Nedim, 297

Güzin Abla, 211

H

Hacıoğlu Lahmacun, 137

Haydarpaşa project, 294, 301

Headscarf, 226, 346-347, 402

health, 10-11, 13-14, 17-18, 22-23, 40, 42-44, 46, 50, 52, 110, 208, 308, 326, 329-331, 334, 358, 381, 407
    commercialization of health, 110, 326, 329, 331, 358
    healthy body, 8, 10
    healthy food, 13
    healthy life, 10, 18, 46, 310
    healthy nutrition, 131

Heavy Metal, 233, 237

Hey, 206, 231

hip-hop, 236

holiday, 88-90, 96-97, 99, 174, 398, 403-404, 407
    resorts, 89-90, 96, 98, 407

homosexuality, 26, 200, 205, 210, 212

Horkheimer, Max, 121

house, 34, 40, 52, 62, 76, 93-94, 99, 117-118, 122, 127-128, 160-170, 174, 176, 179, 181-182, 189, 200, 208, 253, 271, 274, 287, 301-302, 310, 315, 322, 354, 364, 370, 385, 394
    home cooking, 140, 382
    household, 127, 163-164, 169-170, 269, 271, 282
    housewives, 14, 40, 46, 48, 54, 140, 164, 167-168, 170, 179
    housework, 29, 163-164, 169-170, 174, 179
    rationalization of housework, 163
    housing problem, 310, 317

I

identity, 6, 29, 31, 40, 52, 62, 70, 84, 96, 131, 137, 140, 156, 182, 185, 205, 237, 244, 289, 302, 369, 379, 404, 412, 415, 419-420, 422

İleri, Selim, 380, 385

İlhan, Atillâ, 269, 373

image, 66, 81, 93, 96, 137

IMF, 60, 102, 105-106, 329

individual, 18, 40, 43, 50, 52, 71, 144, 160, 211, 244, 339, 373
    individualism, 18, 43, 62
    individualization, 6, 8, 43, 70-71, 144, 149, 269, 279, 368

informal sector, 274, 364
    informalization, 329

internet, 7, 94, 181, 197, 199, 248, 266, 271, 274, 279-281, 393, 397
    internet cafe, 122, 276, 279

İnsel, Ahmet, 339

installment sales, 109-110, 112, 164, 170, 316, 325

insurance, 394, 397, 308, 326-330

İplikçi, Müge, 271, 377

Iraq, 358

Islam, 176, 319, 398, 402, 404
    Islamic, 67, 76, 106, 205, 226, 358, 398, 402, 404, 419
    Islamic ascendence, 402

Istanbul, 31, 75-76, 81-82, 88, 99, 128, 131, 134, 137, 140, 152, 181-182, 211, 230, 236, 240, 244, 294, 297, 301-304, 315, 322, 336, 362, 364, 382

Istanbul Court Martial Commandership, 336

İzgü, Muzaffer, 315

J

Jacobs, 282

jazz, 236, 240, 244

jogging, 10, 181

K

Kadınca, 10, 42, 162, 207

Kapital, 65

Karay, Refik Halid, 144

Karum, 75

Kaya, Ahmet, 192

Kemalism, 420

Kemer Country, 322

Kentmen, Hulusi, 65

Keyder, Çağlar, 297, 310, 315

Kırlı, Cengiz, 287

Kimse Yok mu?, 334

Klein, Naomi, 379

Koç, 66, 72, 75, 105-106

Koç, Rahmi, 392

Korukent, 322

Kozanoğlu, Can, 6

Kudret, Cevdet, 34

Kurtlar Vadisi (Valley of the Wolves), 34, 364

Kurukahveci Mehmet Efendi, 282

Kutgün, Cemile, 233

Kutlu, Ayla, 331

Kurds, 189, 415

L

labor, 46, 106, 117-118, 144, 163, 169, 174, 319, 329, 331-334, 370
    invisibility of woman's labor, 46, 179

Lacoste, 80-82

Lady Diana, 219

lahmacun restaurants, 134, 137-138

Laila, 230, 243

Lambada, 233, 237

language, 52, 62, 184, 186-192, 194, 197, 205, 284, 347, 412, 415

leaping into the future (çağ atlamak), 160, 370

Levi's, 72

liberalization, 43, 189, 282, 357

lifestyle, 5-7, 29, 31, 34, 66, 70, 76, 131, 134, 137, 170, 190, 219, 240, 250, 284, 289, 316, 318-320, 368, 370, 380, 382, 408

light erkek, 29

limitless choices, 70

lounge bars, 240

to lose weight, 12, 16, 18-20, 23, 406

Lowenthal, David, 377

lower middle class, 225, 316, see also middle class

luxury, 28, 56, 80, 82, 88, 96, 110, 147, 152, 159, 219, 222, 240, 298, 318, 385

M

Macro, 72

Maçka, 81-82

macho, 29-31, 36, 39

maganda (coarse, un-refined male), 31, 156, 419

Mağden, Perihan, 76, 179

"make it big", 43, 274

Mansız, İlhan, 33

Mardin, Şerif, 398

Marie Claire, 10, 15, 55, 214, 277

market, 5, 7-8, 13-14, 17, 22, 29, 31, 33, 36, 43, 50, 52, 60, 62, 66, 72, 75-76, 81-82, 84-85, 87, 94, 96, 102, 105-106, 109-110, 117-118, 122, 131, 137, 140, 156, 164, 170, 174, 185, 189, 192, 200, 219, 223, 226, 250, 256, 269, 271, 282, 284, 302, 304, 324, 329, 342, 347, 350, 364, 368, 370, 379, 394, 417, 420, 422
    blackmarket, 151

market research, 81, 84

Marks and Spencer, 75

Marx, Karl, 126, 370

masculinity, 26, 29, 31, 34, 36, 156, 170

Mashattan, 294, 301

mass, 82, 127, 149, 157, 269, 287, 316, 358, 364, 373, 420
    mass consumption, 128
    mass media, 6, 208, 266, 269, 279, 419
    mass production, 137, 149
    mass tourism, 88, 93, 96
    massification, 71

Mass Housing Administration, 316

MBA, 62, 350

McDonald's, 128, 130-131, 134, 137, 140-141

McLuhan, Marshall, 248

mechanization, 164, 169

media, 6-8, 14, 33, 46, 65, 82, 94, 164, 181, 191, 197, 200, 208, 211-212, 219, 236, 240, 248, 250, 259-260, 266, 269, 279, 319, 358, 362, 390, 398, 419, *see also* mass media

Mercedes, 149, 152

Meryem, Hatice, 169

Metro, 72, 77

Metrosexual, 26-29, 31, 34, 37

middle class, 14, 62, 81-82, 85, 92, 99-100, 128, 131, 152, 182, 282, 284, 308, 315-317, 321, 364, 385, 407, *see also* lower middle class, new middle class, upper middle class

Middle East Technical University, 62

migration, 134, 310, 315, 322
    forced migration, 134
    migrant, 156, 301-302, 319, 358, 362, 364, 418
    racism against migrants, 358

Migros, 75

militarism, 117, 155, 339

military *coup* of March 12, 1971, 253, 354

military *coup* of September 12, 1980, 8, 33, 40, 43, 189, 253, 309, 336, 339, 354, 357, 370, 379, 419

Ministry of Education, 163, 342

Ministry of Finance, 216

Ministry of Health, 334

Ministry of Interior, 276

Ministry of Tourism, 296

modern, *see also* postmodern
    modernity, 22, 33, 36, 82, 131, 134, 144, 147, 155, 160, 205, 226, 269, 287, 289-290, 315, 377
    modernization, 34, 147, 160, 163, 250, 279, 354, 402, 412

money, 56, 58, 60, 63, 66-67, 73, 75-76, 93, 103, 106, 114, 116-118, 121, 137, 140, 152, 163, 174, 219, 223, 226, 233, 240, 316, 348, 367, 398, 420

Moore, Michael, 358

Mungan, Murathan, 13, 29, 84, 211

motherhood, 200

multiculturalism, 192

Müldür, Lale, 373

Municipality of Şişli, 420

MÜSİAD, 66

Mydonose tent show center, 190

myth, 6, 152, 156, 169, 219
    mythical, 362, 364
    mythical time, 373

N

National Lottery, 117-119, 123-124, 145, 189, 320

national developmentalism, 90, 319

nationalism, 34, 189, 192, 212, 342, 369, 419-420, 422

Navaro-Yaşın, Yael, 75-76, 163

neo-liberal, 56, 60, 274
    neoliberalism, 62, 326, 332, 339, 347-348

Nescafe, 282, 284

Nestle, 14

neo tribalism, 244

NeoTurkism, 412

new middle class, 62, 66, 93, 284, 329, *see also* class, middle class, upper middle clas

new world economic order, 105

New York, 62, 289, 297, 304, 358

Nike, 380

Nine West, 75

Nişantaşı, 81-82

nostalgia, 369-370, 376-377, 379, 398, 404, 407-408

O

obesity, 14, 20, 131

Oker, Celil, 274

Oktay, Ahmet, 197

Olivium, 75, 84

Öncü, Ayşe, 29, 31, 315, 322, 404

orta direk, 62

other, 31, 40, 81, 122, 155, 205, 266, 284, 302, 304, 334, 364, 373
otherization, 334
otherness, 31, 131, 319

Ottoman cuisine, 382, 393, 397

Ottoman Empire, 34, 287-290, 296, 310, 393

Ottoman Turkish, 186

outlet stores, 82, 87, 410

outskirts of the city, 84, 301, 319

Özakman, Turgut, 422

Özal, Semra, 225

Özal, Turgut, 60, 150, 317

Özer, Kemal, 302

Özkök, Ertuğrul, 332

Özlü, Tezer, 10, 176, 289

Öztürk, Yaşar Nuri, 404

Özyeğin, Gül, 170

P

Para, 59, 65

Parla, Jale, 147, 155

passion for cars/love affair with car, 127, 147

pavyon, 240

Pekkan, Ajda, 244, 379

performance centers, 240

Peters, John Durham, 266

Philip Morris, 14

Pizza Hut, 128

place, 76, 81-82, 88, 93-94, 99, 126, 140, 182, 223, 240, 244, 253, 284, 286-287, 289-290, 294, 302, 362, 385, 390

planning, 81, 121, 182

pleasure communities, 240, 244

polarization, 65, 81, 200, 308, 319, 368, 408

popular culture, *see also* culture

populism, 332

pornography, 208, 276, 279

postmodern, 244, 354, *see also* modern

post-modern *coup*, 354

poverty, 82, 118, 128, 131, 135, 174, 233, 259, 319, 326, 332, 334, 364, 407
representations of poverty, 332, 334

power, 6, 8-9, 29, 36, 43, 62, 66, 105, 155-156, 169, 185, 226, 253, 275, 336, 339, 390, 404, 415

Prince Charles, 219

private schools, 66, 344-345, 347, 364

production, 6, 14, 70, 84, 96, 105-106, 117, 137, 140, 144, 149, 282, 319, 329, 336, 379, *see also* mass production
production becoming secondary, 117
relations of production, 106

productivity, 52, 163

Profilo, 83-84

propaganda, 44, 253, 338

private space, 271

privatization, 60, 297, 308, 329, 347, 357-358

privatization of security, 357-358

public space, 76, 271, 289, 302, 354

Q

quick meals become fast food, *128, 140*

R

race, 412,

racism, 192, 358

radio, 7, 40, 52, 106, 114, 152, 176, 181, 188-189, 192, 235, 250, 266, 269, 279, 284, 287, 316, 357, 377, 379, 387, 398, 402, 404

Ramadan, 402, 404, 407-408

rape, 26, 212, 354

rating, 259

rationality, 163, 342

reality show, 259

recreation, 94, 96, 181-182, 302

Red Turks, 419

Reggae, 233, 236

representation, 5-7, 82, 144, 155-156, 289, 304, 332, 334, 362, *see also* representations of poverty

Rifat, Oktay, 163

risk, 14, 62, 105-106, 109, 114, 118, 259, 419

rock, 233, 236, 242

Rockistanbul, 236

Roseberry, William, 284

Rutherford, Jonathan, 26

S

Sabancı, 56, 58, 66, 72

Sabancı, Sakıp, 56, 58

Şafak, Elif, 75, 96, 382

Samsonite, 82

Sassen, Saskia, 297

savings, 105, 124, 152, 316

Secularism, 402, 420-421

sefertası movement, 128, 137, 140

Selçuk, Münir Nurettin, 303

September 11, 358

service sector, 70, 88, 134, 140, 294

sexuality, 26, 29, 46, 200-201, 203, 205, 208, 211-212, 412

Seyfettin, Ömer, 34

shopping malls, 71, 74-76, 81-82, 84, 149, *see also* new shopping spaces

Simmel, Georg, 373

simulation, 96, 256, 266

slang, 33, 190, 192, 196-197, 370

slow food, 137

social assistance, 326, 329, 408

social exclusion, 110, 301

social polarization, 308, 319, 368, 408

social roles, 179

social security, 105, 308, 326-327, 329-335, 358

Sodexho, 140

Sofra, 140

Şok, 75

Somer, Mehmet Murat, 88, 244

Soysal, Sevgi, 128

spare time, 164, 174, 179, 181, *see also* time

speculation, 117

squatterization, 310, 315, 319

standardization, 94, 137, 339

Starbucks, 288-289

state, 34, 36, 60, 88, 176, 186, 197, 211-212, 233, 253, 256, 287, 326, 336, 339, 347, 390, 398, 412
   state and economy, 105, 117-118, 297, 310, 315, 319, 326, 331, 342, 347, 350, 379
   state and family, 212, 216
   state and social services, 308, 310, 315, 326, 329, 331, 408
   state and violence, 354, 357-358
   welfare state, 331

status, 5, 14, 18, 82, 84, 96, 99, 131, 144, 149, 155-156, 170, 219, 274, 287, 315, 373, 385, 415

step, aerobic, 10, 12, 15, 22, 25

stock market, 60, 117-118, 122, 274

Strange, Susan, 105

stress, 15, 18, 46, 48, 52, 55, 236

structural adjustment policies, 105

Stüdyo 54, 230-234

style, 5, 31-34, 36, 76, 129, 149, 170, 197, 207-208, 211, 215, 219, 287, 358, 380, 387, 395-396, 420
   stylized, 284

symbol, 93, 96, 134, 137, 274, 284, 315, 420

symbolic economy, 304

Şu Çılgın Türkler, 422

Sun Language (*Güneş-Dil*) theory, 186

Suner, Asuman, 271, 274

supermarket, 14, 17, 52, 65, 72, 75, 82, 282, 393, 410-411, 422

Süreya, Cemal, 415

T

Tamer, Ülkü, 394

Tanpınar, Ahmet Hamdi, 121, 144

Tanyeli, Uğur, 322

Tarkan, 33, 196

taş fırın erkek (Marlboro Man), 29

Tatlıses lahmacun, 137

Tekbir shopping center, 76

TEKEL, 282

Tekfen, 72

Tekin, Latife, 144, 315

telecommunication, 269, 297

telephone, 266, 269, 271-272, 280

television, 5-6, 10, 14, 18, 29, 46, 52, 65, 82, 93, 110, 114, 117, 121, 176, 190, 200, 211, 219, 223, 233, 236, 240, 248-250, 253, 256, 259-260, 262, 266, 269, 274, 289, 310, 322, 326, 332, 347, 357, 362, 364, 377, 379, 382, 387, 398, 404
   private television, 197, 233, 256, 404

terror, 203, 319, 358
   terrorist, 40, 354, 358, 362

tesettür, 76

Teşvikiye, 81-82

time, 6, 18, 76, 126-127, 140, 155-156, 163-164, 169-170, 174, 176, 179, 181-182, 189, 197, 226, 370, 373, 382, 390, *see also* spare time
   acceleration of time, 126, 140, 182
   synchronic forms of time, 174

timeshares, 92-93, 99

Tiryaki, 282

TOBB, 66

Toblerone, 72

Tommy Hilfiger, 380

Top Shop, 75

Toptaş, Hasan Ali, 290

tourism, 88, 93-94, 99, 294, 297, 302, 304
   tourism sector, 71
   mass tourism, 88, 93, 96
   tourism and investments, 88, 301
   sub-sectors of tourism, 88-89, 94, 96

Toys "R" Us, 72, 77

traditional, 14, 29, 34, 62, 137, 140, 211, 225-226, 279, 310, 331, 382, 402

traffic issue, 48, 108, 145, 147, 152, 155-156, 253, 407

traffic monster, 152

transsexuality, 26, 200

transvestism, 200

TRT, 213, 236, 250, 253, 257, 262, 347, 357, 379, 415

TÜBİTAK, 271

Tunç, Ayfer, 131, 250

Türk Dil Kurumu, 186

Türk-İş, 84

Turkcell, 420

Turkification policies, 189, 415

Turkish coffee, 282

Turkish National Information Infrastructure Master Plan, 271

Türkmenoğlu, Fatih, 152

türkü bars 240

TÜSİAD, 66

U

Ümit, Ahmet, 240, 393

Uncertainty, 31, 40, 66, 297

underground clubs, 240

unemployment, 118, 287, 331, 348, 352

uniform/uniformity, 36, 94, 350

Unilever, 14

upper class, 72, 117, 192, 216, 219, 364,
   upper middle class, 31, 60, 131, 152, 170, 319

Uras, Güngör, 316

urban transformation, 249, 294, 301, 304, 318

Urban Transformation Project, 294, 301, 318

Urry, John, 93

Uyar, Tomris, 96, 140, 190

Uyurkulak, Murat, 117, 189, 357

Uzun, Mehmed, 189

V

Versace, 82

villager, 65, 311, 316

violence, 7, 36, 40, 43, 106, 134, 192, 211, 226, 244, 308-309, 319, 342, 354, 357-358, 362, 364, 402, 420
   domestic violence, 223, 364
   violence against women, 36, 212
   symbolic violence, 36

vocational schools for girls (*Kız Enstitüleri*), 163

W

wealth, 56, 60, 66, 89, 117-118, 134, 147, 152, 155, 216, 219, 226, 286-287, 296

West, 5, 34, 52, 160, 164, 233, 331, 348, 402, 412, 415, 419
   negative influences of excessive Western aspirations, 33
   West and East, 287, 310, 426
   Western, 33, 70, 75, 76, 134, 164, 176, 186, 189, 230, 282, 287, 289, 310, 316, 377, 407, 415, 420
   Westernization, 33, 147, 160, 163-164, 186, 205, 315

white goods, 109, 170

White Turks, 408, 419

Williams, Raymond, 259

woman, 13, 18-19, 21, 25-26, 29, 33-34, 156, 164, 179, 205, 207, 211, 420
   liberation of woman, 10, 169

womanhood, 211, 310

World Bank, 60, 105, 329

world music, 236

Y

Yaşın, Mehmet, 4123

Yemez, Yücel, 387

Yenal, Zafer, 387

Yeni Demokrasi Hareketi (New Democracy Movement), 66

Yeşilçam, 65, 147, 213

Yöndem, Ertürk, 211, 347

Yumoş, 170

yuppie, 59-60, 284

Yücel, Doğu, 269

YÖK, 339

Z

Zekeriyaköy, 322

Zontellektüel, 33

Zukin, Sharon, 304

© 2006, Ottoman Bank Archives and Research Centre